Laura Wallace

The Arts and Skills of English

English

4

TEACHER'S EDITION

Owen Thomas

Holt, Rinehart and Winston, Inc.
New York · Toronto · London · Sydney

Author:

Owen Thomas   Professor of English, Indiana University, Bloomington, Indiana

Consultants:

Juanita Abernathy   Coordinator of English and Reading, Georgia State Department of Education, Atlanta, Georgia

Alexander Frazier   Faculty of Early and Middle Childhood Education, The Ohio State University, Columbus, Ohio

Nancy Redkey   Teacher, formerly of Westport School System, Westport, Connecticut

Evelyn Mlodzik   Teacher, Duluth Public Schools, Duluth, Minnesota

Sr. Margaret Shea   Teacher, Hall of the Divine Child, Monroe, Michigan

Cover Design:

Ursula Pross

Table of Contents

Introduction: The Arts and Skills of English

The English Curriculum

The title of this series reflects a basic assumption about the content of the English curriculum, namely, that the content can, and should, be divided into two major areas. One area relates to the arts of English (for example, literature and creative composition), and the second relates to the skills of English (punctuation, spelling, and so on). In discussing this curriculum, we will focus first on the arts and skills as the proper subject matter or content. Then we will focus on the various ways in which this content can be presented effectively to children.

Content

The primary arts of English consist of literature, composition, and the nature of language. In studying these arts, we encounter universal concepts in a form that is both immediate and accessible. Literature, for example, provides a variety of insights into the human condition—the nature of man with all his strengths and weaknesses, the individual's interactions with his fellow men, and his relationship to the society which he has structured and within which he must live. An understanding of such significant topics can be the work of a lifetime, and the earlier one begins, the better he will be able to relate to himself and his social environment.

In recent years much attention has been focused on improving the ability of people to communicate with each other. Through the study of the processes involved in composition, an individual can learn to communicate his ideas and perceptions of reality with the force of conviction and originality. This capacity affords every person —whether child or adult—the opportunity of simultaneously structuring his experiences and sharing his perceptions with others.

The basis of such communication is, of course, language. Most scholars in the field agree that language is <u>natural</u> to man. That is, a child learns language without having to be formally drilled in its rudiments, and, by the age of five or six, he is already capable of producing an infinite number of sentences that are unique to him. The child who recognizes this fact has a significant glimpse into the marvel of his own mind. Equally important, such recognition can help him achieve confidence in his worth as an individual.

But literature, composition, and language are not the only subjects which belong in the English curriculum. Children should also master those practical skills which are useful for all members of our society. In particular, children need to acquire locational and organizational skills which will facilitate their learning in all areas of the curriculum. As they learn to read, and even more as they learn to write, children also need to learn the conventions which apply to such things as abbreviations, letters and addresses, capitalization, punctuation, spelling, and so on. The skills are different in kind from the arts, but they constitute an important part of the English curriculum.

We can represent the content of the English curriculum by a triangle of arts and a circle of skills.

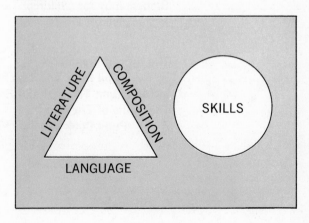

Process

In discussing the process of teaching, we can use four well-established terms: listening, reading, speaking, and writing. Each term refers to a specific <u>action</u> which teachers and children perform. And each specific action is one way of approaching the content of the English curriculum. For example, children can read literature on their own, or they can listen while a teacher reads to them. Composition may sometimes be oral, and at other times children can write their compositions.

While each action is a way of approaching the content of this series, all four (listening, reading, writing, and speaking) are in fact interdependent and multidimensional. Listening and reading —the decoding processes—are requisite to every lesson in this series. These are the actions whereby a child forms perceptions and receives impressions. The encoding processes—speaking and writing— are also an integral part of most lessons. These are the actions that the child generally uses when he "performs" or expresses himself. And the quality of his performance will be vitally affected by the kind of stimuli he receives from listening and reading.

We can understand the multidimensional aspects of the process by looking more closely at one of the actions, listening, for example. Before a child is asked to read a literature selection, he generally listens to it. The primary object, of course, is to listen for understanding. But each child is also encouraged to participate actively in the listening. The following is a typical example, taken from the teacher's notes which accompany one of the poems in Book Three: *Before reading the poem, encourage the children to react as they listen. "If you think the poem is spooky and you want to shiver, then go right ahead. . . ."* In other words, the child's response is a key factor in the process of his listening.

Listening and speaking are basic actions, and each child begins to develop proficiency in them before coming to school. We can—and should— capitalize on this fact in teaching English to children. This permits us to develop the children's oral language experiences. Reading and writing, on the other hand, are actions which most children learn in school. Teaching the mechanics of these two activities is certainly an important aspect of the total language arts program. But as children acquire the ability to read and write, they also must learn how to apply these two actions toward becoming more sensitive readers and more creative writers.

The interrelationship between the content and the process of the English curriculum can be illustrated as follows:

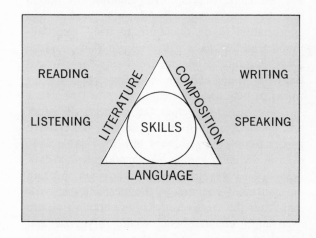

In this diagram, the content of the curriculum is represented by the merging of the triangle of arts and the circle of skills. The complete process of teaching—and learning—is represented by the terms in the shaded area of the diagram. While listening and reading are actions which are quite closely associated with the topic of literature, and speaking and writing are closely associated with the topic of composition, all four actions are equally vital to the total process.

In this series, then, the content and the process of the curriculum are fused together. This fusion engages each child actively in learning so that he or she comes to recognize that literature is one of the great accomplishments of man, that composition is an important way of thinking, and that language itself is perhaps man's most precious gift.

English in the Schools

Having established the content and the process of the English curriculum in general, we can now turn to the question of appropriateness and ask what we can reasonably expect of children in the elementary grades.

In working with children, my consultants and I adopted Jerome Bruner's familiar hypothesis that many key concepts of a subject can be taught effectively in some intellectually honest way to any child. In working with children, we found that they could respond with understanding and appreciation to the literature of truly great authors. Children have active imaginations, and all great literature is imaginative. Poetry, in particular, helps young children see themselves and their world in new and different ways.

We also found that the concepts of order and selectivity, which are the heart of the creative process, could be presented in a reasonable way, even in the early grades. We found that most children like to compose, particularly when they are not constantly confined by the mechanics of writing. After the creative aspects of composition are over, most children seem willing to revise and recopy their work, and so this fact was incorporated into the program. Additionally, we developed many opportunities for children to compose without writing.

The fact that children come to school with an innate capacity for making and understanding sentences has important implications for their study of literature and composition. But it is the very foundation of the language strand of this series. By helping a child to discover the nature of language, by providing insight into the way language works, we hope to increase a child's understanding of his own mind. And such an understanding should enable a child to develop a positive attitude toward his own linguistic ability.

In developing the lessons on literature, composition, and language, my consultants and I have carefully considered studies in children's maturation. These studies indicate, among other things,

that the age of six is nearly ideal for beginning relatively formal instruction in school. By the age of five, most children have begun to develop "concept mastery"; that is, their world no longer has an exclusive personal orientation where events happen "by personal causation." As Nicholas Anastasiow has said, "The six-year-old still has difficulty with abstractions such as time, but he can handle concepts and symbols such as print." And he adds, "The five- to six-year-old has integrated his emotional, language, thinking, motoric, and interpersonal skills into a unity that is a functioning whole—ready for academic tasks." (These concepts are developed in Nicholas Anastasiow's book, *Oral Language,* an effective and comprehensive summary of recent research in the field, published in cooperation with IRA, under the direction of ERIC.)

This recent research is reflected in the content and structure of Books One and Two which provide a wide variety of opportunities for children to extend their "concept mastery" as well as their various skills. For example, most six- and seven-year-old children are highly imaginative in their use of puppets and they generally respond with equal enthusiasm to role playing. These forms of concept manipulation enable a child to become directly involved with both literature and composition and they also help to develop greater facility in the use of language.

Similar studies (such as those of Jean Piaget and his colleagues) indicate that by the age of eight children are able to work with both physical and verbal symbols. They have matured beyond the age when learning consists primarily of activity; they can begin to work with representations of things. In other words, these children are ready to move beyond mere experience to the higher levels of awareness and verbalization. They can not only do things, they can begin to understand that doing sometimes has a symbolic meaning, and frequently they can bring such understanding to the level of verbalization. More specifically, they can move beyond the simple experience of literature, composition, and the use of language.

They can begin to talk about these things, and such talk can help to increase the value of the experience. This fact provides the organizing principle for every lesson in Books Three through Six.

Naturally, the level of verbalization can be subdivided almost indefinitely. In fact, educational development, from kindergarten through postgraduate study, consists in learning to make increasingly subtle verbalizations about increasingly abstract subjects. Obviously, children cannot discuss all of the subtleties inherent in such things as poetic metaphor, compositional form, or linguistic competence. But they can experience these things, and they can begin to bring this experience to the level of verbalization, particularly with respect to the foundations of these experiences.

The Structure of the Series

The books of this series form the basis of a spiral curriculum. In the beginning of the Arts Section of each book, we establish the foundations of literature, composition, and language. Then, in later lessons of each book, as well as in later books in the series, we constantly "turn back on" these foundations and make them more explicit. This is true also for the skills. The skills presented at one level are repeated and, wherever possible, extended at the next level.

Literature

The lessons on literature aim to establish the foundations of mature—and critical—appreciation. More specifically, a child learns that literature is a unique and valuable way of perceiving the world, and he also learns that the basis of literature is metaphor, in the broadest meaning of this word. In this sense, metaphor refers to any one of the many ways we can see one thing (or situation) in terms of another. This includes all of the traditional types of figurative language, such as metaphor (in its restricted sense of an implied comparison), simile, personification, apostrophe, metonymy, and so on. It also includes

entire works of literature, such as allegory, parable, fable, and myth. (For a fuller discussion, see Owen Thomas, *Metaphor and Related Subjects,* New York, Random House, 1969.)

The emphasis on metaphor is central to the program and is amplified throughout the series as the child becomes aware that literature can take many different forms. Thus, the children begin with the simplest kinds of metaphor, those that occur in lyric poetry. For example, the first two poems in the third book of the series are Christina Rossetti's "Who Has Seen the Wind?" and Carl Sandburg's "Fog." The following excerpt is taken from the discussion in the child's text: *Think about the words "the trees bow down their heads." When the poet sees the wind bending the trees, it makes her think of a man bowing down his head. One thing sometimes makes us think about another thing. And when we put the two things together, we have a metaphor.* Through this discussion (and similar ones in the fourth, fifth, and sixth books), the teacher helps a child bring his experience with metaphor to an initial level of awareness. As the literature strand in later lessons develops, this initial awareness is expanded and enriched.

Throughout the series, the literary selections have been chosen to engage a child's interest and response, no matter what his background. They draw upon the experience that each child already has of himself and his physical world, and they acquaint him with new and fresh ways of perceiving these experiences, ones that are generally common to all men. Metaphor is an enabling fact in the process of perception—the process of understanding the world.

In this context, we can also note that on the most immediate level, understanding requires a reader to know the meanings of words and sentences. In a larger sense, understanding is "linear"; that is, a reader must comprehend a story line, a setting, characters—in brief, the content of a literary work. In a third sense, broader than the other two, understanding occurs when a reader brings his experience and his view of the world to a literary work, and these help to determine his response.

More particularly, as a child comes to understand a work (in the third sense), he imposes his own experience on it. And there is a reciprocal action: As he discusses a work, he imposes an order on his previous experience. This process —a movement from self to work to self—expands his perceptions and enriches succeeding experiences, both literary and personal. And in this sense, understanding develops gradually over a period of years as each child becomes increasingly adept at perceiving higher levels of abstraction, and indeed as he comes to a fuller understanding of the nature of humanity.

In the broadest sense, understanding is related to imagination, which is another foundation of the literature strand. The focus can best be illustrated with a particular example. In Chapter Two of Book Three, there is a poem which begins: "The rainbow is the fishing line of the king of dragons." First, the children consider the metaphor itself, and then, in the discussion material that follows, they read this question: "What fish could you catch with a rainbow?" Quite literally, any answer which a child gives to this question must involve his imagination. And such an approach (which occurs in all books in the series) frequently elicits the most satisfying response.

These questions, and similar ones in other strands, are also valuable in another way: They have no "right-or-wrong" answers. They help children increase their understanding of literature; they also help them to develop their own imaginative capabilities. But they accomplish these goals without imposing the fear of failure. In other words, in following a method which encourages a child's active participation, a teacher provides support for each child's own response so that he develops confidence in his ability to respond. Such confidence is an essential ingredient in developing a life-long, active interest in literature.

We can also note that the literature strand does not neglect the more traditional duties of the classroom teacher. Thus, the discussions in the child's text and the notes in the teacher's edition sometimes include information concerning vocabulary and comprehension. Additionally, a few technical terms such as *stanza* and *rhyme* are introduced when they are appropriate to the discussion, but these terms—like the literary forms themselves—are only means, not ends. That is, they are introduced chiefly as a means of facilitating discussion and not as ends in themselves.

Composition

Like other key terms we have already considered, the word *composition* has several meanings. It can refer either to an act or to the result of that act. It is always creative, even though a particular composition may be factual, and it can be written, oral, or in pantomime. In any of these senses, composition has two fundamental properties: The first is order, and the second (which presents one of the most serious challenges in teaching composition) is selection. These two concepts—order and selection—form the foundations of the composition strand in this series.

As the children read the individual lessons on composition, they come to realize that every writer must give order to his material. This is a basic principle in all composition, from haiku to the novel. It applies with equal force to the writing of children and to the work of professional authors. And it is also a key to the great creative paradox: Order provides freedom.

Appropriately, this paradox relates directly to the structure of the individual lessons in composition. Embedded in these lessons is a quite formal structure which removes the problem of finding "something to write about" by providing a wide variety of topics that relate directly to the immediate experience of all children. Additionally, there is sufficient structure to provide a natural framework for response, thereby removing the problems inherent in the search for a proper form. In other words, the order within each lesson provides freedom for each child to respond in his own way.

The development of the concept of order can be illustrated by referring to specific examples from different books in the series. In one composition lesson in the third book, a child sees a set of simple pictures. The pictures can be arranged so they tell a story. But this is the key fact: There is no "right-or-wrong" arrangement. That is, the pictures can be arranged one way to tell one story, another way to tell another story, and so on. The child himself brings order to the composition, and yet at the same time he has the freedom of selecting any order that pleases him. In the fourth book, order continues to be treated in terms of simple arrangement of items and information. But in the fifth book, the concept is considerably broadened. The student begins to discuss chronological order, as opposed to other legitimate possibilities, and he discovers that other kinds of order necessitate finding new ways of presenting essential information. He comes to realize that order is influenced by other factors, such as audience. For example, a child might describe a cave one way to a friend and quite another way to a parent. Book Six further refines the concept of order by introducing some fundamental concepts of causation.

As the children study composition, the concept of selection is first implied rather than stated. In the facsimile compositions in the beginning of the third book, for example, it is clear that not all details are included in the compositions. Another implicit treatment of the concept occurs in the "Someone Game," where the children describe a person by selecting a few things that the person is, has, and does. When selection is formally presented, some lessons later in Book Three, it is —again—introduced through pictures. The children are asked to tell a story using some—but not all—of the five pictures in the book. In the fourth book, the children have an opportunity to alter details in a story, for example, to change a sad ending into a happy one, and vice versa. In an informal way, they begin to perceive that point of view also influences the selection of details. A cat, for example, won't notice quite the same

things about a beach that a child or a dog would. In the fifth book, selection is influenced by still other factors when concepts of research—in news stories and biographies—are introduced. The student then learns to select data on the basis of accuracy as well as audience appeal. In the sixth book, the student meets the subject "head on" when he reads the following: *There's one kind of composition that almost everybody finds hard to write. It's the "anything at all" composition. The real problem with the "anything at all" composition is choosing. Of all the millions of things that there are in the world, which one do you want to write about?* In short, the concept of selection develops in the series from the level of experience to the level of awareness and finally in the sixth book to the level of verbalization.

Language

The language strand of this series seeks to provide each child with an understanding of the nature of language and to develop his confidence in using it. The strand itself consists of a strictly pedagogical grammar, which incorporates many pertinent findings both from language studies of the past and from contemporary linguistic research. To provide a context for examining the key features of the strand, we will trace, briefly, the history of language study.

The term traditional grammar has three different meanings. First, it refers to those grammars written in ancient Greece and Rome. One of the most important of these is the grammar of the Roman scholar, Donatus, from whom we trace the notion that a sentence "expresses a complete thought." Second, the term refers to certain grammars written in continental Europe during the sixteenth and seventeenth centuries. These were philosophical grammars; that is, they attempted to explain the nature of language rather than simply describe it. Third, traditional grammar refers to those grammars written in England during the seventeenth and eighteenth centuries. These were prescriptive grammars, since their authors established "rules" for speakers and writers to follow. (The "rule" against splitting infinitives was formulated at this time.) Until quite recently, most of the grammars used in elementary and secondary schools were based on this third type of traditional grammar—that is, on the work of eighteenth century English grammarians.

American structural linguistics came into prominence in the 1930's, and it was a major force in the study of language for more than thirty years. While English traditional grammar was prescriptive, American structuralism was descriptive. The structuralists sought to describe and catalog all the observable features of language. They were determined to make the study of language objective, or, in their terms, "scientific." And, in their attempt to describe the way language is, the structuralists were frequently critical of those traditional school grammars which sought to define the way language should be.

The generative linguists (frequently called the transformationalists) reacted against the goals of the American structuralists. They believe that the structuralist descriptions of language are inadequate because these descriptions focus only on the surface of language. The goal of the generative linguists is to explain the nature and function of language. In this respect, their goal is similar to that of the second type of traditional grammarian—the philosophical grammarians of sixteenth century Europe.

In terms of goals, then, there are three different kinds of so-called grammars: (1) those which prescribe usage (the eighteenth century English grammars); (2) those which attempt to describe observable features (the American structuralist grammars); and (3) those which seek to explain the nature of language (the generative and "philosophical" grammars). The language strand of this series employs much of the terminology of traditional English grammar, and it also incorporates some of the insights of American structuralism. It draws most heavily, however, from the research findings of generative grammar, and it puts these findings to practical use.

In particular, the generative linguists agree that every school child has competence in language. Briefly, competence refers to that knowledge which every native speaker possesses about his language and which enables him to understand and create an indefinitely large number of sentences. Generative linguists distinguish, however, between competence and performance. Where competence refers to the internalized knowledge of rules, performance refers to the use of those rules in the acts of reading, writing, speaking, and listening. The language strand of this series enables each child to understand that he has linguistic competence, and this fact is used to develop his confidence in his own knowledge. The series then builds on this confidence in several ways that seek to improve a child's performance abilities.

But how does a child learn that he has linguistic competence? That was the major challenge in writing this series. Obviously, it is not sufficient simply to tell a child that he has competence. Rather, the fact must be demonstrated to him in a way which engages him actively. It is my belief that we can help a child develop awareness of his competence by showing him that he is able to structure—to manipulate—language in rather complex ways. As each book in this series both states and demonstrates, every child knows—in his head—the rules for using language.

Each book begins by establishing that children can distinguish sentences from non-sentences. From this, the children discover that they already understand the concept of sentence. Each book then introduces a pedagogical device called a *sentence model,* which permits the children to "talk about" the knowledge they have in their heads. In other words, the model not only develops awareness, it also provides a vocabulary which enables each child to verbalize his experience and awareness.

This model is so structured that all teachers can use it easily and effectively. The model has two parts: the rules and a lexicon. (This second term is quite old, and children have no difficulty learning it; most children seem to like any word that has an *x* in it.) In the beginning, the lexicon is limited to a few simple sets of nominals and verb phrases. The children are then presented with the basic rule in the grammar: A sentence has a nominal and a verb phrase. The text demonstrates how the nominals and the verb phrases in the lexicon fit together to form sentences. The children then experiment in forming sentences of their own.

Eventually the basic rule is replaced by another which represents the fact that sentences frequently contain other sentences within them. This slightly more complex rule is stated as follows: A sentence has a nominal (and another sentence) and a verb phrase. As explained carefully in the text, the parentheses indicate that so-called embedded sentences are optional. In discussing these rules, emphasis is constantly on the fact that they represent something that the children already know. And these are the only two rules given through Book Five. And there's a simple reason for this: Formal linguistic rules aren't necessary in teaching a child that he has linguistic competence.

In working with the sentence model, children learn to distinguish between two major types of sentences: basic and derived. Again, these are pedagogical labels which can be easily illustrated. The following sentences are all basic:

1. The boy ate the hamburger.
2. Robert is happy today.
3. The baby cried.

In traditional terms, basic sentences are simple, active, and declarative. They include no negatives; nor do they include prenominal adjectives (for example, the *tall* boy). As the second example indicates, however, a basic sentence may incorporate an adverbial in its final "position."

In the sentence model, all other kinds of sentences are treated as derived sentences. These include various kinds of questions, imperatives, passive sentences, and sentences containing negative elements. Additionally, compound sentences and those containing relative clauses are also derived sentences, as are those which contain prenominal adjectives. Of course, not all of these are discussed at every grade level.

As part of his linguistic competence, every child possesses the ability to produce an unlimited number of new and unique sentences. Partly, this is because some of the rules that a child has in his head are recursive; that is, they can be used repeatedly in the generation of a single sentence. There are various kinds of recursive rules, but most importantly the rules which enable a speaker to embed one sentence inside another are all recursive. For example, we can take two basic sentences:

The boy got a prize.
The boy won the race.

and we can make the second into a relative clause and then embed it into the first:

The boy who won the race got a prize.

This process can be repeated indefinitely. Thus, given *The boy gave the prize to his mother,* we can create another relative clause and ultimately get, through embedding:

The boy who won the race got a prize which he gave to his mother.

All school children have a knowledge of recursive rules and have considerable experience using them. For the child, what is important is the fact of recursiveness, rather than the form which particular recursive rules might take. And throughout the series, the language strand emphasizes the fact of linguistic competence rather than the form which particular rules might have.

In particular, children learn (again, by doing) that they can combine two or more sentences to form a single new sentence. The fact is presented quite simply in Book Three when the children work with relative clauses and prenominal adjectives. The concept is developed in subsequent books, and eventually children recognize that a single sentence may have considerable density: that is, a single sentence may actually consist of a number of basic sentences which are combined and embedded in a variety of ways. The following example, taken from Book Five, consists of ten basic sentences which are combined through recursive rules:

> Ebenezer Plunkett, a small, blue frog who likes square lollipops, invented a strange machine which talks to people who live in round houses.

The children also learn that mature writers and speakers use sentences of considerable density when the situation requires that they do so.

In addition to a presentation of the rules, there are also lessons on the constituent parts of sentences—that is, the categories in the lexicon of the sentence model. Books Three through Six all contain lessons on the nature of nominals and verb phrases. Various terms are introduced (for example, *noun, verb, adjective, adverbial,* and *auxiliary*), but in every case these terms are described as being "useful" when we want to talk about language. Technical terminology is kept to a minimum, and with few exceptions most of the terms will be familiar to nearly all teachers. One exception is the category of "be" words (*am, is, are,* and so on) which are not grouped with verbs since, in English, they function quite differently from words like *climb* and *eat.* The texts also use the term *morpheme,* which is convenient in discussing any part of language that has semantic meaning (for example, words, suffixes, and prefixes). Virtually all other terms used in the series have been employed by grammarians for hundreds of years.

Each text also distinguishes between grammar and usage. Everyone has an innate grammar, which we can categorize pedagogically as a set of rules and a set of morphemes. But no two people are identical, and this fact gives rise to differences in usage. (This was the primary concern of the English grammarians of the eighteenth century; it is also the concern of many texts used in schools today.) In this series, the subject of usage is presented in terms of dialects. Linguists have established that dialects are self-consistent varieties within a single language; that is, no dialect is a "corruption" or "sub-standard form" of another dialect. They have also established that persons can sometimes learn to speak more than one dialect, if they want to.

In sum, the language strand helps each child understand that, in his head, he has a knowledge of English. It helps him talk about this knowledge, and it strives to give him confidence in his ability to use this knowledge.

Blending the Major Strands

Although we've discussed the three major strands separately, they are actually woven together in each book so they reinforce and extend each other. In other words, literature, composition, and language are not separate subjects; they are parts of a whole. And this unity is constantly emphasized throughout each book and throughout the series.

We can use the fundamental concept of *order* to illustrate how this blending functions. Order is formally introduced in an early composition lesson in Book Three. Shortly thereafter, the concept is used in a language lesson which discusses the order of words in a sentence: The words cannot be in random order, and the rules specify which order must be followed. The concept of order also appears in the literature strand. For example, the children read the delightful poem "Bubblegum," and then they read the following: *Like stories, and like your own compositions, a poem has some kind of order. Read the first line of the poem again. Is it a good place to begin? Why? . . . How does the poem end? Do you think this is a good ending?* Once the concept is introduced into each strand, it is developed with frequent references to the use of the term in the other strands.

The tri-strand development of the concept of order continues in Books Four, Five, and Six. In each case, the concept is treated in a more sophisticated way. For example, in Book Five children discuss ordering groups within a composition and also the ordering of elements in complex sentences. Additionally, they discuss order in several different kinds of literature: poetry, drama, nonfiction, and so on. In Book Six, the concept appears again in the composition and language strands, and is particularly emphasized in the literature strand. After reading a short story by Ernest Hemingway, for example, the children have the opportunity to discuss the ordering of events in the story.

Similar examples could be presented for the tri-strand development of the concepts of metaphor, imagination, and even memory. Many of these interrelationships are indicated in the teacher's notes which accompany particular lessons, so any teacher can make additional connections when these would be useful.

The Arts and Related Topics

In addition to the three major strands—literature, composition, and language—each book in the series also contains, in the Arts Section, several lessons on "related topics." These lessons provide a link between the humanistic and the social study of English.

In each book, there are special lessons dealing with the history of our language and with the many varieties of spoken English. In Book Three, emphasis is on the fact that language changes. Children examine how the spellings of some words, and occasionally the meanings, have changed, and these lessons help explain the irregular forms of some nouns and verbs. The origins of English words are explored further in Book Four and children are made aware of the work of the etymologist. Book Five has a number of fully developed dialect lessons which are designed to help children develop respect for the varieties of English used in different regions of our country and in different countries of the English-speaking world. The discussion of dialects is continued in Book Six. Children also consider the notion of "appropriateness" as it applies to language, particularly with regard to idioms and slang expressions.

In every book there are lessons which teach children how to use the dictionary to determine the spellings, pronunciations, and meanings of words. Early in Book Three children are introduced to all of these uses of the dictionary. They learn some of the skills involved in using a pronunciation key, particularly as it applies to monosyllabic words. The pronunciation of polysyllabic words is taken up in Book Four, and the children also learn the function of double-entry words. In Book Five, the children examine the multiple meanings of some words as well as how to deal with run-on entries. In Book Six, children learn something about the history of the dictionary, and they also compare the pronunciation keys used in different dictionaries.

In addition to the many lessons on the use of the dictionary, the books in this series also introduce the children to other reference tools. In Book Four, for example, there are lessons in locating books in the library, and in Book Five there are suggestions on using encyclopedias, almanacs, and bibliographies.

Some of the other "related topics" include reading and writing codes in Book Three, a number of lessons on the newspaper in Book Five, and an introduction to the science of logic in Book Six. In every book in the series, there are special lessons on homophones and homographs, synonyms and antonyms, and so on. And many of these related topics are followed up with additional discussion material in the Skills Section of each book.

Taken together, these lessons underscore an important point: While it is useful to divide the content of English into arts and skills, it is nonetheless true that there are many significant connections between the two parts.

The Skills of English

As we've already noted, the skills of English are also an integral part of the curriculum. For easy reference, the skills in this series are presented —alphabetically—in a separate section of each book. Although primary focus in the Skills Section is on the essential rules of written composition, such as using capital letters and punctuation marks, there are also lessons which present the structural forms of letters and announcements and which give suggestions for locating and organizing information.

The specific skills in each book are selected for their appropriateness to a particular grade level. (See the scope-and-sequence chart on pages T–24 and T–25.) Although there is no single order in which the skills should be taught, many of the lessons are cross-referenced in the child's text and in the teacher's notes. When a specific skill is introduced, the lesson includes a discussion of the skill, a set of illustrative examples, and one or more sets of exercises which provide practice for those children who need it. Every skill presented in one book is repeated, and wherever possible extended, in the next book of the series.

Teacher's Notes

This teacher's edition includes notes to accompany nearly every page in the Arts Section of the child's text. It also includes, in the special introduction, various suggestions for teaching the lessons in the Skills Section.

The notes which accompany the lessons on literature provide many activities for involving the children in the material, and they stress the fact that such involvement should be presented in stages so that the children are asked to do only one thing at a time. Specifically, the literature notes provide many opportunities for dramatic experiences—experiences which contribute to making the literature more meaningful to the children. The emphasis in these activities is constantly on understanding and imaginative involvement.

The notes on composition suggest many kinds of oral experiences and supplementary writing activities. They also suggest that each child maintain a file of his composition work. Several lessons require a child to revise an earlier composition. There are also suggestions that each child be permitted, on occasion, to keep a particular composition "private"; that is, to show it to no one unless he wishes.

The notes which accompany the lessons on language are intentionally specific. The illustrative material has been chosen with extreme care. Thus, the nominals used in the sentence model are of a particular kind, and other nominals may not work in the model. The notes generally provide ample additional illustrative material for you to use. Please remember that the material is illustrative: a means whereby each child can gain some insight into the nature and extent of his own linguistic competence.

Supplementary Materials

Although each text is complete in itself, most teachers will want to supplement it with the Daybook/Skillsbook, which is available for each level beginning with the third. These consumable books provide materials which reinforce the concepts presented in the basic text and also provide considerable flexibility in establishing a program.

As its name suggests, the Daybook/Skillsbook is actually two books in one. The Daybook accompanies the Arts Section of the text, and the Skillsbook accompanies the Skills Section. The material in the Daybook is imaginative and frequently innovative. For example, there are exercises in each book which guide the children in making their own metaphors. There is "freedom through order" in such exercises, and consequently no "right-or-wrong" way of completing them. The kinds of exercises included in the Skillsbook are quite traditional in form, although particular care has been taken to make them fresh and interesting for the children. In both the Daybook and the Skillsbook, the exercises are structured so they may be done independently by the children.

An evaluation component for each of the books in this series is also available. (See Guidelines for Evaluation for a fuller description of this component.)

Guidelines for Evaluation

A teacher should know what to expect from a program. Only then is it possible to determine, objectively, whether a child is making satisfactory progress within that program.

Here again, there is a distinct advantage in separating the arts from the skills of English. The skills, by their very nature, permit us to establish precise and readily measurable performance objectives. Thus, specific objectives for each of the skills are included in the teacher's notes which accompany the skills lessons.

But the same degree of specificity does not apply to the arts of English. In other words, because the arts and skills are different, we need to establish different kinds of objectives for the two parts of the program.

Objectives have been established for the arts segment of the program. These objectives are less specific than the skills objectives, but they are no less real. They also may be creative, judgmental, discriminative, and occasionally even social; that is, there is a wide variety of objectives which relate to the arts. In contrast, the highly specific performance objectives which relate to the skills are generally of one kind and pertain chiefly to the conventions of writing (abbreviations, punctuation, and so on); other than these, there are a few skills which focus on "tools" (for example, those which relate to the use of the dictionary).

Here we can refer to a distinction made earlier. Many of the implicit, non-specified arts goals are humanistic, and they relate to the fact that man thinks, feels, and needs to communicate. The skills are social in the sense that they enable man to achieve these goals within a particular society. In this sense, the skills are discrete. For example, a child either knows—or doesn't know—that the word *September* is abbreviated using four letters whereas all other abbreviations for the names of the months use only three letters. In contrast, there is no precise point at which we can say that a child understands—or doesn't understand—the value of literature. Most children have had experience with stories, nursery rhymes, fairy tales, and various other literary forms before coming to school. The fact that they respond to these indicates that, on the simplest level, they already understand the "value" of literature. But clearly, every child—and for that matter, every adult—can develop his understanding of literature and can learn to respond more fully to increasingly "valuable" works. Additionally, such development takes place at variable rates. Nearly all teachers can recall a case in which a child suddenly plunges into lyric poetry, or art, or music. Perhaps his enthusiasm lasts a few days, or even a few months. Then just as suddenly, the enthusiasm is gone. If we are sensitive to these times, then we can help the child profit from these enthusiasms, and we can certainly hope that they will emerge again in later years. But we can't absolutely plan on these things happening. Therefore no specific objectives or related evaluation materials are given for these affective changes.

The broader our objectives, the more sensitive must be our judgments and evaluations. We can easily determine whether a child has made progress in learning to use contractions and abbreviations. A misspelled word seems to leap off the page. These are absolutes. (But if teaching were concerned solely with absolutes, it would indeed be dull.) Yet how do we determine whether a child is making—or has made—"progress" in studying the arts?

Some negative answers to this question are clear. It is often difficult to determine progress from one day to the next. And we cannot assume that all children will demonstrate progress in the same way. Thus, at some times—and for some children—the response to a poem might well be silence, while other children might want to dramatize the poem and still others might want to discuss its structure. Similarly, in studying a composition lesson which calls for children to dramatize a myth, one child may wish to develop dialogue for the characters, another might wish to add new adventures to the story, a third might want to direct the final production, and a fourth might prefer to work on scenery or to act. No single one of these ways of responding is absolutely better than any other, and no child should be expected to exhibit all these forms of behavior. Finally, no teacher should be unduly concerned if, during the course of a year, a child fails to make significant progress in some one area. In many cases, this is not evidence of failure to teach or to learn; it may well be that the child is simply not ready, and that spectacular growth may take place at some later time.

There are two stages in evaluating progress and growth in studying either the arts or the skills of English. First, we need to specify those verbs which characterize particular types of performance. (To borrow a term from the language strand of the series, these verbs are all "do" words.) Second, we need to list a variety of ways in which performance can be demonstrated.

Consider an example from Book Three in which the children are presented with a set of three pictures. These pictures can be arranged in any order so they "tell" various stories. The children then read two simple compositions which employ two of the possible arrangements. Next, the children discuss these compositions, relating the order to the pictures, and then have the opportunity to use a second set of pictures to "tell" other stories. The following verbs might apply to the objectives of this lesson: *analyze, recognize, demonstrate, rearrange, reorder, revise, structure,* and so on. Some children—the talkative ones—can *explain* the difference in order that results from rearrangement. Others can *demonstrate* their understanding of the principle of order through the stories they compose. And still others *display* their understanding through informal *dramatizations* of possible stories or perhaps by *drawing* their own pictures in various arrangements.

Nor do these verbs and types of behavior exhaust the possibilities. Some children can *analyze* the arrangements used by other children; they can *retell* the same "story" in various ways; they can *defend* their own choices; they can *compare* their choices with others; and so on. This means that no list of verbs can be complete when they apply to

evaluations of the arts. Many of these "performance verbs" are incorporated into the discussion and activity materials in the arts lessons of the children's text; many others are included in the side-column notes of the teacher's edition. The following examples are typical:

Here are some more pictures. First, put the pictures in any order that tells a story. Then write a story about the pictures. If you want to, you can draw the pictures to show what order you used. (Book 3, Chapter 3, Lesson 2)

Try to think of another way that Perseus could have tricked Atlas. Then write another ending for the myth. (Book 4, Chapter 7, Lesson 1)

Try to explain how to make the "tag" at the end of this question. (Book 5, Chapter 3, Lesson 3)

Find three other sentences which show that the authors used facts in their writing. Then find three sentences which show that they also used their imaginations. (Book 6, Chapter 4, Lesson 5)

As already noted, each of the substantive chapters in any book contains a review lesson, and these lessons also incorporate many performative verbs: *use, compare, describe, explain, ask, answer, write, select,* and so on. There are also various synonyms for these verbs, or—particularly at the earlier levels—more informal ways of stating the same idea. For example, instead of asking children directly to *explain* the difference between plays and stories, the Book Three text says: "How are plays different from stories?" Such questions as these (and each book contains literally hundreds of them) serve the same purpose as the more formally stated performance questions.

In general, and in the context of the cautionary observations already given, a teacher can evaluate progress in studying the arts. This book includes a Statement of Goals which teachers can use to develop their own evaluation programs. This statement consists, first, of the broad objectives which apply to each of the major strands in the Arts Section, and, second, of narrower and more specific performance objectives. (The Statement of Goals may be found in the side columns of this guide, beginning on page i.) Of course, no child should be expected to do all of the things listed in this structure. Nor do the "guidelines" exhaust the possible ways that a child can demonstrate growth in a particular area. The performance objectives list a variety of things that a teacher might look for in observing the individual children in the class. Such observation can be an effective basis of evaluation for the Arts Section.

A separate evaluation component is available for the arts of English (Literature, Composition, Language, and some of the Related Topics). It's designed to aid the teacher in assessing conceptual growth. These materials are in the form of spirit duplicating masters. Of course, teacher instructions are included.

The Skills Section lists specific performance objectives for each skill. Professionally designed tests have been constructed from these objectives and are also included in the evaluation component.

In sum, the series incorporates performance objectives in three separate ways. First, and most importantly, the children's books include hundreds of direct and indirect questions and activities that call for children to demonstrate their progress, understanding, and degree of mastery of both the arts and the skills. Second, the teacher's notes which accompany each lesson also include hundreds of performative verbs that apply directly to evaluating a child's progress. And third, there are specific lists of performance objectives for both the Arts Section and the Skills Section of each book in the series.

Scope and Sequence

The table on the following pages indicates the scope and sequence of the material contained in Books Three through Six. This table includes the most important topics taught at each grade level, as well as the appropriate page references in the children's text. It also indicates how the concepts are developed from one book of the series to the next.

Literature

Book Five

POETRY

Lyric poetry, 2, 6, 60, 102, 148, 154, 169, 178, 210, 220, 232, 300
Narrative poetry, 138, 154, 188
Nonsense poetry, 14
Haiku, 80, 104
Ballads, 158, 276
Songs, 264
Metaphor, 8, 22, 62, 82, 180, 220, 234
Rhyme, 264, 267
Stanza, 221, 234, 267

PROSE

Fantasies, 25, 198
Diaries, 35, 46, 65
Autobiographies, 48, 52, 65, 217
Biographies, 90, 217
Myths, 68, 203, 243
Plays, 112, 279
Speeches, 252
Tall tales, 129
Folktales, 286

ASPECTS OF LITERATURE

Imagination, 27–28, 62, 123, 132, 138, 178, 212, 234, 279, 304
Humor, 14, 52–53, 131, 192, 255
Hero, 74, 188, 191, 243, 245
Public vs. private writing, 35, 65, 176
Mood or feelings, 104, 180, 212, 232, 234, 255
Sounds, 232
Dialect and slang, 142, 158, 160, 297
Moral, 172

Book Six

POETRY

Lyric poetry, 3, 4, 74, 175, 183, 192, 297
Ballads, 134, 148
Concrete poetry, 139
Metaphor, 43, 158, 277, 301
Similes, 195, 277, 301
Rhyme, 176

PROSE

Diaries, 8, 30, 148
Journals, 8, 13, 20, 22, 76, 148
Autobiographies, 40, 43, 51, 55, 62
Biographies, 62, 67
Myths, 85, 97, 148, 161
Folktales, 109, 116, 125, 127, 148, 161
Legends, 161, 167
Short stories, 222
Fairy tales, 236
Newspaper stories, 248, 260
Dialect stories, 270, 285, 287
Speeches, 202, 212
Letters, 30, 32, 39

ASPECTS OF LITERATURE

Imagination, 13, 22, 55, 64, 67, 148, 270, 276
Humor, 192, 194, 236, 241
Hero, 85, 109, 116, 134, 148, 161, 167
Public vs. private writing, 4, 148
Mood or feelings, 262–263
Point of view, 55, 214
Theme, 227
Audience for, 39, 76

Composition

Book Three

Book Four

Book Five

ORGANIZATION OF COMPOSITIONS
Selecting and ordering parts for a composition, 9–10, 23, 66, 235–236, 293–294
Paragraphing, 357–358, 365–366
Outlining and using outlines, 161–163, 173, 176, 213, 218
Selecting and ordering facts, 96–98, 132, 136
Selecting and classifying people, things, and ideas, 192–194, 197, 218, 222

DESCRIPTIONS
Writing descriptions by using the describers (*is, has, does*), 17–19, 23, 66, 213
Using metaphors, 62, 83, 235–236, 240, 256–257, 262
Different point of view and different audiences, 104–107, 111, 269–271

OTHER COMPOSITIONS
Written and oral compositions, 218, 304
Public and private compositions, 35, 62, 65
Writing compositions that answer the questions Why? How? or What?, 293–294
Writing a book review, 345
Telling a story, 28–29
Keeping a diary, 41–42, 47
Writing about feelings, 104, 111
Writing an autobiography, 54–55
Writing a biography, 96–98, 132, 136
Writing a tall tale, 132
Writing a fantasy, 202
Writing newspaper stories, 185–187, 208–209, 246, 250–251, 261, 280, 284
Putting on plays, 123–124, 143, 203, 279
Writing poetry, 75–76, 82–84, 88, 182, 235–236, 257
Writing haiku, 82–84, 88
Using onomatopoetic words, 181–182
Revising and recopying compositions, 63–64, 136, 150–151, 292, 304

Book Six

ORGANIZATION OF COMPOSITIONS
Selecting and ordering ideas, 89–90, 94
Selecting and classifying things and ideas into groups, 228–290, 294

DESCRIPTIONS
Using metaphor, 43, 150, 195, 200, 277–278, 294
Using the senses, 185–186, 195–196, 200
Using the imagination, 22, 196, 276
Writing a description in dialect, 287

OTHER COMPOSITIONS
Giving attention to subject and details, 23–24, 28, 150, 302
Using the describers (*is, has, does*), 24, 28
Writing an imaginary conversation, 22
Expressing actions and feelings, 43
Writing according to audience, 76, 150
Explaining a point of view, 177, 180, 302
Writing a speech, 214
Writing a personal essay, 264–265, 268
Keeping a journal or diary, 13–14, 28, 149
Writing a personal sketch, 33, 48, 149
Telling about actions and feelings, 55
Writing biographies, 67, 68, 72, 149
Writing a myth, 101, 122, 150
Writing a folktale, 116, 128, 144, 150
Writing a legend, 167
Writing a fable, 168–169, 180
Writing newspaper stories, 252–253
Writing a short story, 228–229, 246
Writing dialogue for a play, 89
Composing pantomimes, 241–242, 246
Writing a ballad, 55–56, 72, 150
Using onomatopoetic words, 117–118, 122
Writing poetry, 139–140, 144, 215, 277
Writing a speech, 204–206, 220
Writing letters, 32, 44, 48, 149
Revising and recopying compositions, 77, 94, 144, 150, 302

Language

Related Topics and Skills

Introduction: Book Four

Book Four in the series, although complete in itself, is also a continuation of the program begun in earlier books. This program has several goals, which give form to the lessons in each book and also to the sequence of lessons in the series:

- To provide experience in literature, composition, and the nature of language.
- To bring this experience to the level of awareness as the children discuss the literature, engage in composition, and manipulate the language.
- To provide a vocabulary which will help children talk about their own awareness at any of several levels of verbalization.
- To apprise children of the need for mastering certain basic skills.
- To make these fundamental skills available to them.

In this introduction, we will examine the structure of Book Four to see how these goals are achieved. And, in addition to a discussion of the content of the fourth book, you will also find some suggestions concerning its teaching. Suggested guidelines for evaluation begin on page *i*.

The Structure of Book Four

Book Four is divided into two major parts: an Arts Section (consisting of 243 pages) and a Skills Section (consisting of 92 pages). The Arts Section is divided into sixteen chapters containing a total of 102 individual lessons. The Skills Section contains lessons on 18 skills and includes a separate section on usage.

In the Arts Section, there are three major strands: literature, composition, and language. The lessons in each strand form a well-ordered sequence, with later lessons building on—and generally reinforcing—earlier lessons. Thus, each

strand in the Arts Section forms a spiral in itself, and the three spirals are interwoven to form a unified whole.

More specifically, the Arts Section can be divided into two halves, with eight chapters in each half. And each half contains three different kinds of chapters: introductory, substantive, and summary. The introductory chapters in each half —Chapters 1 and 9—each contain a brief lyric poem. In the children's text, little or no discussion accompanies these selections. Thus, the teacher has considerable freedom in beginning each half-year in a way that seems most appropriate for the children in a particular class. The introductory chapters also point up to the children the reasons for studying language, and they serve to reinforce the understanding that children already have a knowledge of this language "in their heads." Each substantive chapter contains eight lessons, arranged in this order:

1. Literature
2. Composition
3. Language
4. Related Topics
5. Literature
6. Composition
7. Language
8. Review

Finally, the three summary chapters—Chapters 5, 13, and 16—insure that each spiral "turns back on itself," and they also provide a means for interweaving the spirals.

As noted above, each substantive chapter contains—in addition to lessons on the three major arts—two other kinds of lessons: one on related topics and a review. The lessons on related topics are concerned with what we can call the minor arts of English, for example the study of the dictionary or the uses of the library. The review lessons serve a dual purpose: They enable a child to check his own progress and they also help him to see how the three major arts are related.

The Literature Strand

The *Introduction: The Arts and Skills of English* includes a discussion of the fundamental concepts that underlie the literature lessons in this series. Book Four begins with the concept of metaphor, which is the foundation of the literature strand. Three of the first four literature lessons focus on lyric poems which contain easily recognizable metaphors. As the children come to realize what metaphor is—that it is natural to literature and that it is based on everyday experience—a variety of types of literature are presented to extend the concept.

Thus, in addition to poetry, the children also read a variety of types of prose, including folk literature, excerpts from historical and scientific writing, an autobiography, and diaries written by other children. In all of these, there is strong emphasis on the role played by imagination—both the author's and the child's. Most importantly, the children are encouraged to see that literature provides an important way of looking at the world, one which carries over into their everyday life.

In addition to a wide variety of literary types, this strand also contains selections of distinctive literary merit. For this reason, most children will enjoy reading them. But no reader can be expected to enjoy every work of literature, and so the text encourages but does not require appreciation.

Finally, the literature strand also provides each child with a vocabulary for talking about literature. This permits the children to share their feelings about poems and stories, which is certainly one of the most important aspects of the English language arts.

The Composition Strand

The first composition lesson in Book Four presents a practical definition that provides a starting point for discussion. The importance of "talk" is stressed at the very beginning and throughout the strand. The first lesson introduces the concept of order as a foundation for all forms of composition—oral or written. Children learn to impose order by rearranging pictures to tell a simple story. And there is no "right-or-wrong" order in which these pictures can be arranged. Then the concept of order is combined with selection and extended to writing a variety of different kinds of compositions. In all this, there is a natural movement from "talk" to writing and back again.

The development of the child's creative imagination is another important aspect of the composition strand. The children use their imaginations when they supply pictures to complete a story and also when they create dialogue and settings for their stories. They use their imaginations to change the endings of stories—their own as well as other people's. And they use their imaginations to write poetry.

The text also introduces the describers—Isabella Is, Harry Has, and Dudley Does—as a means of organizing data. These are first used by the children to describe someone or something in their immediate environment. Then they are extended to include descriptions of the heroes in literature and of the children's own imaginary heroes.

Thus the lessons in this strand contain opportunities for both structured and informal experiences in composition. In addition, there are numerous activities in the literature lessons and in the reviews which further involve children in the composition process. There is also strong emphasis throughout on revising and recopying earlier compositions.

The Language Strand

Because of the subject matter, the language strand is the most structured of the three major strands. For this reason, the simplest way to discuss the development of the strand is through a chapter-by-chapter analysis. The fundamental purpose of each lesson is the same: to help each child realize the nature and extent of his linguistic competence.

Chapter 1: Introduces the concept of word order in sentences and demonstrates to children that they can distinguish between sentences and groups of jumbled words.

Chapter 2: Presents grammar as a study that helps a child understand how he uses his knowledge of the rules of language and introduces the sentence model as a device for discussing this internalized grammar.

Chapter 3: Extends the discussion of the most basic rule of language (A sentence has a nominal and a verb phrase) and illustrates that each child already possesses the ability to combine sentences.

Chapter 4: Further illustrates the child's sentence-combining ability and provides labels for three kinds of nominals: regular nominals, names, and pronouns.

Chapter 5: Reaffirms the existence of each child's linguistic competence and also provides a cumulative review of the grammatical concepts already presented.

Chapter 6: Illustrates some varieties of verb phrases which every child uses and provides labels for verbs, "be" words, and adjectives.

Chapter 7: Illustrates one way that adjectives work in the sentence-combining rule and introduces the concept of sentence positions.

Chapter 8: Illustrates that everyone knows rules for making questions and provides labels for three kinds of adverbials: when-adverbials, where-adverbials, and how-adverbials.

Chapter 9: Reviews the functions of the sentence model and illustrates that, like all models, it is incomplete.

Chapter 10: Introduces some of the auxiliaries which every child uses and illustrates another kind of question: the tag question.

Chapter 11: Distinguishes between basic and derived sentences, introduces the idea of negative elements in sentences, and extends the discussion of tag questions.

Chapter 12: Introduces the concept of morpheme as a part of language that has a single meaning.

Chapter 13: Reviews the reasons for studying language.

Chapter 14: Further illustrates the child's sentence-combining ability and applies the concept morpheme to questions and negative statements.

Chapter 15: Further extends the discussion of morphemes to include plural and past tense forms and introduces alternative *wh-* words used in combining sentences.

Chapter 16: Review the fundamental concepts presented in the language strand.

It's important now that we repeat a comment made in the *Introduction: The Arts and Skills of English.* The language strand consists of a pedagogical grammar, one which draws upon several so-called schools of linguistics, primarily the transformational-generative. It also introduces some pedagogically useful apparatus that is not included in scientific grammars; for example, sentence pictures, position pictures, the concept of a basic sentence, and informal rules which are simplifications based on the more elaborate rules of scientific grammar. This apparatus is useful in helping a child learn about his own linguistic competence; it is not intended to train a child in the principles of linguistic science.

As these comments suggest, the language strand seeks to acquaint each child with two important and fundamental facts. First, by virtue of being human, each child possesses linguistic competence; that is, he has an innate knowledge of words and rules. Second, the rules are such that each child is capable of producing a boundless number of different sentences. The model introduced in Chapter 2 and developed throughout the strand helps to bring these facts from the level of experience (where children have been producing sentences for years) to the higher levels of awareness and verbalization.

Teaching Book Four

The subject of teaching English in general is touched upon in the *Introduction: The Arts and Skills of English.* Specific suggestions for teaching individual lessons are given in the side-column material which appears with the pupil pages in this book. This material is divided, for your convenience, into the following categories:

Purpose
Preparation
Presentation
Follow-up

In a few instances, preparatory and follow-up activities have been omitted, and you should feel free to incorporate your own ideas whenever they seem appropriate. In addition to these main categories, there are also lists of Additional Resources which should facilitate your teaching. Answers to the activities (■) are also included wherever they are warranted. Under Follow-up you will find additional practice for any children who have difficulty with a particular lesson, as well as enrichment activities for more able students.

The length of time to be spent on a lesson will naturally vary with the ability and maturity of the children in a particular class. In general, however, each lesson requires about thirty minutes of teaching time. At the rate of three lessons a week, you can cover the entire Arts Section in the course of a regular school year. By adding an occasional fourth lesson in a week, you can cover all of the material in the text and still have some time for many of the supplementary activities suggested in the guide. A five-day-a-week schedule, of course, is ideal and will enable you to make maximum use of the text and the supplementary materials and activities.

There are a few other remarks we should make with regard to using these materials. We have already noted that the arts and skills of English differ from each other in several ways. One difference is particularly obvious: Memorization may be necessary for children to acquire certain skills, but our aim in teaching the arts should be on the development of attitudes. The rules of the sentence model, for example, are not important in themselves, and children should not be asked to memorize them. It is far more important that each child recognize that he has an innate knowledge of the rules. The sentence model is a means of achieving this recognition, permits each child to bring *his* own linguistic experience to the levels of awareness and verbalization.

The most profitable kind of learning involves inquiry and discovery. Such learning is active rather than passive, and the greatest support for it is an enthusiastic teacher—one who enjoys literature and who respects the process of composition and also the marvel of language. Such a teacher encourages children to respond—to move from the level of awareness to the level of verbalization. Such a teacher will also supplement the text with additional poems, stories, compositions. Whenever possible, opportunities should be provided for many kinds of dramatic experiences—role-playing, pantomime, and play production, both formal and improvised.

Since the emphasis throughout the text is on verbalization ("talk"), you should try to use a tape recorder if one is available, particularly in conjunction with the lessons on composition. Children who are still reluctant to write compositions are often willing to compose orally. Children enjoy listening to their own compositions, but they also like to see them written, and for this reason you might want to transcribe as many of these oral compositions as possible. This is time consuming, but the results are worth whatever time you can spare.

The suggestions contained in the side-columns of this Teacher's Edition are provided to save you time and to facilitate your teaching. However, they are only suggestions, and you should feel free to supplement them with your own ideas whenever this seems appropriate. Most certainly, you will want to tailor the activities in the literature and composition strands to meet the needs and interests of the individual children in your class.

As a final word, no text is a substitute for a teacher. The most an author can expect to do—and the most I've tried to do—is to provide materials for you to use. I hope that you and your class find them helpful.

Bibliography for Teachers

Language

Burns, Paul C. and Schell, Leo M. *Elementary School Language Arts: Selected Readings*. Rand McNally and Company.

Chomsky, Noam. *Language and Mind*. Harcourt Brace Jovanovich.

Dinneen, Francis P. *An Introduction to General Linguistics*. Holt, Rinehart and Winston, Inc.

Dixon, John. *Growth Through English*. National Association for the Teaching of English. Reading, England.

Frazier, Alexander. *New Directions in Elementary English*. National Council of Teachers of English.

Jacobs, Roderick and Rosenbaum, Peter S. *Transformations, Style, and Meaning*. Xerox College Publishing.

Hunt, Kellogg. *Grammatical Structures Written at Three Grade Levels*. Research Report Number 3. National Council of Teachers of English.

Katz, Jerrold. *Philosophy of Language*. Harper and Row.

Labov, William. *The Study of Nonstandard English*. National Council of Teachers of English.

Lenneberg, Eric H. *New Directions in the Study of Language*. The M.I.T. Press.

Muller, Herbert. *Uses of English*. Holt, Rinehart and Winston, Inc.

O'Donnell, Roy C., Griffin, William J. and Novis, Raymond C. *Syntax of Kindergarten and Elementary School Children*, Research Report No. 8. National Council of Teachers of English.

Shane, Harold G., Walden, James and Green, Ronald. *Interpreting Language Arts for the Teacher*. National Education Association.

Shuy, Roger W. *Discovering American Dialects*. National Council of Teachers of English.

Literature

Arbuthnot, May Hill. *The Arbuthnot Anthology of Children's Literature*. Scott, Foresman and Company.

Association for Childhood Education. *Sung Under the Silver Umbrella*. The Macmillan Company.

Association for Childhood Education. *Told Under the Magic Umbrella*. The Macmillan Company.

Austin, Mary C. and Mills, Queenie B. *The Sound of Poetry*. Allyn and Bacon.

Baron, Virginia Olsen. *Here I Am!* Bantam Books.

Bogan, Louise and Smith, William Jay. *The Golden Journey: Poems for Young People*. Henry Regnery Company.

Bontemps, Arna. *Hold Fast to Dreams*. Follett Publishing Company.

Bulfinch, Thomas. *The Age of Fable*. Fawcett Publications.

Dorson, Richard M. *American Folklore*. University of Chicago Press.

Dunning, Stephen, Lueders, Edward and Smith, Hugh. *Reflections on a Gift of Watermelon Pickle . . . and Other Modern Verse*. Scott, Foresman and Company.

Durrell, Donald D. and Crossley, Alice B. *Favorite Plays for Classroom Reading*. Plays, Inc.

Emrich, Duncan. *The Nonsense Book of Riddles, Rhymes, Tongue Twisters, Puzzles and Jokes from American Folklore*. Four Winds Press.

Ferris, Helen. *Favorite Poems Old and New*. Doubleday and Company.

Hamilton, Edith. *Mythology*. New American Library.

Hollowell, Lillian. *A Book of Children's Literature*. Holt, Rinehart and Winston, Inc.

Huck, Charlotte S. and Young, Doris A. *Children's Literature in the Elementary School*. Holt, Rinehart and Winston, Inc.

Johnson, Edna B., Sickels, Evelyn R. and Sayers, Frances Clark. *Anthology of Children's Literature*. Houghton Mifflin Company.

Jordan, June. *Somebody Turned on a Tap in These Kids; Poetry and Young People Today*. Delacorte Press.

Joseph, Stephen M. *The Me Nobody Knows*. Avon Books.

Koch, Kenneth. *Wishes, Lies, and Dreams*. Random House.

Larrick, Nancy. *A Teacher's Guide to Children's Books*. Charles E. Merrill Books.

Larrick, Nancy. *On City Streets*. M. Evans and Company.

Lewis, Richard. *Journeys; Prose by Children of the English-speaking World*. Simon and Schuster.

Lewis, Richard. *Miracles; Poems by Children of the English-speaking World*. Simon and Schuster.

Lewis, Richard. *Out of the Earth I Sing*. W. W. Norton and Company.

Lomax, John A. and Alan. *American Ballads and Folk Songs*. The Macmillan Company.

Martignoni, Margaret E. *The Illustrated Treasury of Children's Literature*. Grosset and Dunlap.

Merriam, Eve. *Finding a Poem*. Atheneum Publishers.

Merriam, Eve. *It Doesn't Always Have to Rhyme*. Atheneum Publishers.

Morton, Miriam. *A Harvest of Russian Children's Literature*. University of California Press.

O'Faolain, Eileen. *Irish Sagas and Folk-Tales*. Henry Z. Walck.

Pellowski, Anne, Sattley, Helen and Arkhurst, Joyce. *Have You Seen a Comet? Children's Art and Writing from Around the World*. The John Day Company.

Petitt, Dorothy. *Poems to Remember*. The Macmillan Company.

Read, Herbert. *This Way, Delight*. Pantheon Books.

Richards, Laura E. *Tirra Lirra*. Little, Brown and Company.

Ross, David. *Illustrated Treasury of Poetry for Children*. Grosset and Dunlap.

Rugoff, Milton. *A Harvest of World Folk Tales*. The Viking Press.

Sheldon, William D., Lyons, Nellie and Rouault, Polly. *The Reading of Poetry*. Allyn and Bacon.

Untermeyer, Louis. *The Golden Treasury of Poetry*. Golden Press.

Walter, Nina Willis. *Let Them Write Poetry*. Holt, Rinehart and Winston, Inc.

Withers, Carl. *A Rocket in My Pocket: Rhymes and Chants of Young Americans*. Holt, Rinehart and Winston, Inc.

Sources of Audio-Visual Materials

Recordings

Caedmon Records, 505 Eighth Avenue, New York, N.Y. 10018.

Columbia Records, 51 West 52 Street, New York, N.Y. 10019.

Decca Records, 445 Park Avenue, New York, N.Y. 10022.

Folkways Records, 117 West 46 Street, New York, N.Y. 10036.

Folkways/Scholastic Records, 906 Sylvan Avenue, Englewood Cliffs, New Jersey 07632.

Spoken Arts Records, 59 Locust Avenue, New Rochelle, N.Y. 10802.

Films and Filmstrips

Bailey Film Associates, 11559 Santa Monica Blvd., Los Angeles, Calif. 90025.

Coronet Films, Coronet Building, 65 E. South Water Street, Chicago, Ill. 60601.

Educational Enrichment Materials, Division of Teaching Resources Corp., 83 East Avenue, Norwalk, Conn. 06851.

Encyclopaedia Britannica Films, 425 North Michigan Avenue, Chicago, Ill. 60601.

Eye Gate House, 146-01 Archer Avenue, Jamaica, N.Y. 11435.

Jam Handy Instructional Materials, Scott Educational Division, The Plastic Coating Corp., Holyoke, Mass. 01040.

Learning Corporation of America, 711 Fifth Avenue, New York, N. Y. 10022.

McGraw-Hill Text Films, 330 West 42 Street, New York, N.Y. 10036.

Society for Visual Education, 1345 Diversey Parkway, Chicago, Ill. 60614.

Sterling Educational Films, 241 East 34 Street, New York, N.Y. 10016.

Texture Films, 1600 Broadway, New York, N. Y. 10019.

Weston Woods, Weston, Conn. 06880.

Bibliography for Children

Additional listings can be found under Additional Resources in lessons throughout the book.

Alexander, Lloyd. *Coll and His White Pig.* Holt, Rinehart and Winston, Inc.

Arora, Shirley L. *What Then, Raman?* Follett Publishing Company.

Atwater, Richard and Florence. *Mr Popper's Penguins.* Little, Brown and Company.

Bridges, William. *Zoo Doctor.* William Morrow & Company.

Buck, Pearl. *The Big Wave.* The John Day Co., Inc.

Carpenter, Edmund, editor. *The Story of Comock the Eskimo.* Simon & Schuster, Inc.

Clark, Ann Nolan. *Paco's Miracle.* Farrar, Straus & Giroux, Inc.

Cleary, Beverly. *Ribsy.* William Morrow & Co. Inc.

De Angeli, Marguerite. *The Door in the Wall.* Doubleday & Co., Inc.

De Jong, Meindert. *Wheel on the School.* Harper & Row, Publishers.

Dickens, Charles. *The Magic Fish-Bone.* Harvey House, Inc., Publishers.

Dodge, Mary Mapes. *Hans Brinker or the Silver Skates.* The World Publishing Company.

Estes, Eleanor. *The Moffats.* Harcourt Brace Jovanovich, Inc.

Fritz, Jean. *Brady.* Coward-McCann, Inc.

Gannett, Ruth Stiles. *My Father's Dragon.* Random House, Inc.

George, Jean. *My Side of the Mountain.* E. P. Dutton & Co., Inc.

Godden, Rumer. *The Dolls' House.* The Viking Press, Inc.

Grahame, Kenneth. *Wind in the Willows.* Charles Scribner's Sons.

Johnson, Annabell J. and Edgar R. *The Grizzly.* Harper & Row, Publishers.

Lampman, Evelyn S. *The Shy Stegosaurus of Cricket Creek.* Doubleday & Co., Inc.

Lawson, Robert. *Rabbit Hill.* The Viking Press, Inc.

Lenski, Lois. *City Poems.* Henry Z. Walck, Inc.

Lewis, C. S. *The Horse and His Boy. The Last Battle. The Lion, the Witch and the Wardrobe. The Magician's Nephew. Prince Caspian. The Silver Chair. The Voyage of the "Dawn Treader."* The Macmillan Company.

Lewis, Richard. *I Breathe a New Song: Poems of the Eskimo.* Simon & Schuster, Inc.

Lindgren, Astrid. *Pippi Longstocking.* The Viking Press, Inc.

Mary-Rousseliere, Guy. *Beyond the High Hills: A Book of Eskimo Poems.* The World Publishing Company.

McCloskey, Robert. *Homer Price.* The Viking Press, Inc.

Monjo, F. N. *The Jezebel Wolf.* Simon & Schuster, Inc.

Morton, Miriam, editor. *Twenty-two Russian Tales for Young Children by Leo Tolstoy.* Simon & Schuster, Inc.

Mulock, Dinah Marie. *The Little Lame Prince.* The World Publishing Company.

Norton, Mary. *The Borrowers.* Harcourt Brace Jovanovich, Inc.

Pearce, Philippa A. *The Minnow Leads to Treasure.* The World Publishing Company.

Selden, George. *The Cricket in Times Square.* Farrar, Straus & Giroux, Inc.

Shotwell, Louisa R. *Roosevelt Grady.* Scholastic Book Services.

Singer, Isaac Bashevis. *When Shlemiel Went to Warsaw and Other Stories.* Farrar, Straus & Giroux, Inc.

Spyri, Johanna H. *Heidi.* The Macmillan Company.

Thompson, Eileen. *The Golden Coyote.* Simon & Schuster, Inc.

Weik, Mary Hays. *The Jazz Man.* Atheneum Publishers.

Wilder, Laura Ingalls. *By The Shores of Silver Lake. Little House in the Big Woods. Little House on the Prairie. On the Banks of Plum Creek.* Harper & Row, Publishers.

Wojciechowska, Maia. *Shadow of a Bull.* Atheneum Publishers.

The Arts and Skills of English 4

Owen Thomas

Consultants:
Juanita Abernathy
Alexander Frazier

Holt, Rinehart and Winston, Inc.
New York · Toronto · London · Sydney

Statement of Goals

On pages *ii–x* (and also on pages 337–342) are the objectives which relate to the literature, composition, language, and related topics strands of this book. They consist of a few broad objectives for each strand, followed by a number of more specific performance objectives through which children can demonstrate progress in studying the arts of English. Because of the nature of the arts, and because of the organization of this part of the curriculum, the performance objectives are grouped according to blocks of chapters, but in fact these objectives are cumulative. That is, an objective stated for Chapters 1–5 is also applicable to Chapters 6–9, and so on. Of course, no child should be expected to do <u>all</u> of the things listed; nor is the list exhaustive. (For a fuller discussion, see Guidelines for Evaluation in the *Introduction: The Arts and Skills of English.*)

i

Literature

Demonstrates an understanding of the concept of metaphor through one or more of the following:

Chapters 1–5

1. Recognizing that metaphor helps us see things in new ways.
2. Locating simple metaphors in lyric poems.
3. Identifying the two things being compared in a metaphor.
4. Using a metaphor frame to construct original metaphors.
5. Locating the main metaphor on which an entire poem may be based.

Chapters 6–9

Objectives 1–5 listed previously
6. Specifying ways in which a metaphor can be extended.
7. Locating metaphors in prose as well as poetry.
8. Creating original metaphors about suggested topics.

Chapters 10–13

Objectives 1–8 listed previously
9. Finding the human qualities that are attributed to non-human things in given metaphors.
10. Identifying metaphors that appeal to senses other than sight.
11. Creating original metaphors which appeal to the sense of hearing.

Chapters 14–16

Objectives 1–11 listed previously
12. Using the term *metaphor* during discussions.
13. Describing *metaphor* in terms of "putting one thing together with another thing that it reminds you of."

Author
Dr. Owen Thomas: Professor of English, Indiana University, Bloomington, Indiana.

Consultants
Mrs. Juanita Abernathy: Coordinator of English and Reading, Georgia State Department of Education, Atlanta, Georgia.

Dr. Alexander Frazier: Faculty of Early and Middle Childhood Education, The Ohio State University, Columbus, Ohio.

Illustrations: Vincent Ceci, Seymour Chwast, Margaret Coro, Paul Degen, William Holleran, Mona Mark, Judy Markham, William Naegels, Paula Scher, Emanuel Schongut, and Barry Zaid of Push Pin Studios; Robert M. Quackenbush; Michigan Conservation Department (photo, page 151).

Acknowledgments

Grateful acknowledgment is hereby made to the following authors, publishers, agents, and individuals for their special permission to reprint copyrighted material.

BELKNAP PRESS of Harvard University Press for "A Bird Came Down the Walk," from Thomas H. Johnson, Editor, *The Poems of Emily Dickinson*, Cambridge, Mass. Copyright 1951, © 1955, by the President and Fellows of Harvard College. Reprinted by permission of the publishers and the Trustees of Amherst College.

THE CHRISTIAN SCIENCE MONITOR, for "Unfolding Bud" by Naoshi Kariyama, copyright © 1957 by The Christian Science Publishing Society. All rights reserved. Reprinted by permission.

COWARD-MCCANN, INC., for excerpts from *Tall Tale America* by Walter Blair, copyright 1944 by Coward-McCann, Inc. Reprinted by permission.

DOUBLEDAY & COMPANY, INC., for "pete at the seashore" from *The Lives and Times Of Archy and Mehitabel* by Don Marquis, copyright 1935 by Doubleday & Company, Inc. Reprinted by permission.

PAUL S. ERIKSSON, INC. and INTERNATIONAL FAMOUS AGENCY, INC., for excerpts from *Small Voices* by Josef and Dorothy Berger, copyright © 1966 by Josef and Dorothy Berger. Reprinted by permission.

Reveals an active response to literature through one or more of the following:

Chapters 1–5

1. Identifying how and why people react differently to different literary selections.
2. Participating in group discussions about the selections in the text.
3. Referring to or recommending literary selections other than those found in the text.
4. Participating in the choral reading of poetry.
5. Reading in a way that reflects the mood of a given poem.

Chapters 6–9

Objectives 1–5 listed previously

6. Comparing the personal feelings expressed by an author with one's own feelings.
7. Demonstrating physical motions appriate to a particular selection.
8. Reading dialogue from prose excerpts in an appropriate manner.

Chapters 10–13

Objectives 1–8 listed previously

9. Participating in the dramatization of literary selections.

Chapters 14–16

Objectives 1–9 listed previously

10. Identifying and responding to the humor in a particular selection.
11. Participating in the singing of ballads and the reading of tall tales.

Demonstrates the use of imagination in discussing literature through one or more of the following:

Chapters 1–5

1. Making inferences based on a particular literary selection (for example, suggesting where Maurice found the things described in the story).
2. Creating dialogue for the inanimate objects of a particular selection.
3. Dramatizing the story of a myth.

Chapters 6–9

Objectives 1–3 listed previously

4. Creating alternative endings for myths —orally or in writing.
5. Identifying thoughts and feelings that might be included in a diary.
6. Identifying topics of conversation that are appropriate to a particular historical figure.
7. Describing animals in terms of human qualities and feelings.
8. Applying the metaphors from a particular poem to additional situations.

Chapters 10–13

Objectives 1–8 listed previously

9. Dramatizing how a story character might act in a particular situation.
10. Composing dialogue that a story character might use in a given situation.

Chapters 14–16

Objectives 1–10 listed previously

11. Expressing one's own feelings about the subjects of poems.
12. Describing the subject of a poem from a different point of view.

Table of Contents

The Arts of English

Demonstrates comprehension of content through one or more of the following:

Chapters 1–5

1. Discovering that every word in a poem is important.
2. Defining some of the new vocabulary "by example" (showing how a mouse *nibbles,* and so on).
3. Discussing the meanings of poems.
4. Describing some of the things that a story character is and has and does.
5. Dramatizing or illustrating the sequence of events of a given story.
6. Reacting to the irony in a particular selection (for example, the comment of the stool in the folktale "Talk").

Chapters 6–9

Objectives 1–6 listed previously
7. Applying the concepts of order and selection to prose selections.
8. Distinguishing between the factual and the imaginative aspects of literature.
9. Defining the role played by imagination in the re-creation of an historical event.

Chapters 10–13

Objectives 1–9 listed previously
10. Comparing and contrasting the heroes of different literary selections.
11. Comparing and contrasting similar events as they are described in fiction and nonfiction.
12. Making inferences and predicting outcomes from the information provided in a given excerpt.

Chapters 14–16

Objectives 1–12 listed previously
13. Describing the "action" in a ballad.
14. Identifying exaggeration in a tall tale.
15. Identifying some of the special characteristics of scientific writing.

Demonstrates an understanding of some of the structural aspects of literature through one or more of the following:

Chapters 1–5

1. Contrasting the rhythms of different poems.
2. Differentiating unrhymed poems from those that rhyme.
3. Identifying rhyming words when they occur in poetry.
4. Identifying stanzas in given poems.
5. Defining a refrain as repeated lines at the end of a stanza.
6. Identifying refrains in given poems.

Chapters 6–9

Objectives 1–6 listed previously
7. Describing how some poets exercise considerable freedom with regard to the mechanics of writing.
8. Distinguishing between words that rhyme and words that almost rhyme (slant rhymes).
9. Locating examples of slant rhymes in given poems (for example, *crumb/ home*).
10. Recognizing the rhyme scheme and rhythm pattern of a limerick.
11. Identifying the hero, the villain, and the action of a given myth.

Chapters 10–16

Objectives 1–11 listed previously
12. Identifying the special form of most English haiku poems.
13. Counting out—either verbally or through some physical motion such as clapping—the syllables of a given haiku poem.
14. Recognizing that many ballads are written in four-line stanzas.
15. Recognizing repetition as a poetic device.

Demonstrates an understanding of the variety of types of literature through one or more of the following:

Chapters 1–5

1. Distinguishing between poetry and prose.
2. Distinguishing between serious and humorous verse.
3. Locating particularly vivid descriptions in given prose selections.
4. Defining folktales as a prose form belonging to our oral literary heritage.

Chapters 6–9

   Objectives 1–4 listed previously
5. Identifying the limerick as one form of nonsense poetry.
6. Defining a diary as a private form of writing.
7. Locating "explanations" of things in some myths.
8. Including well-written history among the forms of literature.

Chapters 10–13

   Objectives 1–8 listed previously
9. Defining haiku as a form of poetry in which the subject is generally drawn from nature.
10. Distinguishing a ballad from other forms of poetry.
11. Distinguishing an autobiography from other prose forms.
12. Recognizing that Biblical stories are part of our literary heritage.

Chapters 14–16

   Objectives 1–12 listed previously
13. Listing accuracy and completeness as important features of scientific writing.
14. Defining a tall tale as a variety of folk literature which deals with the "impossible."

Composition

Demonstrates an awareness that composition can assume a variety of forms through one or more of the following:

Chapters 1–5

1. Defining a composition to include oral, written, or pantomime forms.
2. Creating compositions which describe real or imaginary things.
3. Distinguishing between compositions that describe and those that tell stories.

Chapters 6–9

Objectives 1–3 listed previously
4. Defining a diary as a record of events and feelings.
5. Writing diary entries.
6. Participating in both formal and informal dramatic experiences.
7. Using the special form given for writing plays.
8. Adapting given stories for dramatic presentation.
9. Creating original plays, orally or in writing.
10. Writing limericks.

Chapters 10–13

Objectives 1–10 listed previously
11. Writing an original haiku poem.
12. Writing a friendly letter.
13. Writing an autobiography or an autobiographical poem.
14. Distinguishing between public and private compositions.

Chapters 14–16

Objectives 1–14 listed previously
15. Conducting an interview.
16. Writing a newspaper story based on an interview.
17. Using pantomime to communicate ideas and to tell stories.

The Skills of English

Demonstrates an understanding of some of the essential elements of composition through one or more of the following:

Chapters 1–5

1. Ordering a given set of pictures to create both oral and written compositions.
2. Reordering sets of pictures to create alternative compositions.
3. Selecting and describing details of given pictures.
4. Using the describers is, has, and does to describe people and things.
5. Describing the sequence of events in a story.
6. Creating the middle or the ending for an incomplete story.
7. Telling a story from two different points of view..

Chapters 6–9

Objectives 1–7 listed previously

8. Creating alternative endings for stories.
9. Drawing pictures and ordering them to tell a story.
10. Creating a fanciful setting and cast of imaginary characters for a story.

Chapters 10–13

Objectives 1–10 listed previously

11. Describing given objects in terms of sound, taste, feel, and smell.
12. Applying the concept of order to the writing of an autobiography.

Chapters 14–16

Objectives 1–12 listed previously

13. Using who, what, when, where, and why as the bases for interviews and newspaper stories.
14. Creating stories in pantomime.

Demonstrates the ability to improve compositions through one or more of the following:

Chapters 1–5

1. Distinguishing between recopying and revising compositions.
2. Recopying one's own compositions.
3. Suggesting how given compositions can be revised by adding dialogue and action.
4. Suggesting other ways to revise one's own compositions.

Chapters 6–9

Objectives 1–4 listed previously
5. Creating specific settings for stories.
6. Revising pictures in a set to alter the endings of stories.
7. Revising informal dramatic presentations.

Chapters 10–13

Objectives 1–7 listed previously
8. Including sensory descriptions in compositions.
9. Adding interest to previously written compositions through the creation of dialogue.

Chapters 14–16

Objectives 1–9 listed previously
10. Revising a play presented in pantomime.

(Continued on page 337)

The Arts of
English

Purpose To provide a common experience with literature.

[Intentionally, there is no discussion of the poem in the child's text. The purpose of this omission is to focus the lesson on <u>experiencing</u> the poem, since experience must always precede awareness and verbalization. Also, it's best to begin the text in a relaxed atmosphere, one in which the children can simply enjoy the poem. Later lessons provide ample opportunity for discussion, but children first need to learn that silence is sometimes an equally appropriate response to literature.]

Preparation Although the poem is about a tide in a river, you may wish to begin by discussing tide changes in an ocean, particularly if you live near the coast. You can ask the children what happens at high and low tide, what effect the tide has on floating objects, swimmers, boats on the beach, and so on. In any case, you should turn the discussion to the subject of rivers before reading the poem. You might include some questions such as these:

1. What happens when a river overflows its banks?
2. What happens when a boat on a river makes waves?
3. What happens when you float a stick on a river?

Finally, point out the difference between an ocean tide and a river tide, suggesting that the latter is much calmer and quieter.

Presentation While the children still have their books closed, read "The Tide in the River" to them. Try to add as much feeling as possible to your reading, perhaps acting out a small "shiver" as you read the fourth line of the poem. Then have the children turn to page 3 and read the poem with you. (Generally, each poem in this

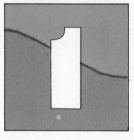

2

A Poem

The Tide in the River

The tide in the river,
The tide in the river,
The tide in the river runs deep.
I saw a shiver
Pass over the river
As the tide turned in its sleep.

ELEANOR FARJEON

book should be read twice: first, to the children, and then again with them. There are many reasons for reading poetry to children. In the first place, poems are meant to be said. The Irish poet, Padraic Colum, once said this about poems: "They are for our voices, not just for our eyes." Another reason for reading to children is that, as a teacher, you serve as probably their most important model. If, in your reading, you show that you like poetry, then chances are the children will like it too. Finally, by reading to the children, you provide them with an essential listening experience.)

After you've read "The Tide in the River" at least once with the children, you can request volunteers to read the poem aloud.

Follow-up After reading the poem in the text, you might want to have the children listen to some of Eleanor Farjeon's other poems. (See Additional Resources.)

Additional Resources

Books Farjeon, Eleanor, *The Children's Bells,* Walck. Farjeon, Eleanor, *Eleanor Farjeon's Poems for Children,* Lippincott. Hallowell, Lillian, *A Book of Children's Literature,* Holt, Rinehart and Winston. This anthology contains "The Sounds in the Morning" and other poems by Eleanor Farjeon. Larrick, Nancy, compiler, *Piping Down the Valleys Wild,* Dell. This paperback collection also contains a number of poems by Eleanor Farjeon.
Recordings *A Gathering of Great Poetry for Children, Volume 2,* 1–12″ LP, cassette, Caedmon. This collection of poems, superbly read by Julie Harris, Cyril Ritchard, and David Wayne, includes a number of poems by Eleanor Farjeon.

Purposes (1) To help children see that they "know" what a sentence is (that is, they can distinguish sentences from non-sentences); (2) To illustrate that everyone makes sentences by arranging words in order.

Preparation Have on hand a library book, if possible one the children read in an earlier grade. On the chalkboard, re-arrange the words in the first two or three sentences from the book so that they're in a jumbled order. Help the children see that, although they know what the individual words mean, the sentences don't make very much sense because the words are "jumbled up." Then read the sentences from the library book, or have a volunteer do it for you. Finally, ask the class if the words make more sense as the author has arranged them in the book.

Presentation Give the children a few minutes to scan page 4 of their books, pointing out that there are two important words and these are printed in very dark type. Write the words *sentences* and *words* on the chalkboard. Then you can say: "Everyone knows what a word is, and some of you have already learned some things about sentences. Today we'll learn some more about these two things."

Read the first half of page 4 with the children, pausing so they can answer the questions. Then have them try to make two different sentences, using the words in the illustration. If a child forms a question —"Is peanut butter good?"—be sure to accept it. Then call the attention of the class to the first sentence of the lesson, which states that a sentence can say things or ask things. Finally, point out to the children that they know how to make sentences because something "in their heads" tells them how.

Sentences

When people say things and ask questions, they use **sentences.** People also read sentences in books. They write sentences in stories and letters. Every day you use hundreds and hundreds of sentences.

When you got up this morning, did you say anything? Do you remember what you said? What did you say on your way to school? What did you say in school? Most of the time when you were talking, you were using sentences.

If you can talk in sentences, then you must know how to make sentences. But what do you need to make a sentence? First of all, you need some **words.**

Here are some words. Try to put the words together to make two sentences.

Using these words, we can make these two sentences.

Peanut butter is good.
I walked to school.

But we can't take just any bunch of words and make them into a sentence.

Here are some more words. There's no way to make a sentence from these four words. They just don't fit together. You can try, if you want to. But <u>nobody</u> can make a sentence from these words.

To make a sentence, we need words. But they must be words that fit together.

■ Here are some more groups of words. But these words are not in order. Try to make them into sentences.

1. shoe her lost Mary
2. funny smells Chalk
3. elephants teacher My likes
4. balloon a Fred found

If we don't put words in the right **order,** they sound silly. If we do put them in the right order, we get sentences.

● Every sentence has words, and the words must be in the right order.

■ Here are some more words in a jumbled order. Now try to make them into sentences.

1. Maria tree climbed a
2. finger hurts My
3. policeman shoe the The found
4. eyes Swimming my hurts
5. hair my cut Bobby

Read the last sentence on page 4 and the first paragraph on page 5 with the children. In working with the illustration on page 5, some children may try to add words so they can make sentences. You can avoid this problem by printing each word on a separate card and then asking the children to work with just the four cards. Reassure the class by saying that nobody can make a sentence from just these four words. Then read aloud the sentence beneath the illustration to emphasize the major point of the lesson.

The first activity (■) can be done orally by the entire class. Afterwards, emphasize the word *order,* and have the class discuss other things where order is important (for example, in playing a game).

The second activity (■) can be done on either an individual or group basis.

Follow-up As a follow-up activity, you can have the children look through other library books for sentences to "jumble up." After jumbling the words, they can exchange papers with their friends and try to rearrange the jumbled words so that they do form sentences. Finally, the children can compare the sentences they have made with the "originals" in the books from which they were selected.

Answers

For the first activity, children will probably suggest the following:
1. Mary lost her shoe.
2. Chalk smells funny.
3. My teacher likes elephants.
4. Fred found a balloon.

These sentences are most likely to result from the second activity:
1. Maria climbed a tree.
2. My finger hurts.
3. The policeman found a shoe.
4. Swimming hurts my eyes.
5. Bobby cut my hair.

Purposes (1) To introduce the idea of metaphor; (2) To experience the poem, "The Mouse Whose Name Is Time."

[You'll notice that in this book we use the term *metaphor* in its broad sense rather than in its narrow, restricted sense. In the broad sense, a metaphor is any verbal comparison. The formal distinction between a metaphor (in its narrow sense) and some other figure of speech, such as a simile or personification, isn't important here. We'll call all such things metaphors at this point and make distinctions later in the series. For your own information, you may wish to read *Metaphor and Related Subjects* by the author.]

Preparation All children have sometimes had the experience of feeling that time passes very quickly—and, on other occasions, very slowly. A discussion of such occasions provides an excellent preparation for this vivid poem. If the children seem to need some prompting, you can suggest such times as playing a game, or going to see the dentist, and so on.

After helping the children see that the way time seems to go by is relative, you can turn their attention to things that change with time. How are the children different from the way they were last summer? From the way they were "this morning at breakfast"? Then tell the children that today's poem is about time and how things change, but that before they read the poem, they'll need to learn two new words.

Write the words *seer* and *sibyl* on the chalkboard, and then say "If you were a seer, then you'd be a magician who could see into future time. If you were a sibyl, then you'd be a woman magician who could also see into future time." You might also ask if anyone would like to be a seer or a sybil—and why.

Daybook: Metaphors, page 1

6

A Poem

Sometimes a poem is like a picture made of words. If you try to <u>see</u> what the poet is talking about, then you can get a picture in your head. This poet once thought about the ways a mouse and time are alike. A mouse eats, little by little. And time is always going by, little by little. Here's what the poet wrote.

The Mouse Whose Name Is Time

The Mouse whose name is Time
Is out of sound and sight.
He nibbles at the day
And nibbles at the night.

He nibbles at the summer
Till all of it is gone.
He nibbles at the seashore.
He nibbles at the moon.

Yet no man not a seer,
No woman not a sibyl
Can ever ever hear
Or see him nibble, nibble.

And whence or how he comes
And how or where he goes
Nobody dead remembers,
Nobody living knows.

ROBERT FRANCIS

Presentation   As suggested earlier, first read the poem to the children while their books are closed. Then have the children turn to page 7 and read the introductory paragraph. When they've finished, ask them to try to describe the tiny bites a mouse takes. (You can also comment on the difference between "nibbling" and "gobbling.") This can be followed by thirty seconds of silent clock watching.

Now read the poem with the children, encouraging them to read with a "mysterious tone" in their voices.

Next, read the discussion material on page 8. Try to underscore the fact that all poets "pretend" when they write. The third paragraph on page 8 is the most important one. Write the word *metaphor* on the chalkboard and help the children pronounce it. Some children will be familiar with the descriptive definition used in Book Three and you can adapt it here: "Sometimes one thing—like time—makes us think of another thing—like a mouse. If we put the two things together into a word picture, then we have a metaphor."

You can develop the discussion by referring to "The Tide in the River" on page 3. "A river made that poet think of a person who was sleeping, and she put the two of them together into a metaphor."

In the activity (■), the children use a "metaphor frame" to help them create metaphors about the rain. You can copy the frame on to the chalkboard, and then have volunteers suggest various things that the rain makes them think of. Encourage the children to tell how the two things put together to make each metaphor are alike. Then have the children use the metaphor frame to write their own metaphors about the rain.

Finally, read the poem once more before you end the lesson.

Follow-up On the bulletin board, you can post a metaphor frame similar to the one in the activity on page 8. In place of "rain," you can use some of the following: clouds, snow, fog, sunshine, wind, cold, lightning, thunder, night, and so on. As the children write their metaphors, encourage them to think about the similarities in the two things being compared. Later, you can make a bulletin board display of the children's metaphors, and perhaps even a metaphor "file box" where the children can browse during free time.

Additional Resources

Books Francis, Robert, *Come Out into the Sun: Poems New and Selected,* University of Massachusetts Press. You may want to select two or three other of Francis's poems to read to the children. Hannum, Sara and Gwendolyn E. Reid, compilers, *Lean Out of the Window,* Atheneum. Robert Francis is one of the poets whose works are included in this anthology. Morrison, Lillian, *Sprints and Distances, Sports in Poetry and Poetry in Sports,* Crowell. Children interested in sports will find this collection intriguing. The works of both ancient and modern poets are included—among them, Robert Francis.

Recordings *A Gathering of Great Poetry for Children,* Volume 2, 1–12″ LP, cassette, Caedmon. Included in this collection is "The Mouse Whose Name Is Time," as well as another of Robert Francis's poems, "Night Train." Volume 3 of this same series contains Francis's poem "Catch."

When you read a poem or a story, it's important to know what all the words mean. You probably know what it means to be "out of sight." But what does "out of sound" mean? A *seer* is a kind of magician. He's someone who says he can see into the future. A *sibyl* is a woman seer. And *whence* is a special word that poets sometimes use. It means "from where."

Of course, time really isn't a mouse. But the poet pretends that it is. He says that the way the day goes—little by little—is like the way a mouse nibbles food. What other things does the mouse nibble at in the poem?

There's a special word for this way of talking and writing. The word is **metaphor.** When the poet pretends that time is a mouse, he's using a metaphor. The poem says that the mouse whose name is Time cannot be heard or seen. How is this like a mouse? How is it like time?

The poem about the tide in the river also has metaphors. The poet says, "the tide turned in its sleep." A tide doesn't really sleep. And a river can't "shiver." When the poet says these things, she's using metaphors.

You can almost always find metaphors in poems and stories. We'll find lots of them this year. You can also make your own metaphors. Think about the rain. Here are two metaphors about the rain.

Rain is like soft, silver thread.
Rain is like leaves falling from the clouds.

■ What do you think the rain is like? What does it make you think of? Try to write your own metaphor about the rain. Here's a sentence to help you.

The rain makes me think of _____ because both of them _____.

Kinds of Writing

This book is about the different ways that people use language. So far, we've talked about talking. We've read two poems. We've even written some metaphors. Whenever you write something, you use language.

You can write stories, poems, and plays. You can write letters to friends. You can write reports about the things you're learning in school. There are many different kinds of writing that you can do.

There's a special word for the things you write. They're called **compositions.** You probably wrote several compositions last year. There are even compositions that you don't write at all. You can tell a story without writing it. You can put on a play without writing it. You can even "talk with your hands," without using words at all.

There are many different kinds of compositions. One kind describes something. You can describe an animal or a toy. You can describe what you see from your window in the morning. There are many other things to describe.

Purposes (1) To introduce the concept of composition; (2) To suggest that there are many varieties of composition, both written and oral.

Preparation Write the word *composition* on the chalkboard, and then comment that—even though some children may not know the word—they already know how to make compositions.

Arrange beforehand for a child to pantomime a simple composition (for example, skipping rope, pouring cereal into a bowl and eating it, and so on). Have the rest of the class try to guess what the child is doing. Then you can say: "He acted a composition."

Also prearrange for a child to describe some object in the room, perhaps the flag. Then say: "He just spoke a composition."

Finally, have the children turn to page 3 and reread the poem, "The Tide in the River." Then comment: "This poem is a written composition."

Presentation As the children read page 9 in their texts, call their attention to the contextual definition of *composition* in the third paragraph. To reinforce the idea that composition may be written, oral, or in pantomime, you can then refer back to the activities done during the preparation for the lesson. You can also ask what kind of composition the children in the illustration are involved in. Of course, all of them are writing compositions, and you may want to discuss in greater detail the varieties of written composition pictured. You can ask questions such as these:

1. Besides writing about it, how else could the boy present his science report?
2. Besides writing a letter, how could the girl send someone else a message?
3. How else could the boy tell a story about his cat?

9

Next, have the children read silently the sample composition on page 10. Then they can try to guess what the composition describes. Be sure that the children understand that a "description" is one kind of composition.

The first sentence beneath the composition can lead to an interesting class discussion. Try to encourage descriptive metaphors by using the frame:

Our schoolyard in winter (*or spring or fall*) reminds me of _____ because both of them _____.

Then have each child choose one picture from the four on page 10. Divide the class into groups of children who have chosen the same picture, and have each group choose a secretary. The members of each group can then jointly prepare a description of their picture, which the secretary can record and later read to the rest of the class.

Follow-up It's important that each child keep a folder of his own compositions. Even though the children may not have written individual compositions as part of this lesson, they can prepare for doing so by making folders which include their names. You can then arrange these in a brightly colored box that the children have easy access to.

Whenever you have free time, you can draw an object on the chalkboard and then have the children write a class composition about it. You might also want to set off a special section of the bulletin board on which you can post each day a different "picture for writing."

Throughout the year, you should try to provide the children many opportunities for oral composition. In addition to pictures, you can also use appropriate films and filmstrips to inspire your class.

10

Here's part of a composition that a nine-year-old girl wrote. Try to guess what she's describing.

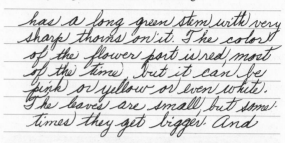

has a long green stem with very sharp thorns on it. The color of the flower part is red, most of the time, but it can be pink or yellow or even white. The leaves are small, but sometimes they get bigger. And

Do the seasons change in the place where you live? Here are some pictures of trees. Each picture shows how a tree can look at different times of the year.

■ Now choose one of the pictures. Then describe how the tree in the picture looks. Or, if you wish, you can think about a real tree and describe it.

Grammar

In your head, you know how to make sentences. You can also learn to talk about sentences. Here are two important things you've learned about making sentences:

- Every sentence has words.
- The words must be in the right order.

■ Here are some more groups of words. First, put the words in each box together so they don't make a sentence. Then, put them in order so that they do make a sentence. (The first group of words has already been done for you.)

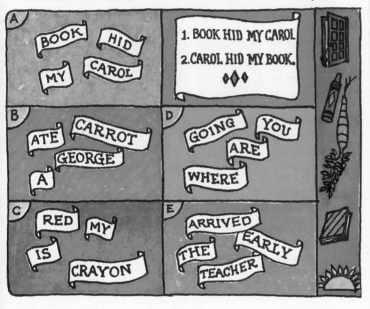

A
BOOK HID
MY CAROL

1. BOOK HID MY CAROL
2. CAROL HID MY BOOK.
◆◆◆

B
ATE CARROT
GEORGE
A

D
GOING YOU
ARE
WHERE

C
RED MY
IS
CRAYON

E
ARRIVED
THE EARLY
TEACHER

Daybook: Rules About Sentences, page 3

Purpose To introduce *grammar* as the study of how we use words and rules to make sentences.

Preparation Remind the children that they've already read one lesson about sentences. In that lesson, they learned that every sentence has words in it, and that the words must be in an order that makes sense.

Then, on individual cards or in boxes drawn on the chalkboard, write some jumbled words which can be rearranged to make sentences (for example, *dog, cat, the, chased, the*). Ask the children what they see on each card (or in each box). Then say: "You know that we use words to make sentences. Can you rearrange these words to make a sentence?" When the children have suggested a sentence, ask: "Can you put the words in another order to make a different sentence?" (The words suggested above can be put in more than one order, but they can't be put in just any order.) Ask: "Can you arrange the words in any way at all and still have a sentence?" (Help the children see that this is impossible.)

Presentation Read the text on page 11 with the children, stressing the first sentence. The Preparation above will help them grasp the "two important things" about making sentences.

Work the activity (■) on page 11 with the entire class, perhaps having the children write each answer before saying it aloud. (For the second part, accept any sentence that makes sense.)

Then go on to read page 12, stressing the first paragraph. At first, many children find it difficult to believe that they know so many words and rules. That's a primary reason for studying grammar—so they can learn about the words and rules they have in their heads.

11

After reading the paragraph below the symbol (●), discuss briefly with the children how knowing "special terms" can facilitate a discussion. You can say: "Whenever we want to talk about something, we need to use special words. What special words would you need if you wanted to talk about a spaceship? Or about a TV set?" As the children make suggestions, write the words on the chalkboard. Then point out that the special terms on page 12 can help them talk about their language. (While it's not important that the children memorize these terms, you can suggest that they add the words to their personal spelling lists.)

The activity (■) on page 12 can be done individually or in small groups. The "first word" of each sentence has already been capitalized, but you may need to remind the children to use a period at the end of each sentence that is a statement.

Follow-up If you wish, you can use the following sets of jumbled words to reassure the children that they already know how to make sentences.

1. THE WAGON OX PULLED A
2. LIVE I BUILDING IN TALL A
3. AT HOWLS MY THE DOG MOON
4. FROG LOG SAT ON THE A
5. PRESIDENT IS GEORGE THE
6. MOLE HOLE LIVES A IN A
7. UNCLE A MY FISH CAUGHT
8. HAIRCUT YAK THE A NEEDS
9. PAJAMAS STRIPED ZEBRA THE WORE

Answers

The children will probably suggest the following sentences:
1. My cat walks backwards.
2. Agnes forgot her lunch.
3. I broke my pencil.
4. The mayor likes oranges.
5. My bicycle is purple.

In your head, you know thousands and thousands of words. You also know hundreds of rules that help you put the words in order.

To make sentences, you need to use both the words and the rules. When we talk about the words and rules and sentences, then we're talking about **grammar.**

● The study of grammar helps us understand how we use words and rules to make sentences.

When you study grammar, you'll use many special words. These words will make it easy for you to talk about sentences. Here are some special words that we've already used.

    rule   order   sentence   word

■ Just for practice, try to put the following words in the right order so that they make sentences.

1. backwards cat My walks
2. lunch Agnes her forgot
3. pencil I my broke
4. mayor likes oranges The
5. purple My is bicycle

Arts and Skills

This book has two important parts. It has an *arts* part and it also has a *skills* part. Do you know the difference between them? The arts are the <u>what</u> of English, and the skills are the <u>how</u> of English.

The arts of English are the important things people do with language:

The <u>poems</u> and <u>stories</u> other people write
The <u>compositions</u> you write
The <u>grammar</u> we all use

We can say this a short way. The arts of English are literature, composition, and grammar.

The skills of English are different. They are the things we need to know when we speak and write. Here are some things you should know how to do:

Write abbreviations
Use contractions
Put words in alphabetical order
Address letters
Proofread your written work
Use punctuation marks

These skills help us to speak and write so that other people can understand us easily.

Right now, you're reading the arts part of this book. Look in the Table of Contents to find out where the skills part begins. Notice that the skills are arranged in alphabetical order. Why do you suppose they're arranged this way? What other books have things in some special order?

When you study the arts, you'll probably read chapter by chapter, just like a storybook. But you'll skip around in the skills part, just as you do in a dictionary.

Daybook: Dividing the Parts, page 4

Purpose To introduce the distinction between the arts and skills of English.

Preparation This is an ideal time to have the children examine their textbooks physically, noting the title, recognizing the division between the arts and skills in the Table of Contents, and finding the special title page at the beginning of the Skills Section of the text.

Presentation As the children read this lesson, you should give them the opportunity to ask questions. Some might ask whether the arts are "better than" (or "more important than") the skills. If the question does arise, it's certainly best to say that the two things can't be compared. You might comment that it's like asking whether an apple is better than a typewriter.

You should encourage the children to discuss the questions in the next to last paragraph. You might want to suggest some small group discussions, with each group reporting its answers to the class.

Follow-up Because this lesson is brief, you may have time for some of the follow-up suggestions made in earlier lessons.

Purposes (1) To increase a child's experience with variety in literature through a nonsense poem; (2) To introduce some technical terms that facilitate the discussion of literature.

[Children have varied experiences with literature, but even those with the widest experience sometimes think that literature must always be serious or even teach a lesson. One aim of the literature strand of this series is to increase each child's awareness of the scope of literature, and Lewis Carroll's delightful poem can help to achieve this purpose.]

Preparation Despite its obvious appeal to children, nonsense poetry generally requires very careful preparation. You may need to help some children relax and just enjoy the poem, without being concerned about its "meaning." Most children are familiar with "counting-out rhymes" or "choosing rhymes," and also with "rope-skipping rhymes." You can discuss these with the class, and perhaps have volunteers recite one or two such rhymes.

In addition, you might read one or two short nonsense poems, such as those of Edward Lear. (See Additional Resources.) Encourage the children to listen for the "music"—the "special sounds"—of these poems.

Presentation As you read the introduction on page 15 to the children, write the italicized words on the chalkboard. Some are defined in the text; you can illustrate the meanings of the other words or have volunteers check their definitions in a dictionary. So that children aren't discouraged by the number of "new" words in this selection, remind them that, in a nonsense poem, it's not always important to understand every word the first time they hear the poem. It's more important to listen for the music.

Daybook: The Last Word, page 6

14

A Poem

Here's a poem from the book *Alice's Adventures in Wonderland*. The book was written by Lewis Carroll. The poem is about a kind of square dance that was popular many years ago. It's called a *quadrille*. But in this silly poem, people don't dance the quadrille. Some sea-animals do. In the poem, two of these animals—a whiting and a snail—even talk. Do you know what kind of fish a *whiting* is?

There are some other words in the poem that you may not know. A *porpoise* is a sea animal that looks like a small whale. On many of the beaches in England, there are smooth, round stones called *shingles*. If a beach has these stones, then people call it a *shingle*.

Here are some more words you may not know: *tread, advance, notion,* and *askance.* You can look them up in a dictionary.

This poem is fun for the whole class to read aloud. If you listen carefully as you read it, you can almost hear the music of the quadrille.

The Lobster Quadrille

"Will you walk a little faster?" said a whiting to a snail.
"There's a porpoise close behind us, and he's treading on my tail.
See how eagerly the lobsters and the turtles all advance!
They are waiting on the shingle—will you come and join the
dance?
    Will you, won't you, will you, won't you, will you join the
    dance?
    Will you, won't you, will you, won't you, won't you join the
    dance?

Then read the poem to the children. Every touch of drama and excitement that you can get into your voice will add to the children's enjoyment. In particular, try to achieve a contrast between the spoken and the narrative lines; the refrain can be very bouncy, if you wish.

The chief point is this: The children should feel that you like the poem and enjoy reading it. As already noted, if children are to enjoy literature, then they must see that significant adults also enjoy it. Many children will look to you for clues on how to respond. If you like the rhythms and the rhymes, then they will too.

When the children are comfortable with the poem—and particularly with its rhythm—then you can discuss the "story" of the poem. Remind the children of other stories they know where animals talk. Then ask how one would get to France from England. (Be sure to have a map of Europe ready to help clear up any confusion that arises when children mention cars as well as boats and airplanes.) Then explain how keeping a picture of the map in their heads will help them understand the poem as they read it.

Now read the poem again as the children follow along in their books. Encourage them to join in the refrain at the end of each stanza.

If the lesson is running long, you can save the rest of the discussion for another day. This will help preserve the children's enthusiasm for the poem when you do return. It will also reinforce the notion that you can return—again and again—to good literature and enjoy it anew each time.

The discussion material on page 17 emphasizes three important points. The first paragraph stresses the importance of close reading—understanding the story of the poem. Most nonsense poems tell a simple story, if they tell one at all, but even so, understanding the story can increase one's enjoyment of the poem.

The second and third paragraph provide illustrative examples of terms, such as *stanza, rhyme,* and *refrain,* which are useful in discussing poetry. In introducing these terms, you should try to repeat them frequently and to provide as much context for them as possible. You can say: "There are some lines in the poem that are repeated several times. These repeated lines are called a *refrain.* Who can find the refrain—the repeated lines—on pages 15, 16, and 17?" When someone has identified the refrain, you can write the word *refrain* as a heading on the chalkboard, and then write the actual lines under the heading.

The same process will also work in discussing rhyming words. When you come to *askance,* you might say: "This is a real word, but even so, the poet probably used it because he liked the way it sounds—and because it rhymes with *dance.*"

The fourth paragraph focuses on the subject of the poem—worrying (rather than on the story of the poem). Be sure to provide ample time for a discussion of the questions contained in this paragraph.

Follow-up This is a particularly good poem to follow-up with an art activity. The children can work individually, illustrating the entire poem or just one of the stanzas. Or you can divide the class into three groups, with each group responsible for illustrating one stanza. Then you can arrange the pictures sequentially to form a small mural.

If you haven't already done so, you might want to read two or three other nonsense poems to the class. (See Additional Resources.) Again, encourage the

"You can really have no notion how delightful it will be,
When they take us up and throw us, with the lobsters, out to sea!"
But the snail replied "Too far, too far!" and gave a look askance—
Said he thanked the whiting kindly, but he would not join the dance.
Would not, could not, would not, could not, would not join the dance.
Would not, could not, would not, could not, could not join the dance.

"What matters it how far we go?" his scaly friend replied.
"There is another shore, you know, upon the other side.
The further off from England the nearer is to France—
Then turn not pale, beloved snail, but come and join the dance.
  Will you, won't you, will you, won't you, will you join the
    dance?
  Will you, won't you, will you, won't you, won't you join the
    dance?"

LEWIS CARROLL

    In the poem, the whiting tells the snail to hurry up. Are snails always slow? What makes you think so? Did the snail want to join the dance? What did the whiting say to try to make the snail change his mind? To get from England to France, you have to travel across water. That's why, in the poem, the whiting says, "The further off from England the nearer is to France."

    This poem, like lots of others, is divided into **stanzas.** How many stanzas are there in "The Lobster Quadrille"? This poem also has words that **rhyme** with each other. In the first stanza, *tail* rhymes with *snail. Advance* rhymes with *dance.* In the second stanza, what rhymes with *be*? What rhymes with *replied* in the third stanza?

    In some poems, the lines at the end of the first stanza are repeated. These lines are called a **refrain.** What is the refrain in this poem? In which stanza are the words of the refrain a little different? What other poems or songs do you know that have refrains?

    In "The Lobster Quadrille," the whiting tells the snail not to worry. But everyone worries sometimes. What do you worry about? Do you think it's good to worry <u>all</u> the time? When people want to stop worrying, sometimes they dance. What else could they do? What do you do?

children to listen for the "music" of each poem as you read it. Perhaps some of the children would even like to participate by reading short poems that they have selected themselves. Suggest that they practice beforehand, and, if a tape recorder is available, they can even "listen" to themselves before reading to their classmates.

Additional Resources

Books Opie, Iona and Peter, *Lore and Language of School Children,* Oxford. Withers, C. A., *A Rocket in My Pocket: Rhymes and Chants of Young Americans,* Holt, Rinehart and Winston. Both of these books contain some "counting-out" and "rope-skipping" rhymes, such as are mentioned in Preparation. You'll find more of Lewis Carroll's amusing poetry in Ferris, Helen, compiler, *Favorite Poems, Old and New,* Doubleday, and Untermeyer, Louis, compiler, *The Golden Treasury of Poetry,* Golden Press. Other fine collections of humorous verse include Ciardi, John, *The Reason for the Pelican,* Lippincott; Lear, Edward, *The Complete Nonsense Book,* Dodd, Mead; Love, Katherine, compiler, *A Little Laughter,* Crowell; and Richards, Laura, *Tirra Lirra,* Little, Brown.

Recordings *Discovering Rhythm and Rhyme in Poetry,* 1–12″ LP, Caedmon. This recording, by Julie Harris and David Wayne, is an excellent way to introduce children to rhythm, rhyme, and repetition in poetry. *Nonsense Verse of Carroll and Lear,* 1–12″ LP, 2-track tape, cassette, Caedmon. "The Lobster Quadrille" is just one of the many verses read by Beatrice Lillie, Cyril Ritchard, and Stanley Holloway. *The Simon Sisters Sing The Lobster Quadrille and Other Songs for Children,* 1–12″ LP, Columbia.

Purposes (1) To emphasize the importance of <u>order</u> in composition; (2) To provide on open-ended experience in using order to create compositions.

Preparation Remind the children that, in an earlier lesson, they put words in order to make sentences. (You might repeat an example from page 11.) Then ask a volunteer to tell—in order—the things he did to get ready for school that morning. Then have someone else, who did similar things in a different sequence, tell—in order—about his preparations.

Presentation Have the children turn to page 18, and then ask them if they have ever done what the girl in the set of pictures is doing. Then read the first paragraph on this page with the children. Ask for a volunteer to explain the first sentence of the paragraph, as well as each sentence in the rest of the paragraph.

Then call the children's attention to the activity (■) at the bottom of page 18. Encourage them to see that the pictures can be arranged in more than one way; that is, there's more than one way to tell almost any story. The children can discuss various ways to arrange the pictures, and then decide which one they'd like to use as the basis for a class story. Then, as the children describe what's happening in each picture, you can write the class story on the chalkboard.

Next, read the first paragraph on page 19 with the children. In working with the pictures on this page, you can describe them, one at a time, and have the children identify the picture you're describing.

Order in Compositions

Sometimes compositions describe things. Sometimes they tell stories. But no matter what kind of composition you're writing, it's always a good idea to put the parts of the composition in order.

Here are some pictures that you can use to tell a story about a girl.

■ First tell what's happening in each picture. Then put the pictures in order and use them to tell a story.

Daybook: Moving Pictures, page 8

18

Sometimes, we can put pictures in more than one order to tell more than one story. Here are some more pictures. Try to describe what's happening in each picture.

■ First put the pictures in an order that tells a story. Then write your story. Now change the order so the pictures tell a different story. Write your new story.

The activity (■) on page 19, can be done individually, in pairs, or in small groups. (If done in groups, it's a good idea to have a secretary for each group.) After the writing, have two or three volunteers read their compositions to the class. (Try to choose children who have selected different orders of arrangement.)

In "correcting" the children's compositions, try to make two or three written comments on each paper. (More than three tend to be distracting.) Be sure to include at least one specific, positive comment (for example, "This is good because . . ."). Criticism is best worded in terms of questions, suggestions, or examples.

Follow-up You may want to use the second part of the activity on page 19 as a follow-up. But it's best to wait a day or so, until the children have "recovered" from the stimulus of writing their first stories, before asking them to rewrite their stories using a different order.

This would be a good time to set up in your room a special "composition corner." (A small table or even an extra desk will do.) Here you can display a variety of things to stimulate creative expression. Then, whenever the children have free time, they can come to the "corner" to gather ideas for composition. You might want to begin by displaying pictures cut from magazines which the children can put in order. These pictures should be carefully chosen, since the lesson stresses the fact that we can frequently arrange things "in a different way."

Purpose To introduce the sentence model as an effective way of talking about language.

[For children who have not used Book Three, the concepts presented in this lesson may be new. To reassure them, you can compare learning to use the model with other kinds of learning, for example, riding a bike. You might say: "It takes time to learn new things, but after a while it's easy."]

Preparation Remind the children that—in their heads—they already know many things about sentences. If necessary, you can repeat some of the exercises from previous lessons.

Then display a variety of kinds of models: a plane or car, a dress pattern, a recipe, a globe, and so on. Encourage descriptions, comparisons, and contrasts of these models. Finally, write the word *model* on the chalkboard and explain that the plane, the pattern, and so on are all models. Then say: "Today we'll learn about another kind of model—the sentence model."

Presentation Have the children examine the illustration on page 20. (They'll probably need some help with terms such as *excursion* and *module*.) Then compare this model with some of the others discussed during the Preparation. Finally, ask the children to suggest ways that such models can be useful.

Read the first three paragraphs on page 20 with the children, and then ask for volunteers to answer the questions in the third paragraph. You should probably read the last paragraph to the children as they follow along in their books. You can write the words *lexicon* and *rules* on the chalkboard, and then explain that a lexicon is something like a dictionary, or "a place where we keep words."

20

A Sentence Model

In your head, you know thousands of words. You also know lots of rules. The rules tell you how to put the words in order so that they make sentences. When you study grammar, you learn to talk about words, rules, order, and sentences. But the words and rules are inside your head. You can't see them. How can we talk about things we can't see?

One way is to make a **model.** There are many different kinds of models. A globe is a solid model. A photo of the surface of the moon is a picture model. A recipe is a model that has only words. Some models have both pictures and words, like this one of a spaceship of the future.

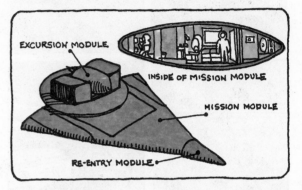

Does this model tell everything there is to know about spaceships? What doesn't it tell? Most models tell only about the important parts of a thing.

To help us talk about sentences, we can use a **sentence model.** A sentence model tells about two important things: the **lexicon** and the **rules.** The lexicon has words in it, just as you have words in your head.

Daybook: Lexicons and Rules, page 10

Here is a very simple sentence model.

A SENTENCE MODEL	
Lexicon	Rules
Nominals: the boy the chicken the teacher the girl the frog *Verb Phrases:* fell asleep found a peanut broke the chalk dropped a book dug a hole	A sentence has a nominal and a verb phrase.

This model doesn't show everything that you know—in your head—about sentences. But it does show some important things. It shows that you have words in your head. It shows you can make these words into **nominals** and **verb phrases.** The model also shows that you have rules in your head. One rule says that, if you put a nominal and a verb phrase together, then you'll have a sentence.

Here are two sentences we can make using the sentence model.

The boy broke the chalk.
The chicken fell asleep.

■ Now you take some nominals and verb phrases from the lexicon. Put them together as the rule says. Try to make at least five different sentences.

Examine the sentence model on page 21 with the children, helping them see that it's divided into two parts: a lexicon and some rules. Then read the paragraph below the model with the children. You can ask for volunteers to read the lexicon words listed under *Nominals* and also those listed under *Verb Phrases.* Then proceed with the examples in the text, and have the children find *the boy, broke the chalk, the chicken,* and *fell asleep* in the lexicon.

The activity (■) on page 21 can be worked as a class exercise. (You can use oaktag cards for each nominal and verb phrase; these can also be used with later lessons.)

Follow-up To provide children with additional practice combining nominals and verb phrases, you can add these to the lexicon:

Nominals	*Verb Phrases*
the spider	blew a horn
the kangaroo	laughed out loud
the dancer	wore galoshes
the clown	likes bananas
the centipede	lives next door

(At this early stage of the language program, it's best for the children not to make up their own nominals and verb phrases. For now, you should also restrict your examples to those given in the text.)

The children might enjoy illustrating some of the more humorous sentences that they have made using the model.

Answers

The following are just a few of the sentences that can be made from the model:
1. The boy fell asleep.
2. The boy found a peanut.
3. The boy broke the chalk.
4. The boy dropped a book.
5. The boy dug a hole.

Purposes (1) To introduce the importance of reviewing one's work; (2) To review the concepts metaphor, composition, and grammar (the sentence model).

[The review lessons in this book are not designed to "test" a child's progress in studying the arts of English. However, they can help you to determine, in a general way, the children's understanding of certain basic concepts, and thus serve as a guide to teaching future lessons.

In order to assess an individual child's growth in studying the arts, you should begin to observe the child's performance during subsequent lessons. In particular, you should become familiar with that section of the Statement of Goals (beginning on page *i*) which applies to the first few chapters of this book. This statement indicates a number of ways that children can demonstrate the acquisition of new learnings. As mentioned in the discussion Guidelines for Evaluation in the *Introduction: The Arts and Skills of English,* we should not assume that all children will demonstrate progress in the same way. Nor should we expect any child to do all of the things listed in the goal structure. By the time children have completed Chapter 5, however, they should be exhibiting one or more of the performance objectives included under each broad objective for Literature, Composition, Language, and Related Topics.]

Preparation The first paragraph on page 22 provides the motivation for this lesson, although you may want to expand the discussion of "review" before proceeding. (Many people, including children, have the misconception that reviewing is only for slower students, when actually people review things all the time.) You might say: "Whenever we discuss things we've already done, then we're reviewing." You

Review

This section has a special name: **review.** You may already know that *review* means "to look again" or "to look back." When you're learning about anything, it's a good idea to stop once in a while. Then you can look back and think about what you've read.

There are two good reasons for this. You learn so many new things in school that you might forget some of them. A review helps you remember these things. And a review helps you see how the different things fit together.

This book has many different things in it. But three kinds of things are particularly important:

Literature
Composition
Grammar

When we review, we'll look at each of these things.

Literature

When you read anything—and particularly when you read poems, plays, and stories—you need to know what each word means. Most of the time, you already know the words. But sometimes you'll find a new word. In this chapter, we used a word that you may not have known before. The word is *metaphor.* Do you remember what a metaphor is?

■ Here's another chance to make metaphors. Try to think of something that the sun reminds you of—maybe a big balloon or a yellow marshmallow. This sentence may help you:

The sun makes me think of _____ because both of them _____.

Composition

In this book, there's a special word for the things you write. They're called *compositions*. A composition can be almost anything you write. And there are even compositions that you don't write.

When you make up compositions, you put things in *order*. What does putting things in order mean?

■ Look again at the pictures on page 19. Try to think of a different order to put them in. Then use them to write another composition.

Language

People use sentences when they write poems. You use sentences when you write compositions. When you study about how to make sentences, then you're studying *grammar*.

One way to talk about sentences is to use the *sentence model*. A sentence model has *rules* and a *lexicon*. What is in the lexicon? What do the rules show?

■ Here's one nominal that we have in the lexicon: *the frog*. Try to put it with each of the verb phrases on page 21. You should be able to make five different sentences.

If you could look inside your head, then you wouldn't need a sentence model. But nobody can <u>see</u> inside his own head. How can we <u>talk</u> about something we can't see?

 When you make sentences, you must put words in order. What else must you do when you <u>write</u> sentences? Look on pages 306–315 to find out how to punctuate sentences.

Answers

1. The frog fell asleep.
2. The frog found a peanut.
3. The frog broke the chalk.
4. The frog dropped a book.
5. The frog dug a hole.

can also suggest reviewing some of the trips children have taken, games they've played, and so on.

Presentation After discussing other things we review, return to the third paragraph on page 22 and stress the fact that the Arts Section of this book contains three major parts: Literature, Composition, and Language (or Grammar).

Read, or have a child read, "The Tide in the River" again, and ask what "picture language" is used. Then discuss the Literature Review. You can add other "metaphor frames," using the words *leaf, bird,* and even *toenail,* in place of *sun.*

As you've probably noted, the text generally avoids asking for "formal definitions" of technical terms such as *metaphor, stanza,* and *lexicon.* It's more important that children be able to use these terms appropriately.

Notice that the Composition Review doesn't ask what "order" means, but asks rather what "putting things in order" means.

In presenting the Language Review, you can reproduce the sentence model on page 21 and, if you wish, include the additional nominals and verb phrases given in the notes on page 21. Here are some other nominals and verb phrases you can also use:

Nominals	Verb Phrases
the farmer	reads books
the mouse	broke a leg
the zebra	looks silly
the judge	ran away
the monkey	eats ice cubes

At the end of each review lesson, you'll find a cross-reference to the Skills Section. These references should help to remind the children of the relationships between arts and skills.

Purposes (1) To extend and enrich the concept of metaphor; (2) To demonstrate that metaphor helps us see things in new ways.

Preparation An ideal preparation (or follow-up activity) consists in having a chemical garden of real plants for the children to observe, noting daily any changes. (An amaryllis plant is both beautiful and rapid growing.)

The series of pictures on pages 24–25 also provide excellent preparation. Have the children discuss the differences they observe in each successive "frame."

Presentation Tell the children that there are some words in the poem which they may not understand at first, but you'll return to them later. Then read the title and the poem to them. (A brief pause at the end of each line can add to the effect of the poem by suggesting the stages in the opening of the bud.) After reading the poem, you might write the poet's name on the chalkboard and help the children to pronounce it: Nā ō′ shē Kor′ ē yam′à.

Then read the first paragraph on page 24 with the children. Ask each child to make a fist and then open his or her hand slowly, with the palm facing up. Ask the children to describe the difference in the sizes of their hands as they opened them and to relate this to the way a bud becomes a flower. Without getting too technical, explain the meanings of the italicized words in the second paragraph on this page.

Now read the poem to the children again as they follow along. (Some might prefer to look at the pictures rather than read.)

The first two paragraphs of the discussion material on page 26 are closely related. You may want to let the children

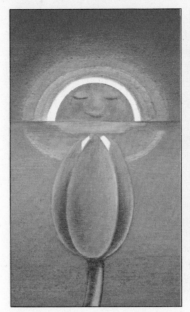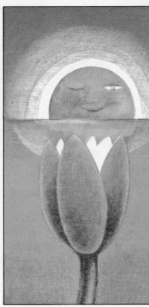

A Poem

In "Unfolding Bud," Naoshi Koriyama looks at poetry in a new way. She uses a metaphor to show how a poem is like a water-lily bud. The bud opens up very slowly, and it takes several days to blossom into a flower. Each day the flower is a little different. It gets richer in color, and as the poet says, it takes on "new dimensions."

What are *dimensions*? What does *tight-closed* mean? As something *unfolds*, does it *reveal* more of its *inner self*? Knowing these words will help you understand the poem.

Daybook: Metaphor and a Metaphor Game, page 12

Unfolding Bud

One is amazed
By a water-lily bud
Unfolding
With each passing day,
Taking on a richer color
And new dimensions.

read them silently. If you do discuss the question at the end of the first paragraph, be sure to encourage a variety of answers, and help the children see that there's no "right-or-wrong" answer to questions such as this.

The final paragraph on page 26 is, perhaps, best read along with the children. The first two sentences make the important point that even people who like poetry (or music, art, food, and so on) don't always like the same things. Children frequently feel that they should like all poetry, and they sometimes find it difficult to admit—even to themselves—that they don't particularly enjoy everything they read.

Follow-up As suggested under Preparation, this would be a good time to have children observe some rapid growing plants and to observe the changes that take place. Some children may want to write about these changes; others may want to record them with a camera.

After discussing some of the things that a poem reminds them of, the children can try to write an original metaphor to describe a poem. With some children, you may want to use the following frame:

A poem makes me think of _____

　　　　a diamond　　a cocoon　　a rainbow

because both of them _____

If you haven't already done so, you should certainly begin now to display books of poetry for the children to browse through during their free time. Listed below are some collections containing poems which, like the one in the text, reveal the beauty of "simple" things. Also suggested are poems from each of these books that you may want to share with the children.

Additional Resources

Books Arbuthnot, May Hill, editor, *Time for Poetry,* Scott Foresman, for "A Word" by Emily Dickinson and "Be Like the Bird" by Victor Hugo. Coatsworth, Elizabeth, *Poems,* Macmillan, for "Poems of Praise." Frost, Robert, *You Come Too,* Holt, Rinehart and Winston, for "Dust of Snow." Hughes, Langston, *The Dream Keeper and Other Poems for Young People,* Knopf, for "Dreams." Teasdale, Sara, *Stars Tonight, Verses Old and New,* Macmillan, for "Night" and "The Coin." Untermeyer, Louis, compiler, *The Golden Treasury of Poetry,* Golden Press, for "Leisure" by William Henry Davies. Larrick, Nancy, compiler, *City Streets,* Evans, for any number of poems which speak of the beauty hidden in familiar city sights. Lewis, Richard, *The Moment of Wonder,* Dial. This last book is a collection of Chinese and Japanese poetry, which typically reflects the beauty of nature.

One is not amazed,
At a first glance,
By a poem,
Which is as tight-closed
As a tiny bud.

Yet one is surprised
To see the poem
Gradually unfolding,
Revealing its rich inner self,
As one reads it
Again
And over again.

NAOSHI KORIYAMA

Naoshi Koriyama says that a poem reminds her of a tiny water-lily bud. Both a poem and a bud open up very slowly. When a water-lily bud opens, you can look inside and see more and more of the flower. What happens when you read a poem again and again?

If you think about it, there are lots of amazing things in this world. When you think how a tiny seed grows into a plant, that's amazing. When you think how a bud becomes a flower, that's amazing. And when you read a poem, think how it can help you see pictures of things in your head. That's amazing, too.

Different people like different poems. There may be a poem that you like but that someone else doesn't like at all. When you really like a poem, you'll probably read it over and over again. Then it begins to open up, just like a flower. A poem may remind you of a bud that opens and grows. It may remind you of blocks that you can make into a house, or a piece of cloth that you can make into a dress. Try to think of some other things a poem reminds you of.

The Describers

Here are three things to think about. Think very hard. Try to get a good picture of each of them.

hat   truck   dog

What color is the hat? Does it have something special on it? Does it keep you warm? What about the truck? What kind of load does it have? What jobs does it do? And what kind of dog are you thinking about? Does it have a collar, or a spot over one eye? Does he know any special tricks?

One way to describe someone or something is to tell what the person or the thing is and has and does. Suppose you want to describe a hero. You could do it this way.

My hero is kind.
He has freckles.
He writes poems after school.

The first sentence tells one thing the hero is. The second sentence tells one thing he has. And the third sentence tells something he does.

There are three special **describers** that can help you tell about someone or something. Their names are Isabella Is, Harry Has, and Dudley Does.

ISABELLA IS   HARRY HAS   DUDLEY DOES

Daybook: The Describers, page 14

Purposes (1) To develop the concept of description in composition; (2) To introduce a method of describing people and objects.

[The "describers" are a major innovation of this series and are used frequently in later lessons of this book. You should prepare three cardboard name tags, one for each of the describers. These will serve as useful instructional aids in this lesson as well as in other lessons to follow.]

Preparation Suggest that each child draw and color a picture of a tree. When the pictures are finished, you can tape some of them onto the chalkboard and have the children discuss the different things people "picture" when they think about a tree.

Presentation Read the first paragraph on page 27 with the children, pausing long enough for two or three responses to each of the questions. During the discussion, focus first on the word *hat*, then on *truck*, and finally on *dog*. Again, the children should recognize that the pictures they get—in their heads—aren't identical. Help the children to see that this is why labels aren't enough; we also need to describe things.

In reading the description of the hero in the middle of page 27, emphasize is and has in the first two sentences, and help the children see that the third sentence tells one thing the hero does (even though we don't use the word *does* in the sentence). To be certain that the children understand this, you can ask them to suggest some other things that the hero could do.

Write *is, has,* and *does* on the chalkboard, and then comment that there's a special term we can use to talk about these words. Direct attention to the last paragraph on page 27, and have the children locate the word written in "very dark type." Then call their attention to the illustration, and have them identify Isabella Is, Harry Has, and Dudley Does.

Next, have the children turn to page 28 and identify the describers in the illustration on this page. You can use the three name tags and have volunteers read the appropriate parts from the illustration. Then ask the volunteers to describe a car, a bike, a pencil, and so on, making sure that each one uses the appropriate form (*is* for "Isabella," and so on).

Another volunteer can then read the facsimile composition on page 28. Ask the class which sentence tells what the flag is, which tells what it has, and which tells what it does. (The final sentence says something about the writer, rather than the flag.)

The activity (■) on page 28 can be played as a class game. Choose a child in the class, but don't tell them who you've chosen. Then the children can ask questions which can be answered with a "yes" or "no" (for example, "Is the someone a boy? Has the someone got red hair? Does the someone ride the bus to school?"). Record the data under *is, has,* and *does* on the chalkboard. When a child thinks he knows who the "someone" is, he can ask directly ("Is it Bill Jones?"). If a child guesses incorrectly, then he can't ask any more questions.

Follow-up Divide the class into groups of three and have each group choose a "subject." Then assign a describer to each child, which he or she can use to write about the subject. As each group finishes, someone from the group can put the sentences together to form a descriptive composition.

Here are the describers showing what something <u>is</u> and <u>has</u> and <u>does</u>. Can you guess what something is?

Here's a composition that uses the describers.

> The Flag
> Our country's flag is red, white and blue. It has fifty white stars and thirteen stripes. Each stripe stands for one of the first states. I feel good when the flag waves in the wind.

■ Now <u>you</u> think of someone. The someone can be real or imaginary. Make a list that tells three things the someone <u>is</u>, three things the someone <u>has</u>, and three things the someone <u>does</u>. Then write a composition that uses what's on your list.

A Picture of the Model

Do you remember what the study of *grammar* is?

● The study of grammar helps us understand how we use words and rules to make sentences.

In your head, you know lots of words. You also have lots of rules. You use the words and the rules to make sentences. But you can't see inside your own head. You need a model to help talk about what goes on in your head when you make sentences.

Most of the time, models show only the important things. The sentence model shows that—in your head—you have words and rules. One very important rule says that a sentence has a *nominal* and a *verb phrase*. We can show a picture of the rule, like this.

Daybook: Practice with the Sentence Model, page 16

Purposes (1) To develop the concept that the sentence model provides a useful means for talking about language; (2) To present the "sentence picture" as an equivalent of the rule: A sentence has a nominal and a verb phrase.

Preparation Discuss with the children how pictures can help us learn about things we've never actually seen. You might ask: "Do you know what George Washington looked like? Did you ever meet him? Do you know what an igloo looks like? Have you ever been to Alaska?" If possible, have a picture of each of these available.

Presentation Have the children examine the illustration on page 29, and then suggest that this looks like a rule of the sentence model that they've already talked about. You may want to refer the children back to the "model" as it appears on page 21 of their text. Then have the children turn again to page 29 and note the title of this lesson: A Picture of the Model.

Before proceeding, ask the children if they can find the sentence on page 29 that tells what the study of *grammar* is. Have a volunteer read the sentence aloud. Then have the children read page 29 silently. When they've finished, you can discuss the illustration with them.

Then have the children turn to page 30, and help them see that the first illustration is merely a simplified version of the one on page 29. (The birds, of course, are simply decorative. Whenever you—or the children—draw sentence pictures, you should feel free to decorate them also.)

Read the last paragraph on page 30 with the children, pausing so they can answer the questions. If they seem unsure of the answers, you can direct them to read the first paragraph on page 31.

29

At this point, you might duplicate the simple sentence picture on the chalkboard, adding a rectangle beneath the "nominal box" and another beneath the "verb phrase box." In the rectangle below NOMINAL, write *The chicken*, and in the one below VERB PHRASE, write *found a peanut*.

To help the children learn to use the sentence picture, erase *The chicken* and ask them to choose a nominal from the list on page 31. Write that nominal inside the rectangle where you formerly had written *The chicken*. Ask for a volunteer to read the new sentence. Then repeat the process by erasing *found a peanut*, asking for a verb phrase from the list, and writing it inside the rectangle.

Volunteers can then go to the chalkboard and repeat the process. (You can appoint a class secretary to record each of the sentences that the class makes.) Then the children can work in small groups to complete the first activity (■) on page 31.

Next, have a child read the paragraph that follows the first activity. Ask the children if they'd like to try to make one hundred different sentences. If so, you can divide the class into ten groups, assign a nominal to each group, and then have each group add their nominal to the ten verb phrases. Each group can have one child act as secretary to record and count the sentences, and then the secretaries can add their numbers together.

We can also make a simple picture, like this.

These pictures both show the same thing that the rule says.

● A sentence has a nominal and a verb phrase.

Here's a picture that's a little different from the first picture. Can you see how it's different? How is the <u>nominal</u> part of the picture different? How is the <u>verb phrase</u> part different?

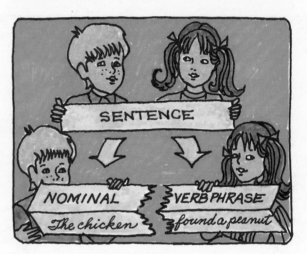

The boy is holding one of the nominals from the lexicon of the sentence model. The girl is holding one of the verb phrases. Suppose you put them together as the rule says to. What sentence do they make?

Here are some more nominals and verb phrases we can add to the lexicon.

Nominals:	*Verb Phrases:*
the dog	ate my lunch
the fish	climbed a tree
the doctor	sang a song
the bird	tickled my foot
the mailman	won a prize

■ Now try to put these nominals and verb phrases together. How many different sentences can you make?

Suppose you put these nominals and verb phrases together with those from the lexicon on page 21. Then you'd be able to make one hundred different sentences! If you don't believe this, here's something for you to try.

■ Take the first nominal from the first lexicon: *the boy*. Put this nominal together with each of the verb phrases from the lexicon on page 21. Then put it together with each of the verb phrases from the lexicon on this page. How many different sentences could you make?

Now suppose you do the same thing with the second nominal in the lexicon: *the chicken*. How many sentences could you make?

How many nominals are left? How many sentences can you make with each one? Now do you see how we can make one hundred different sentences using just these few nominals and verb phrases?

Follow-up There are many ways you can vary the activity in which children combine nominals and verb phrases to make sentences. Here are just a few suggestions:

1. Divide the class into two teams: "the nominals" and "the verb phrases." Provide each child on the "nominal" team with a nominal and also a number. Provide each child on the "verb phrase" team with a verb phrase and a matching number. Then, as you call out the numbers, the "nominals" and the "verb phrases" can come forward to read the sentence they make. (You can make the game competitive, if you wish.)

2. Divide the class into any number of teams and provide each with the same set of nominals and verb phrases. Challenge the teams to make up as many sentences as they can in a specified time.

3. Have the children choose just one nominal to work with. Then have them combine this nominal with as many different verb phrases as they can. (Or you can choose one verb phrase and as many nominals as possible.)

Answers

In response to the first activity, the children can make a maximum of twenty-five different sentences, including the following:

1. The dog ate my lunch.
2. The dog climbed a tree.
3. The dog sang a song.
4. The dog tickled my foot.
5. The dog won a prize.

Purpose   To introduce the idea of homographs.

[In this series, the distinction is made between homographs and homophones. A homograph is a word that has the same spelling as another word, but a different origin and meaning (for example, *record* meaning "a disk" and *record* meaning "to write down"). A homophone is a word that has the same pronunciation as another, but a different origin, meaning, and usually spelling (for example, *blue* and *blew*).]

Preparation   Ask for volunteers to write these sentences on the chalkboard as you read them:

1. The boy swung the bat.
2. A bat eats insects.
3. She didn't bat an eye.

Call the children's attention to the use of *bat* in each of these sentences. You can ask: "Is the word *bat* spelled the same way in each sentence? Does it mean the same thing?" You can comment that it might seem strange to have words that are spelled alike but mean different things. Then add that today's lesson will help them understand why this is so.

Presentation   Have the children turn to page 32 and suggest that they try to pronounce the "words" in the first illustration. Then have them try the "words" in the second illustration. Encourage them to explain why it's easier to say the "words" in the second set. Volunteers might even try to make two or three nonsense "words" of their own.

Now have the children read the text on page 32. Be sure to stress the numbers in the final paragraph on the page. Point out that to spell all the words differently, we would have to put the 26 letters together in 500,000 different ways.

Same Letters, Different Words

Suppose you have twenty-six boxes. In each box are some wooden letters. One box has lots of *A*'s in it. Another box has lots of *B*'s. And so on.

Now suppose you are the Great Word Maker. You can take letters from any of the boxes. You can put them together to make words. You might do something like this.

These words might be fun to make. But they're hard to say.

So you decide to put vowel letters in every word. Now you can make words like these.

These aren't all real words, but at least you can say them.

Now there's another problem. In English, there are more than 500,000 words. But there are only five vowel letters and twenty-one consonant letters. So how can you spell all these words?

Daybook: Two Silly Stories, page 18

You could figure out a way to spell every word so that they're all different. Most of the time, that's what happens in English. But sometimes you use the same letters—in the same order—to spell words. The words *look* the same. But they may not *sound* the same. And they mean different things.

Here's an example.

Judge Sanchez makes fair decisions.
Did you go to the country fair?

What words look the same in these sentences? In the first sentence, what does *fair* mean? What does it mean in the second sentence? There are really two words spelled *f-a-i-r*. The two words look alike, but they mean different things. There's a special name for words like this. They're called **homographs.**

Here's another example of homographs.

The branches bent in the wind.
Did you wind my clock?

Now what two words are spelled the same? Do they sound the same? Do they mean the same thing?

To show that there's more than one word with the same spelling, many dictionaries put numbers after words, like this.

> **pitch er**[1] (pich′ ər), a container with a handle on one side and a lip for pouring on the other.
> **pitch er**[2] (pich′ ər), a member of a ball team who throws the ball for the batter to hit.

■ All these words have more than one meaning. First look each one up in the dictionary. Then make up sentences to show all the different meanings for each word.

1. ring	3. light	5. root	7. ground
2. maroon	4. like	6. peck	8. rock

Next, have the children read the first three paragraphs on page 33 and answer the questions about the homographs *fair* and *wind*. Write the word *homograph* on the chalkboard, and, if necessary, help the children pronounce this special term. You can use the examples containing the word *wind* to help the children understand that—sometimes—homographs are not pronounced alike.

Then explain that some dictionaries use a special method to show that there's more than one word with the same spelling. Call the children's attention to the small superscript numbers following the entry word *pitcher* in each definition. Then have the children read the text and explain the purpose of these numbers.

You may want to begin the activity (■) on page 33 with the class as a group. If so, then the last few items can be done individually or in small groups.

Follow-up This would be an appropriate time to teach the lesson on Homographs on pages 284–285 in the Skills Section. In addition, you can construct an exercise similar to the one on page 33, using these homographs:

junk	ash	hawk
heel	lie	mail
dock	batter	present
reel	refund	bow
scale	insult	bill
jet	lightness	school
sow	content	spike

After the children have used these in sentences, you can ask them to distinguish between those homographs which sound alike and those which do not.

Some children might also enjoy drawing pictures, perhaps even cartoons, to illustrate the meanings of some of these homophones.

Purposes (1) To provide experience with descriptive literature; (2) To demonstrate how all authors use essentially the same method of description.

Preparation Remind the children of the descriptions they wrote in the last composition lesson. (You may want to read one or two of these compositions to the class before proceeding.) Then review the three describers: Isabella Is, Harry Has, Dudley Does. Ask the children how they might use these describers to talk about their classroom. Then announce that today you'll read an excerpt from a book in which the author describes a boy's room. (If possible, have a copy of the book *Maurice's Room* on hand to display.)

Presentation Read the selection in the text to the children while their books are still closed. Encourage them to try to imagine what Maurice's room looks like. When you have finished, ask the children to try to describe their impressions of the room. Ask if they would like to live in such a room.

Then have the children turn to the illustration on page 35. You can comment: "This is how one artist thought Maurice's room looked." Then you can have the children identify a few of the things included in the illustration. In particular, you should have the children locate the following items as you list them on the chalkboard: *raccoon tail, plate of mealy worms, cactus, chicken-wire roof, garter snake,* and *lizard.*

To provide additional preparation for rereading the selection, you can also write these words and phrases on the chalkboard: *powdery drift of white moths, butterfly bolts, filaments from electric-light bulbs, salamanders, hinges, octopus,*

A Description

Here's a description from the book, *Maurice's Room.*

In his room Maurice had a bottle full of dead beetles, a powdery drift of white moths in a cup without a handle, a squirrel hide tacked to a board, a snakeskin on a wire hanger, a raccoon tail, a glass of shrimp eggs, a plate of mealy worms, a box of turtle food.

There were things with which to make other things, such as nails of different sizes, screws, wire, butterfly bolts, scraps of wood, sockets, filaments from electric-light bulbs, cardboard from grocery boxes, two orange crates, a handsaw, and a hammer. On the top of a chest of drawers Maurice kept stones and pebbles, dried tar balls, fragments of brick, pieces of colored bottle glass that had been worn smooth, and gray rocks that glistened with mica.

On his window sill there was a heap of dried moss next to a turtle bowl in which several salamanders lived half hidden by mud and wet grass. On the same sill he kept some plants from the five-and-ten-cent store. They looked dead. Now and then a cactus would put out a new shoot.

In another bowl on a table covered with yellow oilcloth were four painted turtles that were getting quite soft in the shell, and in a corner, in a square fish bowl with a chicken-wire roof, lived a garter snake and a lizard.

An old hamster in his cage slept or filled his pouches with dried carrots or ran on his wheel. The wheel, which needed an oiling, screeched all night, the time the hamster preferred for exercise. But the noise didn't keep Maurice awake, only his parents. In a pickle jar, a garden spider sat in a forked twig, her egg sack just below her. Maurice also had a bird. It was a robin, blind in one eye and unable to find food for itself.

magnifying glass, expeditions, and *fixtures.* You might have on hand such things as butterfly bolts, light-bulb filaments, hinges, and a magnifying glass. You can use pictures from science books or an encyclopedia to help the children define *moth, salamander,* and *octopus.* And you can use the context of the story itself to help them define *expeditions* and *fixtures.*

When you feel that most of the children are familiar with the vocabulary, you can read the excerpt from *Maurice's Room* again, with the children following along in their books. Or you might want to have volunteers read certain paragraphs to the rest of the class.

After this second reading, you can turn to the first paragraph of the discussion on page 36. Ask the children what Maurice <u>is</u>, and then write their response on the chalkboard. Then suggest that Maurice <u>has</u> a great many things, and ask how many of these things they can remember. Remind the children that <u>is</u> and <u>has</u> are two of the describers. Finally, ask for responses to the final sentence of the paragraph.

Encourage the children to use their imaginations in responding to the questions in the second paragraph of the discussion. Since these require the children to make inferences, their answers may vary widely.

Before beginning the activity (■), each child should choose the three things that he or she wishes to write about.

Follow-up You may want to select other passages from the book *Maurice's Room* to read to the class. You should also encourage the children to read more and more on their own. Listed under Additional Resources are a number of books that most children will enjoy.

Additional Resources

Books Calhoun, Mary, *Katie John,* Harper. This book and its sequel, *Honestly, Katie John!,* relate the adventures of a ten-year-old girl growing up in a Missouri town. Cleary, Beverly, *Henry Huggins,* Morrow. The Henry Huggins series, a favorite with children, begins when Henry adopts a stray dog. Other books in the series include *Henry and Beezus, Henry and Ribsy, Beezus and Ramona, Henry and the Paper Route,* and *Henry and the Clubhouse.* Enright, Elizabeth, *The Saturdays,* Holt, Rinehart and Winston. Other books about the Melendy family include *The Four-Story Mistake, Then There Were Five,* and *Spiderweb for Two.* Estes, Eleanor, *The Moffats,* Harcourt. The adventures of the Moffat family are continued in *The Middle Moffat* and *Rufus M.* Fox, Paula, *Maurice's Room,* Macmillan. Krumgold, Joseph, *And Now Miguel,* Crowell. This is an excellent book, but one that you will probably want to read to the children. McClosky, Robert, *Homer Price,* Viking. Most children delight in the "misadventures" of Homer, who grows up in a small Midwestern town. Neville, Emily Cheney, *It's Like This, Cat,* Harper. This is another excellent book—about a New York City boy—to read to the children. Taylor, Sidney, *All-of-a-Kind Family,* Follett. This family's adventures are continued in *More All-of-a-Kind Family* and *All-of-a-Kind Family Uptown.* Weik, Mary Hays, *The Jazz Man,* Atheneum. This moving story tells of the friendship between a lame black boy and a jazz musician.

On the floor were coffee cans with things in them; an eggbeater with a missing gear, a pile of dead starfish, cigar boxes, clockworks, hinges, and a very large grater with sharp dents on all four of its sides. The grater was orange with rust, and it stood in the middle of the room beneath the octopus. You would have to use a magnifying glass to see all the other things Maurice had found.

His bed had two blankets and a pillow without a pillowcase. Sometimes a small goose feather pricked its way through the ticking, and Maurice would put it away in an envelope. He had used two pillowcases for his collecting expeditions, and after that his mother wouldn't give him any more.

There was one tidy corner in Maurice's room. It was where he has pushed his Christmas toys. They were a month old now, and the dust covered them evenly. They were like furniture or bathroom fixtures. Maurice felt there wasn't much to be done with them.

PAULA FOX

Do you remember the three describers? Can you find them in the story? The story tells about things that Maurice <u>has</u>. He has a bottle of dead beetles. What are some other things that he <u>has</u>? Try to think of something Maurice <u>is</u>. You know one thing he <u>does</u>. He collects things. Try to think of something else he probably does.

Maurice has lots of interesting things in his room. And he has some toys that he got for Christmas. How do you know that he doesn't care much about these toys? What things does he like better? Where do you suppose he found these things? The story doesn't tell, but you can use your imagination.

■ Pretend you're Maurice. Then use your imagination to make up a story about finding three different things.

Imagination

Here's a chance for you to use your imagination in a different way. First, look at the pictures below. Try to figure out which picture shows the beginning of the story. Which picture shows the end of the story? Now think of some things that could happen in the middle of the story.

Purposes (1) To introduce the concept of imagination as an important element in the composition process; (2) To establish a connection between imagination and order.

Preparation You can remind the class that they have already used their imaginations to make up metaphors, and then tell them that, today, they'll have a chance to use their imaginations in another way.

Presentation Have the children examine the three pictures which show the monkey. Ask volunteers to describe each picture as fully as possible, but avoid having them make connections between any of the pictures.

After the children have described each picture, read the opening paragraph of the lesson along with them. Have the children determine, by discussion, which picture comes first. (Most children will probably select the lower left picture.) You can duplicate this picture with stick figures on the chalkboard, leaving room for other pictures to follow. Then have the children determine which picture comes last (the upper right one), and ask the children to give reasons to support their decision. If possible, duplicate this picture on the chalkboard also, leaving room between the first and last pictures to draw the other two.

Now focus the class's attention on the upper left picture and also on the question mark. Remind them of the description they gave earlier of the upper left picture, and ask for suggestions for another picture—in place of the question mark. Most probably, someone will see that the fourth picture could show the monkey stacking boxes or climbing on stacked boxes, but accept any other plausible idea for getting the banana.

Now have the class read the first four paragraphs on page 38. Note that it suggests three different ways to tell the story: from the point of view of (1) the main character (the monkey), (2) an onlooker (a scientist), and (3) an inanimate object (the banana). You can also treat the subject by asking the children to imagine themselves as the director of a TV show or film. Suggest that the director is the person who decides where to put the camera, which pictures to use, and so on. Ask for different ways to make a TV show from the monkey-banana story.

Some children may prefer to do the activity (■) alone; others may prefer to work in groups to prepare a TV show. This last group could work with simple hand puppets.

The last paragraph in this lesson is particularly important. Every writer occasionally writes things "just for himself," and providing children with this option helps them learn that their writing must satisfy themselves as well as others. In discussing this paragraph with the children, it might be useful to have them consider why they often want to share their work.

If children show their compositions to you, your comments should follow the guidelines given on page 19. Probably most children will be eager to share their compositions, but you should avoid calling attention to those few who aren't.

Follow-up You may want to include a large manila envelope labeled "Private" in each child's composition folder. Then the children can use their envelopes to save those compositions which they don't wish to share with anyone.

Your imagination can help you figure out what happens in a story. It can also help you when you want to tell a story. There's <u>always</u> more than one way to tell a story.

Suppose you were the monkey. How would you tell the story? Where would you begin? What would you say first?

Suppose you were a scientist, and you were watching the monkey through a window. How would you tell the story? What would you say?

Suppose you were a talking banana and you were telling the story to another banana. What would you say?

■ Now, use your imagination to write a story about the monkey and the banana. Pretend to be the monkey, or a scientist, or a banana, or anything at all. Try to think of a good title for your story.

When you have finished you can read your story to your friends. You can show it to your teacher if you want to. But you don't have to read it or show it to anyone. You can keep it just for yourself. People sometimes write stories and poems just for themselves.

Combining Sentences

Have you ever heard a child who is just learning to talk? When very young children put words together, they like to use the word *and*.

Daybook: Putting Sentences Together, page 20

38

Young children also use *and* a lot when they put sentences together. Using *and* is the easiest way of combining sentences.

THE GIRL STOOD UP AND SHE SANG A SONG AND SHE WON A PRIZE AND SHE WAS HAPPY.

Most very young children know only one way to put sentences together. But you know more than one way. You can put one sentence <u>after</u> another, like young children do.

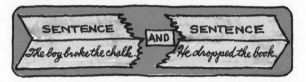

SENTENCE AND SENTENCE
The boy broke the chalk. He dropped the book.

But you also know the rule for combining two sentences by putting one sentence <u>inside</u> the other.

If we want to put one sentence inside another, we can't use just any sentences. But we can do it when both sentences have the same nominal. What nominal does each of these sentences begin with?

The boy broke the chalk.
The boy dropped a book.

Purposes (1) To help children recognize that they know rules for combining sentences; (2) To introduce the concept of a "sentence-combining rule."

[Again, this lesson uses the sentence model not to teach a rule but rather to demonstrate an extremely important fact of language, namely, that every speaker has innate rules which permit him to combine sentences.

For the most part, the sentence model is a device to be used; that is, it is not a repository of terms and definitions. Having children memorize definitions is rarely effective in teaching. For this reason, the child's text avoids presenting formal definitions of such concepts as a *basic sentence* (a simple, active, declarative sentence, always affirmative, and having no internal modification, such as dependent clauses, prenominal adjectives, and the like); *recursiveness* (a property relating to a set of rules which permits those rules to be applied repeatedly within a single set of operations so long as certain specified conditions are met); and *regular nominal* (a common noun generally preceded by one or more determiners). Definitions are frequently included in these side-column notes as an aid to those teachers who may wish to broaden their own understanding of this particular model of language.]

Preparation If possible, make a tape recording of the speech of a four- or five-year-old to demonstrate how young children frequently use the word *and*. While listening to the tape, the children can raise their hands each time they hear the child say the word *and*. Alternatively, you can transcribe the speech of a young child and read it to your class, having the children raise their hands as you read.

39

Presentation   Ask for volunteers to read the text and illustrations at the bottom of page 38 and the top of page 39. Another volunteer might count the number of times that the word *and* is used in the illustrations.

The main point of the lesson is contained in the paragraph which begins above the second illustration on page 39 and continues directly below it. What is important is that the children have the rule in their heads. The rest of the lesson merely provides a means for talking about this internalized knowledge.

Read the final paragraph on page 39 with the children, and help them to see that the two sentences at the bottom of the page begin with the same nominal: *the boy.*

Before the children read page 40, you can say: "This book has a special way of showing how one sentence fits inside another." You might also want to copy the sentence problem given on page 40 onto the chalkboard, following this procedure:

1. Write only the two sentences to be combined, one over the other. Add the "+ sign" and draw a line under the bottom sentence.
2. Put an "X" through *The boy* in the bottom sentence and write *who* above the "X." Draw the brace which shows where the bottom sentence fits into the top one.
3. Write the single new sentence as the "answer" to the problem.

As you perform each step, explain the procedure to the children. Then read page 40 with the children. When they've finished, ask for a volunteer to explain what happens at each of the three steps.

Here's a good way to show how one sentence fits inside another sentence. We can write the sentences, one on top of the other. Then we can add a plus sign so that the sentences look like a problem in addition.

> The boy broke the chalk.
> + The boy dropped a book.

Here's how we add these sentences together.

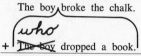

The boy who dropped a book broke the chalk.

First, we found the nominal that's the same in both sentences. Then we crossed out the nominal in the bottom sentence, and we wrote in the word *who*. Finally, we pulled the top sentence apart. And we put the bottom sentence inside the top sentence.

Here are the three steps again.

Step One:

> The boy broke the chalk.
> + The boy dropped a book.

Step Two:

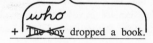

Step Three:

> The boy   who dropped a book   broke the chalk.

■ Here are some more sentence problems. In each problem, both sentences begin with the same nominal. Try to add the sentences together to make a new sentence. (The first one has been done for you.)

1. The boy fell asleep.

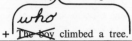

+ ~~The boy~~ climbed a tree.

   The boy who climbed a tree fell asleep.

2. The girl broke the chalk.
  + The girl ate my lunch.

3. The teacher dropped a book.
  + The teacher sang a song.

4. The mailman won a prize.
  + The mailman found a peanut.

5. The frog sang a song.
  + The frog ate my lunch.

6. The fish fell asleep.
  + The fish ate my lunch.

■ Perhaps you'd like to write your own sentence problems. You can make some like the ones you just solved. Use the nominals and verb phrases from the lexicon on page 31. For each problem, write two sentences. Make sure that both sentences begin with the same nominal. Then add your sentences together using *who*.

Maybe you'd rather exchange your sentence problems with a friend. Then you can try to solve each other's problems.

Answers

2. The girl who ate my lunch broke the chalk.
3. The teacher who sang a song dropped a book.
4. The mailman who found a peanut won a prize.
5. The frog who ate my lunch sang a song.
6. The fish who ate my lunch fell asleep.

The first activity (■) on page 41 is best done orally, either in groups or with the entire class. Encourage the children not to take "short cuts" at this stage, and have them explain all three steps for each of the sentence problems.

The second activity (■) can be done in small groups or individually. You should move among the children as they are working, giving help as required.

Before concluding the lesson, remind the class of the main point of the lesson: They already know the rule in their heads and the sentence problem is only a way of showing them what they know.

Follow-up Here are some additional sentences to use:

1. The elephant smiled happily.
   + The elephant sat on the sandwich.

2. The dancer broke a leg.
   + The dancer wore galoshes.

3. The clown cried all day.
   + The clown lost the race.

4. The spider looks silly.
   + The spider reads books.

5. The mouse ran away.
   + The mouse ate my lunch.

6. The monkey won a prize.
   + The monkey reads books.

7. The zebra broke a leg.
   + The zebra climbed a tree.

8. The judge rode a bicycle.
   + The judge carried a cane.

9. The lion roared loudly.
   + The lion jumped through the hoop.

10. The cow munched on some grass.
    + The cow wore a bell.

Purposes (1) To re-emphasize the concept of metaphor and the importance of close reading in literature; (2) To restress description and point of view in composition; (3) To reiterate that children have an internalized knowledge of the sentence-combining rule.

Preparation Remind the children that each long chapter in the text ends with a review, and then discuss briefly the purposes of these lessons.

Presentation By now the children have had a number of experiences working with metaphor. They have read poems which contain metaphors, and they have created some metaphors of their own. You can review the concept of metaphor with the children, now and at various times throughout the year, by using a "metaphor frame" like the one on page 8 of the children's text. Occasionally, you may want to suggest some alternatives from which the children can choose— if they wish—in making their own metaphors. Here are some examples you can use.

1. A river makes me think of _____
   a ribbon   a knife   tumbleweed
   because both of them _____.

2. A snowflake makes me think of _____
   a star   a daisy   a good-bye
   because both of them _____.

3. A seashell makes me think of _____
   a fan   a ruffle   a china dish
   because both of them _____.

4. A rainbow makes me think of _____
   a bridge   a dream   a smile
   because both of them _____.

5. Thunder makes me think of _____
   wild horses   laughter   hands clapping
   because both of them _____.

Review

Literature

In this chapter, you read a poem about poetry. What metaphor did the poet use to describe a poem? Can you know all there is to know about a poem the first time you read it? How do you really get to know a poem?

You also read part of a story about a boy's bedroom. How would you describe Maurice's room? Does it make you think of your room?

■ Now think for a while about some of the things in the room where you sleep. Make a list of as many of the things as you can think of. Where are these things? Are they on a table? Are they on the floor, or in a corner? Then use your list to write a description of your room.

Composition

One good way to talk about something—or to write about something—is to use the *describers*. What are the three describers? What does each one help you do? How would you use the describers if you wanted to describe a person? How would they help you if you wanted to describe a fire engine or an airplane? How would they help you describe an imaginary animal?

■ Do you remember the story you wrote about the monkey and the banana? Did you pretend that you were the monkey? Or were you the scientist? Or the banana? Pretend to be someone or something else and tell the story in a different way.

Language

Everybody talks and writes in sentences. And everybody puts sentences together to make new sentences. Do you remember how young children put sentences together?

When children get older, they learn new ways of putting sentences together. One way is to use the sentence problem.

■ Here are some more sentence problems for you to solve.

1. The boy climbed the tree.
    + The boy ate my lunch.

2. The girl won a prize.
    + The girl sang a song.

3. The dog found a peanut.
    + The dog dug a hole.

4. The teacher dropped a book.
    + The teacher fell asleep.

5. The fish tickled my foot.
    + The fish fell asleep.

 In this chapter, you used the dictionary to help you with words called *homographs*. But do you know how to find words quickly in the dictionary? For practice with *alphabetical order,* look on pages 256–262. And for more about homographs, turn to page 284.

In discussing the Literature and Composition Review, you should help the children see the relationship between the descriptions they read in literature and the descriptions they write themselves. (One of the purposes of the chapter reviews is to show the relationship between various concepts presented in the text.) For the first activity (■) on page 42, help the children see how they can use the describers is, has, and does to talk about the rooms where they sleep.

If you feel that the children need more practice combining sentences, here are some additional problems you can use:

1. The girl writes books.
    + The girl lives next door.

2. The mailman plays the flute.
    + The mailman likes music.

3. The acrobat smiled happily.
    + The acrobat sailed through the air.

4. The nurse won a prize.
    + The nurse collects butterflies.

5. The kangaroo fell asleep.
    + The kangaroo jumped a mile.

6. The beetle carried a cane.
    + The beetle fell off a leaf.

7. The clown laughed out loud.
    + The clown turned a somersault.

Answers

1. The boy who ate my lunch climbed the tree.
2. The girl who sang a song won a prize.
3. The dog who dug a hole found a peanut.
4. The teacher who fell asleep dropped a book.
5. The fish who fell asleep tickled my foot.

Purposes (1) To continue the study of metaphor; (2) To examine carefully a poem based on one main metaphor.

[Both adults and children are familiar with the condition known technically as *conflict*—the choice between two equally attractive options. Everyone has had considerable experience with this emotion, which is the subject of Frost's poem, "The Road Not Taken."]

Preparation Ideally, a walk in the woods should precede this poem. At the end of the walk—and before returning to the classroom—you can read the poem to the children.

Additionally, you can prompt a brief discussion related to the predicament of choosing (for example, between a dog and a bicycle). You can also elicit from the children examples of other difficult choices. During the discussion, try to evoke the feelings that occur when people are faced with such choices.

Presentation Before rereading the poem to the children, discuss with them that "The Road Not Taken" is about a man walking in the woods. The man comes to two roads, and he must choose between them. (At this point, you might want to refer the children to the illustration on pages 44–45 of the text.) Tell the children that this is really a metaphor: The man is talking about choosing between <u>any</u> two things, which is something that people often must do.

Then, while their books are closed, read the poem again to the children. After this reading, you can comment that there were probably some words in the poem that the children didn't recognize. Then write the following phrases on the chalkboard: *two roads diverged, bent in the*

A Poem

This poem is by Robert Frost. It describes a man walking along a road in the woods. He comes to a place where the road *diverges* or "goes two different ways." He looks down one road as far as he can see. But then he takes the other road. It's grassy because fewer people have walked on it. The man thinks the grassy road has the "better claim" because it's less worn. He does notice that there are fresh leaves on both roads. So he knows that nobody else has walked on either road that day. Still, he chooses the road that is less traveled on.

Here is the poem Robert Frost wrote.

Daybook: Choosing Your Way Through, page 22

The Road Not Taken

Two roads diverged in a yellow wood,
And sorry I could not travel both
And be one traveler, long I stood
And looked down one as far as I could
To where it bent in the undergrowth;

Then took the other, as just as fair,
And having perhaps the better claim,
Because it was grassy and wanted wear;
Though as for that the passing there
Had worn them really about the same,

undergrowth, was grassy and wanted wear, leaves no step had trodden black, and *ages and ages hence.* Then you can read the poem again to the children, this time stopping to explain the meanings of these phrases. Wherever possible, use the content of the poem itself to explain the meanings.

Then read the introduction on page 44 to the children, and finally reread the poem, this time having the children follow along in their books.

By now the children should be ready for the discussion material on page 46. Since most of the questions are open-ended, you should encourage a wide variety of responses. (Some children may wander into the area of choosing between "right" or "wrong," which is not what the poem is about. Without rejecting such responses, remind them that the poem is about the predicament of choosing between two things when you really want both of them.)

Follow-up Some children might enjoy hearing one or two other poems by Robert Frost, but you should choose them carefully. *You Come Too,* listed under Additional Resources, contains some of Frost's poetry especially selected for children. Or you may want to play a recording of Robert Frost reading some of his own poetry.

Although it is certainly not important that children learn biographical facts about any author whose works are contained in this text, some children might enjoy hearing selected parts of Doris Faber's biography of Robert Frost. Those sections which deal with Frost's life as a boy growing up in Massachusetts would be particularly appropriate.

Additional Resources

Books Faber, Doris, *Robert Frost, America's Poet,* Prentice-Hall. Frost, Robert, *You Come Too,* Holt, Rinehart and Winston.
Recordings *Poems by Robert Frost,* LP Recording, Decca.

And both that morning equally lay
In leaves no step had trodden black.
Oh, I kept the first for another day!
Yet knowing how way leads on to way,
I doubted if I should ever come back.

I shall be telling this with a sigh
Somewhere ages and ages hence:
Two roads diverged in a wood, and I—
I took the one less traveled by,
And that has made all the difference.

ROBERT FROST

In the first stanza, the poet says he's sorry he can't travel both roads. Why do you think he's sorry? Have you ever wanted to do two different things at the same time? Have you ever had to choose one or the other?

The poet takes the less traveled road. Suppose you were the poet. Which way would you go? The poet says he'll try the first road "another day." Do you think he will? What do you think he means when he says:

"Yet knowing how way leads on to way,
I doubted if I should ever come back."

How does this make the poet feel? How do you know?

In the last stanza, the poet says that having taken the road less traveled by has made all the difference. What do you think this means? Do you think the poet is sorry that he chose the second road?

You know that lots of poems have metaphors. In a metaphor, a poet describes one thing by telling about something else it reminds him of. Do you think the "road" could be a metaphor? Besides a road, what could Robert Frost have been thinking about?

More Imagination

Part I

Here's another chance to use your imagination to tell a story. Look at these pictures.

The first picture shows the beginning of a story. What do you think the boy is saying? What could the girl say? The second picture shows the middle of the story. But the last picture—the end of the story—is blank. Try to think of a good ending for the story.

Purpose To provide additional opportunities for using imagination in writing stories and poems.

[The two parts of this lesson are unified in that they both deal with using imagination in the process of composition. Nonetheless, each part is complete in itself, and you may wish to teach them on different days. For this reason, there is a separate Preparation, Presentation, and Follow-up for each part.]

Preparation (Part I) Have the children differentiate between some things that are real and some things that are imaginary. Ask them to imagine what would happen if, yesterday, there was a heavy snowfall. Or what would happen if all the lights in the city went out. Encourage the children to become aware of their ability to use imagination in thinking of things that could happen.

Presentation (Part I) Have the children read the text and examine the pictures on page 47. Encourage a variety of answers to the two questions in the paragraph below the pictures. Encourage a similar variety in imagining a good ending for the story. Try to emphasize that people can use their imaginations in many different ways.

The set of pictures on page 48 is very open-ended; that is, there's no implied story at all. For this reason, the children must impose a story on the pictures, and in doing this, it's best to treat each picture thoroughly. Be sure to emphasize the role-playing aspect of the directions beneath the pictures. Then have the children complete the activity (■) at the bottom of page 48. Among other things, asking the children to imagine themselves as the zebra avoids the problem of their having to use quotation marks when they write their stories. (The use of quotation marks is not treated until a later lesson.)

Follow-up (Part I) When the children have finished writing, you can ask for volunteers to share their stories with the rest of the class. There should be considerable variety among them, and this will help the children to grasp the significance of the role played by imagination in the composition process.

Here's another missing-picture story. The first picture shows the beginning of the story. The last picture shows the end of the story. But the middle picture—the middle of the story—is blank. Try to think of a good middle for a story about a zebra.

Suppose you were the zebra. And suppose you could talk. What would you say in the beginning of the story? What would you do in the middle? What would you say at the end?

■ Now write your story. Pretend that you're the zebra. Tell what you would <u>say</u> in the beginning and at the end. Tell what you would <u>do</u> in the middle of the story.

48

Part II

In this part, you can use your imagination to write a poem. There are many different ways to write poems. One good way to begin is to read some poems that were written by other children.

Here's a poem that one nine-year-old girl wrote. She used her imagination to pretend that she was a flag. This is the poem she wrote.

If I Was a Flag

If I was a flag
I would feel like April
With the colors red, white and blue,
I would feel happy flying like a bird,
Swing on air, with the breath of air.
I would feel pretty good standing on a pole with the
    people saluting at me.

Here's a poem by a boy who used his imagination to pretend he was a blackboard.

A Blackboard

How does it feel to be a blackboard?
I think it would feel funny.
Always being written on.
Always having examples erased off.
What do you see?
You see many, many kids.

Preparation (Part II)   Remind the children that there are many different ways to use their imaginations to think of things. Ask them to imagine that they are flags on the top of poles. "What could you hear? What could you see? What could you feel?" Next, have the children imagine themselves as chalkboards, and again ask them what they would see, hear, and feel.

Then suggest that imagination not only helps you think of many different things, it also helps you write things in different ways. "You can use your imagination to write a story, or you can also use it to write a poem."

Presentation (Part II)   Ask for volunteers to read and discuss the text and the poems on page 49, and compare the poems with the answers which the class gave during the Preparation. Use the differences to stress the fact that people use their imaginations in different ways.

Then ask the children what they would like to be if—all of a sudden—they could be anything at all. Tell them that there are some questions at the top of page 50 that will help them. When they begin the activity (■) on page 50, encourage them to make a list of several things they'd be able to see, hear, and feel before they start their poems.

Follow-up (Part II)   For other excellent suggestions for ways to engage children in the writing of poetry, see Kenneth Koch's book, listed below.

Additional Resources

Books   Koch, Kenneth, *Wishes, Lies and Dreams,* Random House.
Recordings   *Wishes, Lies and Dreams,* 1-12″ LP, Spoken Arts.

Purposes (1) To provide additional experience in discussing the sentence-combining rule; (2) To introduce the terms *matrix* and *insert* as convenient labels to use when discussing the sentence-combining rule.

[This lesson continues the practice of introducing technical terms as useful means of talking about language. Although you might want to have the children find the meanings of *insert* and *matrix* in a dictionary, there is no purpose in having them memorize these definitions. Additionally, it's a good idea to use the terms *insert* and *inside* interchangeably, as well as *matrix* and *outside*, not only in this lesson but also in the ones that follow, until the children are comfortable with the technical terms. As usual, the terminology is less important than an understanding of the operations involved.]

Preparation Since page 50 is essentially a review of the previous lesson on sentence combining, there's no need for special preparation. You may want to work some sentence problems on the chalkboard, following the procedure outlined in the notes on page 40.

Presentation When you're certain that the children understand the process involved in combining sentences, call their attention to the last paragraph on page 50, which presents the most important point of the lesson. You can ask for volunteers to try to state the rule in their own words, and then have them read the rule at the top of page 51.

You should probably spend a few minutes discussing this rule with the children. On the chalkboard, write the "first" rule that the children learned: *A sentence has a nominal and a verb phrase.* Then write the "new" rule directly below it. As

Here's a chance for you to really use your imagination. If you could be any <u>thing</u> at all, what would you be? Would you be a happy thing or a sad thing? What would you do? Would you do something silly or something smart? Could you see or hear anything special?

■ Now pretend that you <u>are</u> the special thing. Write your poem, telling how you'd feel and what you'd do. You can write a title for your poem, if you want to.

The Sentence-Combining Rule

You already know how to combine two sentences that have the same nominal. We can put one sentence inside the other, like this.

> The dog fell asleep.
> + The dog ate my lunch.
> ———————————————
> The dog who ate my lunch fell asleep.

What nominal is the same in these two sentences? Do you remember how we put one sentence inside the other? We did it like this.

> The dog who ate my lunch fell asleep.

This sentence problem shows how two sentences can fit together to make a new one. Since you know how to solve the problem, there must be a rule—in your head—that tells you how to do it.

Daybook: Putting More Sentences
Together, page 24

50

We can write the rule this way.

- A sentence has a nominal (and another sentence) and a verb phrase.

We can use special words to help us talk about combining sentences. The sentence inside the parentheses is sometimes called the **insert sentence.** And the sentence outside the parentheses is called the **matrix sentence.** The *insert sentence* goes inside the *matrix sentence.*

Here's a sentence we can use for a matrix sentence.

The doctor laughed loudly.

We can spread the matrix sentence apart, like this.

The doctor (   ) laughed loudly.

And then we can add an insert sentence.

The doctor (the doctor tickled my foot) laughed loudly.

We cross out the nominal of the insert sentence and write in the word *who.*

The doctor (~~the doctor~~ *who* tickled my foot) laughed loudly.

When we take away the parentheses, we have a new sentence.

The doctor who tickled my foot laughed loudly.

Here's another example. Try to explain what happens each time we rewrite the sentence.

The boy began to sneeze.
The boy (   ) began to sneeze.
The boy (the boy ate the pizza) began to sneeze.
The boy (who ate the pizza) began to sneeze.
The boy who ate the pizza began to sneeze.

the children compare the two rules, help them to see that all we've really done is to make the "first" rule longer. Direct their attention to the new words that have been added to the rule and to the use of parentheses. Be sure to explain that, when we have parentheses in a rule, we use the part inside the parentheses only if we want to. You can reinforce this point by saying: "Every sentence must have a nominal and a verb phrase. But not every sentence must have another sentence inside it." Then you can summarize the discussion by saying: "The new rule tells you even more about what goes on in your head when you use language. It says you can make sentences. And it also says that you can combine sentences."

After the children have read the paragraph which follows the rule, write the words *insert* and *matrix* on the chalkboard. Help the children pronounce each of these terms, and then add on the chalkboard:

insert = inside
matrix = outside

Emphasize that the special words help us talk about what happens in our heads when we combine sentences.

After the children have studied the first example on page 51, you may want to write it on the chalkboard in the form of a sentence problem:

The doctor laughed loudly.

+ ~~The doctor~~ *who* tickled my foot.

The doctor who tickled my foot laughed loudly.

Help the children to see that this represents the same thing as the example given in their books, the only difference being in the format.

Work the example on the bottom of page 51 with the entire class, asking for comments on each step. Then call for volunteers to solve the problem on the top of page 52.

The activity (■) on page 52 can be worked in pairs or in small groups.

Follow-up To provide further practice, you can have the children use the method presented in this lesson to combine the following sentences:

1. MATRIX: The fish found a peanut.
   INSERT: The fish tickled my foot.
2. MATRIX: The dog dug a hole.
   INSERT: The dog won a prize.
3. MATRIX: The doctor fell asleep.
   INSERT: The doctor ate my lunch.
4. MATRIX: The bird dropped a book.
   INSERT: The bird climbed a tree.
5. MATRIX: The mailman broke the chalk.
   INSERT: The mailman sang a song.
6. MATRIX: The boy found a peanut.
   INSERT: The boy ate my lunch.
7. MATRIX: The chicken climbed a tree.
   INSERT: The chicken broke the chalk.
8. MATRIX: The teacher sang a song.
   INSERT: The teacher dropped a book.
9. MATRIX: The girl won a prize.
   INSERT: The girl dug a hole.
10. MATRIX: The frog tickled my foot.
    INSERT: The frog fell asleep.

Answers

2. The chicken who crossed the road found a worm.
3. The lady who broke my balloon said she was sorry.
4. The girl who lives next door caught a fish.
5. The fish who ate the worm swallowed the hook.
6. The boy who caught the fish ate his lunch.

Now here's one for you to try. Suppose we have this matrix sentence.

The girl (   ) likes to whistle.

And we want to add this insert sentence.

The girl sits next to me.

Which nominal do we cross out? What word do we use instead of the nominal? What new sentence can you make?

■ Now try to combine these sentences. (The first one has been done for you.)

1. MATRIX SENTENCE: The dog slept all day.
   INSERT SENTENCE: The dog barked all night.

   The dog (   ) slept all day.
   The dog (the dog barked all night) slept all day.

   who
   The dog (~~the dog~~ barked all night) slept all day.
   The dog who barked all night slept all day.

2. MATRIX SENTENCE: The chicken found a worm.
   INSERT SENTENCE: The chicken crossed the road.

3. MATRIX SENTENCE: The lady said she was sorry.
   INSERT SENTENCE: The lady broke my balloon.

4. MATRIX SENTENCE: The girl caught a fish.
   INSERT SENTENCE: The girl lives next door.

5. MATRIX SENTENCE: The fish swallowed the hook.
   INSERT SENTENCE: The fish ate the worm.

6. MATRIX SENTENCE: The boy ate his lunch.
   INSERT SENTENCE: The boy caught the fish.

What Does "Meaning" Mean?

Did you ever see a young child just beginning to learn words? He points at things and asks, "What's that?"

For small children, pointing is an important way of learning new words.

But as children get older, they learn to read. Then there are other ways they can find out the meanings of words. One important way is to use a dictionary. Word meanings that we find in a dictionary are called **definitions.** And there are some things you should know about definitions.

In a dictionary, definitions have two parts. The first part tells what group or family a thing belongs to. Suppose we have an apple, a banana, a grape, and a pear. All of them are alike in one way. They're all fruits. So we can say they belong to the family of "fruits." A canary, an eagle, and a sparrow all belong to the family of "birds."

Daybook: Members of the Family, page 26

Purposes (1) To suggest that there are many ways to learn the meanings of words; (2) To illustrate how the definitions of nouns are usually arranged in dictionaries; (3) To explain the use of pictures in a dictionary.

[Many people, particularly children, assume that most of the meanings we know are acquired by consulting dictionaries. This lesson suggests that such an assumption is false, but at the same time it demonstrates the importance of using a dictionary for this purpose.]

Preparation Children should know the alphabet well before beginning this lesson. If necessary, you can refer some children to the skills lesson, Alphabetical Order, beginning on page 256. In addition to the exercises on alphabetizing given in the Skills Section, you may wish to have the children arrange spelling words and the names of class members in alphabetical order.

It's also useful to display various types of dictionaries in the classroom so the children recognize that all dictionaries are not alike. (In particular, most school dictionaries do not provide full definitions of words.)

Presentation After the children have read the first half of page 53, ask for volunteers to tell about younger children in their families who ask questions similar to those in the illustrations.

Then write the word *definition* on the chalkboard, and read the first paragraph under the second illustration, which explains what the word means. Comment that, in a dictionary, many definitions have two parts. Then have the children read the final paragraph on page 53 silently to find out what the first part of the definition tells.

53

When they've done so, write the key sentence from that paragraph on the chalkboard: *The first part tells what group or family a thing belongs to*. Then have the class work the activity (■) on page 54.

Next, have the children read the paragraph below the activity to learn what the second part of a definition tells. Also have them read the definition of *hammer* and answer the questions in the paragraph below the definition. Repeat the process with *hive*. You can then have the children check *hammer* and *hive* in a classroom dictionary and compare the definitions with those given in the text.

If your classroom dictionary has illustrations to accompany *hammer* and *hive,* then you might want to discuss the usefulness of these pictures before proceeding with the material in the text. If not, then you can select an illustrated definition—preferably one which is unusual—and then read the definition to the children. Ask if they can get a good picture of the item you're defining from the words alone. You might even want to have a volunteer try to draw a picture of the item on the chalkboard. Then have the children examine the illustration which accompanies the entry in the dictionary.

Then continue with the material on the bottom of page 54 and the top of page 55, allowing plenty of time for the children to study and compare the illustrations. Help them to understand that sometimes a dictionary will include not only a picture with a definition but also an explanation of the picture as well.

The activity (■) on page 55 works particularly well with small groups.

■ Try to tell what family each of these groups of things belongs to.

1. rose, lily, petunia, daisy
2. hammer, saw, chisel, pliers
3. ant, bee, fly, mosquito
4. drum, trumpet, violin, piano
5. maple, oak, elm, willow

The first part of some definitions tells what family a thing belongs to. The second part tells how that thing is different from all the other things in the same family. How is a trumpet different from a drum? How is an apple different from a grape?

Here's part of a definition of *hammer*.

hammer a tool with a metal head and a handle, used to drive nails and to beat metal into shape.

Which words in this definition tell what family a hammer belongs to? Which words tell how a hammer is different from other tools?

Here's part of another definition.

hive a house or box for bees to live in.

Which part of this definition tells the family? Which part tells how a hive is different?

Sometimes, the words of a definition tell you all you need to know. But at other times, the words of a definition aren't enough. Then a dictionary gives both a written definition and a picture, like this.

har mon i ca (här mon′ə kə), a small musical instrument with metal reeds which is played by the mouth. See the picture.

harmonica

A picture can be a very important part of a definition. (Many people say that a picture is worth a thousand words.)

Besides definitions and pictures, some dictionaries give even more information about a word. They describe the picture, like this.

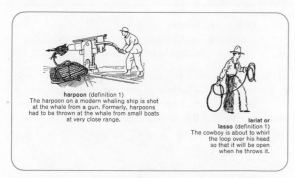

harpoon (definition 1)
The harpoon on a modern whaling ship is shot at the whale from a gun. Formerly, harpoons had to be thrown at the whale from small boats at very close range.

lariat or
lasso (definition 1)
The cowboy is about to whirl the loop over his head so that it will be open when he throws it.

■ Here are some words that you may not know. Look them up in the dictionary. Which part of the definition tells the family each thing belongs to? Which part tells how the thing is different from the other members of the same family?

1. bellows
2. plume
3. flute
4. chowder
5. dolphin
6. bison
7. dormer
8. helmet
9. ostrich
10. ladle
11. pontoon
12. silhouette
13. mushroom
14. troupe
15. yam

Did the dictionary use a picture to help you understand the meaning of any of these words? How did the picture help? Were there any words to describe the picture? How did these words help?

Follow-up Suggest that the children begin making their own dictionaries to which they can add throughout the year. (These dictionaries can be either books or small file boxes.) Encourage the children to try writing their own definitions, using the guidelines established in this lesson. Occasionally, they can also add pictures to help clarify the definitions.

Answers

A slash separates the group to which each thing belongs from the features which distinguish it from other members of the same group. Answers may vary somewhat, depending on the dictionary used.

1. Instrument / for producing a stream of air.
2. Feather / usually large and wavy.
3. Musical instrument / long and pipelike; played by blowing across a hole.
4. Soup / made from fish, clams, and vegetables.
5. Whale / small; with a beaklike snout.
6. Four-legged animal / with a big head; a shaggy mane; short, curved horns; and a humped back.
7. Window / upright; set in a sloping roof.
8. Covering for head / usually made of metal; for protection.
9. Bird / fast-running; large; with a long neck, long legs, and small wings.
10. Spoon / cup-shaped; with a long handle; for dipping.
11. Boat / low; with a flat bottom.
12. Outline drawing / filled in with solid color, usually black.
13. Plant (fungus) / small; top shaped like an umbrella.
14. Group of people / usually made up of actors, singers, or acrobats.
15. Root / starchy; used for food; grows in warm countries.

Purposes (1) To provide experience with another literary form—the folktale; (2) To illustrate the use of conversation in stories.

Preparation Ask the children to describe briefly some stories they know in which animals talk. Encourage them to tell about characters from comicstrips as well as from literature they may have read. Discuss some of the different ways the animals talk in these stories, and then comment that the authors had to use their imaginations to think of things for these animals to say.

Presentation It's best to read the story to the children the first time. Be as dramatic as you can in reading the dialogue, perhaps varying the volume and pitch of your voice for the different characters.

A Folktale

In every country, in every part of the world, people tell stories. Sometimes these stories are so old that nobody knows who made them up. And sometimes, the stories aren't even written down.

> One parent tells his child,
> and that child grows up and tells his child,
> and <u>that</u> child grows up and tells his child,

and so on. Then one day someone does write the story down so that other people—people all over the world—can read it.

Here's a story from West Africa. It's probably hundreds of years old. But it wasn't written down until a short time ago.

Talk

Once, not far from the city of Accra on the Gulf of Guinea, a country man went out to his garden to dig up some yams to take to market. While he was digging, one of the yams said to him, "Well, at last you're here. You never weeded me, but now you come around with your digging stick. Go away and leave me alone!"

The farmer turned around and looked at his cow in amazement. The cow was chewing her cud and looking at him.

"Did you say something?" he asked.

The cow kept on chewing and said nothing, but the man's dog spoke up.

"It wasn't the cow who spoke to you," the dog said. "It was the yam. The yam says leave him alone."

Daybook: Who Said That? page 28

Then write the word *folktale* on the chalkboard, and direct the children's attention to the title of the lesson on page 56. Read the introduction to the children, helping them to see that a folktale is a story that was handed down by word of mouth for many years. You can also comment that such stories were often changed a little each time that someone else told them. If you wish, you can then point out West Africa on the world map or globe and help the children locate the Gulf of Guinea.

To prepare the children for reading the story themselves, write the following words on the chalkboard: *yam*, *cud*, *palm*, *gazelle*, and *community*. You can explain that a *yam* is a kind of sweet potato, and then point out the yams in the illustration on page 57. You can also use the illustration to help the children define *palm*. Then have volunteers check a dictionary for the meanings of the other words.

For the second reading of the story, you can have volunteers read the lines spoken by the various characters. If you decide to do this, then you will need readers for the following:

farmer	weaver
yam	fish trap
dog	bundle of cloth
palm tree	man bathing
palm branch	river
stone	chief
fisherman	stool

You, or one of the children, can read the narrative parts of the story. (Before beginning to read, help the children to understand that they say only what is inside the quotation marks. They can also omit such phrases as "he asked" and "the dog said." This may take a little practice at first, especially if the children haven't had experience with this kind of reading.)

The man became angry, because his dog had never talked before, and he didn't like his tone besides. So he took his knife and cut a branch from a palm tree to whip his dog. Just then the palm tree said, "Put that branch down!"

The man was getting very upset about the way things were going, and he started to throw the palm branch away, but the palm branch said, "Man, put me down softly!"

He put the branch down gently on a stone, and the stone said, "Hey, take that thing off me!"

This was enough, and the frightened farmer started to run for his village. On the way he met a fisherman going the other way with a fish trap on his head.

"What's the hurry?" the fisherman asked.

"My yam said, 'Leave me alone!' Then the dog said, 'Listen to what the yam says!' When I went to whip the dog with a palm branch the tree said, 'Put that branch down!' Then the palm branch said, 'Do it softly!' Then the stone said, 'Take that thing off me!'"

"Is that all?" the man with the fish trap asked. "Is that so frightening?"

"Well," the man's fish trap said, "did he take it off the stone?"

"Wah!" the fisherman shouted. He threw the fish trap on the ground and began to run with the farmer, and on the trail they met a weaver with a bundle of cloth on his head.

"Where are you going in such a rush?" he asked them.

"My yam said, 'Leave me alone!'" the farmer said. "The dog said, 'Listen to what the yam says!' The tree said, 'Put that branch down!' The branch said, 'Do it softly!' And the stone said, 'Take that thing off me!'"

"And then," the fisherman continued, "the fish trap

said, 'Did he take it off?' "

"That's nothing to get excited about," the weaver said. "No reason at all."

"Oh, yes it is," his bundle of cloth said. "If it happened to you you'd run too!"

"Wah!" the weaver shouted. He threw his bundle on the trail and started running with the other men.

They came panting to the ford in the river and found a man bathing. "Are you chasing a gazelle?" he asked them.

The first man said breathlessly, "My yam talked at me, and it said, 'Leave me alone!' And my dog said, 'Listen to your yam!' And when I cut myself a branch the tree said, 'Put that branch down!' And the branch said, 'Do it softly!' And the stone said, 'Take that thing off me!' "

The fisherman panted, "And my trap said, 'Did he?' "

The weaver sneezed, "And my bundle of cloth said, 'You'd run too!' "

"Is that why you're running?" the man in the river asked.

"Well, wouldn't you run if you were in their position?" the river said.

The man jumped out of the water and began to run with the others. They ran down the main street of the village to the house of the chief. The chief's servants brought his stool out, and he came and sat on it to listen to their complaints. The men began to recite their troubles.

"I went out to my garden to dig yams," the farmer said, waving his arms. "Then everything began to talk! My yam said, 'Leave me alone!' My dog said, 'Pay attention to your yam!' The tree said, 'Put that branch down!' The branch said, 'Do it softly!' And the stone said, 'Take it off me!' "

After the second reading, have the children turn to the discussion on page 61. In answering the questions, encourage the children to refer to the folktale itself whenever necessary. Also try to encourage variety in their answers, especially to such open-ended questions as the one about the reason for the stool talking last.

If the lesson is running long, you can postpone the activity (■) at the bottom of page 61 until another time.

Follow-up This is another good selection to have the children illustrate. Each child could select one "scene" from the story to portray, and then the finished pictures can be arranged sequentially on the bulletin board.

You can also extend the discussion of how folktales are often changed somewhat as people retell them. You might suggest that the children add some things of their own to the story—perhaps another person and another talking object. After the children have added their own "scenes," they might enjoy dramatizing the entire folktale, perhaps using puppets. These can be as simple as cardboard cutouts stapled to tongue depressors or as complicated as papier mâché figures, depending on the time you have available.

This would also be a good time to read to the children some other folktales. (See Additional Resources.)

"And my fish trap said, 'Well, did he take it off?'" the fisherman said.

"And my cloth said, 'You'd run too!'" the weaver said.

"And the river said the same," the bather said hoarsely, his eyes bulging.

The chief listened to them patiently, but he couldn't refrain from scowling. "Now this is really a wild story," he said at last. "You'd better all go back to your work before I punish you for disturbing the peace."

So the men went away, and the chief shook his head and mumbled to himself, "Nonsense like that upsets the community."

"Fantastic, isn't it?" his stool said. "Imagine, a talking yam!"

HAROLD COURLANDER AND GEORGE HERZOG

In the story, the first <u>person</u> to talk is the farmer. Who is the last person to talk? The first <u>thing</u> to talk is the yam. What's the last thing to talk?

Why does the storyteller make the chief the last person to talk? What does the chief say? What is the "nonsense" he is talking about? How would such nonsense upset the "community"?

Why does the storyteller make the chief's stool the last thing to talk? What does the stool say? Do you think that the chief is surprised when the stool talks? Why? Is there anything funny about what the stool says? If you were reading the story aloud, how would you read this last line?

■ Now think about two other objects in your classroom. Imagine that these two things are talking to each other. What are some of the things they could say? Write a story about your two objects. Have them both talking.

Additional Resources

Books   There are many excellent books of African folklore available, including Arkhurst, Joyce Cooper, *The Adventures of Spider, West African Folk Tales,* Little, Brown; Carpenter, Frances, *African Wonder Tales,* Doubleday; Courlander, Harold, *The Hat-Shaking Dance,* Hale; Courlander, Harold and George Herzog, *The Cow Tail Switch and Other West African Stories,* Holt, Rinehart and Winston; Guillot, René, *René Guillot's African Folk Tales,* Watts; Habte-Mariam, Mesfin, *The Rich Man and the Singer,* Dutton; and Kamerman, Sylvia E., *Dramatized Folk Tales of the World,* Plays.

Recordings   Children will usually enjoy Boris Karloff reading some of Kipling's famous *Just So Stories,* 1–12″ LP, 2-track tape, cassette, Caedmon. A dramatized version of these stories is available on *Just So Stories: Rudyard Kipling (Dramatized Version),* 1–12″ LP, Spoken Arts. And a musical adaptation of the *Just So Stories* is available on Columbia Records. Other fine recordings of myths and folktales include *Folk and Fairy Tales from Africa,* Miller-Brody; *Folk Tales from West Africa,* Folkways; *Folk Tales of the Tribes of Africa as told by Eartha Kitt,* Caedmon; and *The Rain God's Daughter and Other African Folktales,* Caedmon.

Filmstrips   *African Folk Tales,* 6 color filmstrips, 3 records, Holt, Rinehart and Winston. This set includes such stories as "Why the Bush Fowl Calls at Dawn" and "Why the Flies Buzz."

Purpose To provide additional practice with description.

Preparation If your library has a book of riddles for children, you might display the book and then ask the children to answer a few of the riddles. Then write the word *describers* on the chalkboard and ask for a volunteer to name three describers. You can also refer to the compositions which the children wrote using the describers.

Presentation The first half of the page can be done orally, as a class. You can duplicate the riddle on the chalkboard, adding the suggestions which the children make for additional things that a spaceship <u>is</u>, <u>has</u>, and <u>does</u>. Be sure the children understand that, in the riddle, the spaceship is "talking" (that is, each line begins with the word *I*). Help them see, also, that the first line is restricted to <u>is</u>, the second to <u>have</u>, and the third to <u>does</u>.

You might begin the activity (■) orally by asking for volunteers to look out the window, choose an object, and then describe it in the form of a riddle. When the class understands the form of a riddle, they can work in pairs and groups to write their own riddles.

Follow-up After the children have asked their riddles, they can revise and recopy them. They might even want to make an illustrated booklet of riddles to share with another class.

Additional Resources

Books Emrich, Duman, compiler, *The Nonsense Book of Riddles, Rhymes, Tongue Twisters, Puzzles and Jokes from American Folklore*, Four Winds. Leeming, Joseph, *Riddles, Riddles, Riddles*, Watts.

The Riddle Game

Here are the *describers* again. This time they're talking about a spaceship.

Try to think of one other thing that a spaceship <u>is</u>. Think of another thing it <u>has</u>. Think of something else it <u>does</u>.

Now add your own words to what the describers say. You can make them into a riddle.

I am tall and shiny and _____.
I have a nose cone and a _____.
I take off slowly and then I _____.
What am I?

■ You can use the describers to make up your own riddles. First, think of a "secret something." Tell one or two things the secret something <u>is</u>. Then, tell one or two things it <u>has</u>. And finally, tell one or two things it <u>does</u>. Write the answer to your riddle on the back of your paper. If you want, you can exchange papers with your friends. Then you can try to guess the answers to each other's riddles.

Three Kinds of Nominals

Part I

Here's a sentence we can make using the model.

The boy tickled my foot.

You already know that *the boy* is a nominal.
Here are some other nominals.

the girl   the frog   a doctor
a chicken   a fish   a mailman

Nominals like these have two parts. There's a special name for the first part. It's called a **determiner**. (Words like *the* and *a* are both determiners.) The second part has a shorter name. It's called a **noun.** When we put a determiner and a noun together, we get a nominal.

● One kind of nominal has a determiner and a noun.

If a nominal has a determiner and a noun, then we call it a **regular nominal.**

In your head, you know thousands of nouns. Here are some of them.

baby   chair   school   wagon
tiger   nurse   pie   lady

What are some of the nouns that we have in the lexicon on page 31?

Now we can add some more words to the lexicon. If we put a determiner with each of the nouns in the list above, then we'll have these nominals.

the baby   my chair   this school   her wagon
a tiger   the nurse   the pie   that lady

Daybook: Practice with Nominals, page 30

Purposes (1) To distinguish three kinds of nominals; (2) To provide labels for the three kinds of nominals.

[Children begin using three different kinds of nominals when they are two—or at the most three—years old. That is, they have many years of experience in using these nominals. In this lesson, that experience is first brought to the level of awareness (as the children distinguish the three types) and then to the level of verbalization (as they learn the names for the three types).

The lesson is divided into two parts to provide you with the option of teaching the lesson on separate days.]

Preparation On the chalkboard, write one sentence that the children have already used, perhaps *The boy broke the chalk.* Then elicit the two parts of the sentence and also the names for these parts (nominal and verb phrase). Repeat with two or three other sentences.

Presentation Proceed slowly and deliberately with page 63. A child can read the first third of the page, and then you can read the middle third as they listen. When you come to the rule (●), write it on the chalkboard and help the children pronounce the words *determiner* and *noun*.

The sentence under the rule introduces the term *regular nominal,* but until the children read page 64, they have nothing to compare this term to. Thus, some children may not recognize the usefulness of this term until they've read the next page.

After the children have identified some of the nouns in the lexicon on page 31, have them identify the determiners and nouns in the list at the bottom of page 63.

Copy the two example sentences at the top of page 64 onto the chalkboard. Ask for a volunteer to identify the nominal in each sentence, and then have another volunteer identify the two parts—determiner and noun—of each nominal.

Now erase the two nominals from the sentences on the chalkboard and in their place write *Barbara* and *Pokey*. Then have a volunteer read the first third of page 64. Ask for another volunteer to suggest one way that a name is different from a regular nominal. (There's no determiner in a name; the first letter of a name is always written as a capital letter.) The first activity (■) on page 64 can then be done orally.

Call attention to the paragraph following the first activity. You can make a list of names on the chalkboard as the class suggests them. Encourage the children to include the names of pets as well as people.

The second activity (■) on page 64 can be completed individually, using the names already on the chalkboard. The children should feel free to use other names as well, including their own.

Part II: Read the first sentence on page 65 and ask for examples of regular nominals and names. Also ask for someone to identify the two parts of a regular nominal.

On the chalkboard, write the three example sentences given at the top of page 65. Then have the children answer the questions pertaining to the examples.

Here are two sentences that have regular nominals.

The girl tickled my foot.
The frog tickled my foot.

But in many sentences, we don't use a determiner and a noun. What else can we use?

Barbara tickled my foot.
Pokey tickled my foot.

When we talk about people and pets, we sometimes use their **names.** Names are another kind of nominal.

■ Which of these sentences have regular nominals? Which have names?

1. The doctor was tired.
2. Oscar can't swim.
3. Ellen looks pretty.
4. The wagon is broken.
5. Rusty is always hungry.
6. Mr. Williams works hard.

A regular nominal has a determiner and a noun. Another kind of nominal is a name. In your head, you know lots of names. What are some of these names?

■ Now use names to complete these sentences. (Remember that when you write a name, it must always begin with a capital letter.)

1. _____ doesn't like marshmallows.
2. Mr._____ fell in a hole.
3. _____ buried a bone.
4. _____ is a nurse.
5. _____ went on a picnic.
6. _____ pulled my tooth.

Part II

You've learned about *regular nominals* and you've learned about *names*. There's a third kind of nominal that's important, too.

Here are three more sentences.

The boy fell down.
Jack fell down.
He fell down.

Which sentence begins with a regular nominal? Which begins with a name? Now look at the first word in the last sentence. It's not a regular nominal. It's not a name. It's another kind of nominal—a **pronoun.**

● Names and pronouns are also nominals.

Everybody knows lots of nouns and lots of names. But nobody knows very many pronouns, because there aren't very many. Here are some of them.

I   she   you   he   we   it   they

■ The nominals have been left out of these sentences. Try to add the right kind of nominal to each one.

	Nominal	Verb Phrase
1.	(regular nominal)	found a peanut.
2.	(name)	likes buttermilk.
3.	(pronoun)	climbed a tree.
4.	(regular nominal)	danced on the desk.
5.	(pronoun)	slept all day.

Next, call their attention to *He* in the third sentence. Then say: "It's not a regular nominal. There's no determiner. And it's not a name. We need to use another term to talk about words like *he, she,* and *it.*"

(In many older texts, you'll find the inaccurate statement that a pronoun is a word used in place of a noun. This statement is only rarely true. In the example on page 65, *He* is not used in place of the noun *boy* but rather in place of the entire regular nominal—*The boy.* In general, it's best to avoid such statements, since several of them are not entirely accurate and can be confusing to children.)

The activity (■) on page 65 can be done as a class. Try to encourage a number of different responses for each item in the exercise.

Follow-up You can easily extend the activity on page 65 by selecting additional verb phrases from previous lexicons. But one word of caution: The verb phrases in the sentence model have been selected so they will fit with any third-person-singular nominal. This is true for all verb phrases in the present tense. The nature of English is such that—with one exception—any verb phrase in the past tense will fit with any nominal (singular or plural; first, second, or third person). The exception is the past tense form of *be*, where *was* is used with first- and third-person-singular nominals and *were* is used with all others. Thus, it's best to choose verb phrases in the past tense (but not *was* or *were*) when asking the children to select a pronoun for the exercise.

Purposes (1) To review the use of imagination in literature and composition; (2) To reinforce the concept of nominal and to review the sentence-combining rule.

Presentation To vary the presentation of the Review, you can assign three children to act as "Review Teachers." Each of these children can be responsible for a particular section: Literature, Composition, or Language. Similarly, you can divide the class into three groups and have each group prepare a set of answers, such as the following:

metaphor	pronoun
imagination	regular nominal
Harry Has	determiner
sentence problem	folktale

Then the children can also prepare questions to go with these answers. (Frequently, they'll be able to form more than one question for a given answer.) Each group can then ask the other children in the class to answer the questions.

To provide some additional practice with nominals, you can make up sentences similar to those in the activity on page 65 for the children to complete. You can use regular nominals and verb phrases from the lexicons on pages 21 and 31 of the text. And you can use the children's own names.

Review

Literature

People who write poems and stories always use lots of **imagination.** Sometimes they even think up things that could never happen. You've walked on lots of roads. Have you ever been on a road through some woods? What was it like? Do you think about roads differently since you read "The Road Not Taken"?

■ Now think about a road that you'd like to travel on. It can be a real road or an imaginary one. What kind of road is it? Are there trees on either side? Or are there tall buildings? Or do you see something else as you walk along your road? Where does the road lead? Will it take you to a strange place? Write a story that tells about your road.

Composition

You can use your imagination to tell stories. Another good way to use your imagination is to made up riddles. Here's part of a riddle. Try to add some words to complete it. Then write an answer for the riddle.

I am long and _____.
I have an eraser and a _____.
I make lines and _____.
What am I?

■ That's an easy riddle. Now try to make up a harder one. Think again about a "secret something." Don't forget to use the describers to tell two things your secret something <u>is</u> and <u>has</u> and <u>does</u>.

Language

Do you remember the sentence-combining rule?

● A sentence has a nominal (and another sentence) and a verb phrase.

What do we call the sentence inside the parentheses? What's the name for the sentence outside the parentheses?

■ Use the rule to try to put these sentences together.

1. MATRIX SENTENCE: The lady caught a fish.
   INSERT SENTENCE: The lady found a worm.

2. MATRIX SENTENCE: The boy found a nest.
   INSERT SENTENCE: The boy climbed the tree.

3. MATRIX SENTENCE: The girl won the race.
   INSERT SENTENCE: The girl ate the spinach.

■ Now look again at these sentences. Make a list of all the nominals. What kind of nominals are they? Rewrite each matrix sentence using names. Then rewrite them again using pronouns.

 Using a *dictionary* is one of the most important skills you can learn. For more practice with the dictionary, look on pages 275–283.

You can ditto the following exercise to provide additional practice with the sentence-combining rule:

1. MATRIX: The gorilla read a book.
   INSERT: The gorilla sat in a tree.
2. MATRIX: The mongoose fell asleep.
   INSERT: The mongoose ate some snakes.
3. MATRIX: The lady climbed a tree.
   INSERT: The lady saw a mouse.
4. MATRIX: The whale carried an umbrella.
   INSERT: The whale was getting wet.
5. MATRIX: The crocodile smiled.
   INSERT: The crocodile swallowed a whale.

Answers

The answers for the first activity are as follows:
1. The lady who found a worm caught a fish.
2. The boy who climbed the tree found a nest.
3. The girl who ate the spinach won the race.

For the second activity, the children should list the following nominals:

the lady	a fish	a worm
the boy	a nest	the tree
the girl	the race	the spinach

All of these are regular nominals. For the last part of this activity, the children should write the following:
1. She caught a fish.
2. He found a nest.
3. She won the race.

Purposes (1) To provide an example of an extended, well developed metaphor; (2) To provide additional experience with lyric poetry; (3) To suggest that <u>order</u> plays an important role in literature.

[This lesson is the first one in the second quarter of the book, and Vachel Lindsay's poem is particularly suitable at this time. It demonstrates how the three strands—literature, composition, and language—fit together and reinforce each other. First, the poem is a good example of literature which draws on native traditions; second, it clearly demonstrates the importance of order in the composition process; and third, it illustrates in a simple way how we use language in building metaphors.]

Preparation If possible, show several pictures of a single thing (for example, a tree or a house) at different times of day and at different seasons of the year. Perhaps your school librarian can help you find collections of photographs; many photographers have photographed a single subject under varying conditions. Help the children see both the basic similarities in the pictures as well as the differences.

Additionally, the children may consult a dictionary or an encyclopedia for the meaning of *Indian Summer*. Help them to see that, even though the weather may be very mild, Indian summer is really part of autumn, and generally doesn't last more than a few days. (Some sources require that a frost occur before we can legitimately call such a warm spell "Indian Summer.") Explain that during Indian summer days the sun shines dimly

A Poem

Here's a poem about the sun. Do you know what Indian Summer is? This poem tells how an Indian might think about the sun late in the summer.

Indian Summer Day on the Prairie

In the Beginning

The sun is a huntress young,
The sun is red, red joy,
The sun is an Indian girl,
Of the tribe of the Illinois.

Mid-Morning

The sun is a smoldering fire,
That creeps through the high gray plain,
And leaves not a bush of cloud
To blossom with flowers of rain.

Noon

The sun is a wounded deer,
That treads pale grass in the skies,
Shaking his golden horns,
Flashing his baleful eyes.

Sunset

The sun is an eagle old,
There in the windless west.
Atop of the spirit-cliffs
He builds him a crimson nest.

VACHEL LINDSAY

and softly, and the air is usually smoky and still. You can also discuss an Indian summer that the children may have experienced. Then you can compare the sights, the sounds, and the feelings of different times of the year and let the children decide on their favorite seasons.

Presentation As usual, your reading of a poem can provide a valuable experience in listening for the children. In this case, the listening can be quite active. For example, as the children listen they can pretend to be Indians. Encourage them to try to hear sounds, to see "visions," and to feel themselves growing older on an Indian summer day.

First, read the poem aloud to the children while their books are closed. Then ask them to turn to page 69 and call on a volunteer to read the short introduction. Then the children can follow along as you read the poem again. The more "dramatic feeling" you can get into your reading, the more the children will be able to listen actively.

Speaking is the most natural complement to listening, and the discussion on page 70 encourages the children to "talk about" both the poem and their individual responses to it. Some of the questions require close reading; others encourage children to use their imaginations in responding to the poem.

Since the discussion of the poem is somewhat long, you may want to postpone reading the last paragraph and working the activity (■) until another day. If so, you should reread the poem a final time before concluding the lesson.

Follow-up Some children might enjoy illustrating the poem "Indian Summer Day on the Prairie." You can have each child choose a particular stanza, and then you can arrange the finished pictures sequentially to show the sun at various times of the day. Other children might prefer to illustrate their own metaphors about the sun.

Additional Resources

Books Hampson, Alfred L., editor, *Poems for Youth,* Little, Brown. You may want to read "Sunset" by Emily Dickinson to the children. Lindsay, Vachel, *Johnny Appleseed and Other Poems.* This book contains poetry of Vachel Lindsay especially selected for young readers.
Recordings *Poetry,* 1–12″ LP, Caedmon. Some of Vachel Lindsay's best-known poems are read on this recording by the poet's son. *Vachel Lindsay Reading,* 1–12″ LP, cassette, Caedmon.

Why do you suppose the poet divided "Indian Summer Day on the Prairie" into four stanzas? Notice that each stanza has a title. What does each stanza tell about? Each stanza begins with the same words: "The sun is . . . ." But each stanza tells about a different time of the day.

What is the title of the first stanza? What time of day is this? Here the poet uses three metaphors to describe the sun. What are they?

What time of day is mid-morning? In this stanza, what is the metaphor about the sun? Is the "high gray plain" really a plain? What else could it be? What does the poet call the clouds? How does he talk about the rain?

What metaphor does the poet use for the sun at noontime? Instead of a plain, how does the poet describe the sky now? How does the color of the sun change in the third stanza? What are "baleful eyes"?

What kind of animal is the sun at sunset? What does an "old eagle" make you think of? How does the color of the sun change now? Sometimes, to an Indian, cliffs are not just cliffs. What are they?

First the sun is a young girl. Then it's a smoldering fire. In the third stanza, it's a wounded deer. And at the end of the day, it's an old eagle. What does this tell you about what happens to the sun as the day goes by?

Suppose a sailor wanted to write a poem about the way the sun looked at different times of the day. What would be a good metaphor for how the sun appears "in the beginning"? Try to think of some good metaphors for the sun at other times of the day.

■ Now <u>you</u> choose three times of the day to tell about. Think of how the sun looks at each of these times. What does it remind you of? Try to think of a metaphor for the sun at each of the times you have chosen.

Public and Private

Sometimes a composition is **private.** You write it for yourself. But sometimes a composition is **public.** If someone else is going to see it, then your composition should be neat. It should be easy for the other person to read.

If you want other people to read your composition, then you should do these things:

Spell all the words correctly.
Put capital letters in the right places.
Use the right punctuation marks.
Make your handwriting neat.

That's what you do when you **recopy** a composition. You copy it again, neatly. Then you can show it to anyone.

When you look back at a composition, you may think of a way to make it more interesting. Then you can **revise** your composition. One way to make a composition more interesting is to tell more about what's happening.

Here's a silly composition. It doesn't tell much and it isn't very interesting. It was written to help you think about revising. How could you revise it?

One day someone Number One saw Someone Number Two.

Someone Number One said, "I have been somewhere."

Someone Number Two said, "I was there some-time."

Then someone Number One asked, "Did you see something?"

Someone Number Two answered. So Someone Number One and Someone Number Two did something.

Purposes (1) To help children realize that compositions have different purposes; (2) To provide reasons for recopying some compositions; (3) To distinguish between recopying and revising.

Preparation Try to find some typographical errors in a daily newspaper which you can use to demonstrate that almost everyone makes mistakes in writing. You can ask the children how they would correct these mistakes, and then comment: "When people want to correct their mistakes, then they must recopy their work."

Presentation Read the first paragraph on page 71 with the children, helping them distinguish between public and private compositions. Then, after the children have read the second paragraph, you can ask them to give reasons why some written compositions should be neat.

Then ask the children to look at one of the poems or other compositions in their folders. Suggest that perhaps they wish they had said something in a different way. Ask if they can think of any new ideas they might have used. Then read the rest of the lesson with the children, helping them to see the difference between recopying and revising.

One way to work with the "silly composition" is to write each paragraph on the chalkboard and then erase particular parts as the children suggest revisions. This will produce a fully revised story which can then be recopied.

Follow-up This is an appropriate time to introduce the lesson on Proofreading in the Skills Section. You might want to help the children formulate individual check-lists of things to "look for" when they are recopying. These can be kept and expanded as the year progresses.

Purpose To provide a cumulative review of the grammatical concepts presented in the first four chapters.

Preparation Ask for a volunteer to give words which name parts of an airplane or an automobile, and list these on the chalkboard. Then ask another volunteer to give words which name parts of a school or a house, and put these words in a second list. Then challenge someone to talk about the first object (for example, the airplane) without using any words from the first list; to make it even more interesting, you can have a child try to talk about the first object using words from the second list. Then reverse the procedure and challenge someone to talk about the second object (for example, the school) using only words from the first list. The children will probably enjoy discovering that there are special words for talking about almost anything.

Presentation Pages 72 and 73 will help children understand the need for a special vocabulary when they discuss sentences. In reading the first paragraph, encourage the children to use their imaginations to think of themselves as being very, very small—small enough to walk around inside someone's head.

One way to revise this silly composition is to tell who the Someones are, what they said, and what they did. Can you think of a good name for the Someones? Where did Someone Number One go? When did Someone Number Two go there? What questions did Someone Number One ask? What did Someone Number Two answer? What did they do?

■ Now revise the composition. Don't forget to tell who the Someones are, what they said, and what they did.

■ Look over the compositions you've written this year. Is there one that you'd like to revise? How could you make it more interesting?

Talking About Sentences

Suppose you were very small. Suppose you were smaller than the point on the end of a pencil. And suppose you could walk around inside someone's head. Of course, you'd need to have a light with you so you could see everything. What do you think you would see?

There are some things you wouldn't see. You wouldn't see a special part of the head that said *lexicon*. You wouldn't see any *rules*. You wouldn't see any *sentence pictures* or how words fit together to make sentences.

Nobody, not even the most famous scientist in the world, knows exactly what people do when they make sentences. So what does a scientist do when he wants to talk about how people make sentences?

The best thing that a scientist can do is to use a *sentence model*. The model can help us talk about sentences. It can tell us what special words to use when we talk about language.

Suppose you want to talk about painting a picture. Or suppose you want to tell someone about a car. But you don't know any of the right words to use. Here are some words you could use.

frame	easel	body	pencil
brush	motor	brake	eraser
wheel	window	yellow	fender
door	paper	blue	gasoline
paint	water	seat	smock
battery	mirror	black	red

Can you talk about paintings and cars without using <u>any</u> of these words? When you want to talk about something, you almost always need special words.

■ These sentences have some of the special words we've used so far. The special words are underlined. Try to tell what each of the underlined words means.

1. When you make sentences, the words must be in the right <u>order</u>.
2. Besides words, you also need <u>rules</u> to make sentences.
3. One part of the sentence model is called the <u>lexicon</u>.
4. Very young children generally know only one <u>sentence-combining</u> rule.
5. What is the difference between a <u>matrix</u> <u>sentence</u> and an <u>insert</u> <u>sentence</u>?
6. Here is an example of a regular nominal: "the boy." Which part is the <u>determiner</u>? Which part is the <u>noun</u>?

 On page 303, there's a list of questions to help you in *proofreading*. Whenever you *recopy* a composition, it's a good idea to refer to this list.

The activity (■) on page 73 provides an excellent opportunity for teaching the use of an index. Children can use the Index which begins on page 337 to find examples that illustrate the meanings of the key terms.

Evaluation By this time, most children should begin to demonstrate one or more of the performance objectives included under each broad objective relating to the arts of English. These objectives are listed under Statement of Goals, beginning on page *ii* of this guide and continuing on page 337. During each lesson, you should be observing individual children in terms of these objectives. As mentioned earlier, such observation is one of the most effective means for assessing the performance of children. (See Guidelines for Evaluation in the *Introduction: The Arts and Skills of English*.)

If the evaluation component which accompanies this book is available, then you may wish to select the material appropriate for use at this time. You should also become familiar with the additional performance objectives which apply to Chapters 6–9.

Purposes (1) To introduce the diary as another literary form; (2) To demonstrate the historical permanence of literary forms; (3) To illustrate how a diary is an example of private writing which records a person's feelings and thoughts.

[Children of nine or ten are just beginning to develop a sense of history. As they do, they should see that literature is an important part of history, not only because it helps us understand the past but also because—in its permanence—it provides a link between the past and the present.]

E. Schongut

Two Diaries

You know there are two different kinds of writing: public and private. When you keep a **diary,** the things you write are almost always very private.

You probably know that a diary is a special book you write in every day (or almost every day). You write about the things you've done. You tell the way you feel and perhaps even the special things you dream.

Preparation You can ask the children if they have done anything special lately that they would like to remember for a long time, maybe "forever." Then you can ask each child to jot down one thing that made him or her happy, angry, sad, or whatever on the previous day.

After several children have shared their experiences, you can ask the class if they think they will remember these things next year, in ten years, in fifty years. Then suggest that, today, they'll read about what some people do when they want to remember the special things they've done or the feelings they've had.

Presentation Have the children turn to page 75 and read the first two paragraphs of the introduction. Then ask them to suggest some other things people can put into diaries. In reading the rest of the introduction (on page 76), lead the class to discover "the most important thing any writer can learn." A volunteer might give some reasons why honesty is important for any writer.

Have the class read the entries from the first diary silently. Ask them to pick out a few errors that Mary Scarborough Paxson made in writing the diary. Have a volunteer explain why such errors aren't particularly important in a diary. Try to elicit again that a diary is private writing, and so the author doesn't need to worry about someone else not understanding it.

Most people who keep diaries don't make them public. But sometimes a person will let others read his (or her) diary. There may be words misspelled, and the punctuation may not be right. But in a diary, that's not so important. It's much more important to be honest and say exactly what you want to.

Here are parts of two diaries. Both of them were written by young girls.

The first diary was written by a girl who wanted to "make books" when she grew up—but she never did write them. That's too bad, because her diary shows that she knew how to write honestly. She said exactly what she felt. And that's the most important thing any writer can learn.

January 15, 1880. i got laughed at in school today and i dident like it, the teacher asked me what is the smallest fur berring annimal and i said a catterpiller and i ought to say a mouse and i dont care a catterpiller is littler than a mouse and it has fur on it.

January 16. mama says I mustent forget to make cappital eyes when I mean me.

February 7. Maggie and I went to the liberry and we got little women to read, we love the books that Louisa Alcott makes. when I am grone up I am going to make books like Louisa Alcott does.

February 21. I am eight years old today. mama gave me a book and that is the most I got, Maggie gave me a bottle of colone and papa gave me a little pocket book with 25 cents in it, that is the most money I ever had all at once before.

March 21. I let a little mouse out of a trap today, nobody saw me do it.

June 18. Maggie and I went fishing today and we got our feet soking wet, we dident catch any fish only one bull frog and we dident know what to do with it. so we cut the line, and it was an awful wicked thing to do to let it go with the fish hook fast in its stummick. we were afraid to take it off of the hook. Maggie said it was my bull frog because I caught it and I said it was her bull frog because she told me to dangel the worm in front of it.

October 7. It is Maggie's birthday and she is ten years old and she is fat and I am lean.

December 25. It is Christmas and its another holliday that dident come on a school day. They dont any hollidays ever come any more only on Saturdays and Sundays and they are hollidays anyway.

February 1, 1881. I like all my lessons but mental arithmetic. I like my dolls only I havent any real nice ones any more. I have only five and there is something the matter with all of them. I want a new one terribly bad but Mama says I must be patient, thats what you have to wait for til you Mothers and your Fathers get ready.

MARY SCARBOROUGH PAXSON

In this diary, Mary tells how she feels about the things she did at school. She tells about the books that she got from the library. What kind of books did she like? She also tells about going fishing and about birthdays and holidays. How does she feel about holidays? How does she feel about her dolls?

Think about some things that you might like to tell about. Has anything good—or bad—happened to you at school recently? What kinds of library books do you like? How do you feel about holidays?

Next, discuss some of the specific entries in this diary and ask if the children have ever had similar experiences or feelings. Have them compare Mary's feelings about books, birthdays, holidays, lessons, and so on with their own feelings about these things. Encourage each child to assert his own sense of values as he states his feelings. (But be sure the discussion atmosphere is such that the children feel no fear of ridicule.) The discussion at the bottom of page 77 provides a guide to the kinds of questions you can ask.

At this point, you might want to mention to the children that in the next composition lesson they'll learn how to keep a diary. Then they'll have a chance to write down some of their own thoughts and feelings.

You might wish to save the second selection—the diary by Susan Robben—for another day. Again, you can begin by having the children note some of the errors, and you can use these to reinforce the distinction between public and private writing. On page 79, the first two paragraphs provide a guide to the kinds of questions you can ask about the diary entries and also about the children's own feelings.

You can help the children understand that you respect their privacy by <u>not</u> having them discuss the final paragraph on page 79.

Follow-up   The composition lesson which begins on page 80 is a natural follow-up to this lesson.

Some children might also enjoy other literary selections composed by young people. (See Additional Resources.)

Here's the second diary. It was written almost a hundred years later. This girl was also honest when she wrote about her feelings.

February 24, 1963. Today my daddy, two sisters and I went to Bethpage park. It was snowing. It was a beautiful day. We walked four miles. The snow sounded like rain.

February 27. I marked the papers for the teacher at school. It is realy very fun.

February 28. Today I went to a restaurant. I had a boy friend there. His name was Jim. He gave me ice cream. He gave me flowers. He was a very nice man. He was the sheff. I think he cooks.

March 6. Last night my daddy brought me home a prisom. I brought my prisom to school.

March 9. Today I was very sick. I think I have the mumps.

March 10. Today I was sick too. But I felt fine. I felt like I was not sick. But I think I was sick. But I realy felt good. I felt like running and jumping all over.

May 1. I picked flowers for a May basket for my mother. And do you know what waked her up? The fresh flowers I picked!

May 11. Today my father moded the law. I raked it. I like to moe the lawn. I have lots of fun every day.

May 13. Today is catacisom. We had a examination test. I am positif I got 100.

May 14. Today we brought Figaro our cat to the animal hospital.

May 15. Today we got Figaro our cat back. And I think he

does not want to be home. He cannot go outside or eless he might get into another fight.

June 8. Today Robert Corbet knocked my tooth out by bumping into my mouth. My father said I might get about 50 cents for that, or 25 cents. I will tell you on the next page how much I get.

June 9. I got 35 cents.

June 10. At music we had to sing by ourselves. I sang a song that its name was Where Does It Come From? I will sing it to you.

Where does it come from?
Where does it come from?
I tell it to you now.

Sponges come from the botom of the sea.
Bananas they grow on the tall banana tree.
Gather cocoa beans and what you've got?
Pleanty choco-lot
For putting in the pot.

SUSAN ROBBEN

In this diary, Susan tells a lot about her friends and her family. She also tells a lot about herself. What are some of the things she likes to do?

One of the things Susan writes about is a trip to the park. Have you ever taken a trip to the park or to the zoo or to somewhere else? Do you remember some of the things you saw there? Do you remember *all* of the things? A diary would help you remember.

What did you do yesterday that would be good to tell about in a diary? What you write in a diary doesn't have to be very important. It can be anything at all.

Additional Resources

Books Barnstone, Aliki, *The Real Tin Flower: Poems About the World at Nine,* Macmillan. Berger, Josef and Dorothy, *Small Voices,* Eriksson. Larrick, Nancy, compiler, *Green Is Like a Meadow of Grass: Children's Pleasure with Poetry,* Garrard. Lewis, Richard, compiler, *Journeys: Prose by Children of the English-speaking World,* Simon and Schuster. Lewis, Richard, compiler, *Miracles: Poems by Children of the English-speaking World,* Simon and Schuster.

Recordings *Miracles: Poems Written by Children,* Collected by Richard Lewis, 1–12″ LP, 2–track tape, cassette.

Purpose To provide an opportunity for diary writing.

Preparation Remind the children of the excerpts that they read from the diaries of Mary Paxson and Susan Robben. Then ask them to recall some of the things they did in school last year. A free discussion will remind some children of things they had forgotten. Encourage them to express their opinions about these things.

Presentation Read the first two paragraphs with the class. The questions in the second paragraph may remind the children of still other things they did last year. Then have the children read the rest of the page by themselves. In discussing the kinds of questions that they can ask themselves, help the children see that the key to keeping a diary is to "think about the day in little bits." Encourage them to do this as they complete the activity (■).

The suggestion to write in a diary "before you go to bed" is admittedly ideal, and one worth striving for. Some children might achieve it, especially if they have cooperative parents and if they genuinely want to keep a diary. A more realistic plan would be for you to allow for "diary-writing time," perhaps the last few minutes of each day. Remember that it's important to respect the privacy of each child's diary, unless the child indicates otherwise.

Follow-up Some children might want to make special booklets, which they can use just for writing diary entries.

Keeping a Diary

In a diary, you can write anything at all. You can tell what you <u>do</u> and what you <u>think</u> and what you <u>like</u>.

Do you remember what it was like when you were in third grade? Do you remember what you did every day? What did you do in school? Were you sick at all? Did you miss school? Do you remember what you did on your birthday? Did you get any new toys? What were some of your favorites?

If you had kept a diary, it would help you remember all these things. One good way to keep a diary is to think about the day in little bits.

Tonight, just before you go to bed, write the answers to these questions.

> What time did I get up today?
> Was it a special day (like someone's birthday)?
> What did I do after breakfast?
> What friends did I see?
> What happened in school?
> What did I do after school?
> What games did I play?
> What did I do after dinner?

And don't forget that in a diary you can also tell about your thoughts and feelings. Try to answer these questions before you go to bed.

> What did I think about today?
> What was the <u>best</u> thing about today?
> What was the <u>worst</u> thing about today?

■ Just for practice write a composition that answers all of these questions for yesterday. If you can't remember what you really did, then you can use your imagination.

One Kind of Verb Phrase

Part I

So far, all the sentences we've been using begin with nominals. There are also nominals that don't come first.

Here's a sentence picture like the ones you've seen.

The boy is holding a nominal. What's the girl holding? Suppose she made the verb phrase into two parts, like this.

In one hand, she's holding the word *broke*. And in the other hand, she's holding a nominal!

- Some verb phrases—but not all—have nominals in them.

In a verb phrase like *broke the chalk,* the first part—*broke* —is a verb. The second part—*the chalk*—is a nominal. This kind of verb phrase has two parts: a verb and a nominal.

Daybook: One Kind of Verb Phrase, page 32

Purposes (1) To extend the children's understanding of the nature of verb phrases; (2) To help them recognize that some verb phrases contain nominals; (3) To introduce the term *verb*.

[Again, children have had considerable experience in using many thousands of verb phrases. Some of this experience has been brought to the level of awareness in earlier lessons, particularly those in which the children used verb phrases from the lexicon of the sentence model to create sentences. This lesson develops additional awareness of the structure of verb phrases and also provides additional practice in talking about different kinds of nominals. A subsequent lesson (pages 91–93) will help children become aware that they also use verb phrases which contain adjectives.]

Preparation Examine the sentence model from an earlier lesson (or any large reproduction you may have made of the model). Then have the children construct three or four sentences using the nominals and verb phrases below:

Nominals	Verb Phrases
the baker	peeled the banana
the cat	cut the meat
a gorilla	picked a flower
my dog	climbed a tree

(If you add verb phrases of your own, be sure that they consist of a verb followed by a regular nominal.)

Presentation Read page 81 with the children, and discuss the two pictures and the rule (●). You may need to reassure some children that it's natural to have nominals in some verb phrases: "It's one of the rules of language that all people have in their heads."

Then direct the children's attention to the verbs listed at the top of page 82, and ask for volunteers to give examples of sentences that use these verbs. Also, ask the children to suggest examples of other verbs, and have them illustrate the use of each one in a sentence. (The proper use of words in sentences is the best evidence that children understand individual words as well as kinds of words.) As usual, remind the children that this lesson merely helps them talk about things they already know in their heads.

The first activity (■) can be done as a class exercise. In Sentences 1, 2, and 4, ask for volunteers to identify the determiner and the noun. The second activity (■) can be done individually or in groups. In Sentence 1, the children need to add only a noun to complete the nominal. In Sentences 2, 3, and 4, you can have them add regular nominals, then names. (Don't ask for pronouns until they have read Part II of this lesson.)

Part II: Have the class read the paragraph at the bottom of page 82 and also the one at the top of page 83. After they've read the five pronouns on page 83, make two columns on the chalkboard, as follows:

she	them
I	us
he	her
we	me
they	him

In your head, you know lots of verbs. Here are some of them. What other verbs can you think of?

build	drive	chase	hit	visit
write	swallow	push	sit	play

■ What nominals come <u>after</u> the verbs in these sentences?

1. The dog ate the pizza.
2. Sam lost a pencil.
3. The girl visited Mary.
4. The truck pushed the car.

■ Here are some more sentences that are not complete. The nominal that comes after the verb has been left out. Try to think of a good nominal for each sentence.

1. The teacher found a _____.
2. I see _____.
3. The chicken tickled _____.
4. The boy hit _____.

Part II

You've learned about nominals that come at the beginning of a sentence. You've learned about nominals that come after the verb. You've also learned about three different <u>kinds</u> of nominals: *regular nominals, names,* and *pronouns.*

Regular Nominal:	<u>The boy</u> found <u>the dog</u>.
Name:	<u>John</u> found <u>King</u>.
Pronoun:	<u>He</u> found <u>him</u>.

We can have a regular nominal, a name, or a pronoun at the beginning of a sentence. We can also have a regular nominal, or a name, or a pronoun after some verbs.

Answers

The answers to the first activity are as follows:
1. the pizza
2. a pencil
3. Mary
4. the car

We can use the pronoun *you* at the beginning of a sentence. We can also use it after a verb. *It* is another pronoun we can use at the beginning of a sentence or after a verb. But most of the pronouns we use after verbs are different from those we use at the beginning. Here are some pronouns that come after verbs.

me   him   her   us   them

■ Now use pronouns after the verbs to complete these sentences.

1. John sees _____.
2. The frog tickled _____.
3. The girl hit _____.

■ Here's something else for you to do. Add a regular nominal, a name, or a pronoun after the verb to complete each of these sentences.

	Nominal	Verb Phrase	
1.	The doctor	saw	(regular nominal)
2.	Paul	found	(name)
3.	My canary	swallowed	(regular nominal)
4.	Mrs. Davis	will call	(pronoun)
5.	The milkman	visited	(name)
6.	The carpenter	built	(regular nominal)
7.	Arnold	likes	(pronoun)
8.	The dog	chased	(pronoun)
9.	My uncle	photographed	(name)
10.	The policeman	will ride	(regular nominal)

Explain that the pronouns in the left column are the ones we use <u>before</u> a verb, and those in the right column are the ones we use <u>after</u> a verb. Then have the children match the pronouns on the left with those on the right. You might do the first one (*she-her*) for them by way of illustration. If you wish, you can explain that the pronouns *you* and *it* don't change after a verb.

The first activity (■) on page 83 can be done as a class exercise. The second activity (■) can be done individually or in small groups. When the children have completed the exercises, you can change the kinds of nominals called for after the verbs. Any of the three kinds already discussed will fit after any of the verbs in the exercise.

Follow-up This would be an appropriate time to use the lesson on Pronoun Forms on pages 335–336.

Here are some additional sentences you can ditto to provide practice identifying the nominals that come after verbs. For each sentence, have the children locate the verb phrase. Then they can underline the nominal in the verb phrase and tell whether it's a regular nominal, a name, or a pronoun.

1. The class laughed at Mary.
2. Figaro ate a goldfish.
3. Maggie likes that book.
4. Maggie and Mary caught a frog.
5. The frog swallowed the hook.
6. Mary didn't keep it.
7. Mary has five dolls.
8. Susan fed Figaro.
9. Her father mowed the lawn.
10. Robert knocked out my tooth.

Purposes (1) To help children recognize some basic characteristics of speaking; (2) To bring experience with speaking to the levels of awareness and verbalization.

Preparation An excellent way to prepare for this lesson consists in speaking to the class in several different ways before they open their books. You might say one sentence in your normal voice; the next in a very high voice; the next in a whisper; and so on. Here's a sequence of sentences that you might use:

1. (*Normal*) Today we're going to learn some things about the way people talk.
2. (*High*) Sometimes people talk one way, and sometimes they talk another way.
3. (*Whisper*) Sometimes they talk very softly.
4. (*Semi-shout*) And sometimes they talk very loudly.
5. (*Deep*) There are special words we can use if we want to talk about talking.
6. (*Normal*) Now open your books and we'll read page 84.

Presentation After you've "broken the ice" for the class, most children will be eager to join in the spirit of the lesson. Page 84 provides a variety of opportunities for humorous, extemporaneous dramatization. Encourage as many children as possible to respond to the questions in the four paragraphs of the text. If you wish, you can whisper "roles" for the children and have the rest of the class try to guess which animal is being imitated.

After the imitations, call the attention of the class to the two special words: *volume* and *pitch*. (You can illustrate the meanings of these words by the way you read the paragraph.)

You can have the class as a whole say the sentence *I like shredded wheat,* varying volume and pitch as suggested

What Did You Say?

Can you make a sound like a happy cat? Try it. Now make a sound like an angry cat. What's the difference between these two sounds?

Now make a sound like a happy cow. How does a happy cow sound different from a happy cat?

Can you make a sound like a little girl giggling? Can you make a sound like a boy whispering a secret? How are these sounds different?

Now try to make a sound like an old lady laughing. Then make a sound like a football player laughing. What makes these sounds different?

There are two special words that can help you talk about sounds: **volume** and **pitch.** You can use *volume* for talking about a soft voice or a loud voice or anything in between. And you can use *pitch* for talking about a high voice or a low voice or anything in between.

Now say this sentence. Use your regular volume and your regular pitch.

I like shredded wheat.

Try saying the sentence in these different ways.
1. Use your regular volume and a high pitch.
2. Use a soft volume and your regular pitch.
3. Use a loud volume and a low pitch.

Here's another word for you to say: *spinach*. Try it these different ways.

1. Say it so you ask a question.
2. Say it as if you really liked spinach.
3. Say it as if you hated spinach.
4. Say it and laugh at the same time.
5. Say it and cry at the same time.

You can change the *volume* of your voice and make it loud or soft whenever you want to. You can change the *pitch* of your voice and make it high or low. You can sound sad or happy or tired or silly. There are lots of different ways to talk.

Most of the time you don't stop to think about how you're going to talk. But there are lots of different ways you can talk. Sometimes, when you're going to say something special, you can stop before you talk. Then you can decide how to talk.

Here are some sentences that you can use to practice saying things in different ways. Say each sentence three times. First, say it as if you were happy. Then say it as if you were sad. And finally say it as if you were tired.

1. My cat is in the tree.
2. I wish we had some ice cream.
3. The frog almost caught the fly.
4. We play the same game every day.

Here's something for you to try. In the beginning of this chapter, you read two diaries. Choose a part of one of the diaries that you think is special. Then decide how it should sound: happy, sad, tired, silly, or whatever. Then try reading it aloud to your friends. What other stories would you like to read this way?

in the text. A tape recorder is particularly useful in doing this activity. In performing alone, timid children may wish to turn their backs to the audience or move to an area away from the classroom. Recording the voices of such children can help them overcome their timidity.

The tape recorder can also be used with the "spinach" exercises on page 85. Try to be sure that the children read and understand the central paragraph on page 85, which contains a statement of the purpose of the lesson. You might conduct a class discussion of the various ways to read this paragraph aloud. (For example, you can stress the underlined words in various ways.)

The paragraph above the four sentences will give the children experience in following instructions. Call on volunteers to explain, first, how they will read a given sentence, and then have them read it in the appropriate manner.

You can then divide the class into groups to read and discuss the final paragraph.

Follow-up The folktale "Talk" is another selection that the children can reread now, experimenting with changes in volume and pitch as they read the dialogue. Volunteers can select the "parts" they wish to read, for example, the yam, the farmer, and so on. If the children have difficulty deciding which variation of volume and pitch to use for each character, you can suggest the following:

1. *Regular volume and regular pitch:* the farmer, the fisherman, the weaver, and the man bathing.
2. *Loud volume and high pitch:* the yam, the dog, the palm tree, the palm branch, the stone, the fish trap, the bundle of cloth, the river, and the stool.
3. *Loud volume and low pitch:* the chief.

Purpose To provide additional experience with lyric poetry and metaphor.

Preparation You might begin by displaying various pictures of birds. Encourage the children to observe the birds' eyes and to suggest things that these eyes look like. Then ask them to describe how a bird's feathers might feel. Also have volunteers describe the movements of a bird, and ask what moving objects the flying of a bird can be compared with. Finally, ask the children what a wild bird would be likely to do if they offered him food.

Presentation Have the children listen as you read the introduction to them. On the chalkboard, you can write Emily Dickinson's name, as well as the italicized words in the second paragraph.

Next, explain to the children that, as they listen to poetry, they should try to get pictures in their heads. (In reading the poem, let your own dramatic talents have full sway; it's the best way to encourage children to read dramatically themselves.)

After reading the poem once, state that you'll read the poem again, and suggest that the children listen for such things as the poet's description of the bird's eyes as well as for the kind of cloth that describes the bird's head. Have them listen also for words that describe the bird's movements. During the second reading, you may want to have the children follow along in their books. (At some point, you may also want to discuss the spectacular —and unusual—illustration which accompanies this poem.)

After the second reading, have the children read the first paragraph of the discussion on page 88. Let them individually find the lines which tell what the bird does in the first two stanzas.

86

Daybook: Some Small Things About Beetles, page 34

A Poem

This poem was written about a hundred years ago. The poet, whose name is Emily Dickinson, was a shy person who spent a lot of time in the garden around her house. Many of her poems are about things she found in her garden.

In this poem, Emily Dickinson watches a bird hopping down a sidewalk. The bird eats an *angleworm*. Then he takes a drink of *dew*. The poet tries to give the bird a crumb of bread. She was *cautious* but the bird gets frightened and flies away. The bird flying away reminds the poet of rowing in the ocean. It also makes her think about the way butterflies "swim" in the air.

A Bird Came Down the Walk

A Bird came down the Walk—
He did not know I saw—
He bit an Angleworm in halves
And ate the fellow, raw,

And then he drank a Dew
From a convenient Grass—
And then hopped sidewise to the Wall
To let a Beetle pass—

Then have the class read the second paragraph of the discussion, and ask them to find the lines about the bird's eyes and head. The last two questions in this paragraph must be dealt with carefully. Try to help the children understand the lines "rowed him softer home than oars divide the ocean"; "the ocean too silver for a seam"; "banks of noon"; and "plashless as they swim." (This will require careful breaking apart of the lines of the poem on your part.) You can compare "rowing" and "motor propulsion" by saying: "A bird's wings are like oars. The wings move softly through the 'ocean' of air." Ask the children what they think *plashless* means. "Is it like any other word you know?" (*Plash* occurs in Webster's 1848 dictionary as a variant of *splash*.)

Since this poem is one that most children like to return to, you might save the activity (■), as well as the paragraph which precedes it, for another day. This final paragraph is a good reference to use before any lesson which requires children to write poetry of their own. You should try to make the children aware of how poets sometimes use words which "almost rhyme" in their writing. (Technically, these are called *slant rhymes*.)

You might also want to discuss Emily Dickinson's unconventional use of capital letters at the beginning of some words in this poem. Remind the children that people have agreed to use capital letters for such things as the first word in a sentence, proper nouns and the pronoun "I," and so on, but that we don't usually use capital letters at the beginning of words such as *walk* or *angleworm* when they occur in the middle of a sentence. Ask the children to try to guess why these words have been capitalized. (There is no "right-or-wrong" answer to this question.)

Follow-up After discussing the metaphors in the poem, you can suggest that the children write their own metaphors to describe a bird (or some other animal). If some children choose the same animal, then you may want to combine some of their metaphors to make a "group poem."

You might also want to read to the children some of the poems listed under Additional Resources.

Additional Resources

Books Aiken, Conrad, *Cats and Bats and Things with Wings,* Atheneum. This book is of particular interest in that it is illustrated by Milton Glaser. Arbuthnot, May Hill, editor, *Time for Poetry,* Scott, Foresman. Included in this collection of children's literature are "Little Things" by James Stephens and "Night of the Wind" by Frances Frost. Frost, Frances, *Pool in the Meadow,* Houghton Mifflin, for "White Season." Frost, Robert, *Collected Poems of Robert Frost,* Holt, Rinehart and Winston, for "The Runaway." Hampson, Alfred L., editor, *Poems for Youth,* Little, Brown, for other poems by Emily Dickinson. Rossetti, Christina, *Collected Poems,* Macmillan, for "The City Mouse and the Garden Mouse" and "Caterpillar."

Recordings *A Gathering of Great Poetry for Children, Volume 4,* 1–12″ LP, cassette, Caedmon. Julie Harris, Cyril Ritchard, and David Wayne read a number of outstanding poems, including Emily Dickinson's "A Bird Came Down the Walk" and "I'll Tell You How the Sun Rose." *Poetry Programs for Children,* 3–12″ LPs, cassettes, Miller-Brody. Volume 3 of this series also contains some of Emily Dickinson's poems.

He glanced with rapid eyes
That hurried all around—
They looked like frightened Beads, I thought—
He stirred his Velvet Head

Like one in danger, Cautious,
I offered him a Crumb,
And he unrolled his feathers
And rowed him softer home—

Than Oars divide the Ocean,
Too silver for a seam—
Or Butterflies, off Banks of Noon,
Leap, plashless as they swim

EMILY DICKINSON

There are some good metaphors in the last three stanzas of this poem. But in the first two stanzas of the poem, the poet doesn't use any metaphors. The poem starts out telling exactly what the bird <u>does</u>. He comes down the walk. He eats a worm. He drinks some water. And then he hops to the wall.

But then the poet uses several metaphors to describe the bird. How does she describe the bird's eyes? How does she talk about his head? Does the poet actually tell you that the bird flies away? Instead, what does she compare the bird's flight to?

Emily Dickinson liked words that rhyme. She also liked words that almost—but not quite—rhyme. In the first stanza, what word rhymes with *saw*? In the fourth stanza what word almost rhymes with *crumb*?

■ Now find two other words in the poem that rhyme. Then find two other words that <u>almost</u> rhyme.

A Play

Here are some pictures that tell a story. You've probably heard the story before. Do you know what the story is? Do you think it's a true story?

One way to tell a story is to show it in pictures. Another way is to write the story down as a composition. A third way is to make the story into a play.

Purposes (1) To introduce the play as a form of composition; (2) To provide an opportunity for making a story into a play.

[Many plays—perhaps most—were originally written as stories and then adapted for dramatic presentation. Shakespeare himself usually adapted his plays from stories, histories, and poems. By choosing a story they already know, the children can concentrate on the dramatic aspects of the composition process.]

Preparation The lesson on volume and pitch is a natural preparation for this lesson. You can begin by reviewing some of the principles which the children learned in that lesson, and ask them how many different ways they could read the following sentences:

1. The cloud is high and far away.
2. The snowman is cold and quiet.
3. The fire is blazing hot.

Then ask if they can also "act out" any of these sentences. Finally, state that today they'll have a chance to do some other kinds of acting.

Presentation Have the children read the opening paragraph on page 89 and then examine the pictures. Ask for volunteers to explain what happens in each picture. Then have them read the paragraph at the bottom of page 89.

Next, tell the children to read page 90 in order to learn how to make a play from the pictures. This will provide additional practice in following instructions. (You'll notice that the children are not asked to write down the words of the play. In a later lesson, the children will learn the accepted form for writing plays. Plays which are presented in this fashion

—where the actors make up the lines as they go along, from a story they already know—were quite popular several hundred years ago.)

Even though this play is "unwritten," you should encourage the cast to rehearse before presenting it to an audience. It's also possible to present the play more than once, with a different cast each time. Probably most children will take the play —and the subject—seriously, but some children may be sophisticated enough to present a humorous production. Both ways have value since they illustrate the variety of literature.

Finally, you should try to tape at least one version of the play which the children present. (This tape can be used as part of the preparation for the next composition lesson.)

Follow-up This lesson suggests just one of the many ways that you can provide children with the opportunity to participate in creative dramatics. You should try to provide other such experiences at various times throughout the year. You may want to experiment with playlets, finger plays, shadow plays, puppets, choral speaking, TV and radio shows, and even pantomime. These can be very informal group activities and for the most part they probably should be. Or they can be more elaborate presentations to which an audience, perhaps another class is invited. You can create an environment that is physically stimulating by making available all sorts of materials and equipment (discarded clothing, old shoes, cardboard boxes, art supplies, scraps of cloth, yarn, and ribbon, and so on). And you should try to be alert to any experience or situation which might lead into a dramatic activity.

The people in a play are called the **cast.** How many people are there in this story? Who are they? In a play, we say that the cast "acts out" the story. Part of the acting out is talking. Another part is showing what people do. In the first picture, what would George Washington <u>say</u>? Show what he'd <u>do</u> when he chops down the tree. Choose someone in the class to act out the part of George Washington.

What would George's father do when he sees that the tree has been cut down? How would his eyes look? Would his mouth be closed tight? Suppose you're an actor. Try to make a face like George's father. How would George's father sound when he called George?

Now choose two members of the class to act out the play. What would George and his father <u>say</u> for each of the pictures in the story? What would they do?

Now suppose that the artist drew one picture, like this one.

What do you think George's father is saying? What do you think his mother is saying? What might his mother <u>do</u>? Have three members of the class act out the whole story.

90

Another Kind of Verb Phrase

You already know about three kinds of nominals. One kind—a regular nominal—has a determiner and a noun in it. The other two kinds are names and pronouns.

But so far you've only learned about one kind of verb phrase. It has a verb and a nominal.

The elephant climbed a tree.
Sarah ate the hamburger.

In each sentence, what is the verb? What is the nominal that comes after the verb?

Here are two more sentences. They have a different kind of verb phrase.

The elephant is big.
Sarah was hungry.

What is the verb phrase in each of these sentences? Words like *is* and *was* are called **"be" words.**

Here are the "be" words that we use most often.

am   is   are   was   were

We can use "be" words after regular nominals. We can also use them after names and with pronouns.

the boy is   John was   I am

After "be" words, we can use words that help describe what *the boy is* or *John was* or *I am*. These describing words have a special name. They're called **adjectives.** In these sentences, adjectives are used to describe someone and something.

My friend is silly.   The hill is smooth.
My friend is short.   The hill is grassy.

Daybook: Practice with Verb Phrases, page 36

Purposes (1) To extend a child's understanding of verb phrases; (2) To illustrate one use of "be" words; (3) To demonstrate that children already know many adjectives in their heads.

[Here again the important point is that children have considerable experience in using different kinds of words—in this case, adjectives. This lesson brings their experience to the levels of awareness and verbalization. Note that this lesson deals only with those cases in which adjectives follow "be" words. The cases in which adjectives precede nouns are discussed in later lessons.

Note also that the text does not treat "be" words as verbs. It is pedagogically simpler, as well as scientifically more accurate, to separate these two kinds of words. Children know—in their heads—that "be words" and verbs function in different ways, and the separation reflects this fact.]

Preparation Remind the children that they've already learned about one kind of verb phrase: the kind which has a verb and a nominal. Depending on the needs of the children, you may want to present the following examples of sentences containing this kind of verb phrase:

1. The man ate a pickle.
2. The dog found my lunch.
3. My brother found a dollar.
4. The cat drank the cream.
5. The teacher wrote a book.

First have the children locate the subject nominal and the verb phrase in each sentence. Then have them identify the verb and the nominal in each verb phrase. In doing this, you might want to suggest that the children use a simplified illustration (like the second one on page 81).

Presentation Have the children read page 91 through the second set of example sentences. On the chalkboard, you can then make two columns—one headed *Verbs* and the other *"Be" Words*. Under *Verbs* write the following words: *build, drive, push, visit, play,* and *hit.* Under *"Be" Words,* write *is, are, was,* and *were.*

Then redirect the children's attention to the two sets of example sentences on the first half of page 91. Elicit that *climbed* and *ate* are verbs, and that each is followed by a regular nominal. Then point out that the words after *is* and *was* are not nominals. Suggest that the children continue reading page 91 to discover the special word to use when they want to talk about words like *big* and *hungry.*

When the children have finished reading, write the heading *Adjectives* on the chalkboard, next to *"Be" Words.* Help the children pronounce the term *adjective,* and then write *big, hungry, silly, short, smooth,* and *grassy* under this heading.

Have the class read the first half of page 92 and examine the first illustration. (As usual, emphasize that they know many adjectives in their heads.)

Then have the class read the rest of page 92 and work the activity (■) at the bottom of the page together. First, have the children choose three or four adjectives from the list at the top of the page; then have them add others "from their heads." You can give the class a useful hint—one which was often used by the American structuralists: Suggest that they insert the word *very* before the blank. Then any word which can follow *very* must be an adjective.

In your head, you know lots of nouns and verbs. You also know many adjectives. Here are some adjectives that you may know.

hungry	big	smooth	silly
long	pretty	short	wiggly
messy	soft	happy	brave

Here's another sentence picture. What is the boy holding? What is the girl holding?

Now look at the sentence picture below. The boy is holding a regular nominal: *the man.* After this nominal, we can use a "be" word. To complete the sentence, we can add an adjective. What "be" word is the girl holding? What adjective would you put after the "be" word?

■ Now use the nominal and the "be" word from the sentence picture. Add other adjectives to make new sentences.

Here's a good way to remember what adjectives are and what they do.

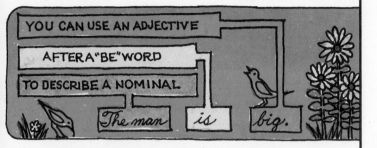

YOU CAN USE AN ADJECTIVE

AFTER A "BE" WORD

TO DESCRIBE A NOMINAL

The man   *is*   *big.*

What does the picture tell you about adjectives? What adjective is shown?

■ Here are some sentences for you to complete. Add an adjective after each "be" word. You can use the adjectives from the list on the top of page 92. Or you can think of some of your own.

1. The teacher was ———.
2. You are ———.
3. My bicycle was ———.
4. Mary will be ———.
5. The snails are ———.
6. A frog is ———.
7. John was ———.
8. They were ———.
9. His kite is ———.
10. I am ———.

■ Here's something else for you to do. Add a "be" word __and__ an adjective to these nominals to make sentences.

1. The turtle
2. Billy
3. She
4. You
5. The elephant
6. Mr. Bailey
7. I
8. They
9. The boy
10. We

Next, have the children examine the illustration on page 93 and ask for a volunteer to explain it.

The entire class can do the first activity (■) on page 93. If any children have difficulty, remind them of the hint about using *very* before the blank space. The second activity (■) on page 93 is suitable for group or written work. Advise the class to use the "be" words that you put on the chalkboard, or else to look back to page 91 where the same words are listed. By way of illustration, you can do the first one for them. (Obviously, the children's answers to all of the activities in this lesson will vary considerably.)

Follow-up You can prepare an exercise similar to the first one on page 93 for those children who you think would profit from the additional practice. You should probably include with the exercise a lexicon of adjectives from which they can choose.

Although synonyms are not formally presented in the text until page 208, this would be a good time to prepare the children for work with synonyms. Write the sentence *The man is very big* on the chalkboard. Then ask the children to suggest another adjective that "means almost the same thing" as *big*. As the children suggest synonyms (*large, huge, tall,* and so on), you can write these words on the chalkboard in place of *big*. Then suggest that the children look again at each of the sentences they made in response to the activities on page 93 and to try to think of "some other adjective that means almost the same thing." Then they can rewrite the sentence, using the synonym.

This would also be a good time to introduce the lesson on Forms of "Be" Words on pages 334–335.

Purposes (1) To review some of the varieties of literary forms; (2) To re-emphasize that diaries and plays are both forms of composition; (3) To review the structure of two kinds of verb phrases.

Presentation It's not always necessary to cover the three sections of any Review with the entire class. For example, those children who did well on the two language lessons in this chapter might omit this part of the Review and focus instead on literature and composition, perhaps working in groups. You could then work with a "language group" without making the children in this group feel that they had fallen behind.

Review

Literature

Almost any kind of writing can be literature. So far this year, you've read several poems, including some silly ones. You've read part of a story about Maurice's room. You've read a folktale from Africa. And in this chapter, you've read parts of two different diaries.

A person's diary can be literature if it's interesting and well written. Try to explain why some people might like the girls' diaries. Would you like to read the diaries of some other people? Whose diary would you like to read?

■ Here's something for you to do. Pretend for a while that you are someone else. Who would you like to be? Would you like to be someone famous? What are some of the things you'd do? How do you think you'd feel? Then use your imagination to write a diary for a day in the life of the person you're pretending to be.

Composition

If you keep a diary of your own, then that's a composition. What kind of things do people put in a diary? What would you put in your diary?

When you make up a play, that's also a composition. You don't have to write it down. You've already made up a play about George Washington. But a play can be about anything at all. It can even have animals instead of people in it.

■ Try to make up a play about something you've read, like "The Lobster Quadrille." Or you can make up a play about something you've written.

Language

In this chapter, you learned about two kinds of verb phrases. One kind has a verb and a nominal. The other kind has a "be" word and an adjective.

■ Here are some verb phrases. Which ones have a verb and a nominal? Which ones have a "be" word and an adjective?

1. saw the elephant
2. was hungry
3. found a penny

4. is sleepy
5. ate the peanut
6. is tall

■ Sometimes people say that an adjective is a word that describes a noun. When you use the describers, you can always put an adjective after Isabella Is. Try to think of some good adjectives to describe a person.

In this chapter, you studied about *pronouns* that come <u>after</u> verbs. You learned that most of these pronouns are different from those that we use at the beginning of a sentence. For more practice with pronouns, turn to page 335.

You also read about "be" words in this chapter. You'll find practice using "be" words on page 334.

Follow-up For those children who need additional practice distinguishing between the two kinds of verb phrases presented thus far, you can use the following:

1. ate a banana
2. was wiggly
3. kicked the ball
4. is wet
5. were hungry
6. rode a bike
7. paints fences
8. is hairy
9. sold the candy
10. are messy

With children who do show need for such practice, it would be advisable to use simplified illustrations like those on pages 81 and 92 of this chapter.

Answers

In the first activity, sentences 1, 3, and 5 have a verb and a nominal. Sentences 2, 4, and 6 have a "be" word and an adjective.

Purposes (1) To introduce the myth as a literary form; (2) To provide an introduction to the structure of myths.

Preparation Remind the children of the lesson (pages 27-28) in which the "describers" were used to tell about a hero. (You might even want to read one or two of the compositions that the children wrote in response to the activity on page 28.) Then lead the children into a discussion of various kinds of heroes—including some of the "super heroes" featured on TV and in the comics.

Next, have the children examine the illustration on pages 96-97 of their texts. Direct their attention to the figure holding the sword and the shield, and identify him as Perseus. Explain that Perseus was a great hero whom the ancient Greeks used to tell stories about. (At this point, you can ask a volunteer to locate Greece on a globe or map.) Then tell the children that a wicked king once tricked Perseus into volunteering to do an almost impossible deed: Perseus was to find the cave where Medusa lived, cut off Medusa's head, and bring it back to the king. Point out Medusa in the illustration, and explain to the children that Medusa had once been a beautiful girl, but, because she was so proud of her beauty, she was changed into a monster. Where she once had golden ringlets for hair, she now had snakes, and anyone who looked at her was instantly turned to stone. Then tell the children that today they'll read about what happened to Perseus after he killed Medusa.

Presentation Write *myth* on the chalkboard, and have a volunteer look this word up in a dictionary. Ask the children if they recall having read any other myths. (Children who used Book Three of this

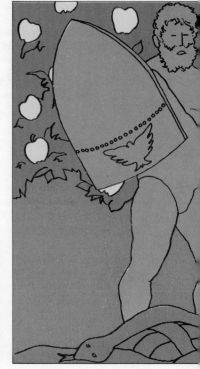

A Myth

A **myth** is an old story. Sometimes it's about nature and how things got to be the way they are. Sometimes a myth is about the olden days in another country and about the heroes who lived then. Here's a famous myth about a Greek hero named Perseus.

Daybook: After Perseus Left, page 38

Perseus and Atlas

Perseus was a great Greek hero who killed Medusa. Medusa had snakes on her head instead of hair, and any man who looked at her would turn into stone. But Perseus tricked her. He used his shield as a mirror, so he didn't have to look the monster in the eye, and he cut off her head with

series will have read myths about the Greek heroes Icarus and Hercules and the African myth "Why the Sun and the Moon Live in the Sky.") Then read the introduction on page 96 with the children.

In presenting the myth, you can divide the class into groups. Many children will be able to read the myth by themselves. (You might appoint one child to act as a "word consultant" should anyone in this group come across an unfamiliar vocabulary word.) Another group of children can work in pairs reading the myth. And still another can use the lesson as a listening experience as you read the myth to them. The children themselves should feel free to join whichever group they prefer.

When the children have finished, bring the groups together so they can all participate in the discussion. In dealing with the first paragraph of the discussion on page 99, direct the children's attention to the fact that there is order in the literature they read as well as in the compositions they write themselves. In answering the question at the end of this paragraph, help the children see why the adventure with Medusa is mentioned at the beginning: "Perseus must use Medusa's head later in the story, and it's better to mention the incident early than to say 'Oh, I forgot to tell you . . .' later on."

You might want to extend the discussion of the concept of order as it applies to this selection. You can say: "First the author tells you who Perseus was and what he did. Next he tells you about Atlas. Who was Atlas? What did he do?" Then help the children outline the order of events as they occur in the story. The questions on the next page can serve as a guide.

1. What did Perseus do when he saw the beautiful garden?
2. Because he was so tired, what did Perseus do when he landed?
3. What was the first thing that Atlas saw when he came into the garden?
4. What did he threaten to do to Perseus?
5. How did Perseus try to defend himself?
6. When he realized that he couldn't hurt Atlas, what did Perseus do?
7. What did Perseus do when Atlas asked him where he was hiding?
8. What happened to Atlas when he looked at the head of Medusa?

After the children have discussed the order of events, you can have them describe the setting of the story. You can also ask what they thought was the most interesting part of the story.

Now return to the second paragraph of the discussion on page 99. Direct attention to the words *hero, villain,* and *action,* and encourage the children to use these words during the discussion which follows. Ask the children to describe some of the hero's characteristics. "Is Perseus strong? Is he brave? How do you know? What else is Perseus?" Then have the children describe some of the characteristics of the villain. "Is Atlas strong? Is he selfish? What else is Atlas?" After the children have answered the questions at the end of this paragraph, encourage them to give other examples of cases where being smart is better than being strong.

The activity (■) can be done individually, in small groups, or as a class. The important element is that the children use their own imaginations to revise stories—both someone else's and their own. (For some people, the word *clever* has the undesirable connotation of "cunning" or even "cheating." Here, of course, *clever* means only "smart and quick.")

his sword. Then he flew away in his magic shoes to the land where Atlas was king, taking the head of Medusa with him.

Atlas was a cruel giant who was so rich that in his garden the apples on the trees were made of gold. Atlas was afraid that someone would steal the apples so he built a high wall around the garden. He was the only person who had a key to the door. Nobody else had ever seen the golden apples or the beautiful garden.

But Perseus, as he was flying, looked down and saw the garden. He flew down and landed. "The garden is beautiful," he said, "and the golden apples are the most beautiful of all. Why is there a wall? Everyone would like to see this beautiful garden." Although Perseus wanted to think of a way to help other people see the garden, he was very tired from his long trip and soon fell asleep.

While he was sleeping, the giant Atlas unlocked the door and came into the garden. The earth trembled as he walked. He was so tall that his shadow turned the day into night. The first thing he saw was Perseus asleep.

"What are you doing in my garden?" roared Atlas. "No one comes into my garden but me. I'm going to kill you."

"I know you are very big," said Perseus. "But I'm not afraid." He picked up his sword and shield and hit the giant.

But Atlas only laughed. "You can't hurt me. I'll step on you and kill you."

Perseus thought quickly. He jumped away from the giant. Then he picked up the head of Medusa and he hid behind a tree.

The giant was very angry. "Where are you?" he shouted.

"Here I am, Atlas," said Perseus, and he held up the head of Medusa. Atlas looked down, right into the eyes of the head. He immediately turned to stone. Since he was so huge, he became an enormous mountain. Birds made nests in his hair, and sheep and goats climbed along his shoulders.

Perseus opened the door to the garden, and everyone came in to admire the golden apples. When people saw how beautiful the garden was, they wanted to thank Perseus. But he put on his magic shoes and flew away to his next adventure. ■

One way to think about a story, is to ask yourself some questions about the *order* of things. First, you learn who Perseus is and about something he did. Why does the author tell you this at the beginning of the story?

First, you read about the **hero** of the story. Then, in the second paragraph, you learn about the **villain.** The villain in this story is the giant, Atlas. The **action** comes when Perseus and Atlas meet. How does Perseus trick Atlas? Who is stronger, Perseus or Atlas? Who is smarter? Is it better to be strong or to be smart? Why?

■ Perseus was very clever. How clever are you? Try to think of another way that Perseus could have tricked Atlas. Then write another ending for the myth.

Writing a Play

Do you remember the play about George Washington and the cherry tree? There were three people in the cast: George, his father, and his mother. Do you remember the exact words that George said in the play? Do you remember the exact words that his father and mother said?

One way to remember the exact words of a play is to write them down. People have written plays down for hundreds of years. Do you know how they do it?

Follow-up After reading the myth about Perseus, the children might enjoy listening to another one of this hero's adventures as told on the recording *Heroes, Gods and Monsters of the Greek Myths, Vol. III.* (See Additional Resources.)

You can also help the children find other myths to read and, perhaps, to report on. (This will also provide an opportunity to introduce the children to the use of reference materials in the library.)

Additional Resources

Books For other myths which you and the children can read together, you might consult these excellent sources: d'Aulaire, Ingri and Edgar Parin, *Book of Greek Myths,* Doubleday. The illustrations in this book are outstanding and the stories are told with a modern flavor. Benson, Sally, *Stories of the Gods and Heroes,* Dial. This very "readable" book is based on Bulfinch's *Age of Fable.* Elgin, Kathleen, *The First Book of Mythology,* Watts. This book, written in a modern style, offers children a good introduction to the world of mythology. McLean, Mollie and Ann Wiseman, *Adventures of the Greek Heroes,* Houghton Mifflin. Again, the language here is simple and the illustrations superb. Price, Margaret Evans, *Myths and Enchantment Tales,* Rand McNally. This is an excellent book for the children to read on their own. Sewell, Helen, *A Book of Myths,* Doubleday. Although this book is too difficult for many children to read, it does offer a fine background of mythology. Helen Sewell's *Adventures with the Gods* would probably be more appropriate for the children's personal reading.

Purposes (1) To provide children with the opportunity to write a play; (2) To introduce some of the mechanics of play-writing.

[As suggested earlier in this guide, you should try to provide the children with as many dramatic experiences as possible at various times throughout the year. Most of these experiences should, of course, be impromptu, thereby encouraging spontaneity on the part of the children. However, there may be a time when you will want the children to write down a play, and this lesson can be taught on such an occasion.]

Preparation If you taped the play about George Washington as suggested during the previous composition lesson, then you can play back the tape now. After the children have listened to the tape, suggest that there are other ways that we can "save" a play, and that today's lesson will show one way to do it.

If you were not able to tape the play about George Washington, then you can use a film or TV tape of a child's program to introduce the lesson. You can initiate a discussion of what goes into the production of such a show by asking:

1. Where does the story come from?
2. Who does the acting?
3. Who tells the actors what to do?

Presentation Have the children open to page 99 and call for volunteers to read the first two paragraphs of the lesson. Review the meaning of the term *cast,* and then write the following words on the chalkboard: *title, scene,* and *lines.* Then direct the children to read the first two paragraphs on the top of page 100 to find out what these words mean. To help the children understand the function of the colon, refer to page 309 of the Skills Section.

First, they give the play a **title.** Then they describe the *cast* of the play. Every play also has a **scene.** The scene tells us when and where the play happens.

Every play also has **lines.** The lines are the words that the people in the play say. The person writing the play make up these lines. He uses a **colon** [:] between the speaker's name and what he says. The writer usually tells what the actions of the people in the play are, too.

Here's the way that children in one class wrote the beginning of the play about George Washington.

George Washington and the Cherry Tree
Cast: George Washington (aged nine), his father, his mother
Scene: the story takes place about two hundred years ago on the farm where George Washington lived.
George: I think I will cut down this cherry tree with my axe.
(He cuts down the tree and goes away. After he is gone, his father walks up to the fallen tree.)

■ Now finish writing this play. What would the father say? What would he do?

Here's another story that you can make into a play.

One day a lion was walking through the forest. When the other animals saw him coming, they ran away because the lion was so strong. Then one day the lion stepped on a thorn. He tried and tried to get it out of his paw, but he couldn't do it. He began to roar, and he frightened all the other animals. But a little mouse saw that the lion was hurt. The mouse was afraid, but he decided to help the lion anyway. He pulled the thorn out of the lion's paw. The lion thanked the mouse. They became good friends, and the lion protected the mouse from the other animals.

If you were going to make this story into a play, who would be in the cast? What would the scene of the play be? What would the title be?

■ Now write down the title, the cast, and the scene of your play. Then write sentences for the lion and the mouse to say. Be sure to tell what they both do.

At this point, you may want to have the children examine an actual copy of a printed play. There may be one in the children's reading books. If not, you will probably be able to find a book of plays in the library and you can use an opaque projector to present a sample page to the class. Point out such things as the scene, the way the names of the actors are written, the fact that there are no quotation marks used in writing a play, and so on.

Then have the children read the beginning of the play about George Washington on page 100 of the text. The activity (■), which involves writing the rest of this play, can then be done as a class activity. As the children suggest additional lines, you can write them on the chalkboard, following the form established in the facsimile. Additionally, some children may want to transcribe from the tape their own version of the play about George Washington. If so, you should probably save the remainder of the lesson for another day.

The second part of the lesson requires that the children change a given story into a play. You can ask for a volunteer to read the story at the top of page 101, and then have the entire class discuss how this story could be made into a play. You can ask: "What would this play need that the play about George Washington didn't need?" If the children don't suggest animal sounds, then you can do so yourself. "How would a lion act? How would a mouse act?"

The activity (■) at the bottom of the page can be done as a class project, then duplicated and presented on another day. Some children might want to make scenery, others can make simple costumes, and so on. The actors should feel free to read their lines, if they prefer.

Purposes (1) To illustrate another use of the sentence-combining rule; (2) To demonstrate that adjectives can be used before nouns as well as after "be" words.

Preparation The preparation can be conducted in two stages: one which reviews the basic sentence-combining rule (first given on page 51), another which reviews the use of adjectives after "be" words. (When discussing sentence combining, be sure to use the terms *matrix* and *insert,* as well as the terms *"be" word* and *adjective.* The children should also understand the difference between *determiner* and *noun.*)

Presentation The first half of page 102 duplicates the preparation suggested above, so you can call on student volunteers to read and explain the material. Be sure they recognize that the verb phrases in the two sentences about the girl each contain a verb and a nominal.

Generally, it's best for you to illustrate the method of inserting adjectives on the chalkboard before the children read the second half of page 102. You can follow this procedure:

1. Write *The boy climbed a tree.*
2. Point out the two regular nominals (*The boy* and *a tree*) and state that each one consists of a determiner and a noun.
3. Under the first sentence, write: + *The boy is tall.* Draw a line to indicate a sentence problem.
4. Label the top sentence *matrix* and the bottom one *insert.*
5. Point out that the same nominal (*The boy*) occurs in both matrix and insert.
6. Point out that the insert sentence has a "be" word and an adjective.

Inserting Adjectives

You now know about two kinds of verb phrases. The first kind has a verb and a nominal. The second kind has a "be" word and an adjective.

You also know how to combine two sentences when each has a verb and a nominal.

   The girl bought a pickle.
+ The girl found a penny.
   The girl who found a penny bought a pickle.

What do we do to the matrix sentences? What do we do to the nominal at the beginning of the insert sentence?

There's a special way to combine two sentences when the insert sentence has a "be" word and an adjective. Suppose we have this "be" word sentence.

   The boy is tall.

We can use it as the insert sentence in this sentence problem.

   The boy climbed a tree.

+ The boy is (tall.)
   The tall boy climbed a tree.

Do you see what we did? When the insert sentence has the first kind of verb phrase, we put it after the noun in the matrix sentence. But suppose the insert sentence has a "be" word and an adjective. Then put the adjective before the noun in the matrix sentence. Try to add these sentences.

   The dog barked loudly.
+ The dog is small.

Daybook: Inserting Adjectives, page 40

102

■ Here are some sentence problems for you to solve. But be careful. The verb phrase in the insert sentence may have a verb and a nominal. Or it may have a "be" word and an adjective. (The first one is done for you.)

1. The teacher sang a song.
    + The teacher is happy.

    The happy teacher sang a song.

2. The girl started to sneeze.
    + The girl dropped the pepper.

3. The lady screamed loudly.
    + The lady saw a mouse.

4. The boy walked backwards.
    + The boy is silly.

5. The mailman ate a pickle.
    + The mailman is hungry.

6. The frog slept all day.
    + The frog is tired.

7. The doctor tickled my feet.
    + The doctor gave me a shot.

8. The kitten frightened a bird.
    + The kitten climbed a tree.

9. The baby fell asleep.
    + The baby is tired.

10. The tiger ate my lunch.
    + The tiger is hungry.

7. Say: "Here's the special thing we do with adjectives." Cross out *The boy is* and then draw a circle around *tall*.
8. Draw an arrow from the circle around *tall* up to the space between *The* and *boy* in the matrix sentence.
9. Finally, write the answer—the single new sentence—beneath the line.

Repeat the entire process—steps 1 through 9—for the sentence problem given at the bottom of page 102.

The activity (■) on page 103 is best done with the entire class. Volunteers can try each problem on the chalkboard, explaining each step they take as you did with the example. Remind the children that they already can do these things "in their heads," and help them use the terms (for example, *adjective* and *insert*) accurately. (If some children need additional practice, you can make new problems by changing the nouns and adjectives in problems 1, 4, 5, 6, 9, and 10 on page 103. Thus, in the first problem, change *teacher* to *cat* and *happy* to *fat*.)

Follow-up   You can use the activity suggested on page 114 of this guide as a follow-up for this lesson.

Answers

2. The girl who dropped the pepper started to sneeze.
3. The lady who saw a mouse screamed loudly.
4. The silly boy walked backwards.
5. The hungry mailman ate a pickle.
6. The tired frog slept all day.
7. The doctor who gave me a shot tickled my feet.
8. The kitten who climbed a tree frightened a bird.
9. The tired baby fell asleep.
10. The hungry tiger ate my lunch.

Purposes (1) To develop further the child's understanding of the nature and function of the dictionary; (2) To acquaint children with the use of the pronunciation key; (3) To demonstrate how a dictionary can be used to determine the spellings of words.

[The development of dictionary skills is an important—even vital—part of instruction in the English language arts. The first dictionary lesson in this book (pages 53-55) focused on meanings. The following lesson provides a solid basis for developing pronunciation skills and also for using a dictionary to determine spellings. If the children have studied any one of the various phonetic systems as part of the reading program in previous grades, then this lesson will provide a useful review. Children who have had no experience with phonetic alphabets will need to work through the lesson slowly, and probably with much guidance. Whatever the children's experience has been, you will probably want to teach the lesson in small groups or, in some cases, individually.]

Preparation The nature of both the preparation and the presentation of this lesson depends, in large measure, on where the children are when they come to your class. But probably the most effective form of preparation focuses on the disparity between spelling and pronunciation in English. You might write the following words on the chalkboard and ask the children to pronounce them: *cough, tough, through, though.* Then you can call attention to the fact that all these words end with the letters *ough,* but that in each word these letters stand for different sounds. Then ask the children to suggest a way they can use to find out "how a word sounds." Someone will probably suggest using a dictionary.

104

The Dictionary: Sounds and Spellings

Part I

In your head, you already know many thousands of words. But what happens when you don't know a word? Then you can use a dictionary to learn these things:

> How to pronounce a word
> How to spell a word
> What a word means

First we'll look at the pronunciation of words.

You already know that we have twenty-six letters to choose from when we spell words. But did you know that we make more than forty different sounds when we <u>say</u> words? There are more sounds than there are letters of the alphabet. Most dictionaries have a **pronunciation key** to show all these different sounds. A full pronunciation key shows <u>all</u> of the symbols and the sounds they stand for. Many dictionaries have a short form of the pronunciation key printed on every right hand page. The short form shows the symbols for all of the vowels and some of the consonants.

Here is the short form of the pronunciation key from the *Thorndike Barnhart Beginning Dictionary.*

hat, āge, cãre, fär;	ch, child; ng, long;
let, bē, tėrm;	th, thin; ŦH, then;
it, īce;	zh, measure;
hot, gō, ôrder;	ə represents *a* in about,
cup, pùt, rüle, ūse;	*e* in taken, *i* in April,
oil, out;	*o* in lemon, *u* in circus

The first column has key words for all of the vowels. Say each word and listen for the sound of the vowel.

Answers
1. grammar: two syllables; first syllable accented; schwa stands for *a*.
2. sentence: two syllables; first syllable accented; schwa stands for *e*.
3. metaphor: three syllables; first syllable accented; schwa stands for *a*.
4. picture: two syllables, first syllable accented; schwa stands for *u*.
5. lexicon: three syllables; first syllable accented; schwas stand for *i* and *o*.

In the second column, there are symbols and key words for five consonants. All of the symbols have two letters. Now say these words.

child   long   thin   then   measure

The *ch* in *child* stands for <u>one</u> sound. But the symbol has <u>two</u> letters. What two letters stand for the one sound that you hear at the end of *long*? Can you hear a difference between the sound for *th* in *thin* and the sound for *th* in *then*? What two letters stand for the sound that you hear in the middle of *measure*?

The last symbol (ə) is special. It's called the **schwa,** and it can stand for any vowel letter. But we use the schwa only in words that have more than one syllable.

Listen for the syllables in these words.

chicken   surprise   partner

Here's the pronunciation for each of these words.

(chik′ ən)   (sər prīz′)   (pärt′ nər)

Look at the pronunciation for *chicken*. You see a small space between each syllable. You also see an **accent mark** after the syllable that is pronounced more strongly. Which syllable is accented in *chicken*? Which syllable is accented in *surprise*? Which syllable is accented in *partner*? In many words, the schwa symbol stands for the vowel in the unaccented syllable.

■ Now try to pronounce these words. Tell how many syllables each word has. Then tell which syllable is accented. If there's a schwa in an <u>unaccented</u> syllable, tell what vowel letter it stands for.

1. (gram′ ər)   4. (pik′ chər)   7. (ad ven′ chər)
2. (sen′ təns)   5. (lek′ sə kən)   8. (jī′ ənt)
3. (met′ ə fôr)   6. (tēch′ ər)   9. (ôr′ dər)

Answers (continued)

6. teacher: two syllables; first syllable accented; schwa stands for e.
7. adventure: three syllables; second syllable accented; schwa stands for u.
8. giant: two syllables; first syllable accented; schwa stands for a.
9. order: two syllables; first syllable accented; schwa stands for e.

Presentation Read the first paragraph on page 104 with the children, helping them to see that a dictionary can be used for things other than finding the meanings of words. Then write the term *pronunciation key* on the chalkboard, and explain to the children that, if they know how to use a pronunciation key, then the dictionary can help them figure out how a word "sounds." (At this point, you can help the children locate the full pronunciation keys in their own dictionaries.)

After reading the second paragraph on page 104, have the children locate the short form of the pronunciation key in their own dictionaries and compare it briefly with the full key. Help them to understand that the short form contains symbols for all of the vowels, but only some of the consonants.

In discussing the short form of the pronunciation key which is reproduced in the text, you should provide each child the opportunity of saying the key words as often as necessary. One way to help the children become familiar with the diacritical marks is to have them draw these marks themselves. But be certain that they do not think they have to memorize the key; rather, it is a device to be used when they're trying to figure out the pronunciation of an unfamiliar word.

Then work through the material on page 105 step by step. If some children have not had previous experience with accented and unaccented syllables, then you may want to extend the preparation before reading the second paragraph on this page. You can write the following words in three columns on the chalkboard:

old   about   radio
fast   letter   cucumber
snow   seven   operate
peaks   control   passenger

Have the children say the words in the first column, and then ask how many vowels they hear in each word. Then have the children say the words in the second column and tell how many vowels they hear in each one. Repeat this procedure with the words in the third column, helping the children to understand that the number of syllables a word has depends on the number of vowels heard in that word. Then explain that, when we pronounce a word that has two or more syllables, we usually say one syllable with more force or stress. You can repeat the words in the second and third columns, stressing the accented syllable in each word a little more than you normally would. Finally, have the children pronounce the words in both columns and identify the accented and the unaccented syllables in each word. (You might suggest that the children make a downward hand movement at the same time that they say the accented syllables.)

Read the rest of page 105 with the children, helping them to understand the function of the schwa. (Be sure to use the term *schwa,* and encourage the children to use it also.)

You will probably need to help the children work the activity (■) on page 105. First, have the children try to say each word, referring to the pronunciation key on page 104 to compare each symbol with a key word. Then have them look at each pronunciation again while you ask:

1. How many syllables does the word have?
2. Which syllable is accented?
3. How can you tell?
4. Which syllable is unaccented?
5. Is there a schwa in this syllable?
6. What vowel letter does the schwa stand for?

Part II

Suppose you want to use a dictionary to find out how to spell a word. You usually know some of the letters of the word. If you know the first two or three, then the word isn't too hard to find. But suppose you don't know them. What then?

These beginning sounds are always spelled the same way in words.

/b/ /d/ /l/ /m/ /p/ /t/ /w/ /v/ /z/

But there are other sounds that we can spell more than one way. Here are a few sounds and some different ways to spell them.

Sounds	*Spellings*
/f/ as in *fan* and *phone*	*f* most of the time, but sometimes *ph*
/j/ as in *jet* and *giraffe*	*j* most of the time, but sometimes *g*
/k/ as in *key* and *cat*	either *c* or *k* most of the time, but sometimes *ch* (*Christmas*) or *qu* (*quart*)
/s/ as in *see* and *city*	either *s* or *c* most of the time, but sometimes *sc* (*scissors*) or even *ps* (*psalm*)

These are all consonants. But suppose the word you want to look up begins with a vowel. Sometimes, it's very easy to tell what vowel letter the word is spelled with.

Daybook: A Symbol Story, page 42

Say these words.

ate   even   ice   open   unit

When you say these words, you can "hear" what vowel letters the words begin with. But you can't be completely sure. There are a few words like *ewe,* which sounds exactly like *you.*

Sometimes, you don't "hear" what vowel letters the word begins with. Then it's harder to guess. These words all begin with different letters.

above   occur   upon

But the sound you hear at the beginning of each of these words is the same. You hear the schwa sound, and you already know that the schwa can stand for any vowel letter. But if you hear the schwa at the beginning of a word, then the word probably begins with an *a* or an *o* or a *u.*

■ Here are some words that are spelled with the special symbols used in the pronunciation key. Try to figure out what the real spelling is for each word.

1. ə round′
2. rē′ ses
3. tə dā′
4. fō′ nə graf
5. lang′ gwij
6. jin′ jər
7. kach
8. ī′ si kl
9. kwī′ ət

Answers

1. around
2. recess
3. today
4. phonograph
5. language
6. ginger
7. catch
8. icicle
9. quiet

Part II: (The second part of this lesson deals with using the dictionary to determine spellings, and you'll probably want to reserve it for those children who are already comfortable with the concepts presented in the first part.)

You might begin by asking the children: "If you don't know how to spell a word, then how can you find it in the dictionary?" The answer, of course, is that sometimes you can't! But you can explain to the children that this lesson will give them some hints that might help.

Read the first two paragraphs on page 106 with the children, and then discuss the "Sounds" and "Spellings" in the middle of the page with them. You might suggest that they try to find words in the dictionary for each of the "sometimes" spellings (for example, *gym,* in which *g* is pronounced /j/). You can also say these words, one at a time: *gem, general, jab, ginger, gentle,* and *judge.* Then the children can look up each word, with half of the group looking under the *J*'s and the other half looking under the *G*'s. Then you can repeat this process for the other sounds in the list.

After working through the rest of the lesson with the children, you may want to spend some time discussing the illustration on page 107. Help the children understand that the children in the illustration are all using "hints" to help them locate words they want to spell.

In doing the activity (■) on page 107, first let the children figure out what they think the spelling is, then have them check a dictionary, and finally have them write the word.

Follow-up To provide additional practice, you can use the lesson Sounds and Letters on pages 316-318 or the activities on page 115 of this guide.

Purposes   (1) To introduce the limerick as a literary form; (2) To provide examples of limericks.

Preparation   There's no particular preparation required for this lesson, but you might want to begin by reading a few short, humorous poems to the children. (The books listed under Additional Resources will give you a variety from which to choose.) If you do follow this preparation, then ask the children how these poems make them feel. (One purpose of this lesson is to help the children understand that literature can frequently be "fun," but it's probably best to let them discover this for themselves.)

Presentation   Read the three limericks on page 108 to the children, giving full vent to your dramatic abilities as you do. It is completely appropriate to read limericks in a "sing-song" manner, pausing at the end of each line and stressing the bouncy rhythm. Try to let your voice range both higher and lower than usual. You should also try to be as "physical" as possible in your reading—move about, jump up and down, wave your arms, and so on.

After you've read each of the limericks on page 108, you can call for volunteers to read them. Encourage the children to be as lively as they feel. If they want to clap their hands, or sway back and forth, or laugh out loud, they should certainly feel free to do so. Then you can have small groups, or even the entire class, read the limericks in unison.

After reading the limericks, ask the children how these poems make them feel. Do they like the bouncy rhythm? Do they enjoy the jokes? Do they like to listen to —and read—poems which they can "act out"?

Limericks

Here are some short, silly poems that are fun to read. They're called **limericks.**

There was an old man who said "Whee!
I can't multiply 7 times 3.
    Though 14 seems plenty,
    It may be past 20.
Oh, why should this happen to me?"

A cheerful old bear at the zoo
Could always find something to do.
    He walked fast and then slow.
    He walked to and then fro.
Sometimes he walked fro and then to.

There was a young girl who said "Why
Can't I look in my ear with my eye?
    If I put my mind to it,
    I'm sure I can do it.
You never can tell till you try."

All limericks start with two lines that rhyme. Then there are two shorter lines that rhyme. Finally, there's a line that rhymes with the first two. In the first limerick, what rhymes with *whee* and *three*? What rhymes with *plenty*? In the limerick about the bear, what two words rhyme with *zoo*? What rhymes with *slow*? What rhymes with *why* in the third limerick? What rhymes with *to it*?

After reading the three limericks on page 108, and perhaps making some general remarks about active listening, you can turn to the discussion at the bottom of the page. (This discussion focuses on the structure of limericks, and serves as a preparation for the composition lesson to follow.) Read the paragraph with the children, pausing so they can answer the questions in the text. The children should have little or no difficulty finding the rhyming words or suggesting other words that also rhyme. You might point out that sometimes only the last syllable of one line rhymes with the last syllable of another line, and sometimes more than one syllable rhymes (*plenty/twenty*).

If the unison reading of the limericks on page 108 has been enthusiastic, then you can begin immediately with unison reading of the two limericks on the top of page 110. You can then request volunteers to read these limericks.

After several readings, you can discuss the rhymes in these two limericks. You might also want to point out that the first, second, and fifth lines of limericks are longer than the third and fourth lines.

Again, ask the children how these limericks make them feel, and encourage a variety of answers in response to the question which concludes the lesson.

Additional Resources

Books Ciardi, John, *The Reason for the Pelican, The Man Who Sang the Sillies,* and *You Read to Me, I'll Read to You,* Lippincott. Clymer, Eleanor, compiler, *Arrow Book of Funny Poems,* Scholastic. Cole, William, compiler, *Beastly Boys and Ghastly Girls* and *Humorous Poetry for Children,* World. Lear, Edward, *A Book of Nonsense,* Little, Brown, and *The Complete Nonsense Book,* Dodd, Mead.

Love, Katherine, compiler, *A Little Laughter,* Crowell. Nash, Ogden, compiler, *The Moon Is Shining Bright as Day,* Lippincott. Richards, Laura E., *Tirra Lirra,* Little, Brown. Smith, William Jay, *Typewriter Town,* Dutton.

Recordings *Anthology of Poetry for Children,* LP Recording, Spoken Arts, *Edward Lear's Nonsense Stories and Poems,* 1–12″ LP, cassette, Caedmon. *Nonsense Verse of Carroll and Lear,* 1–12″ LP, Caedmon.

Purpose To provide children with the opportunity to write limericks.

Preparation Probably the best preparation for writing limericks is to have volunteers read a sampling of limericks to the class. You can choose limericks from the books by Lear and Smith, listed under Additional Resources for the previous lesson, or the "readers" can select their favorites from the text.

Presentation Read page 110 with the children, perhaps calling for a volunteer to read the limerick. Discuss briefly the meaning of the terms *rhythm* and *rhyme,* and then demonstrate the rhythm pattern of a limerick as it is given on page 111. Finally, have the children read these "rhythm lines" in unison, repeating them as often as necessary until the children begin to feel the rhythm. You can also

Here are some more limericks.

I wish that my room had a floor.
I don't care so much for a door.
    But this walking around
    Without touching the ground
Is something that I'll do no more.

There was a young man in Peru,
Who dreamed he had only one shoe.
    He awoke in the night
    In a very bad fright,
And found it was perfectly true.

Many people like to read limericks. Can you explain why they do?

Writing Limericks

Limericks are fun to write, once you know how.

This lesson will show you a way
To find something silly to say.
    Just follow the rule
    And certainly you'll
Have fun while you're learning today.

There are only two rules you need to know.

  1. Limericks have a special **rhythm.**
  2. Limericks have a special **rhyme scheme.**

The first rule means that limericks have a special music, the way a clock does, or a subway.

Daybook: Limericks, page 44

There are two rhythms in a limerick. Lines 1, 2, and 5 have this rhythm:

da DA, da da DA, da da DA

Lines 3 and 4 have this rhythm:

da DA, da da DA

Here's the rhythm for a whole limerick. Practice saying it until you can feel the rhythm inside your head.

da DA, da da DA, da da DA
da DA, da da DA, da da DA
   da DA, da da DA
   da DA, da da DA
da DA, da da DA, da da DA

The second limerick rule tells you how the lines rhyme. The three longer lines end with the same sound. And the two short lines end with the second sound, like this.

First sound
First sound
   Second sound
   Second sound
First sound

Here's a limerick that will help you remember the rhyme scheme.

Suppose that your first sound is "en."
Repeat it in this line, and then
   Look quickly around
   And find one more sound.
Then use the first sound once again.

have the class read the rhythm for the whole limerick silently, using body or arm movements rather than spoken sounds.

Once the children have internalized the rhythm, you can continue with a discussion of the rhyme scheme of a limerick. Help the children see how the limerick at the bottom of page 111 illustrates this rhyme scheme.

In presenting the incomplete limerick on page 112, you should read the four lines aloud several times. After the children have decided which line they prefer for the end of the limerick (both 1 and 3 fit the rhythm scheme), you can read the entire limerick again or perhaps even sing it to a tune you make up.

Probably the best way to prepare for the activity (■) on page 112 is to write a class limerick. The activity itself can then be done in pairs or individually, but you should be prepared to offer help whenever necessary.

Follow-up Most of the children will probably want to share their limericks with others in the class. You might arrange for a few minutes of "limerick reading time" during each of the next four or five days.

Some children might want to experiment with a "chain limerick." If so, arrange the children in groups of five. One child should be prepared to suggest a first line, and then call on someone else in the group to think of a second line. Then the second person calls on a third, and so on.

Purposes (1) To introduce the concept that basic sentences can be divided into positions; (2) To use this concept as a means of illustrating subject and predicate relationships.

[The sentence position picture, adapted from structural linguistics, is a useful device in helping children visualize their innate understanding of the so-called "constituent structure" of simple sentences. In this lesson, the children will learn to use a position picture to help them "talk about" basic sentences. Variations of the position picture have already been used on pages 65 and 83. Even so, you should spend as much time on this lesson as required to provide a good foundation for the next few language lessons, which will use the concept of positions as a means of discussing questions, auxiliaries, and adverbials.]

Preparation You might have the children open their books to page 83 and examine this variation of the position picture. You can point out that this picture shows how we can divide sentences into nominals and verb phrases. You might also remind the children that some verb phrases use "be" words, some use "have" words, and others use "do" words.

Write the word *position* on the chalkboard and ask the children what they think it means. You can demonstrate the meaning by arranging six or seven children in a line—one behind the other—and point out the first position, second position, and so on.

Presentation Call on volunteers to read the two paragraphs on page 112 and the first paragraph on page 113. On the chalkboard, duplicate each new segment of the sentence picture as the children come to it in the text.

Now you're ready to try some limericks of your own. Here's one to help you get started.

There once were two cats of Kilkenny.
Each thought there was one cat too many.
    They scratched and they hit,
    They fought, and they bit,

Which line would you choose for the end of the limerick?

1. Till somebody threw them a penny.
2. And finally one of them got tired and went away.
3. Instead of two cats, there weren't any!

■ Now try to write your own limerick.

Sentence Positions

So far, every sentence we've made with the model begins with a nominal. An easy way to see what comes first is to draw a position picture. Here's part of one.

FIRST POSITION	
The boy	
Andrew	
They	

In the second position, we can have a verb or a "be" word, like this.

FIRST POSITION	SECOND POSITION
The boy	climbed
Andrew	was
They	visited

Daybook: Practice with Sentence Positions, page 46

112

In the sentences we've made with the model, there's been at least one word after the verb or the "be" word. We can show some third position words like this.

FIRST POSITION	SECOND POSITION	THIRD POSITION
The boy	climbed	the tree.
Andrew	was	silly.
They	visited	the zoo.

We can say that the words in the first position are the **subject** of the sentence. Most of the time, the subject is the person or thing we're talking about. All the other words in the sentence are the **predicate.** The predicate usually tells us what the subject is or has or does.

Now look at the first sentence above. What is the subject of this sentence? What is the predicate? Try to find the subjects and predicates of the other sentences.

■ These sentences have been divided into positions. First, find the subject of each sentence. Then, find the predicate.

	FIRST POSITION	SECOND POSITION	THIRD POSITION
1.	The girl	is	tall.
2.	John	ate	the pizza.
3.	I	saw	Robert.

■ Try to find the subject and predicates of these sentences.

1. The boy found a grape.
2. The mailman sang a song.
3. The elephant won a medal.

Now make a position picture like the one above. Try to put all the words in these sentences in the right positions.

Write the words *subject* and *predicate* on the chalkboard, and then read the second paragraph on page 113 with the children. Call on volunteers to answer the questions in the third paragraph on this page. Help the children to see that—in a basic sentence—the first position is the subject, and the other positions make up the predicate. (Don't be concerned with achieving full understanding at this point; there are many opportunities in later lessons to reinforce the concepts.)

The first activity (■) can be worked as an entire class, and then the children can work in pairs or small groups to complete the second activity (■). If you provide additional sentences, be sure that they are basic (statements rather than questions; active rather than passive). It's also best to avoid auxiliaries at this time.

Follow-up First have the children locate the subject of each of these sentences, and then have them divide each sentence into "positions."

1. Maurice found a peanut.
2. The clown was silly.
3. The monkey ate the banana.
4. My cousin read the book.
5. I have a toothache.

Answers

The answer for the first activity are as follows:
1. Subject: the boy
   Predicate: found a grape
2. Subject: the mailman
   Predicate: sang a song
3. Subject: the elephant
   Predicate: won a medal

A slash indicates the positions of the words in each sentence in the second activity.
1. The boy / found / a grape.
2. The mailman / sang / a song.
3. The elephant / won / a medal.

Purposes (1) To review the literary forms of myth and limerick; (2) To provide an additional opportunity for children to compose a play; (3) To re-emphasize the importance of order in language.

Presentation The literature and composition lessons of this Review lend themselves particularly well to group work. The children should feel free to join whichever group they wish—the one writing limericks or the one dramatizing the myth.

The language section of the Review should probably be done with the class as a whole.

You can also challenge some students to create their own insert sentences and then use the special adjective way to combine them with the following matrix sentences. (Of course, the insert sentences will have to begin with the same nominals as are in the matrix sentences. And the nominal in each insert sentence will have to be followed by a "be" word and an adjective.)

1. My uncle rode a bike.
2. The zebra wore a necktie.
3. His brother won a prize.
4. The canary chirped loudly.
5. The monkey scratched his head.
6. The mole dug a hole.
7. My cousin needs a haircut.
8. The fly landed in my soup.
9. The nurse jumped over the fence.
10. The bear climbed a tree.

Review

Literature

In this chapter, you learned about two kinds of literature: *myths* and *limericks*. What is a myth usually about? In "Perseus and Atlas," Atlas is strong, but Perseus is smart. How does Perseus trick Atlas? Do you know any other stories where a hero tricks somebody?

What special *rhythm* does a limerick have? What is the special *rhyme scheme*?

■ Now write another limerick. Perhaps you'd like to make it about a silly hero.

Composition

The myth about Perseus and Atlas would make a good play. The myth already has a *title*. But if you want to, you can make up a different title for it. What other title would be a good one for this play?

Every play has a *cast* and a *scene*. Who would be in the cast of the play about Perseus? Where and when does the play happen?

A play also has *lines*. But you can put on a play without writing down the lines. You don't need to write lines if everyone in the cast knows the story. Then the cast can make up their own lines as they go along.

■ Now choose some people to act out the play about Perseus and Atlas. You can write down the lines, if you want to. Or you can make them up as you go along.

Language

There's an important thing to remember when you study about the "arts" of English. Things have *order*. Literature has order. Composition has order. And language has order. We can see the order when we use the *sentence position picture*.

■ On your paper, make a position picture like the one on page 113. Then try to put the parts of these sentences—in the right order—into the empty positions.

1. Andrew ate the pizza.
2. The boy visited the zoo.
3. I climbed the tree.

There's also order when we combine sentences. When do we put the insert sentence <u>after</u> the noun in the matrix sentence? When do we put something <u>before</u> the noun?

■ Here are some sentence problems for you to solve.

1.   The dog pushed the cart.
  + The dog is clever.

2.   The lady chased the cat.
  + The lady swallowed a canary.

 Do you remember what special mark of punctuation you use when you're writing a play? For more practice using the *colon*, turn to page 308.

Answers

A slash indicates the positions of the words in each of the sentences in the first activity.
1. Andrew / ate / the pizza.
2. The boy / visited / the zoo.
3. I / climbed / the tree.

The answers to the sentence problems are as follows:
1. The clever dog pushed the cart.
2. The lady who swallowed a canary chased the cat.

The following activities can be used after The Dictionary: Sounds and Spellings (pages 104-107):

A. After the children have become familiar with the pronunciation key that is reproduced on page 104 of the text, you can have them compare it with the short form of a key from another dictionary. Then write a number of one- and two-syllable words on the chalkboard. Divide the class into two groups, and have each group use a different key to write the pronunciations. Then the children can compare the pronunciations.

B. Have the children use the key on page 104 to determine what words the following pronunciations stand for. Some children may be able to write the words, spelled correctly. Others can work in pairs, with each child saying the words aloud to his partner. (In this case, you will probably want to divide the words into two separate lists and provide a set of answers to be used by the partners.)

1. boŦH' ər   6. leŦH' ər
2. fā' məs   7. jerm
3. lī' ən   8. o' vər
4. fô' sit   9. rüs' tər
5. fan' tə se   10. sə pōz'

C. Remind the children about some of the hints they learned to help them locate words that they're not sure how to spell. (You may even want to write these hints on the chalkboard.) Then say each word in the list below, and ask the children to tell which hint would be most helpful in finding the word in the dictionary.

1. bravery   6. concert
2. satellite   7. chemical
3. cemetery   8. fantastic
4. scientist   9. generous
5. ache   10. phantom

Purpose To introduce written history as a form of literature.

[In addition to poetry and fiction, many other kinds of writing also achieve the status of literature. This lesson introduces the children to history—a literary form that most of them have probably not encountered before. The selection is excerpted from a full-length book by Samuel Hopkins Adams, and it is especially useful in illustrating how a historian combines fact and imagination in recreating the past.]

Preparation Many nine- and ten-year-old children are just beginning to develop a sense of history. They may fail to recognize that history is being made every day. For this reason, you can introduce this lesson by asking what was the most exciting event that happened in the world during the past year. Perhaps there was an important space flight, perhaps another landing on the moon, perhaps a space station was established.

Ask the children how we learned about the event. In the case of a moon landing, for example, you can discuss live television pictures from the moon and the spaceship. Ask the children to discuss the meaning of "live television." Help them recognize that after something happens they can read about it—and sometimes see pictures of it—in newspapers or magazines (for very recent events) or in books (for events which occurred in the more distant past). You can conclude the discussion by saying: "If an event is very important, then people will still want to read about it many years from now."

Then ask the children if the adults they know ever describe exciting things that happened long ago. "Do the events seem almost real? What's the difference between something that happened long

History

There are interesting things that people write besides poems and stories. Some of the most exciting writing is **history**, which is the story of things that really happened.

Here's part of a history from *The Pony Express*.

The morning sun was trying to break its way through the clouds when Bill Hamilton, the Pony Express rider,

arrived at the exchange station. The night before, Warren Upson, who would take the mail from Hamilton, had selected the fastest horse in the station. Looking at the heavy clouds still blanketing the mountain, he changed his mind. He would be in snow an hour after the start. Upson realized that he needed a horse that wouldn't give up, more than he needed a fast one.

ago and a story that someone makes up in his imagination?" Explain that history is about true things that really happened sometime in the past.

Presentation Have the children turn to page 116 and find the definition of the word *history*. Then, after you've introduced the selection as a true story of something that happened long ago, describe briefly the reasons why there was a Pony Express. (You may want to consult an encyclopedia for more information.)

Depending on the abilities of your class, the presentation of this history can be either a listening or a reading experience. Ask the children to think—as they listen or read—about the fact that this event was both exciting and dangerous when it happened, perhaps as exciting then as a trip to the moon is now.

If you read the selection to the children, try to be as dramatic as possible. You might pretend to be a television announcer describing an important contemporary event. Before reading, you might want to explain these words and phrases:

1. *exchange station:* "a place where one rider passes the mail onto another rider who then continues the journey."
2. *check-point station:* "a place where a rider can get information about the trail ahead."
3. *hump:* "hilly part of a mountain."
4. *avalanche:* "a large mass of snow which suddenly and swiftly slides down a mountain."
5. *Sierras:* "high, rugged mountains in the western part of our country."
6. *pass:* "a narrow opening between mountains."
7. *Mormon settlement:* "a small community of people who believed in one particular religion."

If the children are to read the selection on their own, then you will probably want to do a little more vocabulary preparation. Introduce the two Pony Express riders, Bill Hamilton and Warren Upson. Then explain that the night before Warren was to ride, he looked out and saw "heavy clouds still blanketing the mountain." Ask the children what they think "heavy clouds" are and what a mountain "blanketed" with such clouds might look like. After a brief discussion of the bad weather that was threatening, you can mention that next morning the station master "peered out into the wind-driven mist." Have a volunteer demonstrate *peering* and then ask someone to describe a "wind-driven mist." Point out to the children that the Pony Express riders would look for "familiar landmarks" to guide them as they were riding, but that on this particular trip many of the landmarks were "blotted out by savage snowblasts." Ask someone to explain the words *blotted out* and *savage* as they are used in this context. You can also ask the children what they think some of the *perils* of the trip might be. During this discussion, you can ask: "Do you think there might be dangerous animals abroad?" and explain that *abroad* can sometimes mean "around."

After the children have finished reading or listening, discuss the key events with them to be sure that they understand "what happened." Help them to imagine the danger of being on a horse in the high mountains when the ground is covered with snow. Encourage them to imagine how they would feel in this situation.

Then have the children turn to the discussion on page 120. (This discussion focuses on the nature of history and on the problems that a historian faces in writing history.)

He saddled up the strongest animal in the stable. The station master had breakfast ready at seven. Then, peering out anxiously into the wind-driven mist, he asked, "You going to try it, Warren?"

The young man looked at him with surprise. "Certainly I'm going to try it."

"The trail's blocked," the station master said. "This is only rain here. It'll be snow in the pass and long before you get to the pass. You'll be lucky if there *is* any pass."

"If there isn't, I'll go over the hump," Warren Upson said cheerfully.

The other ran to the door. "Here she comes! Here's Bill! Half an hour early. Good man!"

Jumping for his bearskin cap and elbow-length gloves of beaver fur, the rider got into his jacket. He said "Hello" to Bill Hamilton and soon was on his way to the check-point station at the foot of the mountain.

Here there was news from the mountaintop. A trapper who had come over reported twenty-foot drifts in the 9,000-foot-high Johnson's Pass. He advised Upson to give up the trip.

"If you can make it, why can't I?" the young man said.

"I came on snowshoes. You can't put those on a horse."

Upson agreed, but he was not to be discouraged. He left his rifle and even his revolvers at the station. Every ounce saved would be a help.

He was familiar enough with the landmarks; here a dead pine, there a jutting rock, farther along a scar on a distant mountain face. Now these were blotted out by the savage snow-blasts beating down from the high peaks. Only his compass and the mustang's instinct were left to guide him.

For long reaches the winds had swept the ground bare, and Upson could put his mount to a gallop. But bare ground in one place meant piled-up snow in another. The gallant pony struggled knee-deep, then body-deep. The rider dismounted and picked his way up the steep slopes, pulling the tired animal after him.

They had reached a turn around a cliffside where the snow was shallow. Swinging into the saddle, Upson urged the pony to speed. But the animal, for once, would not go on. Its body stiffened under him. Upson could feel it trembling.

Puzzled, he got off again and looked about. No dangerous animal would be abroad on those heights and at that season. Yet the horse had sensed some peril. Upson stood and waited, alert for what might come. He had not long to wait. A few seconds before, the wind had died down. Now the air seemed to shiver. There was a tremendous, soft "Swoo-oo-oo-ssshhh!" and the snow mass came sliding down from above. Gliding slowly at first, it quickened. It plunged down the slope, hid the road under thousands of tons of snow, and went thundering on into the valley below.

If they had gone fifty yards farther, horse and rider would have been carried away by the on-coming avalanche. Their bodies might have been found after the snow had melted off. Or they might have been lost without a trace.

The pass was now hopeless. Upson's problem was to find a way across the high and rocky shoulder. At Friday's there would be a fresh pony. But the station was seven miles away, perhaps longer by the pathless route that he must take across-country.

After he had traveled some distance, he realized he was lost. East and north by compass he went. He still did not know where the wagon route was until suddenly he saw it in front of him.

The sun was shining and the snow melting on the eastern slope of the Sierras. The station keeper urged Upson to warm himself and take a little rest. He refused. Time

After the children have read the first two paragraphs of the discussion, ask how the writer—the historian—knew what happened. (The Pony Express riders kept notes and diaries.) Emphasize that the historian couldn't change anything that was true: "He couldn't say that George Washington was a Pony Express rider. And he couldn't say that Warren Upson went eighty miles if he really only went fifty." But make certain that the children also understand that a historian sometimes needs to "guess," particularly when he writes conversation. Ask the class to suggest other things—besides what people say—that a historian may have to guess.

You can expand the discussion in the text by asking why a historian needs to make up things. "Why would the writer need to have a good imagination? Why would he need to know a lot about the times he was writing about?"

After reading the third paragraph of the discussion, you can request volunteers to read the dialogue in the history to see if the words "sound right." The children can also discuss other things a rider might talk about—and then try to explain how they know that a rider would be interested in these things.

The last paragraph of the discussion focuses on selection, which is one of the important concepts presented in the composition strand. You can ask the children to discuss the reasons why the historian selects some details and leaves out others.

The activity (■) on page 120 is intended to encourage children to become interested in research and in learning how to do research. You can help them gather encyclopedias, biographies, history books, pictures, ballads, and perhaps—if you live near a sizable library—even newspapers from a hundred years ago.

Follow-up With some children you may want to explore further the use of imagination in this selection. Not only does the historian create dialogue, but he also includes a number of metaphors in his writing. You can have the children locate the following metaphors in the selection, and then try to tell what two things have been "put together" to make each one:

1. "clouds blanketing the mountain"
2. "foot of the mountain"
3. "scar on the distant mountain face"
4. "(landmarks) blotted out"
5. "the wind had died down"
6. "the air seemed to shiver"
7. "(the avalanche) went thundering on"
8. "rocky shoulder (of the pass)"

This would also be a good time to introduce the children to some works of historical fiction that they can read on their own. (See Additional Resources.)

Additional Resources

Books Buckmaster, Henrietta, *Flight to Freedom: The Story of the Underground Railroad,* Dell. Bulla, Clyde Robert, *Indian Hill,* Crowell. Carr, Mary Jane, *Children of the Covered Wagon,* Crowell. Ceder, Georgiana D., *Winter Without Salt,* Marrow. Dalgliesh, Alice, *The Courage of Sarah Noble,* Scribners. Hoff, Carol, *Johnny Texas,* Follett. Field, Rachel, *Calico Bush,* Macmillan. Latham, Jean Lee, *This Dear-Bought Land,* Harper. Mason, Miriam E., *Susannah, the Pioneer Cow* and *Becky and Her Brave Cat,* Macmillan. Meadowcraft, Enid, *By Wagon and Flatboat,* Crowell. Meigs, Cornelia, *The Willow Whistle,* Macmillan. Moody, Ralph, *Riders of the Pony Express,* Dell. Steele, William O., *Flaming Arrows,* Harcourt. Zagoven, Ruby, *Venture for Freedom,* Dell.

enough had been lost already. The rider had to go on.

At the Mormon settlement in Genoa, it was the same way. Fourteen miles to go before he would reach his final stop, and the sun already low over the peaks. He made the two-minute change and hit the trail for Carson City.

He came in at 6:45 in the morning. If it had been anyone but Warren Upson, the townspeople might not have believed that he had come across the pass. He had covered eighty-three miles of distance, including twenty miles of "impassable" trail under "impossible" conditions of weather.

SAMUEL HOPKINS ADAMS

In most of the literature you've read this year, the writer has used his imagination to make up a story or poem. But a history is a true story. And the historian—the person who writes history—must tell about things that really happened.

But sometimes a historian does make up a few things. Bill Hamilton and Warren Upson were really Pony Express riders. Warren Upson really did ride through the snow. All that is true. But nobody knows the exact words that they said on that snowy day. The historian has tried to guess what they might have said.

Do the words sound right to you? Do you think that's the way a Pony Express rider would talk? What else do you think he might talk about?

A historian doesn't always tell everything that happened. Sometimes he leaves things out. When you read this history, can you tell what kind of clothes Warren Upson was wearing? What kind of saddle did he have? The history doesn't tell you these things. If you wanted to find out more, where could you look?

■ Now try to find more information about the Pony Express. Where was it used? How long did it last?

Sad and Happy Endings

Here are two sets of pictures. They're already in order. Use each set of pictures to tell a story.

Purposes (1) To develop the concept of revision as an important element in the composition process; (2) To provide additional opportunities for children to use their imagination in writing.

Preparation If you teach this lesson soon after the children have read the excerpt from *The Pony Express,* you can begin by asking whether the true story of Warren Upson had a happy ending or a sad ending. Encourage the children to use their imaginations to make up a sad ending for this story. Then ask the children if they prefer stories that have happy endings or sad endings—and why.

Presentation Have the children tell the story of the first four pictures in play form: three boys planning to play ball, breaking a window, and being scolded by the shop owner. This can be extemporaneous or you can help the children work it out beforehand. Because the second set of pictures is more tragic, a longer discussion is appropriate. (Perhaps the class will even want to add more pictures.)

Then the class can turn to the first activity (■) on page 122 and discuss possible revisions for each story, after which another set of actors can present the revised story.

The second activity (■) on page 122 is much less structured than similar activities in other composition lessons, and thereby provides a greater range of choice for each child. But not all children will respond enthusiastically to such freedom of choice, and you might suggest that they use an episode from their own lives, perhaps turning an unhappy ending into a happy one.

Follow-up Help the children find other sets of pictures they can use to tell or write some original stories.

Purposes (1) To help children recognize that they have internalized rules which enable them to ask questions; (2) To illustrate one way to represent these rules in the sentence model.

[In teaching this lesson, you should try to say "yes-or-no question"—rather than simply "question."]

Preparation Have one child look out the window and then state one thing he sees; have another open the door into the hall and then state one thing he sees; have a third child look in his desk and tell one thing about it. When all three children have finished, you can then make "yes-or-no" questions from the statements they gave. (Thus, if the first child says, "I see a tree," you can say, "Did Mark see a tree?") Ask for volunteers to answer your questions, and then have them explain how they knew the answers.

Then, on the chalkboard, write the following:

1. The leaves are falling.
2. Are the leaves falling?
3. The dog will find the bone.
4. Will the dog find the bone?

Ask the children which of these sentences are statements and which are questions. Then comment that today's lesson will help them talk about some things they already know—in their heads—about these kinds of sentences.

Presentation Either read—or have a volunteer read—the first two paragraphs of the lesson. Then review the sentence model in sufficient detail so the children recall what it is and why we use it. Remind the children that the model "helps us talk about things we know in our heads about language." Also help the children understand that the model is not

Both of these stories have sad endings. But if we revise some of the pictures, we can change the stories. We can give them happy endings.

■ Look again at the first set of pictures. How could you revise them to give the story a happy ending? You can change both Picture C and Picture D completely, if you want to. Then look at the second set of pictures. Tell how you could change these pictures to make a happy ending for the story.

■ Now choose the kind of story you like best—either a sad one or a happy one. Draw the pictures that tell the story. Then write your story.

Asking Questions

It's easy to make sentences. You make hundreds of them every day. But sometimes it's not easy to talk about sentences. That's why we use the sentence model.

The model we started with was very simple. It had only a few nominals and verb phrases. It also had one rule.

● A sentence has a nominal and a verb phrase.

The model told us some important things about what you know inside your head. But you know a lot more than the model shows. So we made the model bigger, and we talked about different kinds of nominals and verb phrases. That's a good thing about the model. We can keep adding new parts to it.

Here's another important thing you know. In fact, you've known it since you were two years old! You can make different kinds of sentences. One kind of sentence says something. It's called a **statement.** Another kind of sentence asks something. It's called a **question.**

Daybook: Practice with Questions,
page 48

■ Here are some sentences without any punctuation at the end. First try to tell which ones are statements and which ones are questions. Then put a period after each statement and a question mark after each question.

1. The lady swallowed a fly
2. Do you like pizza
3. Is this sentence a question
4. The doctor tickled my foot
5. Have you seen my lunch
6. The mailman fell asleep
7. The boy fell asleep, didn't he
8. Did Tony climb the tree
9. You know how to make questions, don't you
10. What's the answer to this question

There is one important thing you already know about questions. You can make any statement into a question. But the easiest kind to make is one that can be answered with "yes" or "no." It's called a **yes-or-no question.**

Here's a statement.

The boy combed his hair.

And here's the yes-or-no question we can make from it.

Did the boy comb his hair?

If you can make questions in your head, then we can put them in the sentence model. Here's how we do it. We'll use the capital letter **Q.** And we'll say the Q stands for "the idea of a question." Q in front of a statement sentence is a sign to make it into a question. We'll use a special double arrow to point to the question that's made.

Q + The teacher dropped the book.
⟹ Did the teacher drop the book?

Answers

Sentences 1, 4, and 6 are statements. Sentences 2, 3, 5, 7, 8, 9, and 10 are all questions.

fixed, permanent, and unchangeable; we can always add things to it. You can compare the model to the map of a city or state; there are always details we could add to a map, and we might want to add things if they would make the map more useful.

Next, read the final paragraph on page 122 and write the two words—*statement* and *question*—on the chalkboard. If you followed the suggested preparation, then you'll already have some questions and statements on the chalkboard and you can use these again as illustrations. You can also use these sentences to stress the fact that the children already know about questions and statements in their heads.

The first activity (■), on page 123, can be done orally with the entire class. The second half of page 123 makes two important points: first, that there are different kinds of questions, and second, that—in the sentence model—we use a Q to represent "the idea of a question," an idea which the children already have in their heads. (You might discuss other signs, like the skull-and-crossbones representing poison, or a X representing a railroad crossing.)

Then read the rest of page 123 with the children. (The last paragraph will help them understand how a question can fit into the sentence model. If anyone should ask, you can explain that the double arrow can be read as "becomes" or "is changed to.")

The activity (■) on page 124 can be done either individually or as an entire class.

Follow-up For additional statements that the children can use to practice making questions, turn to page 133 of this guide.

Purpose To illustrate the function—and usefulness—of punctuation in writing.

[Everyone knows that writing and speaking are different, but we seldom stop to think about the ways in which they differ. In speaking, we "punctuate" by making our voices high or low, soft or loud, and so on. But we can't put these things on a page, so we use punctuation marks instead.]

Preparation Select a short passage from *Charlotte's Web* or *The Wind in the Willows* and read it to the class with flat expression. Then read it again with all the feeling the passage deserves. Ask the children to compare the two readings and particularly to comment on the difference.

Presentation Have the children open their books to page 124, examine the illustration, and read the words that the boy is saying. Then have them read the first sentence in the first paragraph of the lesson. Most children will quickly recognize that the words in the two sentences are the same. Ask them to find two or three things in the first sentence that aren't in the sentence which the boy is saying (a comma, an apostrophe, an underscore, and a question mark). Then ask why people use marks like these when they write or when they print books.

You can then have volunteers read the two paragraphs on page 124 and the first three paragraphs on page 125. Then the class can try to "solve" the two sentences in the middle of the page. As

 Here's a chance for you to practice changing statements into questions. (The first one is done for you.)

1. Q + The chicken crossed the road.
   ⟹ *Did the chicken cross the road?*
2. Q + The frog slept all day.
   ⟹
3. Q + The teacher walked to school.
   ⟹
4. Q + Mr. Levine hit the ball.
   ⟹
5. Q + Abraham Lincoln liked jokes.
   ⟹

Punctuation

When you read a sentence aloud, what <u>don't</u> you hear? You can hear each word. But there are some things in a written sentence that aren't in a spoken sentence.

Here is a picture of a boy speaking the first sentence of this section. How is it different from the way the first sentence is written or printed?

Answers

2. Did the frog sleep all day?
3. Did the teacher walk to school?
4. Did Mr. Levine hit the ball?
5. Did Abraham Lincoln like jokes?

124

When you speak, your voice goes up and down a little, like music. You also say some words a little louder than others. And from time to time, you stop to take a breath.

But you can't hear sentences that are printed on a page. That's why we use punctuation. Capital letters, periods, commas, and other marks of punctuation are like clues. They help us know how a written sentence would sound if someone read it aloud.

A capital letter can tell us when we are beginning a sentence. A period tells us when we get to the end of a sentence. A comma tells us to stop a little when we are reading a sentence.

Here are two sentences without punctuation. There aren't any spaces between the words.

canyoureadthesesentences
ifyoucanthenyouareagoodreader

Here's what you can do to make them easy to read.

Change a small *c* to a capital *C*.
Change a small *i* to a capital *I*.
Add thirteen spaces to separate all the words.
Add a question mark.
Add a comma.
Add a period.

When someone talks, we can't <u>hear</u> any punctuation. Instead we hear the music of the sentences. When someone writes, we can't <u>see</u> the music. Instead we see the punctuation.

Here are some more sentences for you to write correctly.

1. ilikeapplesbananasgrapesandoranges
2. doyouknowaboynamedsam
3. thisweektheresnoschoolonwednesdaythursdayorfriday

Answers

1. I like apples, bananas, grapes, and oranges.
2. Do you know a boy named Sam?
3. This week there's no school on Wednesday, Thursday, or Friday.

soon as someone is able to read the sentences correctly, divide the class into small groups or pairs and have the children write the two sentences, following the instructions in the text. Each group can pass its results to another group for checking.

The groups can then continue with the unpunctuated sentences at the bottom of page 125. When each group is done, and the results have been checked by another group, the children can explain the corrections they made, in a manner similar to the explanation given in the text for the two earlier sentences.

Follow-up You may want to provide some additional examples of sentences for the children to write correctly. You can prepare a ditto of a passage from a reading book, using no capital letters, spaces between words, or punctuation marks. Then the children can try to rewrite the passage using capital letters, punctuation marks, and so on, in the appropriate places. Such an activity can be combined with a review of the lessons on Capital Letters and Punctuation Marks in the Skills Section.

Alternatively, you can have each child choose one sentence from the text to write without capitals, spacing, or punctuation marks. Then the children can exchange papers with their friends and try to "solve" each other's sentences. The original passage from the text can then be used as a reference to check the correctness of the solution. (It would be advisable to suggest that, for now, the children avoid selecting sentences which contain dashes.)

Purposes (1) To provide additional experience with imaginative verse; (2) To illustrate the use of personification as a literary device.

[The literary device of personification, in which inanimate objects as well as nonhuman creatures are endowed with human properties, is common in literature. Most children are familiar with the device through fairy tales and nursery rhymes. Don Marquis is particularly adept at giving a contemporary tone to personification. The principle is emphasized in this lesson, but it is not recommended that you use the term *personification* with young children.]

Preparation Because children are already familiar with "talking animals" in other stories and poems, little—if any—preparation is needed for this selection. If you feel that some preparation is necessary, then you might begin by having the children discuss what it might feel like to be an animal—a fish, an elephant, an eagle, or whatever.

Presentation In contrast with the usual method of presenting a poem, have the children read page 127 silently. When they are done—and before discussing the poem—you can then read it to them.

After at least two readings, have the children turn to page 128 and discuss the first paragraph. Most children will genuinely enjoy discussing the clever dog—who not only acts like a dog at the beach but can also use a typewriter to say how he feels. Call on volunteers to explain Pete's typing technique. You can encourage a wide-ranging discussion at this point—perhaps wondering what a cat might say or how a fish might use a typewriter. (This poem is particularly useful in prompting a free and relaxed discussion, which can be invaluable for

126

Daybook: What If You Were . . .
page 50

A Poem

Don Marquis is a poet who likes animals. Once he had a puppy named Pete. He wondered what kind of poem his dog might write. Then he asked himself <u>how</u> a dog could write poetry. He decided that a dog could use a typewriter. Here's the poem Don Marquis wrote, pretending he was Pete.

pete at the seashore

i ran along the yellow sand
and made the sea gulls fly
i chased them down the waters edge
i chased them up the sky

i ran so hard i ran so fast
i left the spray behind
i chased the flying flecks of foam
and i outran the wind

an airplane sailing overhead
climbed when it heard me bark
i yelped and leapt right at the sun
until the sky grew dark

some little children on the beach
threw sticks and ran with me
o master let us go again
and play beside the sea

PETE THE PUP

children as they learn to talk before others, as they discover that their ideas have merit, and as they feel a sense of empathy with other readers and even with the poet and perhaps with Pete himself.)

The second and third paragraphs of the discussion will encourage the children to use their imaginations. In addition to the questions in the text, you might ask: "Have you ever wanted to be big? Have you ever tried to outrun the wind?"

There are some children who don't like cats and who might not be responsive to the third paragraph. If this occurs, you can ask about a rabbit stuck in a hole, or about a fish who lives in a river until—one day—he swims into a huge lake. The possibilities are almost endless, both for discussion and for the activity.

If an opportunity presents itself, you might want to relate this lesson to the one on punctuation. Explain to the children that most of the time we need to use punctuation when we write. Except for the poem, for example, this lesson is punctuated properly. But poets and other writers sometimes change language in many different ways when they write—if they have a reason for changing things. (But any comparison with the lesson on punctuation shouldn't be treated at length, and you should certainly discourage any suggestion to punctuate the poem by explaining that it wouldn't be a poem anymore.)

The activity (■) on page 128 can be treated in various ways. Instead of a cat, for example, some children might care to write about a rabbit who eats new tulips, or a monkey who escapes from a zoo, or a baby horse who wants to win a race.

Follow-up If the children enjoyed the activity in this lesson, then you might want to suggest that they repeat the activity, pretending to be some other animal.

Additional Resources

Books Jarrell, Randall, *The Bat-Poet,* Macmillan. Illustrated by Maurice Sendak, this book tells the story of a little bat who makes up poems about his animal friends. Larrick, Nancy, compiler, *On City Streets,* Evans. This anthology includes the poem "freddy the rat perishes" by "archy," alias Don Marquis. Marquis, Don, *The Lives and Times of Archy and Mehitabel,* Doubleday.

Purpose To encourage the development and use of imagination in thinking and writing.

Preparation Ask the children to recall any of the wishes they had when they were much younger. "Did anyone wish for a closet full of candy bars? Did anyone want to be as big as a giant? Did anyone want to go to a star or to the moon?" The children's answers will lead to still other ideas. The more impossible the ideas, the better for the lesson. Try to end the discussion while the level of enthusiasm is still high.

Presentation Have the children read the material on page 128 as well as the facsimile composition on page 129. If someone comments on the handwriting, then you can say: "The boy's handwriting isn't very good, but his imagination is." Then point out that handwriting and imagination are quite different things: Handwriting — penmanship — is one of the skills of English, whereas imagination is one of the arts.

Don Marquis pretended that a dog could use a typewriter to write poetry. But it would be too hard for the dog to make capital letters. If a dog could use a typewriter, then he would use only small letters. What else wouldn't the dog use?

Did Pete really make the sea gulls fly? Did he really outrun the wind? Did his barking frighten the airplane? Did he really make the sky turn dark? Why do you think the poet says all these things? How does he let you know how Pete feels about the seashore?

Suppose you were a cat. You climbed a tree and chased a bird away. Then you couldn't climb down again. How would you feel? What words could you use to describe your feelings?

■ Use your imagination to pretend that you're the cat who climbed the tree. Then write a poem or a story that tells how you feel.

Someplace Else

Here's the best thing about having an imagination. You can think of things that nobody has ever thought of before. But thinking about things that are completely new isn't always easy. How do you begin?

One way is to play the Someplace Else Game. In this game, you use your imagination to make up a whole new place. You can have anything in this place that you want. You can leave out anything that you don't want. You can even change your name, if you want to.

Here are some questions to start you thinking about Someplace Else. Does your Someplace Else have a special name? Is it a city, a country, or a planet? Do you live there?

Here are some answers that one boy gave.

Someplace Else is a special country called Beanland on the planet Theal. I live there all alone and my name is John Gloat.

Now think about Someplace Else. Here are some more questions to help you. What other questions can you think of? Make a list of your answers to <u>all</u> the questions.

Do any girls live in your Someplace Else? Do any boys live there? Are there any adults? How big are the people?

Are there any animals in Someplace Else? What kind? Are there any special kinds of animals that we don't have here? What color are they? Can they talk? What are some things that are <u>not</u> there?

What do people eat there? Do they have television? Are there any stores? Is there any snow? What color is the sky?

What kind of clothes do the people wear? Do they have special kinds of shoes? Why? Where do people live? Do they have any special furniture?

Is there a king or a president? If so, is it a boy or a girl or a man or a woman? Who makes the laws?

How do people get from place to place? Do they walk? Do they ride horses or fish or eagles? Do they have any cars, subways, or airplanes?

■ Now write a composition about Someplace Else. Use your list of answers to help you. Then, if you want to, you can draw a map of Someplace Else, too.

Sometimes the use of imagination should be private rather than public, and for this reason you might prefer <u>not</u> to discuss the questions on page 129 as an entire class. You can suggest that some children work in groups. (The imagination of some children will "take off" immediately from the stimulation offered by the questions.) Other children might prefer to talk to you individually—and privately. Some might find the variety of questions to be too great, and if so you should limit them to three or four questions, with their answers, for the activity (■). Alternatively, you can extend the lesson over several periods, having the children use one set of questions during a single period to write one "chapter" of the composition.

In any case, you should encourage each child to be as fantastic or as serious as he wants. (Some will get quite serious in discussing the laws of Someplace Else. Others will imagine ludicrous and amusing animals. You can stress that <u>all</u> of these responses are good ways to use imagination.)

Follow-up If the children have used only three or four of the questions on page 129 as the basis for their compositions, then you can suggest that at some later time they may want to expand their compositions, perhaps adding more "chapters." (The children themselves will probably have some additional "questions" to suggest.)

In addition to drawing maps, as suggested in the activity, some children may want to illustrate their completed compositions. As with the compositions, encourage the children to be as fantastic or as serious as they wish in drawing the illustrations.

Purpose   To expand the sentence model by introducing the category of adverbial.

[The category of adverbial—like that of nominal—is more inclusive than the corresponding category presented in older textbooks. By using the term *adverbial* (instead of the more limited term *adverb*), we can refer to single words (*today*) and also to phrases (*in the morning*). Although we don't do so at this level, we can also extend the use of the term to clauses (We stopped *when the bell rang*). As usual, the text avoids formal definitions, stressing instead the ways that adverbials can function in sentences.]

Preparation   Review the notion of sentence positions by making a position picture (like the one on page 113) on the chalkboard. Fill in the following basic sentences:

The man/ was/ sorry.
The man/ fixed/ my bike.

Ask the children to identify the kinds of words that occur in each position of these sentences. Then say: "Today we'll learn about another position: the fourth position. There are special kinds of words that go in the fourth position of a basic sentence."

Presentation   Have the children open their books to page 130 and examine the position picture at the top of the page. Have them note that this picture is different from the one you drew on the chalkboard. It has an additional position. Then have the children experiment placing the six adverbials from the center of the page into the fourth position of each sentence in the picture. (Each adverbial will fit into every sentence.)

Adverbials

We've talked about sentences with three positions. And we can add a fourth position, at the end. Look at this position picture.

FIRST POSITION	SECOND POSITION	THIRD POSITION	FOURTH POSITION
The teacher	saw	the rabbit	
Ellen	bought	a duck	
Miss Davis	was	sleepy	
The doctor	ate	a pizza	

Here are some words that we can put into the fourth position. Which ones would you like to use?

at school	here	in the forest
yesterday	there	in the morning

Some of these words tell us "where." Which ones are they? Some tell us "when." Which words are they? Words or groups of words that tell "where" or "when" are called **adverbials.** We can also use the names **where-adverbials** and **when-adverbials.**

Sometimes, we can have another kind of adverbial in the fourth-position. It's called a **how-adverbial.** Here are some how-adverbials.

quickly	slowly	sadly	well
happily	neatly	loudly	poorly

Can you think of some other where-adverbials, when-adverbials, or how-adverbials?

Daybook: Practice with Adverbials, page 52

130

So far, we've looked at two kinds of sentences. One kind has a nominal in the first position, a verb in the second position, and another nominal in the third position. The other kind has a nominal in the first position, a "be" word in the second position, and an adjective in the third position. You know that, with either kind of sentence, you can add an adverbial at the end—in the fourth position. We can show all this in a position picture.

FIRST POSITION	SECOND POSITION	THIRD POSITION	FOURTH POSITION
Nominal	Verb	Nominal	(Adverbial)
Nominal	"Be" Word	Adjective	(Adverbial)

■ Here's something for you to do. Try to add an adverbial to the fourth position of each of these sentences.

	FIRST POSITION	SECOND POSITION	THIRD POSITION	FOURTH POSITION
1.	The nurse	visited	my house	
2.	Mr. Roberts	built	a house	
3.	He	is	happy	

■ Here are some more sentences. Try to divide them into positions. Be careful. One has three positions. The others—the kind with adverbials—have four.

1. The boy found a penny yesterday.
2. My brother saw an elephant this morning.
3. The frog swallowed a fly.

Answers

For the first activity, the children's answers will vary.

The words in the sentences in the second activity fit into the following positions:
1. The boy / found / a penny / yesterday.
2. My brother / saw / an elephant / this morning.
3. The frog / swallowed / a fly.

Follow the discussion in the text of *where-adverbials* and *when-adverbials,* and when the children understand these labels, continue with *how-adverbials,* which are presented on the bottom of page 130. Then let some children jump, sing, laugh, shout, and so on, in front of the class. The rest of the class can then give sentences saying where the thing was done, when it was done, and how it was done. Help the children realize that they already know how to use adverbials. (It's one of the things they have in their heads.) This lesson simply gives a name for these things.

Then request a volunteer to read the first paragraph on page. 131. Have the children examine the sentence position picture as it appears on the top half of this page. (Note that this position picture uses parentheses around the word *Adverbial;* this is the standard way of indicating an optional element.)

Both activities (■) on page 131 can be done either as class or individual work. If, for the first activity, you duplicate the position picture on the chalkboard, then you can add and erase adverbials freely.

Follow-up Here are some more adverbials that you can either write on the chalkboard or include on a ditto sheet. Have the children decide whether each one is a where-adverbial, a when-adverbial, or a how-adverbial.

under the chair	on the ceiling
in the desk	quietly
last year	wisely
in a hurry	every day
at midnight	in the bathtub

After the children have decided what category of adverbial each of these belongs to, they can make some sentences using them.

Purposes (1) To review the wide variety of genre possible in literature; (2) To re-emphasize the importance of imagination in both literature and composition; (3) To review one way of representing questions in the sentence model, and also the category of adverbial.

Presentation In discussing the literature section of this Review, you might want to have the children look back over the selections they have read thus far and classify them according to type (poem, story, myth, and so on). Alternatively, you can list the following in two columns on the chalkboard:

"The Road Not Taken"	history
"Talk"	poem
Maurice's Room	folktale
"pete at the seashore"	poem
"Perseus and Atlas"	story
Pony Express	myth

Have the children match the title of the selection with the genre it represents. Comment on the variety of kinds of literature that the children have already read, and then ask them to tell how the author of each selection used his imagination. (The important point, of course, is for the children to realize that <u>all</u> authors use their imaginations, no matter what genre they choose to write in. It is not particularly important, at this point, that the children be able to identify the various genres.)

You can lead into a review of the composition lessons in this chapter by asking the children to suggest ways <u>they</u> can use imagination in their own writing. You might also want to take this opportunity to have the children write another "chapter" of their "Someplace Else" compositions.

Review

Literature

When people talk about literature, they usually mean stories or poems or folk tales or myths. Most of the time, people are thinking of things that have lots of imagination in them. But literature can be almost anything that somebody has written and somebody else wants to save. A *diary* can be literature. And so can a *history*. What is a history?

In this chapter, you read a history of the Pony Express. It was a true story. Did the author use his imagination at all? How do you think a Pony Express rider would talk? Pretend that you're Warren Upson. How would you describe your horse to a friend?

How did Don Marquis use his imagination to write "pete at the seashore"? Could you pretend to be Pete someplace else? Where would you have Pete be?

■ Try to write a poem or a story pretending that you are Pete.

Composition

When you write your own stories, you can make them end any way you want. And your stories can even happen someplace that isn't real.

Do you remember the Someplace Else you wrote about in this chapter?

■ Now make up a story that happens in your Someplace Else. Decide whether you want the story to have a sad ending or a happy ending. Then write your story.

Language

In this chapter, you learned that we can add *adverbials* in the fourth position of a statement sentence. You also learned about a new kind of sentence: *the question*.

■ Here are some statement sentences with adverbials in the fourth position. Tell what the adverbial is for each sentence.

1. The boy visited the teacher yesterday.
2. The girl found a worm in the garden.
3. The man climbed the ladder quickly.
4. The frog put one foot in the water.

Now make a position picture like the one on page 131. Try to put all the words in these sentences in the right positions.

■ If we add Q to each of these statement sentences, then we'll get questions. Try to do it. (The first one is done for you.)

1. Q + The boy visited the teacher yesterday.
   ⟹ *Did the boy visit the teacher yesterday?*

2. Q + The girl found a worm in the garden.
   ⟹

3. Q + The man climbed the ladder quickly.
   ⟹

4. Q + The dog put one foot in the water.
   ⟹

Why do we use *punctuation* when we write sentences? For more practice using punctuation marks, turn to page 306.

In addition to the activities in the Language Review, you can use the following to reinforce the grammar concepts presented in this chapter. First have the children identify the adverbial in each sentence and tell what kind of adverbial it is. Then have them change each statement into a yes-or-no question.

1. The Pony Express carried mail between Missouri and California.
2. A stage coach made the journey in three weeks.
3. The Pony Express covered the same distance in half the time.
4. Each rider used five different horses every day.
5. The riders changed horses at the exchange stations.
6. The riders used special saddles on their horses.
7. The riders faced many dangers in the wilderness.
8. The riders crossed the country at breakneck speeds.
9. They earned one hundred dollars each month.
10. The telegraph replaced the Pony Express in 1861.

Answers

The following are all adverbials:
1. yesterday
2. in the garden
3. quickly
4. in the water

The words fit into the following positions:
1. The boy / visited / the teacher / yesterday.
2. The girl / found / a worm / in the garden.
3. The frog / put / one foot / in the water.

The following questions can be made:
2. Did the girl find a worm in the garden?
3. Did the man climb the ladder quickly?
4. Did the dog put one foot in the water?

Purposes (1) To provide additional experience with poetic metaphor; (2) To suggest ways in which a metaphor can be extended.

[A good metaphor is open-ended; that is, the more we think about it, the more applications we see. And this means that we must use our imaginations when we consider a metaphor, that we must go beyond the words the poet gives us. "Thunder Pools" provides an unusually good opportunity for the reader to go beyond the image presented in the poem since the subject is a common one but, at the same time, one that everyone has many associations with.]

Preparation You might prepare for this poem by rereading "Unfolding Bud" (pages 25-26) and then discussing the central metaphor of that poem once again. You might also save this poem for a day when there are puddles on the playground or sidewalks. If so, you can ask the children to describe how they feel about puddles. "Do you ever stare into them? Do you like to jump into them? Do puddles make you think of mirrors?" Then you can comment that today's poem is about puddles which the poet calls "pools."

Presentation If you've prepared for the lesson by discussing puddles and pools, then you can begin by having the children examine the illustration on pages 134-135. Help them see how a puddle—or "pool"—both reflects and distorts, and how the distortion can make us think of old things in a new way. Ask the children how they would feel if they were "in" the illustration. "Would you look into the pools? Would you throw small stones to make ripples? How would the air feel? Would there be a breeze?"

A Poem

Here's how one poet sees the earth after a thunder storm. Do you know what *unearthly* means? *Hogsheads* are very large barrels.

Thunder Pools

Now the sudden shower's done,
A new world and a deeper one
Is lying under every tree,
Small blue cousins of the sea.

Made of waters from on high,
These pools of unearthly dye
Show the elm tree's arching crown
And the white clouds upside down.

Such pools are not pools to wade,
It would make the feet afraid
To walk through such a lovely wonder
Poured from the hogsheads of the thunder.

ROBERT P. TRISTRAM COFFIN

Read the poem to the class and suggest that they listen for word-pictures which the poet uses to make them see and feel things. After the first reading, call attention to any words that might be unfamiliar (including, perhaps, *arching crown*). Encourage the children to look for contextual clues to the meanings of these words. You might also focus on the phrase, "a lovely wonder," which the children are apt to treat superficially; try to help them see the power which a word like "wonder" has, if they stop to think about it.

After discussing the words, read the poem again as the children follow along, and then turn to the discussion on page 136. The questions on this page should prompt similar questions from the children—or from you. Help the children see that there are no right-or-wrong answers to most of these questions. The important thing is to be aware of how one feels.

Follow-up You might suggest that the children begin to look for other poems about the weather and its changing moods which they can read to the class on particularly appropriate days. (See Additional Resources for some suggestions.)

Additional Resources

Books Behn, Harry, *The Little Hill,* Harcourt. On a rainy, spring day children might enjoy "Spring Rain." Ciardi, John, *The Reasons for the Pelican,* Lippincott. In "Rain Sizes," John Ciardi describes in a rather amusing way how he feels about the rain. Farjeon, Eleanor, *Over the Garden Wall,* Lippincott. This poet describes the world "After Rain." Field, Rachel, *Poems,* Macmillan. Urban children will recognize the familiar sounds of "City Rain." Fisher, Aileen, *I Like Weather,* Crowell; *Runny Days, Sunny Days,* Abelard-Schuman; and *That's Why,* Nelson. In "Snow Color" from *That's Why,* the poetess describes the variety of colors we see reflected in the snow. Hollowell, Lillian, compiler, *A Book of Children's Literature,* Holt, Rinehart and Winston. This anthology contains a number of poems about the weather, including "January" by Elizabeth Coatsworth, "Spring" by William Blake, and "Autumn Woods" by James S. Tippett.

Purposes (1) To help children distinguish between descriptions and stories; (2) To provide opportunities for writing descriptions, stories, or both.

Preparation Show a picture of a landscape and ask the children to suggest words which describe it. List each word on the chalkboard as it is suggested. Then have the children listen (with their eyes closed) to a sound such as a bell or whistle, and have them suggest words to describe it, adding these to the list on the chalkboard. Again have the children close their eyes and run their fingers through their hair, along their arms, on the surface of their desks, and then have them suggest additional descriptive words to add to the list.

Then, on the chalkboard, write *is, has,* and *does* as column headings. Return to the picture, the sound, the things touched, and this time help the children to group their descriptive words under the headings *is, has,* and *does.* Finally, ask the class to decide whether they told stories about these things or whether they described them.

136

In "Unfolding Bud," you read how a water-lily takes on "richer color" and "new dimensions." In "Thunder Pools," the poet sees a "new world and a deeper one" under every tree. What do you think this means? How is the world in this poem like the lily in "Unfolding Bud"? In "Thunder Pools," the poet calls the puddles "small blue cousins of the sea." How is a puddle like a cousin of the sea?

When the poet looks into the pools, he see reflections of the trees and the clouds. Why do you think he says the clouds are "upside down"? What does the poet mean when he says that the pools are "poured from the hogsheads of the thunder"?

The poet says that thunder pools are not for wading. Why not? Would your feet be afraid to walk through them?

A Description or a Story

One kind of composition is a **description**. A description tells what something or someone is and has and does. Another kind of composition is a *story*. In most stories there is a *hero* who is the person or animal that the story is about.

Here's a composition written by one child.

> Some people think some dogs look alike. I know two black dogs that are sisters but they are different. One of the dogs is mine. She's black all over, and she's bigger than her sister. One ear used to bend over but now it's straight. She has long whiskers and a tail that curves. She sleeps a lot and can run fast.

And here's a composition written by another child.

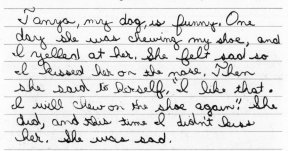

Tanya, my dog, is funny. One day she was chewing my shoe, and I yelled at her. She felt sad so I kissed her on the nose. Then she said to herself, "I like that. I will chew on the shoe again." She did, and this time I didn't kiss her. She was sad.

Can you tell which composition is a description and which is a story?

One composition describes a dog. Can you tell some of the things the dog is and has and does?

The other composition is a story. Who is the hero of the story? How do you know? Is the story real or did the writer make it up? How do you know?

Now you can try a description of your own. What three words should you remember when you write a description? Here are some things you could describe.

a train	a pencil	a telephone
a globe	a TV set	an elevator

If you would rather describe something else, do that instead.

Now write an ending for this story.

> Mark Mindle climbed the tree and walked out onto a branch. There he stepped on a cloud and floated away. Soon he came to . . .

Or, if you'd rather, make up your own story to finish.

Presentation Read through the text to the middle of page 137 with the children, perhaps calling on volunteers to read the two facsimile compositions. Answering the questions in the text will take time. For example, the children must deduce from the dialogue that the composition about Tanya is a story. The writer used his imagination to think of something for the dog to say "to herself." Encourage the children to express a variety of opinions in their answers.

The descriptions can be done orally, using the three-column arrangement as a way of deciding which words to use in descriptive sentences. Remind the children to use senses other than that of sight, as they did in describing how things sound and feel. Help them understand that sometimes it's a good idea to think of descriptive words before beginning to write a composition (and that's the primary reason for using the three columns: *is, has,* and *does*).

The children can work individually or in pairs to complete the unfinished story, or alternatively, the entire class can play a story-completion game. To play the game, each child in turn adds one or two sentences to the story, starts another sentence, and then stops, thereby enabling the next child to complete the sentence, add some of his own, and so on.

Follow-up If you've treated the compositions in this lesson as an oral activity, then you might want to have the children write a description or a story, or both. For their descriptions, the children can choose another item from the list on page 137. You can have the children make up their own stories to complete, or you can use this as a beginning: "As soon as his spaceship landed, Charlie stepped out onto the strange planet and. . . ."

Purposes (1) To review the function of the sentence model; (2) To illustrate that the sentence model, like any model, is incomplete.

[The arts and the sciences (like good metaphors) are open-ended. There is always something new to discover in good literature, and there is always something new to learn in physics and chemistry. Similarly, we can never learn all there is to know about language. Children forget—and are sometimes confused by —this fact. This lesson will remind them that the sentence model is useful, but it will never be complete. It is a mark of education to be challenged rather than discouraged by such a fact.]

Preparation Discuss various models with which the children may be familiar (for example, dress patterns, plans for a house, or an outline for a story.) If possible, display one or more models, and ask the children to explain how they would be <u>used</u> by people.

The sentence model has been referred to in five earlier lessons. Have the children use the Index, looking under the entry *Sentence model,* to locate these. Briefly re-examine each lesson, giving particular attention to the changes and additions. Compare the usefulness of the sentence model with some of the other models discussed earlier.

Presentation Pages 138 and 139 are well suited to oral reading, but be sure to allow frequent pauses to discuss the various points and to examine the map.

The analogy with map making is developed in some detail; help the children see that no map is complete, that we revise maps as we learn more; that we use maps to help us talk about something; and so on. Also help them understand how these facts relate to all models.

A Sentence Model

Here is a very old map of North America.

This map was made before explorers knew very much about North America. No explorer had ever walked from the Atlantic coast to the Pacific coast. No one knew exactly where all the rivers were. No one knew what the Great Lakes looked like. Some people even thought that California was an island.

Little by little, the explorers learned about our country. Little by little, they learned to make better maps.

A map is a kind of model. Nobody—except maybe an astronaut—can see all of North America at one time. But a map helps us get an idea of what the land looks like. A map helps when we want to <u>talk</u> <u>about</u> our country.

A map is a model that tells you about something that's too big to see. A sentence model tells you about something you <u>can't</u> see. It helps you talk about what happens inside your head when you think and listen and talk.

But making a sentence model is a lot like making a map. It took a very long time to explore all of North America. And it's even harder to explore what happens inside someone's head. Scientists are still discovering things about how people make sentences. When they discover something new, they put it in the sentence model.

Suppose you want to learn about the state where you live. Do you need a map that shows all of North America? Do you need a map that shows all of the United States? What do you need? When you study things, you don't always need a complete model. Instead you can use a part of the model—the part that shows what you're studying.

The sentence model which the scientists are trying to make will show <u>everything</u> about sentences. But most of the time we don't need a complete sentence model. We can use parts of the sentence model, just as we can use parts of a map.

 Whenever you're writing about someone you may want to use *possessive nominals*. To learn how to form possessives, turn to page 297.

The emphasis in the final paragraph of the lesson should be on "trying." The scientists will never stop trying because they'll never be done. You might want to relate this fact to other fields of study. (For example, mathematicians don't know all that can be known about arithmetic. They're still learning facts about such apparently simple things as addition and subtraction.)

Follow-up Some children may want to make copies of the sentence model as it appears on page 21, substituting their own personal lexicon for the one given in the text. This can be done as an individual or group activity, and the models can be as simple or as elaborate as the children wish them to be. However you choose to do the activity, you should first review with the children the categories of nominals and verb phrases that they have studied so far. (See pages 63, 81, and 91 of the text.)

Evaluation Because children are different, the rates at which they demonstrate progress will also be different. For some children, additional time and involvement may have been necessary before they were able to "show signs" of mastering certain concepts. But by now, most children will be exhibiting one or more of the performance objectives relating to the arts of English for Chapters 1–9. These objectives are listed under Statement of Goals, beginning on page *ii* and continuing on page 337. Please note that, for the reasons mentioned above, most of the objectives stated for Chapters 1–5 are also applicable to Chapters 6–9.

If the evaluation component is available, you may also wish to use it at this time. And, of course, you should become familiar with the additional objectives for Chapters 10–13.

Purposes (1) To provide an additional example of lyric poetry; (2) To illustrate how literature helps us see familiar things in new ways.

Preparation On the chalkboard, write the German song title *"O Tannenbaum"* and the English translation *"O Christmas Tree."* Then, if possible, play a recording of both versions of the song. After the children have listened to the recordings, you can ask them to describe a decorated Christmas tree by telling some things that it <u>is</u>, <u>has</u>, and <u>does</u>. Then explain that today's poem is about a particular Christmas tree—a "little tree." (It's important that the children do not think that it's about Christmas trees in general.)

Presentation As usual, you should read this poem to the children at least twice. For the first reading, its probably best for them to have their books closed so they won't be distracted by the eccentric appearance of the poem.

Next, have the children examine pages 141 and 142 to discover what's unusual about the poet's use of letters. After they've made a few comments, you can ask the children if, when they were listening to the poem, they could tell that the poet used only a few capital letters. (Undoubtedly, the children will wonder why the poet only wrote in such an unusual way; the discussion on page 142 will help them understand some of the reasons.) Before going on to this discussion, however, you may want to reread the poem while the children follow along in their books. Since there are very few marks of punctuation in the poem, it would be helpful if you read more slowly than usual and if you paused longer (for example, between *see* and *i* in line 7, between *look* and *the spangles* in line 13, and so on.)

140

Daybook: Special Capitals, page 54

A Poem

Suppose you wanted to write a poem about a Christmas tree. Everyone knows what a Christmas tree looks like. How could you make your poem different? The man who wrote this poem helps you think about a Christmas tree in a different way. And he makes people look at his poem in a different way, too.

little tree

little tree
little silent Christmas tree
you are so little
you are more like a flower

who found you in the green forest
and were you very sorry to come away?
see i will comfort you
because you smell so sweetly

i will kiss your cool bark
and hug you safe and tight
just as your mother would,
only don't be afraid

Then read the two paragraphs at the bottom of page 142 with the children, pausing to discuss any questions they may have. In discussing the poet's use of capital letters for the words *Christmas* and *Noel,* you may need to explain that *Noel* is the French word for "Christmas."

To initiate a discussion of the metaphors that the poet uses, you might ask the following questions:

1. What does the poet compare the little tree to in the first stanza of the poem?
2. In the second and third stanzas, the poet talks about the "feelings" that the little tree might have. What are some of these feelings? Do you think a tree could really have such feelings, or do only people have them?
3. The spangles also remind the poet of a person. In the fourth stanza of the poem, what does he say that the spangles do?

Help the children to see how in the fifth and sixth stanzas, Cummings extends the metaphor of the tree as a person: The tree has arms and fingers and feels proud. Perhaps the children will then be ready to suggest other metaphors, other things that a little "human" tree, one with arms and fingers and feelings, might think and do.

To conclude the lesson, you can read the poem once again as the children follow along in their books.

Follow-up The children can use some of the metaphors provoked during the discussion to compose their own poems about a tree. You might want to suggest that some children try writing their poem in the shape of a tree. (This is another way that Cummings occasionally used to make his poems "look special.") The easiest way to do this is to have each child draw a simple outline of a tree, preferably on ruled paper. Then, as they write their poems, they can "fill in" this outline. Remind the children that the larger the outline, the longer the poem will be. Suggest, also, that they might want to revise the outline after they have finished the poem, and they should certainly feel free to do so.

You might also want to read a few other of Cumming's poems to the children, but these should be selected carefully. A few that are particularly appropriate for children include "the sky was," "in just," "o by the by," "i thank You God for most this amazing," and "why did you go?" (See Additional Resources.)

Additional Resources

Books Cummings, E. E., *Poems 1923–1954,* Harcourt. The poems mentioned above are all included in this collection of Cumming's work.

Recordings *A Great Gathering of Poetry for Children,* 4–12″ LPs, cassettes, Caedmon. Volume 2 of this series contains Cumming's poem "o by the by" and Volume 4 includes "i thank You God for most this amazing." *O Tannenbaum,* 1–12″ LP, Decca.

look the spangles
that sleep all the year in a dark box
dreaming of being taken out and allowed to shine,
the balls the chains red and gold the fluffy threads,

put up your little arms
and i'll give them all to you to hold
every finger shall have its ring
and there won't be a single place dark or unhappy

then when you're quite dressed
you'll stand in the window for everyone to see
and how they'll stare!
oh but you'll be very proud

and my little sister and i will take hands
and looking up at our beautiful tree
we'll dance and sing
"Noel Noel"

e. e. cummings

This poet, e. e. cummings, makes his poem look different because he uses language in a special way. He thinks that capital letters should be used only for very special words. (Mr. cummings doesn't even use a capital letter when he writes *I.*) In this poem, there are only two different words that begin with capital letters. What are they? Do you think they both mean the same thing? Why do you think only these words begin with capitals?

Can you think of any other way that e. e. cummings makes his poem special? How does he make you think about a Christmas tree? What are some of the metaphors that the poet uses?

Finishing a Story

Sometimes stories have sad endings. And sometimes they have happy endings. When you write your own stories, you can choose the kind of ending you like best.

Here is the beginning of a story.

The Spider and the Fly

A spider once made a huge web under some stairs. Then he sat in the middle and waited. The longer he waited, the hungrier he got. Finally, a fly got stuck in the web. The spider ran to the fly and looked him straight in the eye.

"Please don't eat me," said the fly.

"Well," said the spider, "if you can give me one very good reason why I <u>shouldn't</u> eat you, then I'll let you go."

So the fly said, ". . .

How could you give this story a sad ending? What would you do to give it a happy ending?

Here's the beginning of another story.

Money in the Puddle

Wilma was on her way to a birthday party. She was wearing a new pink dress, and she had fifty cents to buy a present for her friend. Suddenly she tripped, and her money bounced into the middle of a big puddle.

Do you think this story should have a sad or a happy ending?

■ Now write an ending for one of these stories.

Preparation Briefly discuss some humorous or amusing books that most of the children are familiar with (for example, *Homer Price* or *Henry Huggins*). Then discuss a more serious book (perhaps *Charlotte's Web* or *Bright April*). Ask the children to compare their feelings about the sad and happy elements in such stories. If possible, help the children to understand that a story can be enjoyable even if it's not "happy."

Presentation Read page 143 with the children, perhaps calling on volunteers to read the incomplete stories. After the first one, ask the children to use their imaginations to think of some things a fly and spider might talk about.

Most children will have little difficulty in thinking of possible endings for these stories, and if possible you should help them become aware of this fact. (While it's important for children to develop their imaginations, it's also important for them to recognize when this is happening.)

The children can work individually or in pairs in completing the activity (■).

Follow-up Review the meaning of the term *revise* with the children, and then suggest that they try to revise the compositions that they wrote in response to the activity in this lesson. Those children who used happy endings can rewrite their stories so that the endings are sad; those who wrote sad endings can use a happy ending in the revision.

Purposes (1) To introduce another category of words in the lexicon: the auxiliary; (2) To demonstrate that children already know—in their heads—rules for using auxiliaries.

[Formerly, some textbooks used the term *helping verb* when discussing auxiliaries. While the term is descriptive, it can also be misleading, and there seems little reason not to use a term that the children will need to learn later.]

Preparation On the chalkboard draw a sentence position picture having only three positions. Label each of the positions, and then review with the children the use of the picture. You might want to use the following sentences as examples:

1. The bear/found/a balloon.
2. The giraffe/ate/my popcorn.
3. The goat/likes/my coat.

You can then tell the children that, in today's lesson, they'll learn about some other words that can fit into the second position.

Presentation Have the children turn to page 144, and direct their attention to the title of this lesson. You can write the word *auxiliaries* on the chalkboard and help the children pronounce it. Then comment that auxiliaries are special words we sometimes use with verbs.

Ask for a volunteer to read the first paragraph aloud; then pause to discuss the question at the end. Help the children to see that the second sentence of each pair has an extra word: *has* or *have*. Then examine the position picture in the middle of page 144 with the children,

Auxiliaries

Here are two pairs of sentences. The first sentence in each pair is a little different from the second sentence.

1. The boy visited the teacher.
1a. The boy has visited the teacher.

2. The cats climbed a tree.
2a. The cats have climbed a tree.

Do you see what the difference is?

A good way to see the difference is to divide the sentences into positions.

	FIRST POSITION	SECOND POSITION	THIRD POSITION
1.	The boy	visited	the teacher.
1a.	The boy	has visited	the teacher.
2.	The cats	climbed	a tree.
2a.	The cats	have climbed	a tree.

The differences are all in the second position. The first sentence in each pair has only one word in the second position. That word is a verb. But the second sentence has two words in the second position. It has a verb and also the word *has* or *have*.

There are lots of sentences with *has* or *have* before the verb. And there are several other words that can come before the verb in the second position. These words have special names. They're called **auxiliaries**.

Here are some auxiliaries.

can	should	will	must
may	would	shall	might

Daybook: Practice with Auxiliaries, page 55

144

And here's a position picture that shows how we can use auxiliaries in sentences.

FIRST POSITION	SECOND POSITION	THIRD POSITION
The dog	walked	to school.
The dog	will walk	to school.
The frog	blew	a bubble.
The frog	can blow	a bubble.
The doctor	fixed	the radio.
The doctor	should fix	the radio.

In your head, you know about using words like *have* and *can* and *must* before verbs. You use them every day. But you probably didn't know that they have a special name. When you study grammar, you learn names for things you already know in your head. And you learn how to talk about these things.

■ Now complete these sentences by putting an auxiliary in each blank space. Be careful. Sometimes you'll need *has*. And sometimes you'll need another auxiliary like *can* or *should* or *must*. (The first one has been done for you.)

	FIRST POSITION	SECOND POSITION	THIRD POSITION
1.	The rabbit	*has* eaten	the peanut.
2.	The children	＿＿＿ climb	the stairs.
3.	The dinosaurs	＿＿＿ visited	the king.
4.	Stanley	＿＿＿ paint	a picture.
5.	The doctor	＿＿＿ tickled	my foot.
6.	The girls	＿＿＿ write	a play.
7.	Carol	＿＿＿ finish	her homework.

helping them to see that both *have* and *has* go in the second position, along with the verb. Finally, call for volunteers to read the rest of the page, including the list of auxiliaries at the bottom.

As you work with the position picture at the top of page 145, you can substitute auxiliaries from the list at the bottom of page 144 for those used in the picture. (Each one will fit in every sentence.)

The important point of the lesson is made in the paragraph before the activity on page 145. The word *auxiliary* is a name for something that the children already know about in their heads.

The activity (■) is best done orally with the entire class. Before beginning, you can draw three vertical columns on the chalkboard and then write *has* in the first column, *have* in the second, and *can, will, may, must, should, would, might,* and *shall* in the third. Then you can explain that sometimes *has* will work, sometimes *have,* and sometimes any of the other auxiliaries. (The answers to items 2, 4, 6, and 7 in the exercise will, of course, vary.)

Some children may find it difficult to select auxiliaries, but you can encourage them by pointing out that they certainly know when an auxiliary "sounds right" in a sentence. For example, it wouldn't sound right to say "The children climb must the stairs." The reason they know when it sounds right is that they have the rules in their heads.

Follow-up For follow-up activities which you can use after this lesson, see page 155 of this guide.

Purpose To provide children with information about libraries, particularly with regard to the classification of books.

[This is the first of two lessons on the library. (The second is on pages 164 and 165.) You may want to teach them in succession, particularly if they precede or follow a visit to a library.]

Preparation You may prefer to teach this lesson before visiting a library, and then read it again afterwards. Or you may want to visit a library in preparation for the lesson. (Both ways work equally well.) You can also use any of the materials on the library listed under Additional Resources to prepare for the lesson; in fact, it's useful to show these visual aids more than once. Ideally, of course, you should visit a library several times so the children have ample opportunity to become familiar—in a practical way —with the key terms which are used in this lesson: *fiction, nonfiction, spine, cataloguer, author card, title card,* and *subject card.*

Presentation The lesson is largely expository, and you can have the children read it with you, pausing to discuss the key terms. If the reading follows a visit to a library, you will certainly want to relate the terms to the things the children have seen. You might ask questions like the following:

1. Who remembers where the fiction books were kept?
2. How many of you looked up books in the card catalogue?
3. Who remembers what it said on the cards?

The activity (■) on page 147 can be done in class or in a library. If you choose to do it in a library, you might check beforehand with the librarian to

146

The Library

Suppose you want to find a particular book in a library. Not all libraries are the same. But the books in every library are arranged in some kind of order. And once you learn the order, then you can find the books you want.

Libraries divide books into two kinds: **fiction** and **nonfiction**. A fiction book is a story that a writer has made up in his imagination. All other books are nonfiction.

In most school libraries, the fiction books are grouped together. You can find them in the fiction section. They're arranged in alphabetical order, using the last name of the author. In many libraries, a fiction book has the letter *F* at the bottom of the **spine**. (The spine is the back of the book.)

Sometimes in a town or city library, there is one section for adult fiction and another section for fiction that children enjoy. If there's a special section for children, the books sometimes have a *J* on the spine. *J* stands for *juvenile.*

Here are four books of fiction. Tell which book would come first, which would come second, and so on.

There are many kinds of nonfiction. Most libraries arrange nonfiction books by using special numbers. When a library gets new books, each book is given a number. The books are then placed on the shelves in numerical order.

Here's what happens when a library gets a book. First, the book goes to a **cataloguer**. The cataloguer makes out an **author card** that looks like this.

978	Havighurst, Walter
	The first book of the Oregon Trail; pictures by Helen Borten. Watts, F. 1960 60p col illus map

Then the cataloguer types a second card. This time, he puts the name of the book first. This is called a **title card**.

978	**The first book of the Oregon Trail**
	Havighurst, Walter
	The first book of the Oregon Trail; pictures by Helen Borten. Watts, F. 1960 60p col illus map

Sometimes the cataloguer makes out a third card, called a **subject card.** Here is part of a subject card.

978	**OREGON TRAIL**
	Havighurst, Walter
	The first book of the Oregon Trail; pictures by Helen Borten. Watts, F. 1960 60p col illus map

The cataloguer then gives the book a number. He writes the number on each card. Then he puts the cards—in alphabetical order—into the card catalogue. He writes the number on the spine of the book. And finally he puts the book —in numerical order—on a shelf.

■ Suppose you want to find a nonfiction book. Tell what you would do in each of these situations.

1. You know the exact name of the book.
2. You know the author but not the book title.
3. You want several books about ants, crickets, and wasps.

get some titles of books as well as the names of some authors whose books are on the shelves. You should also help the children see that the various cards list information other than author, title, and subject; for example, the cards indicate if there are illustrations or maps; they give the number of pages; they sometimes say when an author was born; and so on.

Follow-up As suggested earlier, you can arrange for the children to visit a library as a follow-up to this lesson.

Additional Resources

Books Cleary, Florence Damon, *Discovering Books and Libraries,* Wilson. Shor, Pekay, *Libraries and You,* Prentice-Hall.

Filmstrips *The School Library Series,* 6 color filmstrips, McGraw-Hill. This series, designed to acquaint children with the organization of and arrangement of books in a library, includes the following titles: "Using Books," "The Dewey Decimal System," "The Card Catalog," "The Dictionary, Part I," "The Dictionary, Part II," and "The Encyclopedia."

Overhead Transparencies *Library Instruction-2nd Edition,* 26 transparencies, 23 overlays, Scott. This series helps explain the numbering system used for locating books and introduces children to the use of the card catalogue.

Answers

1. If you know the exact name of the book, then you can locate it by first finding its number on the title card in the card catalogue.
2. If you know the author, then you can look in the card catalogue under the author's last name.
3. If you want several books on the same subject, then you can look in the card catalogue under the subject cards.

Purposes (1) To introduce haiku as a literary form; (2) To describe the most common form of haiku poems.

[The only fixed requirement for a haiku poem is that it have exactly seventeen syllables. The number of lines may vary, although the three line arrangement is most common.]

Preparation If a unit on the Far East is being taught in social studies, then this lesson could be taught most effectively as part of such a unit. Perhaps, also, there are some Japanese members of your community who might display and discuss such things as silk screen painting, sumie, origami, kite making, dwarf trees, and so on. You could also display various picture books on Japan, particularly those that show examples of some of the older architecture and the formal gardens.

Presentation Help the children pronounce the work *haiku* (hī′ kü). Then ask for volunteers to read the introductory paragraphs on pages 148–149 of the text. You might read each poem to the class first, and then ask for volunteers to reread each poem.

Haiku

Haiku is a special kind of poetry. A haiku poem is short and serious. It's usually like a little picture. The poet sees something he likes. Then he tries to describe what he sees in a new way. A haiku can be about anything. But most are about the things in nature.

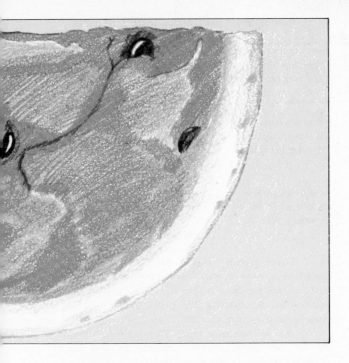

Haiku poems were first written hundreds of years ago in Japan. Now people in other countries like to read and write haiku. Here's one that describes a watermelon.

Cold watermelon:
Thick slices of summer fun
With shiny black seeds.

The discussion on page 150 focuses on the form of a haiku poem. This helps to prepare the children for writing haiku in the composition lesson which follows. If possible, you should also discuss the content of each poem. You might ask questions such as these:

1. How are these poems like other poems you've read? How are they different?
2. When you read haiku, do you "see pictures" in your heads?
3. Do the poets like to think about nature?

In analyzing the form of haiku, encourage the children to respond physically as you count the syllables. They can tap their feet, keep time with their hands, and so on. Children rarely have trouble in getting a feel for syllables (in spite of the fact that there is no completely satisfactory definition of a syllable!).

Before analyzing the form of the final haiku in the lesson, you might want to draw a pattern on the chalkboard and then copy the haiku onto the pattern:

—— —— —— —— ——
—— —— —— —— —— —— ——
—— —— —— —— ——

Follow-up As a follow-up to this lesson, as well as preparation for the next, you might have the class as a whole try to write several haiku poems. Listed under Additional Resources are some books containing other samples of haiku which you may also want to share with the children.

Additional Resources

Books Atwood, Ann, *Haiku: The Mood of the Earth,* Scribner's. Behn, Harry, compiler, *Cricket Songs,* Harcourt. Beilenson Peter, translator, *Japanese Haiku,* Peter Pauper. Issa, Yayu and others, *Don't Tell the Scarecrow and Other Japanese Poems,* Four Winds. Henderson, Harold G., *Haiku in English,* Tuttle. Lewis, Richard, editor, *The Moment of Wonder,* Dial.

Films *The Day Is Two Feet Long,* Weston Woods. This film, in full color, is an excellent example of "cinematic haiku."

Here are some haiku written by Japanese poets.

In spring the chirping
Frogs sing like birds. In summer
They bark like old dogs.
> ONITSURA

When my canary
Flew away, that was the end
Of spring in my house.
> SHIKI

Leaf falling on leaf
On mounds of leaves, rain splashing
In pools of rain.
> GYODAI

You've probably noticed that haiku poetry has a special form. Most English haiku poems have three lines. And every line usually has a particular number of syllables. The first line has <u>five</u> syllables. The second has <u>seven</u> syllables. And the third has <u>five</u> syllables.

Here are two more haiku. They're about autumn. In the first one, the syllables are separated for you. Try to count the syllables in the second haiku.

The / geese / fly/ing / south
In / a / row / long / and / V- / shaped
Pul/ling / in / win/ter.
> SALLY ANDRESEN

At the water's edge
Wet stones, worn smooth and dark by
The rubbing of time.

Writing Haiku

Haiku poems can be about almost anything. You can write haiku about rain or snow, about buildings or trees, about apples or turtles. You can write about anything you want to. But most of the time, haiku are about nature.

Do you remember the one thing that makes haiku special? It's that every haiku usually has seventeen syllables. In most English haiku poems, the first line always has five syllables. The second line has seven. And the third line has five. (5 + 7 + 5 = 17.)

■ Now look at this photograph. Use it to practice writing some haiku of your own.

Daybook: Writing Haiku, page 56

Purpose To provide an opportunity for writing haiku poems.

Preparation The previous lesson, of course, served as preparation for this one. In addition, as suggested in the Follow-up on page 150, it's a good idea to write several haiku as a class activity before asking the children to write such poems on their own.

Presentation The children can probably read the text on page 151 by themselves, but make sure that they understand the requirement of having exactly seventeen syllables. Then suggest that they work either in pairs or individually to write their own haiku. You might display other pictures or ask the children to suggest things they'd like to write about.

Be sure to allow lots of time for the activity (■). Some children will dash off four or five haiku while others are completing one. Tell the children that you'll be pleased to help if they want you to. You should give them the option of keeping their poems private.

Follow-up Perhaps the best follow-up for this lesson is to return to it every so often during the year. After the children have completed a number of haiku, you can gather the poems into a booklet.

If the children want to illustrate the booklet, you might introduce them to sumie, a technique of painting that's very popular in Japan. Examples of sumie can be found in most books about Japan or Japanese art, and instructional books on sumie are also available. If time does not permit you to explore the possibilities of sumie, a similar effect can be achieved by using a monochromatic water-color wash or India ink diluted and applied with a brush.

Purpose To increase the children's understanding of their linguistic competence by illustrating that they know the rules for making tag questions.

Preparation You can begin by discussing with the children how much the sentence model has grown. It began very simply, on page 21, with a few nominals and verb phrases and a single rule, and then expanded gradually as the children learned more terms to use for discussing the language they have in their heads. In addition to statement sentences, it came to include, on page 122, questions that can be answered with a "yes" or a "no." You can conclude the discussion by reviewing the position pictures on pages 144 and 145, calling particular attention to the auxiliaries. Then suggest that, in today's lesson, the children will learn some things about the way auxiliaries work when we make questions.

Presentation On the chalkboard, write the sentence: *George has eaten the pizza.* Then read the first paragraph on page 152 with the children, underlining the auxiliary in the sentence on the chalkboard as the children identify it. Then read the rest of the page with the children, duplicating on the chalkboard each step as it is presented in the text. Then repeat each step as the children read the second example about the girl. This will help them understand the process of making a tag question.

Present one or two additional examples on the chalkboard, and then call for volunteers to repeat the examples, writing the sentences and drawing the arrows. Then introduce the term *tag question* and help the children to see why this is an appropriate name. You might ask: "Do you have little brothers or

152

Another Kind of Question

Here's a sentence with <u>two</u> words in the second position. What is the auxiliary? What is the verb?

George has eaten the pizza.

Suppose we want to make this statement into a question. Then we can add some words at the end. How do we do it?

George has eaten the pizza, ☐ ?

If the subject of the statement is a boy or a man, then the last word in the question will be *he*.

George has eaten the pizza, ☐ he ?

What word goes in the box before *he*? Is it like any other word in the sentence?

Here's a picture of how you make questions like this.

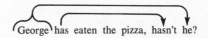

George has eaten the pizza, hasn't he?

If you follow the arrows carefully, then you can understand what happens inside your head. One arrow shows how you change *George* into *he*. The other arrow shows how, at the end, you use the same auxiliary with *n't* added to it.

Here's another example.

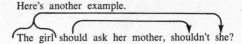

The girl should ask her mother, shouldn't she?

What do we write instead of *the girl*? What happens to the auxiliary?

Daybook: Tag Questions, page 58

Sentences in which the question part comes at the end are called **tag questions**. We can answer them with a "yes" or a "no." Since you know—in your head—how to make tag questions, we can put them in the sentence model. But since they're a little different from the regular yes-or-no questions, we'll have to show them in a special way. We use a Q as the sign for a regular yes-or-no question. For a tag yes-or-no question, we can use Q_{tag}.

■ Now make tag questions from these sentences. (The first one is done for you. The second one is <u>almost</u> done.)

1. Q_{tag} + Patty has gone home.
   $\Rightarrow$ *Patty has gone home, hasn't she?*

2. Q_{tag} + Edward has lost his pencil.
   $\Rightarrow$ *Edward has lost his pencil,* [＿＿＿] *he?*

3. Q_{tag} + The mailmen should finish their work.
   $\Rightarrow$

4. Q_{tag} + I have finished first.
   $\Rightarrow$

5. Q_{tag} + The girl should find her books.
   $\Rightarrow$

6. Q_{tag} + The ladies have built an airplane.
   $\Rightarrow$

7. Q_{tag} + Bobby has two brothers.
   $\Rightarrow$

8. Q_{tag} + That boy has asked for help.
   $\Rightarrow$

9. Q_{tag} + The teacher can sing very well.
   $\Rightarrow$

10. Q_{tag} + This lesson has been easy.
    $\Rightarrow$

sisters who tag along behind you when you go somewhere?"

Then read the paragraph on the top of page 153 with the children. Remind the children that they've already learned about using Q when they make questions. Help them see the difference between Q, which is a sign for a regular yes-or-no question, and Q_{tag}, which is a sign for a tag question.

The activity (■) is best worked with the entire class. Then you can frequently reinforce the point that the children know the rules in their heads. (If the children worked alone, they would probably concentrate on getting the "right" answer rather than on the fact that they know the rules.)

Follow-up For those children who need additional practice making tag questions, you can use the following examples:

1. Q_{tag} + The firemen have taken a bus.
   $\Rightarrow$

2. Q_{tag} + The dentist has lost a tooth.
   $\Rightarrow$

3. Q_{tag} + The giraffe should wear a scarf.
   $\Rightarrow$

4. Q_{tag} + Rory should get a haircut.
   $\Rightarrow$

Answers

2. Edward has lost his pencil, hasn't he?
3. The mailmen should finish their work, shouldn't they?
4. I have finished first, haven't I?
5. The girl should find her books, shouldn't she?
6. The ladies have built an airplane, haven't they?
7. Bobby has two brothers, hasn't he?
8. That boy has asked for help, hasn't he?
9. The teacher can sing very well, can't she?
10. This lesson has been easy, hasn't it?

Purposes (1) To review some of the forms and techniques of poetry; (2) To provide an additional opportunity for children to develop and to revise their own compositions; (3) To review two kinds of questions: regular yes-or-no questions and tag questions.

Presentation You may want to have the children work in two groups to complete the literature and composition sections of this Review.

The Language Review deals only with the two kinds of questions that have been discussed thus far: regular yes-or-no questions and tag questions. Since auxiliaries were also introduced in this chapter, you may want to use one of the activities on page 155 of this guide as a review exercise. Or, if you have already used them as follow-up, you can construct similar activities of your own. You can also adapt the activity on page 155 of the children's text to review auxiliaries. First, have the children decide which sentences already contain auxiliaries. (All the Q_{tag} statements, except number 3, contain auxiliaries.) Then, for those sentences which do not contain an auxiliary, you can have the children add an auxiliary (and change the form of the main verb accordingly if *can, must,* and so on are used).

Review

Literature

So far, you've read many different kinds of poems. You've read short, silly poems, like *limericks*. And you've read short, serious poems, like *haiku*. What is special about the form of most English haiku poems?

In this chapter, you also read a poem that's special in another way. Do you remember the poem about the Christmas tree? How is this poem special? Why do you think the poet changes the regular way of writing things? Would you like to change language when you write a poem?

■ Now look through some books and magazines. Try to find photographs that show things in nature. Then use the pictures to write some more haiku.

Composition

When you write your own poems and stories, you can make them end any way you want. You can give them sad endings or happy endings. And you can also *revise* your compositions to change the endings.

■ Now think about a story you would like to write. Your story can be about anything at all. (You can use pictures in books and magazines to get some ideas if you want to.) Decide whether you want your story to have a happy ending or a sad ending. Then write your story.

■ Did your story have a happy ending? If it did, revise your story so that it has a sad ending. If your story had a sad ending, then change it to make it happy.

Language

You already know how to make *regular yes-or-no questions*. In this chapter, you learned about another kind of question: a *tag question*. What's the difference between a regular yes-or-no question and a tag question?

■ Here are some question problems for you to solve. In some of them, you have to make regular questions. In others, you have to make tag questions.

1. Q + The man fixed the car.
   ⇒

2. Q_tag + Earl can play first base.
   ⇒

3. Q_tag + Frances is very smart.
   ⇒

4. Q + The teacher baked a hundred cookies.
   ⇒

5. Q_tag + Mary can whistle through her fingers.
   ⇒

6. Q + The man washed the windows.
   ⇒

7. Q + The lady painted a picture.
   ⇒

8. Q_tag + Charles should win the race.
   ⇒

 When you write a word, you use letters to stand for the sounds in the word. You can find out more about sounds and letters on page 316.

To provide additional practice with auxiliaries, you can duplicate the following exercise or write it on the chalkboard. Have the children read each group of words and then decide whether the auxiliary is used correctly. If the auxiliary is not used correctly, ask the children what they would do to make a statement sentence that "sounds right."

1. My dog can do many tricks.
2. An elephant eat must a lot.
3. The boys have play that game for hours.
4. He has gone for a walk in the woods.
5. Cars should stop for red lights.
6. It has not rained for days.
7. We not will wait for the bus.
8. A leaf might landed on my head.
9. The old man had lived in that house for years.
10. George can chop down trees.

Answers

1. Did the man fix the car?
2. Earl can play first base, can't he?
3. Frances is very smart, isn't she?
4. Did the teacher bake a hundred cookies?
5. Mary can whistle through her fingers, can't she?
6. Did the man wash the windows?
7. Did the lady paint a picture?
8. Charles should win the race, shouldn't he?

Purpose To help children increase their sensitivity to and awareness of metaphors.

Preparation Reread the poem "Unfolding Bud" once again while the children look at the illustration on pages 24-25. If you used the Follow-up suggestions which accompanied that lesson (such as observing a plant and recording—either with words or with photographs—the changes that take place), then they might be appropriate to discuss here. Primarily, you should seek to re-establish the connection between flowers and poetry, as well as between flowers and metaphors.

Presentation Have the children examine the illustration on pages 156 and 157, and if possible, show them a small sprig of lilies of the valley. Ask the children to compare the flower with others they have seen and also with bells—both large and small—that they've seen and heard. You can even ask if they've ever heard lilies of the valley "ringing in the air." Then comment that today's poem was written by a ten-year-old girl who could "hear the lilies ringing."

Read the poem to the children, and, because it is so short, read it again immediately as the children follow along in their books. Then have the children read the introduction on page 156, and perhaps reread the poem again in unison.

Next, point out the two metaphors in the first seven lines: The flowers are "the dream/of every grassy hill" and also "the bell/of day." Ask the class how a flower can be a "dream," and encourage a wide variety of answers. After the children have had a chance to respond, have them turn to the discussion on page 158.

A Poem

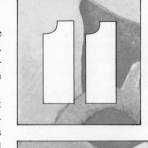

Many people have written poems about flowers. Do you remember "Unfolding Bud"? That was a poem about a water-lily.

Here's a poem about another kind of flower— lilies of the valley. It was written by a ten-year-old girl.

Song

Lilies of the valley,
you are the dream
of every grassy hill.

Lilies of the valley,
ringing in the air,
you are the bell

of day. Ding, dong.
When you are picked
you quietly stop,

little bells of gold,
little bells of gold.
ALIKI BARNSTONE

Daybook: Metaphors You Can Sense,
page 60

Read the first three paragraphs of the discussion with the children. This should prompt additional comments from them. (If the discussion atmosphere is relaxed, then the children should feel increasingly free to make wide-ranging contributions.)

In discussing the fourth paragraph on page 158, try chanting softly the last two lines of the poem rather than simply reading them. (This will help the children hear the *l* sounds "ringing.")

Before turning to the activity, you can ask for volunteers to read the poem again. Three or four different readings would be perfectly appropriate. Help the children understand that poets want other people to read their poems aloud. That's one reason they write poetry: to share their feelings.

The activity (■) can be done as a class, in small groups, or individually. (You can also supplement the illustrations in the text with some taken from magazines or books.) Encourage the children to look carefully at the physical characteristics of each flower. Ask them what the different shapes make them think of, and also ask what sounds the flowers might make—if they could make sounds. (And in metaphors, flowers can make sounds!)

Follow-up This is an ideal time to encourage the children to write their own poems containing metaphors. You might begin by reading a few other poems written by young people. (See Additional Resources.) You can also note that the poem "Song" doesn't use rhyming words, and that their poems don't need to rhyme either.

Additional Resources

Books   Barnstone, Aliki, *The Real Tin Flower,* Macmillan. Koch, Kenneth, *Wishes, Lies and Dreams,* Random House. Hopkins, Lee Bennett, compiler, *City Talk,* Knopf. Read, Herbert, *This Way, Delight,* Pantheon. Walter, Nina Willis, *Let Them Write Poetry,* Holt Rinehart and Winston.

Recordings   *Miracles: Poems Written by Children* (collected by Richard Lewis), 1-12″ LP, 2-track tape, cassette, Caedmon. *Promises to Be Kept: Young poets-to-be read from their works.* 1-12″ LP, open-reel tape, Spoken Arts. *Wishes, Lies and Dreams: Teaching Children to Write Poetry,* 1-12″ LP, open-reel tape, Spoken Arts.

Filmstrips   *Who's a Poet?,* Caedmon. This filmstrip introduces the children to poets as "everyday" people and thereby encourages them to express, poetically, their own thoughts and feelings.

In the first stanza, the poet pretends that a "grassy hill" is like a person. She says that a hill can "dream." If you were a hill, you might dream of having flowers on you. Or you might dream of how you would look in winter. What else might you dream of, if you were a hill?

Then the poet describes how the lilies look. Each blossom looks like a little bell. In this metaphor, there's a word-picture: *The flower is a bell.* There's also a word-sound: *The flower rings.* There are metaphors to see and metaphors to hear.

When someone picks the flower, the ringing stops, quietly. The poet doesn't tell us why the ringing stops. There could be lots of reasons. If lilies really could ring, why would they stop when you pick them?

The last stanza is shorter than the others. The poet uses the same line twice. Read these two lines again. Do you hear all the l sounds? Do you think that—if it really could ring—a lily would sound that way?

■ It's a metaphor to say that lilies of the valley are bells of gold. Here are some other flowers. What word-pictures do they make you think of? Do they make you hear any word-sounds?

Talking About Elephants

Suppose there are four men who have never heard about elephants. You put blindfolds on their eyes. Then you take them to a circus.

You say, "This is an elephant. You can't see it because of your blindfolds. You can touch it, but only for a second."

The first man feels the elephant's trunk. The second man feels his hairy tail. The third one feels a leg. And the fourth one feels the side of the elephant.

Then you say to the men, "Please describe what an elephant is like."

What do you think the first man might say? What might the second man say? What about the third and the fourth?

If the first man said that an elephant is like a fire hose, would the three other men believe him? Why would each man say something different? Can you think of a way to get the men to agree about what an elephant really is?

Purposes (1) To develop further a child's awareness of the principles of description; (2) To emphasize the importance of using senses—in addition to sight —in writing descriptions.

Preparation Put several objects into a paper bag. Then have volunteers feel the objects without looking at them. Ask these volunteers to describe the objects by stating only what they feel, and make a brief list of their comments on the chalkboard. Then remove the objects from the bag and have the children look at the objects. Ask them what else they can say about each object, now that they can see it. Make a parallel list of these comments on the chalkboard.

Presentation Tell the class that, in today's lesson, they'll read about the problems some men had when they tried to describe an elephant which they couldn't see. Ask the children to read page 159 silently. When they've finished, begin a discussion of the questions in the last two paragraphs on the page. Encourage the children to give reasons for their answers.

159

The first paragraph on page 160 will prepare the children for the first activity (■), which can be done as an entire class. Make three columns on the chalkboard, labeled *Is, Has,* and *Does,* and ask the class to suggest things to write in each column. When you have several items under each heading, have the children read the paragraph after the first activity, and also the facsimile letter. After discussing the letter—and what it means to be a "pen pal"—you can suggest that the children can refer to the lists on the chalkboard when they compose an answer to the letter.

This is, of course, an ideal time to refer the children to the lesson on Letters on page 290 of the Skills Section.

Follow-up You might want to read to the children "The Blind Men and the Elephant" by John Godfrey Saxe. (See Additional Resources.) In this humorous poem, six blind men attempt to describe an elephant using only their sense of touch. One describes the elephant as a wall, another as a tree, and so on.

Additional Resources

Books Untermeyer, Louis, compiler, *The Golden Treasury of Poetry,* Golden Press.

Isabella Is, Harry Has, and Dudley Does don't wear blindfolds. If they went to the circus, they could touch the elephant. They could also see him. They could watch him drink. They could even feed him peanuts.

■ Tell three things that Isabella might say about the elephant after she has watched him for a while. Then tell three things that Harry could say and three things that Dudley could say.

Now suppose that you have a friend who lives in another country. He's learning English, and so he writes a letter to you. One day he sends this letter.

Dear Friend,
     Today I read an English book about a zoo. I knew most of the words. But there was one word I didn't know. The word was "elephant". I'm not sure what this animal looks like. In my language we probably use a different word that means the same thing. Can you describe an "elephant" to me?
                    Your pen pal

■ Try to write your friend a letter to help him understand what an elephant is like.

Basic Sentences

Do you remember the first rule of the sentence model?

● A sentence has a nominal and a verb phrase.

Here are some sentences we can make using this rule.

These are all **basic sentences.** They have the right kind of words—nominals and verb phrases—in the right positions.

But we can often change basic sentences by adding ideas to them. Here are some more sentences.

In these sentences, something has been added. When we add something to a basic sentence, we get a **derived sentence.** Any sentence that is not a basic sentence is a derived sentence.

Daybook: Basic and Derived Sentences, page 62

Purposes (1) To introduce into the sentence model two additional terms that facilitate the discussion of language; (2) To introduce the concept of negative as an element in some sentences.

[The distinction between basic and derived sentences is pedagogical, and relates more to our intuitive understanding of sentences than to a scientifically demonstrable fact.]

Preparation Review with the children the sentences that can be made using the simple sentence model on pages 20-21 and 29-31. You might want to write two or three of these sentences on the chalkboard. Then review the two kinds of questions the children have learned to talk about: regular yes-or-no questions (pages 123-124) and tag questions (pages 152-153). If you've written a few sentences on the chalkboard, then you can suggest that the children use these to make some regular yes-or-no questions. Then comment that today's lesson will help us talk about these different kinds of sentences.

Presentation Have the children examine the two illustrations on page 161 and relate them to the sentences they made during the preparation. The ones in the top picture are like those they made using the simple sentence model; the ones in the bottom picture are like the questions they made, and also like the sentences they get when they add sentences together.

Then have the children read the text on page 161 to find out the special names we can use to help us talk about these different kinds of sentences. Help the children to locate and pronounce the two boldface terms. Then, if you've written the sentences on the chalkboard during the preparation, you can label the groups *basic* and *derived.*

The discussion on page 162 repeats the material presented on page 161, but in more detail. The children are already familiar with the types of sentences included on this page; now they'll learn to compare these types. In reading the page, remind the children that they already know how Q changes a sentence, and also how Q_{tag} changes a sentence. Then state that on page 163 they'll learn another way to change a basic sentence into a derived sentence.

Read the first paragraph on page 163 with the children, helping them to understand that we can always add a negative element to a basic sentence. Here are some sentences you can use to supplement the example given at the top of page 163:

1. N'T + Today is Saturday.
   ⇒ Today isn't Saturday.
2. N'T + The girls have solved the puzzle.
   ⇒ The girls haven't solved the puzzle.
3. N'T + The elephant was snoring.
   ⇒ The elephant wasn't snoring.
4. N'T + I can swim a mile.
   ⇒ I can't swim a mile.

Next, compare the position picture on page 163 with the one on page 162, calling attention to the new positions at the right and at the left. Copy the headings of the new position picture onto the chalkboard, and leave room for writing four sentences in the boxes. In the first row of boxes—under First, Second, Third, and Fourth Position—write *Ellen / has found / the elephant / already*. Ask the class what derived sentence you would get if you added Q to this basic sentence. Write this answer in the second row of boxes: *Has / Ellen / found / the elephant / already?* Repeat the process for

We can use a position picture to help us talk about basic sentences.

FIRST POSITION	SECOND POSITION	THIRD POSITION	FOURTH POSITION
The frog	found	the grape	easily.
We	are	hungry	now.
Mary	has lost	her shoe.	
The boys	had	a picnic	in a park.

All of these sentences have a nominal in the first position. In the second position, there's either a "be" word or a verb. And in the third position, there's either a nominal or an adjective. In the fourth position of some of these sentences, there's an adverbial.

These are all *basic sentences*. A basic sentence is one that has the right kind of words—nominals and verb phrases—in the right positions. Some basic sentences have adverbials in the fourth position, and some don't.

We often change basic sentences by adding ideas to them. We've already seen how Q—the idea of a question—can be added to a basic sentence.

Q + John has seen the giraffe today.
⟹ Has John seen the giraffe today?

We can also add Q_{tag} to a basic sentence. Then we get a tag question.

Q_{tag} + Angela can make brownies.
⟹ Angela can make brownies, can't she?

We can add N'T to a basic sentence. N'T stands for the idea of "no" or "not."

N'T + The teacher has eaten her lunch.
⇒ The teacher hasn't eaten her lunch.

A position picture can show these derived sentences.

SPECIAL Q POSITION	FIRST POSITION	SECOND POSITION	THIRD POSITION	FOURTH POSITION	SPECIAL Q$_{tag}$ POSITION
Has	John	seen	the giraffe	today?	
	Angela	can make	brownies,		can't she?
	The teacher	hasn't eaten	her lunch.		

In this picture, we added two new positions. At the beginning, there's now a *special Q position*. And, at the end, there's a *special Q$_{tag}$ position*.

We can change a basic sentence into a derived sentence by adding a Q or a Q$_{tag}$ or an N'T. What basic sentence has been changed in the examples below?

Q + Ellen has found the elephant.
⇒ Has Ellen found the elephant?

Q$_{tag}$ + Ellen has found the elephant.
⇒ Ellen has found the elephant, hasn't she?

N'T + Ellen has found the elephant.
⇒ Ellen hasn't found the elephant.

■ Now add a Q to each of these basic sentences. Then, start again and add a Q$_{tag}$. Finally, start again and add an N'T.

1. My brother has eaten his spinach.
2. That boy has taken my book.
3. Oliver should sharpen the pencils.

Answers

1. Has my brother eaten his spinach? My brother has eaten his spinach, hasn't he? My brother hasn't eaten his spinach.
2. Has that boy taken my book? That boy has taken my book, hasn't he? That boy hasn't taken my book.
3. Should Oliver sharpen the pencils? Oliver should sharpen the pencils, shouldn't he? Oliver shouldn't sharpen the pencils.

Q$_{tag}$ and N'T. Remind the children that, in this exercise, you must go back to the basic sentence—the one in the first row—when you add a new idea. (If you need additional examples, you can select some of the sentences listed under Follow-up.)

Mimeographed forms—perhaps with each basic sentence written in a position picture and with 3 blank rows below—will help the children do the activity (■) on page 163.

Follow-up You can construct an activity similar to the one on page 163, using the following sentences. Again, it would be helpful if you used a position picture to write the sentences, leaving three blank rows below each one. With some children, you may want to do the exercise in three separate stages: first, adding Q; then, adding Q$_{tag}$; and finally, adding N'T.

1. The boy / can kick / the can / over the fence.
2. The rooster / can flap / his wings / wildly.
3. The elephant / brushed / his teeth / daily.
4. The cow / had eaten / the daisies.
5. They / have hidden / the box / under the bed.
6. That rabbit / can eat / carrots / all day.
7. The frog / has swallowed / a fly.
8. The man / had climbed / a tree / in the woods.
9. The beetle / has caught / a butterfly / in his net.
10. The centipede / should polish / the shoes / on his feet.

Purpose To provide the children with additional information about libraries.

[As suggested in the teacher's notes on page 146, this lesson can be most usefully taught immediately following the earlier lesson on the library. The notes that accompany pages 146-147 generally apply here also.]

Preparation Review the earlier library lesson in which the children explored the division of books into fiction and nonfiction and also some of the uses of the card catalogue.

Presentation This lesson builds upon the earlier lesson by providing information about the Dewey Decimal System. You might read page 164 as the children follow along in their own books, pausing to solicit answers to the questions and to expand the discussion, if necessary.

In discussing the illustration on page 165, note that the 100 group is not included, since it's discussed in the next to last paragraph on page 164. You'll probably need to help the children with some of the classificatory words used in the illustration. You might also want to have some of these words checked in a dictionary. As you discuss each category, you can make up titles of books that might be included. (For example, a book called *Fishing for Fun* would be in the 700 category.) Then ask the children to make up titles of their own and fit them into various categories. If you do this orally with the entire class, it will prepare the children to work the activity which follows.

The activity (■) at the bottom of page 165 is best done in small groups or pairs.

Numbers in a Library

You already know that in a library books are divided into *fiction* and *nonfiction*. Fiction books are stories that people make up in their imaginations. All other books are nonfiction, and they can be about almost anything.

How do you find a nonfiction book in the library? Cataloguers give books special numbers to help you. The number that a book gets depends upon its subject. Here's how the special numbers were decided.

About a hundred years ago, a man named Melvil Dewey invented a number code for grouping books. The code is called the **Dewey Decimal System**. It's called a "decimal system" because of the way Dewey used tens. He first divided books into ten subject areas. He gave each subject area a number which is a multiple of one hundred. Dewey then divided each of the ten subject areas into ten smaller areas. And so on.

How did Melvil Dewey decide what hundreds number to give each subject? Here's what he did. He pretended that he was a caveman. And he asked himself questions that he thought a caveman would ask.

The first question Dewey asked was, "Who am I?" And he gave any book that answered this question a number between one hundred and two hundred. On the next page, you'll find some questions like the ones Dewey probably asked. You'll also find the numbers he gave to books that answered each question.

When a new nonfiction book comes into the library, the cataloguer uses Dewey's system to give the book a number. First, he decides what the subject is. That tells him what number in the hundreds the book will get. Then, he looks in his decimal book to find what numbers to put in the tens place, and so on.

■ Suppose you were a cataloguer in a library. Here are some book titles that you want to give numbers to. Try to figure out what hundreds number to give each book.

1. *Fun with Words*
2. *Engineers Did It!*
3. *Shooting Stars*
4. *America Begins*
5. *All About Language*

6. *Desert Life*
7. *The Navajo*
8. *Seven Tales*
9. *Abraham Lincoln*
10. *The First Artists*

Follow-up Working in pairs, the children can make up some additional book titles for their partners to categorize according to the ten main classes of the Dewey Decimal System. Alternatively, some children might want to try to assign class numbers to some of the subject area or general reading books that you have in the classroom.

If your children have had experience using reference materials, then you might suggest that they use these materials to find out more about Melvil Dewey or the Dewey Decimal System. These children can then prepare a report to present to the rest of the class. The report might explain the further subdivision of books according to Dewey's system, including what is meant by a "call number."

If your school has a library, then some children might want to draw floor plans of the room to show where various things, such as the card catalogue, reference materials, the circulation desk, tables, and so on are located. Other children might want to collect pictures of both the interiors and exteriors of different kinds of libraries: public, school, research, bookmobile, and so on.

Additional Resources

Books Cleary, Florence Damon, *Discovering Books and Libraries,* Wilson. Shor, Pekay, *Libraries and You,* Prentice-Hall.

Filmstrips *The School Library Series,* 6 color filmstrips, McGraw-Hill. "The Dewey Decimal System" from this series would be an appropriate filmstrip to use as a follow-up activity for this lesson.

Overhead Transparencies *Library Instruction-2nd Edition,* Scott.

Answers

1. 400	6. 900
2. 600	7. 900 *or* 300
3. 500	8. 800
4. 900	9. 900
5. 400	10. 700

Purpose   To introduce the autobiography as another literary form.

Preparation   Begin a general discussion of books about "the lives of people." Perhaps some of the children have read about sports heroes, scientists, presidents, famous women, and so on. After discussing some of these, you can make a distinction between writing a story about one's own life and writing the story of someone else's life. Then put the words *biography* and *autobiography* on the chalkboard and help the children distinguish between the two.

Presentation   Have the children read the first paragraph of the introduction on page 167. (This paragraph is a continuation of the preparation suggested above; it distinguishes an autobiography from a diary in terms of audience.) Before continuing with the introduction, you can comment that in this lesson the children will read part of the autobiography of Sammy Davis, Jr. Ask if anyone knows who Sammy Davis, Jr., is. (Perhaps some of the children have seen him perform on TV or in the movies.) Then read the rest of the introduction as the children follow along in their books.

An Autobiography

An autobiography is a true story about your own life, or part of your life. It's like a diary, but a diary is private. You write it just for yourself. And an autobiography is public. You write it for other people to read.

Here's part of an autobiography. It was written by Sammy Davis, Jr. When he was very young, he and his family traveled from city to city. His father was a dancer, and he worked as part of a troupe that played in theaters all over the country. A *troupe* is a group of singers, dancers, jugglers, and comedians who put on shows for people to enjoy. The leader of the troupe was a man named Will Mastin.

This is how Chapter Two of the autobiography begins.

We rarely stayed in one place more than a week or two, yet there was never a feeling of impermanence. Packing suitcases and riding on trains and buses were as natural to me as a stroll in a carriage might be to another child. Although I had travelled ten states and played over fifty cities by the time I was four, I never felt I was without a home. We carried our roots with us: our same boxes of make-up in front of the mirrors, our same clothes hanging on iron pipe racks with our same shoes under them. Only the details changed, like the face on the man sitting inside the stage door, or which floor our dressing room was on. But there was always an audience, other performers for me to watch, always the show talk, all as dependably present as the walls of a nursery.

We arrived in Asheville, North Carolina, on a Sunday, and Will gave everybody the day off. We were doing the three-a-day, from town to town, so most of our troupe spent the time catching up on sleep, which was also the cheapest thing they could do. I wasn't tired so I wandered into the

If possible, you should work with small groups in presenting the actual autobiography. There are a number of difficult vocabulary words in the selection, and by working in small groups you can help children acquire the skill of determining definitions from contextual clues. For example, in discussing *impermanence* in the opening paragraph of the excerpt, you can relate it to the comment "We rarely stayed in one place more than a week or two . . ." and also to the word *permanent*.

Reading the selection in small groups also provides a comfortable atmosphere for discussing the informal language used in the dialogue. Help the children realize that the author used informal language because that's the way many children actually talk. Explain that he could have written the dialogue in standard English, if he had wanted to, but then the autobiography wouldn't seem true.

You can also have the children compare the two excerpts included in this lesson. The first one, which ends a third of the way down on page 168, describes various things: how the troupe moved from place to place, how Sammy Davis felt, and so on. The second excerpt, beginning at the middle of page 168, uses a different style, one that's more dramatic. You can suggest that both ways of writing are useful, but sometimes one is more appropriate than the other.

In discussing the dialogue of the second excerpt, you can also relate it to the dialogue in the story of Warren Upson, the Pony Express rider whom the children read about in Chapter 8. You might say something like this: "There, when the author was writing conversation, he tried to find words that sounded right. Sammy Davis, Jr., does the same thing. He probably doesn't remember the exact words that he and the other boys said in the candy store, but he uses words that he might have said. And we 'believe' them because they sound right."

Many children will have had the experience of feeling "dumb," of doing something very silly, and this excerpt can be reassuring for such children. You might even relate an experience of your own, one where you felt as Sammy Davis must have felt in the candy shop.

When the children have finished reading the selection, bring the groups together again to discuss the material on page 171. This discussion focuses on three separate things: (1) asking the

parlor of our rooming house. Rastus Airship, one of our dancers, was reading a paper, and Obie Smith, our pianist, was rehearsing on an upright. I started doing the parts of the show along with him. Rastus left the room and came back with Will and my father and I did the whole hour-and-twenty minute show for them, doing everybody's dances, singing everybody's songs, and telling all the jokes. People were coming in from other rooms and from the way they were watching me I knew I was doing good. When I finished our closing number, Will said, "From now on you're going to dance and sing in the act."

Sammy Davis, Jr. was a good dancer and entertainer. But he was also a boy. He wanted to play with other boys. And he wanted other boys to like him. But it wasn't easy for him to make friends because he moved so much.

Here's another part of the autobiography. This part describes some of the problems young Sammy had in making friends.

I went downstairs to the candy store below our apartment to buy comic books. Some kids from the neighborhood were sitting at the table in the back. I walked over to them. "Hi." They were looking at cards with pictures on them. I watched for a while. "What're those?"

One of them looked up. "You kiddin'?" I didn't answer. "Boy, anyone don't know what these is must be pretty dumb."

"Well, it ain't dumb just 'cause I never saw somethin' before!" I looked around the table hoping to find someone who'd agree with me but they all just shook their heads like I was too stupid to live. I was dying to walk away but I knew if I said, "Well, so long," nobody'd answer.

"These're baseball cards, dopey! Where y'been all your life?"

The most any of them had was about a dozen. I had a ten dollar bill in my pocket. The bubble gum the cards came in was a penny apiece. I bought a hundred of them.

They all stopped talking. I played it big, pulling the cards out of the packages, piling them into one tall stack. The boy who'd first called me dumb came over and looked eagerly at my cards. "Y'wanta trade?"

"Sure. Whattya wanta trade?"

He picked out three. "I'll take these."

"Okay, but what'll you give me for 'em?" I didn't care but I didn't want to look dumb again. He handed me three of his cards and I looked at them as if I knew one from the other.

"Fair 'nuff?" he asked. I nodded. He shouted, "Trade's off 'n no trades back!" and all the other kids burst out laughing. He grinned. "Boy, you really are dumb. Anybody who'd give up a Babe Ruth or a Lou Gehrig for less'n five cards —boy, that's the dumbest thing I ever saw."

This time I even felt dumb. I ran out of there leaving my cards on the counter. I closed the door to my room and played a record, loud, so Mama couldn't hear me crying. I sat on my bed, mad at myself for running out like that and for letting them get the best of me in the first place. And to make it worse I hadn't gotten the comic books. I hated to face them again but they weren't going to keep me from getting what I wanted.

I picked out *Superman, The Flash, Batman* and about twenty others. They were watching me from the table. I had four singles but I gave Mr. Peterson a five dollar bill. They came closer. "Where'd you get all that money?"

"I made it."

"Aww, how'd you ever make five dollars?"

"Dancing."

"Yeah? What kinda dancin' you get five dollars for?"

children to imagine themselves in the role of the hero; that is, encouraging them to feel empathy when they read; (2) suggesting again that literature can take various forms; for example, the same event can be written as a poem, a story, or a play; and (3) stressing the importance of order in any kind of composition.

You might want to read the second excerpt two or three times, having volunteers read the dialogue, before asking the children to consider the activity (■) on page 171, in which they act out the events of the story.

In developing the play, you might want to divide the class into two or three separate groups. Then you can have each group work in a different place, and finally act as its own audience. (This will relieve some of the pressure of performance and also encourage maximum participation on the part of the children.)

Encourage the groups to work on each event singly. The "director" might say: "You're Sammy. And the rest of you are boys with cards. Sammy, you come into the store, see the cards, and ask what they are. What are you going to say?" After finishing this scene, the group can then go on to the next one, perhaps changing roles.

169

Follow-up Since there are not many autobiographies appropriate for children of this age level, you might want to use this opportunity to introduce the children to a similar literary form: the biography. There are many fine biographies—of widely varying reading difficulty—written especially for children. With children who require easier reading materials, for example, you can use any of the d'Aulaire books. And your better readers, especially the boys, will probably enjoy some of the books by Ronald Syme. (See Additional Resources.)

After the children have read some biographies, you might want to plan for the class to have a "Famous Person's Day." The children can pretend to be the characters they've read about, and then write short compositions which describe the characters. (This will result in compositions all written in the "first person.") The children might even enjoy dressing like their favorite characters, and then reading their compositions to the other children, or perhaps to another class.

I put the magazines down and looked him right in the eye. "This kind." I did some of the fanciest tricks I knew and I didn't stop until they were all gaping at me. One of them shrugged. "Well, I guess you c'n dance, but that don't say you get paid no five dollars for it."

I laughed in his face. "Five dollars? I wouldn't even walk out on a stage for only five dollars. Sometimes I make more'n a hundred dollars a week."

"A hundred dollars? You're lyin' through your teeth! My old man's ten times as big as you and he does a man's work loadin' a truck and *he* don't make no hundred dollars."

"Just the same that's what I make."

"How'd you go to school travellin' like you do?"

"I don't hafta go t'school. I work." I knew as I said it that it would kill them.

One of them said, "Here's the cards y'left here before." Another looked enviously at the comic books under my arms. "Y'think I could see those after you're finished with 'em?"

"Sure! Here, you guys can have these." I picked out twenty more for myself and paid for them. "Well, I gotta go upstairs." They walked me to Mama's door.

SAMMY DAVIS, JR.

When you read an autobiography, you get to know about other people and about how they live. Sammy Davis, Jr. traveled a lot when he was young. Would you like to travel the way that he did? Would you like to be a part of a troupe that went from city to city? If you could, what kind of things would you like to do?

Sammy Davis, Jr. sometimes had trouble making friends. This part of his autobiography would make a good play. Some children in the class could play the children in the candy store. Someone else could play Mr. Peterson. And someone could play Sammy Davis, Jr. You don't need to use the exact words. It's more important to make sure that everything happens in the right order.

Here's a list of the things that happen—in order.

1. Sammy Davis, Jr. comes into the store. He sees some boys with cards, and he asks what the cards are.
2. The boys think he's stupid because he hasn't seen baseball cards before.
3. Young Sammy buys a hundred cards. The boys are surprised.
4. One boy trades cards with young Sammy, and Sammy makes a bad trade.
5. He feels bad and runs out of the store. Then he gets mad and comes back. He buys some comics.
6. The boys are surprised that young Sammy has so much money. They talk with him about how he gets the money. They also talk about school.
7. The boys want to make friends with young Sammy so they give the cards back to him. He shares the comics with them, and then they all leave.

■ Now you and your friends can act out this part of the life of Sammy Davis, Jr.

Additional Resources

Books Adoff, Arnold, *Malcolm X,* Crowell. Collier, Edmund, *The Story of Annie Oakley,* Grosset. d'Aulaire, Ingri and Edgar Parin, *Abraham Lincoln; Benjamin Franklin; Buffalo Bill; Columbus; George Washington; Leif, the Lucky;* and *Pocahontas,* Doubleday. Davidson, Margaret, *Frederick Douglass Fights for Freedom,* Four Winds. Graham, Shirley, *Booker T. Washington: Educator of Hand, Head, and Heart,* Messner. Graham, Shirley and George Lipscomb, *Dr. George Washington Carver, Scientist,* Messner. Hunter, Edith Fisher, *Child of the Silent Night,* Dell. Judson, Clara Ingram, *Abraham Lincoln; Andrew Carnegie; Andrew Jackson, Frontier Statesman; Christopher Columbus; George Washington;* and *Thomas Jefferson, Champion of the People,* Follett. Killilea, Marie, *Wren,* Dell. Lawson, Robert, *Ben and Me,* Little, Brown. Masani, Shakuntala, *Gandhi's Story,* Walck. Pace, Mildred M., *Clara Barton,* Scribner. Rudeen, Kenneth, *Wilt Chamberlain,* Crowell. Seymour, Flora W., *Bird Girl: Sacagawea,* Bobbs Merrill. Sterling, Dorothy, *Freedom Train: The Story of Harriet Tubman,* Doubleday. Stevenson, Augusta, *Kit Carson: Boy Trapper,* Bobbs Merrill. Streatfeild, Noel, *Queen Victoria,* Random. Syme, Ronald, *African Traveler, the Story of Mary Kingsley; Cortes of Mexico; John Smith of Virginia; Nigerian Pioneer;* and *Vasco da Gama, Sailor toward the Sunrise,* Morrow. Van Riper, Guernsey, *Lou Gehrig: Boy of the Sand Lots,* Bobbs Merrill. Weir, Ruth C., *Thomas Alva Edison: Inventor,* Abingdon.

Purpose To provide an opportunity for children to write about themselves.

[If you wish, you can use the two parts of this lesson as alternatives, leaving the choice up to each child.]

Preparation If the children have begun to read some biographies, as suggested in the Follow-up for the previous lesson, then you might discuss the characters they're reading about. Encourage the children to tell why they're interested in these people. Additionally, some children may have heard older relatives—parents, grandparents, aunts, and uncles—describe some humorous things they did when they were younger. Discussing these things will help children realize the ways in which biographies—and autobiographies—can be interesting. You can conclude the discussion by commenting: "People are interested in people, and we can read biographies and autobiographies to learn more about other people."

Presentation Even though a child may choose to write a poem rather than a regular autobiography, it would be useful if the entire class read both parts of this lesson before deciding which part they want to do. Ask for a volunteer to read the facsimile composition on page 172. Then write the word *paragraphs* on the chalkboard and help the children pronounce it. (They might also check the meaning of the word in a dictionary.)

The questions in the paragraph after the composition will help the children see one order that they can follow. The final paragraph on page 172 will make the order clearer. The children will probably need individual help in working the first activity (■) on page 173, and this will give you the opportunity to suggest that they make notes before beginning to write.

172

Your Autobiography

Part I

Here is part of an autobiography written by a boy in the fourth grade.

> *The Story of My Life*
>
> My name is Albert Turner. I was born in St. Louis, Missouri on July 7, 1962. I live in Trenton, New Jersey, now. I have one brother. His name is Edward.
>
> I like football, but I'm not very good. I can run fast. I'm almost the fastest runner in my class.
>
> One day, we all went on a trip in a bus. We saw how machines worked.

There are three **paragraphs** in this autobiography. In the first paragraph Samuel Turner tells us his name and where he was born. What else does he tell us in the first paragraph? What does he tell us in the second paragraph? What does he tell us in the third paragraph?

Many autobiographies start by giving the name of the writer. Then they often tell about where and when the writer was born. An autobiography also usually tells what the writer likes and doesn't like. And it almost always tells about some of the things the writer has done.

Daybook: Writing About You, page 64

■ Now try to write your own autobiography. What will you tell in the first paragraph? What will you tell in the second paragraph? What will you tell in the third paragraph? If you want to, you can use your name for the title.

Part II

There's another good way to write about yourself. You can write a poem about your life or part of your life. Here's one that a ten-year-old boy wrote.

What I Want

I really am ten years old
But I want to be a hundred and ten
I really am a boy
But I want to be a whale
I really am smart
But I want to be dumb
I really am a cloud in the sky
But I want to be a dead tree
I really am a potato
But I want to be ice cream

When you look at this poem, you can see that the first line begins with the words "I really am . . . ." And the next line begins with the words "But I want to be . . . ." The other lines in the poem use the same beginning words. What lines would you like to start with?

■ In a poem, you can be anything you really are. And, if you use your imagination, then you can be anything you want to be. Now try to write a poem about yourself.

Tell the children that you will be available to provide help, if they need it. (Some children won't be able to spell the name of the city where they were born. Others may need suggestions to get them thinking about things they like—sports, food, TV programs, playing with a dog, making snowballs, and so on.)

Part II: Have a volunteer read the poem on page 173, and then discuss briefly how the boy who wrote this poem used his imagination. Also help the children see the form of the poem, which is discussed in the paragraph preceding the activity (■).

You can then suggest that each child make a list of four or five things that can follow the words: "I really am . . ." After they've made the list, they can think about things they want to be. Encourage them to use their imaginations—if they want to. In a poem, it's perfectly acceptable to say: "I really am a potato."

In any case, writing an autobiography—even an imaginative one—is difficult for almost everyone, and you should try to provide as much individual help as possible, even more so than with other types of compositions. Some children will need help with mechanics, but nearly all will need some gentle prodding in the form of suggestions or leading questions.

Follow-up Those children who have chosen Part I may want to write an autobiographical poem as a follow-up to this lesson. Perhaps even those children who have already written a poem about themselves will want to repeat this activity.

Additional Resources

Books Koch, Kenneth, *Wishes, Lies and Dreams,* Random House. This book contains many other excellent suggestions for teaching children to write poetry.

Purpose To provide children with an increased understanding of their own linguistic competence.

[This lesson is not intended to expand the sentence model; it seeks, rather, to make children aware of the different ways in which they use rules when constructing sentences. And it reminds them that these rules are already in their heads.]

Preparation Review with the children the earlier lessons on tag questions (pages 152–153 and 162–163). But, during the discussion, be careful to use only examples without an *n't* in the main sentence, such as:

1. The boy has climbed a tree, hasn't he?
2. You can make questions, can't you?
3. These sentences are easy, aren't they?

You can write the main parts of these sentences on the chalkboard, and then have the children make tag questions from them.

Presentation Since this lesson doesn't present essentially new material, you can treat it as a challenge. Remind the children that they know language rules in their heads but that it's not always easy to figure out what rules are. This lesson will present some evidence that—perhaps—will help them figure out one of these rules.

Either working in groups or with the entire class, read page 174 down to the activity (■). Help the children to understand the distinction between knowing a rule "in their heads," and trying to explain what that rule is. Work each of the examples in the activity slowly, asking leading questions as necessary so the children come to realize when—and when not—to use *n't* in the tag. For example, in the first sentence there is no *n't* in the

More About Tag Questions

So far, you've learned about two kinds of questions: *regular yes-or-no questions* and *tag questions*.
Here's a regular yes-or-no question.

Q + Jerry can swim well.
⟹ Can Jerry swim well?

And here's a tag question.

Q$_{tag}$ + Jerry can swim well.
⟹ Jerry can swim well, can't he?

Now look at the tag question again. At the end of the question—in the tag part—there's a word that ends in *n't*.
Here's another tag question.

Q$_{tag}$ + Jerry can't swim well.
⟹ Jerry can't swim well, can he?

Look at this tag question. Is there a word that ends in *n't* in the tag part?

Sometimes there's an *n't* in the tag part, and sometimes there isn't. How do you know when to put *n't* in the tag part of a question and when not to? The answer is easy. You know because there's a rule in your head that tells you. Maybe you can figure out what the rule is.

■ Now add Q$_{tag}$ to each of these sentences. Think about the rule while you're trying to do it.

1. Q$_{tag}$ + Janet is making lunch.
2. Q$_{tag}$ + The man doesn't like ants.
3. Q$_{tag}$ + The girl can wiggle her ears.
4. Q$_{tag}$ + The pencil isn't broken.
5. Q$_{tag}$ + The milk isn't very cold.

Answers

1. Janet is making lunch, isn't she?
2. The man doesn't like ants, does he?
3. The girl can wiggle her ears, can't she?
4. The pencil isn't broken, is it?
5. The milk isn't very cold, is it?

Here are two tag questions. One has an *n't* in the tag, and the other doesn't.

> Manuel can dance well, can't he?
> That frog isn't yours, is it?

In the first sentence, there's an *n't* in the tag. But is there an *n't* anywhere else in the sentence? In the second sentence, there's no *n't* in the tag. Can you guess why we don't put an *n't* in the tag?

■ Here are some more problems for you to try. (The first one is done for you.)

1. N'T + The nurse can stand on her head.
   ⇒ *The nurse can't stand on her head.*

   Now add Q$_{tag}$ to the sentence you just made.
   Q$_{tag}$ + The nurse can't stand on her head.
   ⇒ *The nurse can't stand on her head, can she?*

2. N'T + The mailman is hungry.
   ⇒ _____
   Q$_{tag}$ + _____
   ⇒ _____

3. N'T + The doctor can swim very fast.
   ⇒ _____
   Q$_{tag}$ + _____
   ⇒ _____

4. N'T + The lady has sold her car.
   ⇒ _____
   Q$_{tag}$ + _____
   ⇒ _____

Daybook: Q Tags, page 66

main sentence, so there will be one in the tag. In the second sentence, there is an *n't* in the main sentence, and consequently there is no *n't* in the tag. To help the children talk about this, you can write the first two sentences on the chalkboard, like this:

1. Janet is making lunch, isn't she?
2. The man doesn't like ants, does he?

Then you can write the next two sentences leaving the frame in the tag blank.

3. The girl can wiggle her ears, [   ] she?
4. The pencil isn't broken, [   ] it?

The material at the top of page 175 will help the children generalize about the rule for using *n't* in the tag. As the children begin to make generalizations about the rule, you may need to rephrase their statements.

The activity (■) on page 175 is essentially a review of Q$_{tag}$ and N'T. You may want to use it only with those children who need additional help with these concepts.

Follow-up For additional exercises on tag questions and negative statements, see page 177 of this guide.

Answers

2. The mailman isn't hungry. The mailman isn't hungry, is he?
3. The doctor can't swim very fast. The doctor can't swim very fast, can he?
4. The lady hasn't sold her car? The lady hasn't sold her car, has she?

Purposes (1) To re-emphasize the fact that metaphors can appeal to different senses; (2) To provide an additional opportunity for children to write an imaginary autobiography; (3) To reinforce the notion that children already know how to formulate derived sentences, and to provide practice with tag questions and negative statements, in particular.

Presentation As suggested earlier, you can divide the class into three groups for the presentation of this Review. Each group can then work on a single section of the lesson, perhaps reporting to the others after they have completed the activities. Alternatively, you can discuss the material in the text with the entire class, and then have the children choose which of the activities they wish to do.

Review

Literature

Sometimes, a poet makes a metaphor that's a word-picture. In your head, you can <u>see</u> that kind of metaphor. Sometimes, a poet makes a metaphor you can <u>hear</u>. Here's a metaphor to hear.

When the clouds move in the sky,
I think I can hear a cat laughing.

Can a cat really laugh? How could the clouds be like a cat laughing?

■ Here are some other things that don't make sounds. But suppose they could. Use them to try to make some metaphors you can <u>hear</u>.

1. the sun   3. pencils   5. red jelly beans
2. telephone poles   4. peanuts   6. chocolate ice cream

Composition

An autobiography is like a diary, but it's public instead of private. An autobiography is a true story. You write it for other people to read.

Instead of writing a real autobiography, suppose you pretended to be something or someone else. Then you could use your imagination. You could write an imaginary autobiography of the person—or thing—you were pretending to be.

Suppose you were a whale. What would you call yourself? Where would you live? What would you do every day? Would you do any special things?

Suppose you were the first person to take a trip all the way to the center of the earth. Then what kinds of things would you tell about?

■ Now pretend that you are something or someone else. Use your imagination to write an autobiography about that thing or that person.

Language

Everyone knows how to make derived sentences. That's because—in your head—you know lots of rules.

■ Here are some sentence problems for you to solve. First, add N'T to each basic sentence to make a derived sentence. Then, add Q_{tag} to each derived sentence you made. (The first one is done for you.)

1. N'T + The house is haunted.
   ⟹ *The house isn't haunted.*
   Q_{tag} + The house isn't haunted.
   ⟹ *The house isn't haunted, is it?*
2. Gerald has gone to school.
3. Ruby has baked a cake.
4. Mrs. Nims is my neighbor.
5. My father can ride a camel.
6. Lincoln was a lawyer.

 In this chapter, you wrote a letter to a friend. To learn more about how to write letters, look on pages 290–291.

As a follow-up to the grammar lessons presented in this chapter, you can use the following activity. First have the children identify each sentence as basic or derived, and then have them tell what has been added to each derived sentence —Q_{tag} or N'T or both.

1. The flea rode on a frog.
2. The groundhog saw his shadow, didn't he?
3. The moon danced on a cloud.
4. That monkey doesn't like bananas, does he?
5. That frog hasn't croaked for years.
6. The hippo smiled happily, didn't he?
7. I don't know my zip code.
8. The zebra lost his stripes, didn't he?
9. A hen can't crow, can she?
10. The tortoise didn't fall asleep.

Answers

2. Gerald hasn't gone to school. Gerald hasn't gone to school, has he?
3. Ruby hasn't baked a cake. Ruby hasn't baked a cake, has she?
4. Mrs. Nims isn't my neighbor. Mrs. Nims isn't my neighbor, is she?
5. My father can't ride a camel. My father can't ride a camel, can he?
6. Lincoln wasn't a lawyer. Lincoln wasn't a lawyer, was he?

Purposes (1) To introduce the ballad as a literary form; (2) To identify ballads as poems and songs that tell stories, usually about a hero.

Preparation A day or two before teaching this lesson, you might play recordings of some ballads. Also a few days before teaching the lesson, you can read several ballads to the class, including some that were not originally set to music, for example, "Sam Houston," and "The Pirate Don Durk of Dundee." (See Additional Resources.) This advance preparation will permit the ballad concept to "simmer" in the children's minds before they are asked to talk about a particular ballad.

Presentation Remind the children of the ballads they've already heard, and then read the introduction on page 178 with them. You might want to enlarge on the brief comments about Paul Bunyan, Johnny Appleseed, and John Henry, particularly if you used ballads about these heroes as a preparation to the lesson or if you plan to use them as a follow-up.

If possible, you should first sing the ballad "Casey Jones" to the children, with as much gusto as you can muster. (Remember, you are the model the children look to most when learning to respond to literature.) Another effective alternative would be to invite another teacher into your class to sing the song. If neither of these alternatives is possible, then you should play a lively recording of the song.

After the children have heard the ballad sung, then they can follow along in their books as you read the ballad to them. You may need to explain some of the terms used: A *rounder* is a person who works for the railroad (the name derives from the *roundhouse* where the engines were kept). The *caller* is also known

A Ballad

A poem or a song that tells a story about someone is a **ballad.** Most ballads are written in four-line stanzas.

In almost every country, there are ballads about people who lived long ago and who did exciting things. In our country, there are ballads about Paul Bunyan, who made trees into logs. There are ballads about Johnny Appleseed, who planted many apple trees, and about John Henry, who helped to build the railroads. There is also a ballad about Casey Jones, who was a famous railroad engineer. This ballad tells the story of the last time Casey Jones drove a mail train.

Daybook: Which One Do You Trust?
page 68

178

Casey Jones

Come, all you rounders, for I want you to hear
A story 'bout a brave engineer.
Casey Jones was the rounder's name
On a six-eight wheeler he won his fame.

The caller called Casey at half past four,
He kissed his wife at the station door,
Then mounted to the cabin with his orders in his hand
Took his farewell trip to the promised land.

as the "dispatcher"; it was his job to assign crews to a train and to schedule departure times. The *drivers* are the large wheels on the engine. These are the wheels that move the locomotive; the smaller wheels in front and behind merely help support the locomotive and guide it around curves. (The early locomotives converted water to steam in a boiler and used the pressure from the steam to drive the engine.) You might also want to explain that trains are required, by law, to whistle when approaching a road that crosses; the standard signal is long, long, short, long.

You might want to read the ballad again, or sing it, before turning to the discussion on pages 180–181. This discussion focuses on two things: describing the hero of a ballad, and recognizing that a ballad tells a story. A later lesson on ballads (pages 202–204) concentrates on the form of a ballad, and you may want to postpone a discussion of form until you teach that lesson.

The first paragraph on page 181 suggests one of the many ways in which literary forms are related and, more importantly, suggests that there's more than one way to tell a story.

The activity (■) on page 181 focuses on making literature personal. Children, ideally, should come to feel that writers of poems, stories, songs, and so on are just ordinary people. This can help them develop a more positive attitude toward their own writing.

Follow-up You, or the music teacher, may want to teach the children to sing the ballad about Casey Jones. You can suggest that some children pantomime the action of the ballad while others sing it.

The children might also enjoy illustrating the different stanzas of the ballad.

Additional Resources

Books Carmer, Carl, *America Sings,* Knopf. Lomax, John A. and Alan, *American Ballads and Folk Songs,* Macmillan. Niles, John J. and Helen L. Smith, *Folk Ballads for Young Actors,* Holt, Rinehart and Winston. Rounds, Glen, *Casey Jones: the Story of a Brave Engineer,* Golden Gate. Sandburg, Carl, *The American Song-bag,* Harcourt. Seeger, Pete, *American Favorite Ballads,* Oak. Seeger, Ruth Crawford, *American Folk Songs for Children,* Doubleday.

Recordings *American Favorite Ballads,* 4–12″ LPs, Spoken Arts. Pete Seeger sings some of our best-loved ballads. *Classics of American Poetry for the Elementary Curriculum,* 2–12″ LPs, Caedmon. "Casey Jones" is one of the selections read on this set of recordings. *900 Miles and Other Railroad Songs,* 1–10″ LP, Folkways. On this recording, Cisco Houston sings of the railroad workers. *The Spoken Arts Treasury of American Ballads and Folk Songs,* 6–12″ LPs, Caedmon. Burl Ives sings some favorite American classics. *Treasury of American Ballads and Folk Songs, Sung by Burl Ives,* 6–12″ LPs, cassettes, Miller-Brody.

Filmstrips *American Folklore Series,* 10 sound filmstrips, Holt, Rinehart and Winston. This series includes "Casey Jones," as well as "Paul Bunyan," "Johnny Appleseed," and "John Henry." *Billy Ballad's Hootenanny,* 6 filmstrips and cassettes, Eye Gate. One of the filmstrips in this series deals specifically with ballads. *Casey Jones,* sound, filmstrip, Coronet.

"Put in your water and shovel in your coal,
Put your head out the window and watch them drivers roll,
I'll run her hard till she leaves the rail
'Cause I'm eight hours late with the westbound mail."

He looked at his watch and his watch was slow,
He looked at the water and the water was low,
He turned to the fireman and then he said,
"We're goin' to reach Frisco but we'll all be dead."

Casey pulled up that Reno Hill,
He tooted for the crossing with an awful shrill,
The switchman knew by the engine's moans
That the man at the throttle was Casey Jones.

He pulled up within two miles of the place,
Number Four was staring him right in the face,
He turned to the fireman, said "Boy, you better jump,
'Cause there's two locomotives that's a-goin' to bump."

Casey said just before he died,
"There's two more roads that I'd like to ride."
The fireman said what could they be?
"The Southern Pacific and the Sante Fe."

There really was an *engineer* named Casey Jones. He drove a *six-eight wheeler,* which is a special kind of engine. Casey was killed at the *throttle* of his fast train. He stayed in the *cabin,* slowing down the train as much as he could. In that way, he saved the lives of his crew and his passengers.

Ballads are often set to music. Most of them are songs about a hero. They tell about the dangerous things that the hero does. What are some of the things that Casey does?

Do you remember the story about the pony express rider? That was a true story about another man who carried the mail. How are the two stories alike? How are they different? Which story did you enjoy most? Why?

■ There are lots of real heroes in our country's history. And there are lots of imaginary heroes in our folk tales. Think about a hero you'd like to write about. He or she can be real or imaginary. Then tell some of the things your hero is and has and does.

Telling and Talking

Once a girl wrote this story about her trip to the circus.

Yesterday my father took me to the circus. He bought some peanuts from a man in a white hat. Then he spilled the peanuts in a lady's lap. She got mad, and my father laughed.

After a while, she decided to revise the story.

Yesterday my father took me to the circus. He bought some peanuts from a man in a white hat. Then he spilled the peanuts in a lady's lap. The lady said, "That was a nutty thing to do." My father laughed.

What changes did the girl make when she revised the story? Which story do you like better?

Purposes (1) To illustrate how dialogue can sometimes make a story—or poem—more interesting; (2) To introduce the mechanics necessary for writing dialogue.

[Although the mechanics of using quotation marks are important, it's more important—in this lesson—for children to understand how dialogue can sometimes improve a story by making it more interesting. This fact suggests another point: The lesson is intended as an overview, and the children can't be expected to absorb all the material during the first reading. Thus, you can teach the lesson twice, emphasizing the value of dialogue on the first teaching and the mechanics of writing dialogue on the second.]

Preparation The material on page 181 can serve as preparation for the body of the lesson, which begins on page 182. Call for volunteers to read the two facsimile compositions, and then have the children compare them and identify the differences.

After comparing the two versions of the story, you can have the class consider questions such as these:

1. Do you like stories in which people talk?
2. How does conversation help a story?
3. Do you like to read or act in plays? Why?

Additionally, you can refer back to the literature lesson on autobiography, where the children had the chance to read—and act out—the conversation that Sammy Davis, Jr., had with the boys in the candy store. Then you can discuss with the children how each speaker knew when to begin talking.

Presentation After reading the first paragraph on page 182, you can introduce the children to the two boys in the "picture-story." If possible, duplicate the four pictures on the chalkboard, including the word balloons. Then discuss what happens in each picture, and ask for suggestions about things the boys could be saying. You can write these suggestions inside the word balloons that you've drawn. (Using the chalkboard enables you to erase and change the words easily, thereby stressing the process of revision.)

In teaching the lesson the first time, you can concentrate on eliciting appropriate things for the two boys to say. You might make a record of the children's suggestions, which can then be used when you teach the mechanics of using quotation marks. (If you follow this suggestion, you'll probably want to save page 183 until you teach the lesson again.)

One way to write a story about people is to tell about the things that happen. But you can also tell what the people say. Stories about people are almost always more interesting if the people are talking. And to have people talking in a story, you need to know how to use *quotation marks* when you write.

Here are some pictures of two boys named Billy and Jack. You can use them to tell a story. First, tell what you think is happening in each picture.

Look again at the first picture. What are the two boys doing? What is Jack saying to his friend? What does Billy answer? Suppose you want to include these words in your story. How would you do it?

182

First, we'll write the exact words each boy said.

What's that great smell?
I think it's apple pie.

Then we'll put quotation marks around these words.

"What's that great smell?"
"I think it's apple pie."

To show who said what, we'll add some words to each sentence, like this.

Jack asked, "What's that great smell?"
Billy answered, "I think it's apple pie."

What else did we add besides some words? We added commas to separate *Jack asked* from *"What's that great smell?"* and to separate *Billy answered* from *"I think it's apple pie."* Usually, we use commas to separate the exact words someone says from the rest of the sentence.

Sometimes, we don't use commas when we write quotations. Here are the sentences that the boys said again.

"What's that great smell?"
"I think it's apple pie."

And now look at these sentences.

"What's that great smell?" Jack asked.
"I think it's apple pie," Billy answered.

Now *Jack asked* and *Billy answered* come after the exact words that the boys said. In the first sentence, we didn't use a comma at all. But in the second sentence, there is a comma. We used a comma where the period was in the sentence that Billy said. Why do you think we <u>didn't</u> use a comma in the first sentence? Can you guess why we <u>did</u> use a comma in the second sentence?

The second time through the lesson, you can emphasize the difference between writing conversation in word balloons in a comic strip and using quotation marks —instead of word balloons—in a story. Each way has its advantages. One major advantage of the written form is that it permits the writer to include such things as *Jack shouted, Billy answered softly,* and so on. In other words, the writer can describe the way people speak, which can't be done with word balloons. In teaching this lesson, you may find it useful to say that quotation marks "wrap up" a speaker's exact words.

The activity (■) on page 184 can also be done orally with the entire class, drawing the pictures on the chalkboard.

Follow-up This is a good time to teach the lesson on Quotation Marks on pages 314–315 of the Skills Section.

Purposes (1) To introduce *morpheme* as a useful term in discussing language; (2) To define some of the characteristics of morphemes.

[The pace to follow in teaching this lesson will depend, in large part, on the type of reading instruction that your class has had. It's quite important that the children have considerable experience working with prefixes and suffixes before they are introduced to the terms *prefix, suffix,* and *morpheme.* In general, technical terms should be used to facilitate discussion of things the children already know in a non-technical way.]

Preparation On the chalkboard, write the following words: *review, describer, walked, boys.* Use these words to review the prefix *re-* and the suffixes *-er, -ed,* and *-s.* If you wish, you can draw additional examples of words containing such affixes from spelling and reading lists which the children have used, including those from earlier grades. (If these are unavailable, or if they don't provide a sufficient number of examples, you can find additional ones in most dictionaries.)

Presentation As noted above, the form of presentation will vary considerably from class to class, depending on the background of the children. (You might also want to adapt the suggestions given here so that they follow your presentation of the same topics in reading.) In any case, you should avoid introducing the term *morpheme* until the children are completely comfortable with the terms *prefix* and *suffix.* You can use these terms repeatedly as you discuss the material on page 184. In addition to the examples given in the text, you might want to use those at the top of the next page.

■ Now copy the pictures onto your paper. Think of something for the boys to say in each picture. Write the words that they say right on your pictures. Then use your pictures to write a story about the boys. Don't forget to use quotation marks around the exact words that the boys say.

Morphemes

When you were learning to read, you probably learned about **prefixes** and **suffixes.**

● A prefix is a part of a word that we can add to the front of a whole word.

● A suffix is a part of a word that we can add to the end of a whole word.

Here are some prefixes that you probably know.

mono-   non-   re-   un-

But do you know what these words mean?

monorail   nonstop   rebuild   unfair

Here are some suffixes that you should also know.

-er   -ful   -ish   -less

And here's how we can add these suffixes to words.

farmer   careful   childish   careless

There are also special suffixes for nouns and verbs.

-s   -'s   -ed   -ing

How do they change the meaning of the words they're added to?

boys   man's   walked   speaking

Daybook: Practice with Morphemes, page 70

■ Which of these words have prefixes? Which have suffixes?

1. hopeless	4. doctor's	7. unhappy
2. drinking	5. thankful	8. girls
3. walker	6. nonstop	9. rewrite

Now tell how each prefix or suffix changes the meaning of the word it's added to.

Every prefix means something. Every suffix means something. And every word means something. There's a special name for words or parts of words that mean something. They're called **morphemes.**

● A morpheme is a part of language that has a single meaning.

Here's a letter: *e*. By itself, this letter doesn't mean anything. Now here are three more letters: *c, k, n*. Does *c* mean anything by itself? Does *k* mean anything? Does *n*? Here's one way we can put the letters together: *kenc*. Does *kenc* mean anything in English?

The letters *e, c, k*, and *n* don't mean anything by themselves. So they're not morphemes. If we put them together to spell *kenc*, they still don't mean anything. So *kenc* isn't a morpheme.

Now try to put the letters *e, c, k*, and *n* together so that they <u>do</u> spell something that has meaning. Is the word a morpheme? Why?

■ Try to put these letters together so each group makes a morpheme. Be careful. Sometimes the letters make a whole word. And sometimes they make a prefix or suffix.

1. e, n, s, s	4. i, l, k, m	7. o, r, d, w
2. a, l, k, t	5. y, f, l	8. g, n, i
3. o, n, n	6. n, e	9. d, e

Answers

In the first activity, words 6, 7, and 9 have prefixes. Words 1, 2, 3, 4, 5, and 8 have suffixes.

In the second activity, the letters can be arranged to form the following morphemes:

1. -ness	4. milk	7. word
2. talk	5. fly	8. -ing *or* gin
3. non-	6. -en	9. de- *or* -ed

mono-: monoplane, monotone
non-: nonsolid, nonhuman
re-: repaint, reread
un-: undone, unable
-er: fighter, dancer
-ful: hopeful, fearful
-ish: boyish, greenish
-less: childless, painless

You might also want to explain the meaning of these prefixes and suffixes:

mono-: "one"	*-er*: "one who"
non-: "not"	*-ful*: "full of"
re-: "again"	*-ish*: "like"
un-: "not"	*-less*: "without"

You can do the activity (■) on the top of page 185 orally with the entire class. You might suggest that the children use each word in a sentence to demonstrate how the prefix or suffix changes the meaning of the word it's added to.

Then read the text on page 185 with the children, calling special attention to the sentence after the (●). To add visual impact, you can repeat on the chalkboard the example given in the paragraph which follows. You can also have the children write the letters *e, c, k*, and *n* on separate slips of paper and then try to arrange these letters so that they do make a morpheme.

The activity (■) on the bottom of page 185 can be treated as a game, with the children working in two or more groups.

Follow-up This is a good time to teach the lesson on Plural Words on pages 292–293 of the Skills Section. If you've already taught this lesson, another alternative might be the lesson on Verb Forms on pages 327–329. Additionally, there are two exercises dealing with morphemes on page 197 of this guide.

Purposes (1) To introduce *homograph* and *homophone* as useful terms in discussing language; (2) To distinguish between these two terms.

Preparation Review the earlier lesson on homographs (pages 32–33) with the children. Remind them that homographs are words which look alike but mean different things. Remind them, also, that some homographs (like *f-a-i-r* in *a fair day* and *a country fair*) sound alike, but that other homographs (like *w-i-n-d* in *the wind blew* and *wind the clock*) do not sound alike. Then suggest that, in today's lesson, the children will learn some more things about homographs, and they'll also learn about some other kinds of words.

Presentation Have the children read the first paragraph on page 186, which provides an additional review of homographs. As they're reading, you can write the words *homograph* and *homophone* as column heads on the chalkboard. Help the children pronounce *homophone,* and then have them compare the two terms.

Next, read the second paragraph on page 186 with the children, pausing so they can answer the questions about homophones. As the children read the list of homophones, you can write them on the chalkboard under the appropriate heading. Then you can ask the children to suggest a few other pairs, which you can also add to the list. Finally, you should ask for volunteers to use all of the listed homophones in sentences.

The activity (■) at the bottom of page 186 can be done orally. As the children identify each pair, you can add the words to the list on the chalkboard. (The activity should also enable you to judge how well the children grasp the distinction between the two terms.)

Here are two sentences you've seen before.

Judge Sanchez makes <u>fair</u> decisions.
Did you go to the county <u>fair</u>?

Look at the underlined words in these sentences. They look the same. They sound the same. But they mean different things. What is the special name for words that are spelled the same but have different meanings (and sometimes different pronunciations)? They're called *homographs.* (*Homo* is a prefix that means "same" or "alike." And *graph* means "something written.")

Here are two more sentences.

Sandy sang only <u>one</u> song.
She <u>won</u> the prize anyway.

Say the underlined words in these sentences. Do they <u>sound</u> the same? Do they <u>look</u> the same? Do they <u>mean</u> the same thing? Words that are pronounced alike but are different in meaning and spelling are called **homophones.** (Do you remember what *homo* means?) Can you guess what *phone* means?

Here are some examples of homophones.

| know, no | eight, ate | to, too, two |
| hear, here | son, sun | threw, through |

■ Here are two pairs of sentences. Which pair has homographs? Which has homophones?

1. I dropped my pencil into the <u>pitcher</u> of milk.
   Our team is good, but we need one more <u>pitcher</u>.
2. I put the table over <u>there</u>.
   <u>Their</u> play was good, but our play was better.

Answers

The first pair of sentences has homographs; the second pair has homophones.

■ Here are some homographs. Use the dictionary to find two different meanings for each one.

1. crow	5. junk	9. fast
2. dove	6. mint	10. list
3. duck	7. record	11. desert
4. hatch	8. live	12. object

■ Now here are some homophones. They're written with the special pronunciation symbols used in a dictionary. First write two words for each homophone, using the regular letters of the alphabet. Then use the words in the sentences. (The first one is done for you.)

1. mēt   *meet, meat*
         Did you *meet* John?
         I ate the *meat.*

2. pãr   _____
         I have a new _____ of shoes.
         The _____ tree is pretty.

3. hōl   _____
         Joe fell in a _____.
         He ate the _____ pie.

4. fôr   _____
         I lost _____ marbles.
         Please get it _____ me.

5. flou' ər   _____
         We need _____ for the cake.
         The _____ is growing.

6. nēd   _____
         We _____ some new books.
         We saw the cook _____ the dough.

The activity (■) at the top of page 187 can be done individually or in pairs. Again, have the children use the words in sentences after they've checked the meanings in a dictionary. (Not all dictionaries use separate entries to distinguish between homographs such as *record* and *object*. In such cases, you may need to help the children locate the definitions which apply to two different pronunciations given for each word.)

In working the second activity (■) on page 187, you may want to refer the children to the lesson on the Pronunciation Key in the Skills Section (pages 279–281).

Follow-up This is an appropriate time to introduce the lesson on Homophones on pages 286–287 of the Skills Section.

Answers
Answers may vary somewhat for the first activity.

The answers to the second activity are as follows:
2. pair, pear: I have a new pair of shoes. The pear tree is pretty.
3. hole, whole: Joe fell in a hole. He ate the whole pie.
4. for, four, or fore: I lost four marbles. Please get it for me.
5. flower, flour: We need flour for the cake. The flower is growing.
6. need, knead: We need some new books. We saw the cook knead the dough.

Purpose   To introduce the Biblical story as another literary form.

[The Bible is, of course, the most famous literary work in the world. There are more copies of the Bible—in more languages—than any other book ever written.]

Preparation   Remind the children of some of the heroes that they've already read about (for example, Perseus, Warren Upson, and Casey Jones). Ask if anyone has read other stories about heroes, perhaps Daedalus and Icarus, Hercules, and so on. Then ask the children to suggest what a hero—any hero—must be like. Encourage them to try to describe some of the characteristics that a hero usually has. Finally, suggest that in the Old Testament of the Bible there are many stories about heroes, and that in today's lesson they'll be able to read about one of these heroes—a young boy named David.

Presentation   Read the introductory paragraph on page 189 to the children, giving them brief definitions of the italicized words. You can use the illustration on pages 188–189 to introduce David and Goliath, and then help the children pronounce the names of David's brothers—Eliab, Abinadab, and Shammah—who are also mentioned in the story.

A Biblical Story

One of the most famous parts of the Bible is the story of David and Goliath. David was a young *Israelite* who took care of the sheep while his brothers went off to fight the *Philistines*. One of the Philistines was a giant named Goliath. Here's what happened when Goliath *challenged* the army of Israel.

David and Goliath

The army of the Philistines stood on a mountain on one side of a valley and the army of the Israelites with their king, King Saul, stood on a mountain on the other side. One day there came down from the Philistine side the strongest man of their army—a giant, more than nine feet tall. The giant's name was Goliath. He wore a helmet and a coat of bronze.

Goliath shouted across the valley to the army of Israel, "I am a Philistine. Choose a man to fight with me. Let him come into the valley. If he can conquer me, then we will be your servants. But if I can conquer him, then you shall be our servants." But the Israelites were afraid, and no one answered the giant.

Depending upon the reading ability of your class, you might want to assign the story for individual reading. If so, you will probably need to help the children with words such as *helmet, bronze, conquer, defy, challenge, boastful, courage, shepherd, flock, brass,* and *deliver.* Alternatively, you can read the story aloud as the children follow along in their books.

If the children have read the story individually, then bring the group together again before discussing the questions on page 191. This discussion can be elaborated considerably by asking questions such as the following:

1. How was Goliath dressed? Why?
2. Why did the Israelites fear Goliath?
3. Why did the young boy—David—go to the army camp?
4. How did his oldest brother feel when David said he wasn't afraid?
5. What was the reason that David went before the king?
6. What did he tell the king to prove that he had courage?
7. What did David do when the king gave him a helmet and coat of brass? Why?
8. Why was the giant so angry when he saw David?

Encourage the children to look back at the story for answers to these questions.

After discussing the story in this way, you can go on to ask the children to draw some conclusions from the story. You might ask: "Do you think David was a good king? What did you learn from the story that helps you to answer this question? Why do you think a king might want to write poetry?"

Follow-up This is another good selection for the children to dramatize, but you might want to have them read some other versions of the story first. (See Additional Resources.) If any children are familiar with other Biblical stories, you can give them the alternative of acting out one of these for the rest of the class.

And Goliath shouted again, "I defy the army of Israel. Send me a man from among you that we may fight together." But no one came. Every morning and every evening for forty days the giant shouted his challenge to the Israelites. But no one dared answer him.

Now in the army of the Israelites there were three brothers, Eliab, Abinadab, and Shammah, from the town of Bethlehem. They had a young brother named David, who lived in Bethlehem and watched after the sheep while the older brothers were away. One day the father of the brothers gave David some food to take to the army.

When David got to the camp of the Israelites, he saw both armies standing on the mountains with the valley between them. David found his brothers and gave them the food. Then he heard the loud voice of Goliath, who was shouting from the other mountain. "Send me a man from among you that we may fight together." But no man from Israel would dare to answer him.

And the men near David said to him, "Did you hear this giant who has defied all Israel? If any man is able to kill the giant, then our great King Saul will surely give him a rich reward." David heard all this, and he was not afraid.

Then Eliab, the oldest brother, was angry and said to David, "Why have you come here, and where did you leave your sheep? I know you are too boastful. All you want here is to watch the battle." But David said, "What have I done now? Why do you speak to me like this?" And David turned away from his brothers.

King Saul heard of David's courage and sent for him. Before the king, David said, "Let no man be afraid of the giant. I am small, but I will fight with him." But King Saul asked, "How can you fight this giant? You are only a boy, and Goliath has been a soldier and fighter for many years."

In reply, David told the king a story. "I am only a

shepherd. When a lion or a bear takes a lamb from my flock, then I go to rescue the lamb out of his mouth. The God of Israel has helped me, and God will help me rescue the army of Israel from the giant."

So King Saul gave his helmet and his coat of brass to David. And he gave him his sword and his shield. But they were too heavy for the boy. David said, "I cannot wear these. I am only a boy."

David reached down and took five smooth stones from the brook, and he put them in the shepherd's bag he had with him. Then he took up his slingshot and went out to meet the giant.

When Goliath saw that David was only a boy and not a man, he shouted, "Am I a dog that you come against me with sticks?" And he cursed David and said, "I'll give your flesh to the birds of the air and to the beasts of the field."

David answered the giant, "You come to me with a sword and a spear and a shield, but I come to you in the name of the Lord. This day the Lord will deliver you into my hands." And when David had finished speaking, Goliath drew near him. David took a smooth stone from his shepherd's bag, and put it in his sling and took aim. The stone struck the giant in the forehead, and he fell upon his face on the ground. With a sling and with a stone, David had killed Goliath. ■

Is Goliath a hero? Is David a hero? What makes you think so? Why does David want to use a sling and five smooth stones instead of a sword and spear?

David grew up to become King. He was not only a good king and a good fighter, he also wrote poetry.

■ From what you read about David in this story, tell what you think would make him a good king or a good poet.

Additional Resources

Books Barnhart, Nancy, *The Lord Is My Shepherd,* Scribner. This book contains a number of Old Testament stories simply retold from the King James version of the Bible. Bowie, Walter Russell, *Bible Stories for Boy and Girls: Old Testament,* Abingdon. Children can easily understand the modern language used in the retelling of the Biblical stories included in this book. de Angeli, Marguerite, *The Old Testament,* Garden City. This lavishly illustrated book is an excellent introduction to Biblical stories for children. De Jong, Meindert, *The Mighty Ones: Great Men and Women of Early Bible Days,* Harper & Row. This collection contains another version of the story of David and Goliath which you might want to read to the children. De Regniers, Beatrice, *David and Goliath,* Viking. This is an excellent book for individual reading. Other books about David include Groom, Arthur, *The Young David,* Rou; King, Marian, *Young David,* Lippincott; and Petersham, Maud and Miska, *David,* Macmillan. Other titles by the Petershams include *Joseph and His Brothers, Moses,* and *Ruth.* Untermeyer, Louis, editor, *Songs of Joy: Selections from the Book of Psalms,* World. Werner, Elsa J., editor, *The Golden Bible,* Golden. This book is beautifully illustrated by Feodor Rojankovsky.

Recordings *Bible Stories for Children,* 2–10″ LPs, Folkways.

Purposes (1) To define the nature of a newspaper interview; (2) To illustrate how a writer develops an interview into a story; (3) To provide an opportunity for children to conduct interviews and then write stories based on the interviews.

Preparation Occasionally, a newspaper will print a complete interview, including the reporter's questions, particularly when the person interviewed is famous. You can use such material to illustrate the kinds of questions that reporters often ask. Some children may also have seen interviews on television, perhaps during a news program. If so, you can ask the children what kinds of questions the reporters ask and encourage them to think of reasons for asking questions such as these. Try to elicit the idea that it's part of a reporters job to ask questions. You can then ask the children what a newspaper reporter does after he gets the answers to his questions. Finally, suggest that in today's lesson the children will learn more about interviews and newspaper stories.

Presentation Ask the children how they would feel if they won first prize in a contest of some kind. Then ask how they'd feel if newspaper reporters came to photograph them and ask them questions. Next, read page 192 along with the children, pausing as necessary so the children can answer the questions.

An Interview

Here's a picture of a woman who has just won first prize in a cake-baking contest.

The men who are talking to the woman work for a newspaper. Try to guess why they're talking to her. What do you think they are saying? Why do they have notebooks? What are they writing in the notebooks? What will the men do when they have finished talking to the woman?

The kind of meeting that the newspaper men are having with the woman is called an **interview.** The men are reporters and they are asking her questions. Newspaper men always remember to ask WH questions:

WHo
WHat
WHen
WHere
WHy

Then they use their answers to write a newspaper story.

Daybook: Interviews, page 72

This is part of the story that one of the men wrote after he talked to the woman.

STRAWBERRY–CARROT CAKE TAKES FIRST PRIZE IN CONTEST

Mrs. Hazel Rossi took first prize in the all-state cake-baking contest held yesterday at the city arena. The winning cake was made from strawberries and carrots, and was decorated with peanuts. "This is a secret family recipe," said Mrs. Rossi after the contest. "I always make one for my husband's birthday. He said I should make one for the contest."

Mrs. Rossi lives at 179 Water Street, Apt. D. She has three children. "All of them like my cooking," she said. This is the first time that Mrs. Rossi entered the contest.

Did the reporter remember to ask the right questions? Does he tell who the woman is? Does he tell what the woman has done? Can you tell from the story when and where she did it? Does the reporter tell you why she did it? Does he tell you anything else about the woman?

You can have an interview in your class. Someone can play the part of a famous person visiting your school. Perhaps the person has won a prize. Perhaps the person has written a book or is on television. Perhaps the person has even been to the moon. Try to think of some good questions to ask. Don't forget about who, what, when, where, and why.

■ Now interview the famous person with your classmates. Write down the answers to the questions that are asked. Then write a newspaper story. Be sure that your story tells who, what, when, where, and why.

After the children have read the five WH questions on the bottom of page 192, you can ask them to imagine that they are the reporters in the illustration. What questions would they ask? As the children suggest questions, list them on the chalkboard for later reference. Then call on a volunteer to read the newspaper story on page 193, and discuss the questions in the paragraph that follows. Be sure the children locate specific answers in the news story itself. Also be sure to stress that reporters must be careful when they write their stories.

You can play the part of the "famous person" described in the paragraph preceding the activity (■), but let the class decide what kind of famous person you should be. Then, in small groups, have the children plan their interviews. Each group can then ask you two or three questions, allowing the other groups to listen as you answer. Then each group can write its own newspaper story.

Follow-up A natural follow-up to this lesson is to return to it at another time and repeat the activity suggested on page 193. Alternatively, you might arrange with a few teachers, the principal, or other people working in your school to visit your classroom. Then the children can interview these people and write a news story as a result.

Purposes (1) To develop further the concept of morpheme; (2) To provide an opportunity for children to use the term *morpheme* in discussing language.

Preparation Review the earlier lesson on morphemes (pages 184–185), perhaps by providing more "scrambled morphemes" like those in the activity on the bottom of page 185. Here are some you might want to use:

e, d, k, s	p, a, m, l	u, l, f
e, p, n	e, p, r	s, l, e, s
a, d, w, r	o, n, o, m	o, n, n

Before doing this activity, be sure to remind the children that prefixes and suffixes are also morphemes.

Presentation Have the children examine the illustration at the bottom of page 194. After the children have identified the two figures as cowboys, have a volunteer locate, on a map of the United States, the general area where cowboys live. Point out that this area is known as the Southwest. Ask a volunteer to identify some things in the illustration which indicate that it's a picture of the Southwest. Then write the two words—*south* and *west*—on the chalkboard. Use each word in a separate sentence, and then use the compound word in a separate sentence.

Next, add the suffix *-ern* following the words *south* and *west* on the board, and use the word *southwestern* in a sentence. Help the children understand how you are "building up" the word. Finally, point out that the picture still has two more letters. Add these, and then use the word *southwesterner* in a sentence.

Now you can ask what word in the title of the lesson names the parts of the word you've been building up. Then ask

More About Morphemes

There are thousands and thousands of morphemes in English. Some morphemes are words. Some morphemes are only parts of words. But every morpheme has a meaning.

Here are some words.

baseball   bookcase   houseboat   snowman

Try to take each of these words apart and make it into two other words. Does each smaller word mean something? Is each smaller word a morpheme?

● Sometimes a word has more than one morpheme.

Here's an example. Suppose we have these morphemes.

-er (a suffix meaning "a person who does something")
-ern (a suffix meaning "a place")
south (a whole word)
west (a whole word)

If we put the last two morphemes together, we get *southwest*. If we put the last three together, we get *southwestern*. This is a word we use when we talk about the southwest part of the country. The word *southwestern* has three morphemes in it. If we put all four of the morphemes together, then we get the word *southwesterner*. This word means "a person who lives in the southwestern part of the country."

Daybook: More Morphemes, page 74

194

Here's another word: *cup*. Suppose we divide this word into these two parts: *c* and *up*. The second part means something. But does *c* mean anything all by itself?

If we try to divide a word into morphemes, each part <u>must</u> have a meaning. Suppose we can't divide a word so that each part has a meaning. Then the word has just one morpheme. If we try to divide *cup* into *c* and *up*, one part has no meaning. So *cup* must be only one morpheme.

Suppose we try to divide the word *hand* into more than one morpheme. We can get *and*, but we have *h* left over. And *h* doesn't mean anything by itself. So *hand* has only one morpheme.

■ Which of these words have only one morpheme? Which have more than one?

1. many	5. untie	9. school
2. of	6. rail	10. broil
3. butterfly	7. dairy	11. sandwich
4. frogs	8. nice	12. bagpipe

■ How many morphemes can you find in each one of these words?

1. elephant	5. stomach	9. handful
2. recopying	6. uneasily	10. backwardness
3. typewriter	7. preview	11. handkerchief
4. greenhouses	8. impossible	12. shingle

■ Here are some morphemes. Try to combine them in as many different ways as you can.

1. week	5. break	9. ful
2. less	6. spoon	10. cup
3. day	7. fast	11. end
4. ly	8. er	12. color

them to name each of the four morphemes in the word *southwesterner*.

Read page 194 as the children follow along (or call on volunteers to read particular paragraphs), pausing as usual to discuss the questions. When you come to the discussion of *southwesterner*, you may want to add another morpheme—the *-s* which indicates plural—thereby making a word which has five separate morphemes in it.

The first three paragraphs on page 195 are best done orally. Repeating the "division" of *cup* and *hand* on the chalkboard will add a useful visual impression. The first activity (■) can also be done orally to provide a model for doing the other two. Encourage the children to use a dictionary in working these activities.

Follow-up For additional activities, see page 197 of this guide.

Answers

In the first activity, items 1, 2, 6, 7, 8, 9, 10, and 11 have only one morpheme. Items 3, 4, 5, and 12 have more than one morpheme.

The answers for the second activity are as follows:

1. one	5. one	9. two
2. three	6. three	10. three
3. three	7. two	11. two
4. three	8. two	12. one

Here are some of the words that can be made from the morphemes in the third activity.

weekday	spoonful
weekly	spooner
weekend	faster
lesser	cupful
daily	cupless
daybreak	endless
breakfast	colorless
breaker	colorful
breakfastless	colorfast
spoonless	colorer

Purposes (1) To suggest additional characteristics of literary heroes; (2) To re-emphasize the importance of conversation in composition; (3) To review the concept of morpheme, particularly as it applies to words and parts of words.

Presentation Before discussing the Literature Review, you might want to reread or resing the ballad "Casey Jones," as well as some of the other ballads that the children have learned. Then you can extend the discussion in the text to include these heroes. Additionally, you can have the children compare Casey and David with the heroes that they read about in previous chapters, for example, Perseus, Warren Upson, or Sammy Davis, Jr.

The first part of the Composition Review focuses on the importance of revision. After the children have revised the sample story in the text, you might want to have them try to make one of their own compositions more interesting by adding some dialogue.

You can treat the Language Review as a group game. Additionally, you can have the groups make up lists of "scrambled" morphemes which can then be exchanged with other groups. If you decide to do this, be sure to remind the children once again that a morpheme can be a prefix or a suffix as well as a whole word.

Review

Literature

In this chapter you read a *ballad* about Casey Jones. Do you remember what a ballad is? You also read the biblical story of David. Both Casey and David are heroes. Do you think one was more of a hero than the other? Why or why not? What do you think a hero should be like?

■ Do you know any other heroes? Choose one of your favorite heroes and write a story about him or her.

Composition

When you write a composition, you can tell what people <u>do</u>. And you can also tell what people <u>say</u>.

■ Try to make this story more interesting by thinking of something for the boy and the girl to say.

> A boy and his sister were going ice skating. The pond had a sign, "Danger." They started to skate anyway. The ice broke under the girl. She called to her brother. He pulled her out safely.

Sometimes, you also tell what people say in an *interview.*

■ Suppose that you are interviewing a famous hero. What questions would you ask? Use your imagination to make up answers for your questions. Then write down what the hero might say.

Language

In this chapter, we've talked about *morphemes*. Sometimes a morpheme is a whole word. And sometimes it's a prefix or a suffix, which is only a part of a word.

■ Here are some groups of letters. Try to put the letters together so each group makes a morpheme.

1. p, n, e
2. u, l, f
3. n, a, m

4. t, f, o, o
5. n, u
6. o, b, x

■ Sometimes, a word has more than one morpheme in it. Now put these morphemes together so they make words. Then tell what each word means.

1. re	2. ly	3. finish
ing	un	ed
copy	fair	un

4. ing	5. care	6. re
dis	less	paint
obey	ness	ed

Whenever you're writing, you use *quotation marks* to show the exact words that someone says. Turn to pages 314–315 for more practice with quotation marks.

You can use these exercises to provide additional practice with morphemes.

A. Divide the class into small groups, and then have each group use a dictionary to make as many words as possible from the following morphemes:

1. out
2. land
3. ish
4. in
5. ly
6. board

7. er
8. sick
9. sea
10. side
11. home
12. ward

B. To challenge some of your more capable students, you can ditto the following and have the children unscramble the letters to make morphemes. (Items 2 and 8 cannot be made into morphemes.)

1. e, s, a, t
2. a, o, n, t, k
3. e, v, r, w, e, i
4. o, k, s, o, b
5. w, l, i, y, d, l
6. l, l, b, d, a, a

7. y, s, e, a
8. w, l, m, n, e
9. n, g, i, s
10. k, y, a
11. h, d, r, a
12. e, g, o, s, o

Answers

The following morphemes can be made from the letters given in the first activity:

1. pen
2. -ful
3. man

4. foot
5. un-
6. box

The answers to the second activity are as follows:
1. recopying: writing over again.
2. unfairly: in a way that is not just.
3. unfinished: not done.
4. disobeying: not doing what one has been told to do.
5. carelessness: being without thought in what one says or does.
6. repainted: colored over again with paint.

Purpose To illustrate another type of poetic imagination, one which emphasizes humor.

[This poem can certainly stimulate a discussion of pets that children have or would like to have. But it's also gently humorous, and it encourages the use of imagination. How many of us have ever thought: "It may sound silly, but wouldn't it be nice if . . ."? This poem may help some children realize that such things aren't so silly after all!]

Preparation Encourage the children to discuss their pets—or pets they'd like to have. Ask if they know of any unusual pets and the problems these pets have caused. Ask them to imagine what it would be like to have a very strange pet—perhaps a giraffe, an elephant, or a whale. What would be some of the good things about having such a pet? What would be some of the problems?

Presentation Ask the children to examine the illustration on pages 198 and 199. You might also display a more realistic picture of a yak, and have a child consult a dictionary for a definition.

Then read the introductory paragraph on page 198, commenting on the strangeness of Belloc's title for his book of poems. Without stressing the point heavily, you might suggest that almost everyone gets annoyed—sometimes—by "goody-goody" characters because they just don't seem real.

Before reading the poem, tell the children not to be concerned about any strange words; you will discuss them afterwards. Then read the poem to the children with as much rhythm, expression, and bodily movement as possible. Then dis-

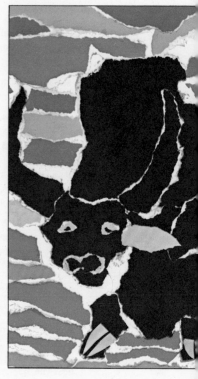

A Poem

Here's a poem from *The Bad Child's Book of Beasts* by Hilaire Belloc. When the poet was a boy, he read lots of poems about happy little children with good little cats and dogs. They were so good that they didn't seem real. So Hilaire Belloc wrote some poems about real animals for real children. This one is about a *yak*.

The Yak

As a friend to the children, commend me the Yak.
　You will find it exactly the thing:
It will carry and fetch, you can ride on its back,
　Or lead it about with a string.
The Tartar who dwells on the plains of Tibet
　(A desolate region of snow)

Has for centuries made it a nursery pet,
  And surely the Tartar should know!
Then tell your papa where the Yak can be got,
  And if he is awfully rich,
He will buy you the creature—or else he will *not,*
  (I cannot be positive which.)

                                    HILAIRE BELLOC

cuss the difficult words and phrases: *commend me* ("I recommend"), *Tartar, dwells, plains of Tibet, desolate, nursery pet.* Finally, read the poem again as the children follow along in their books. Encourage them to respond physically (for example, by shivering when you mention the desolate region of snow), if they wish.

Discuss the questions at the top of page 200, helping the children understand that the poet is intentionally being silly. This will help them be a little silly themselves when they consider the instructions in the activity (■). Encourage them to use their imaginations in thinking of things to do with their yak.

Follow-up If the children enjoyed writing about a pet yak, you can suggest that they choose another unusual pet to tell a story about. Some children might even want to "make up" a creature to write about, perhaps by combining parts of different animals. (For example, they could combine a giraffe and a mouse to make a "girouse," or a butterfly and an elephant to make a "butterphant.") If the children choose to make up animals, they might also want to illustrate their stories.

Additional Resources

Books Belloc, Hilaire, *The Bad Child's Book of Beasts,* Knopf. Ciardi, John, *The Reason for the Pelican,* Lippincott. Nash, Ogden, *The Moon Is Shining Bright as Day,* Lippincott. Smith, William Jay, *Boy Blue's Book of Beasts,* Little, Brown. Starbird, Kaye, *Don't Ever Cross a Crocodile, A Snail's a Failure Socially,* and *Speaking of Cows,* Lippincott.

Purposes   (1) To reinforce the distinction between creating a composition and talking about a composition; (2) To review various types of compositions; (3) To review the purposes of revising and recopying.

Preparation   Have the children look through their folders to find one or two compositions that they particularly like. Then ask them to try to explain what it is that they like about these compositions. As they do so, you can make the distinction between <u>doing</u> something (like writing a composition) and <u>talking about</u> what you do.

Presentation   Read the material on page 200 along with the children. After the first paragraph, you can ask the children to try to describe what they do when they tell a story, write a description, or act out a play. Again, help them understand the difference between doing something and talking about what they do.

After the children have read the second paragraph, you can discuss the meanings of the italicized words and ask the children to give examples of each.

Finally, review the function of the describers by having the children give examples of words and phrases that tell what someone or something <u>is</u>, <u>has</u>, and <u>does</u>. And then ask them to explain the difference between *recopy* and *revise*.

In discussing the activity (■), tell the children that you'll make suggestions for revision, if they want you to. But let the children do the choosing of the composition to be revised. And try to be quite specific in making suggestions. (If, for example, a child chooses to revise an animal story, then you might suggest that he or she revise the story into an autobiography written by the animal.)

A yak is a little bigger than a cow or a horse. Do you think a yak would made a good pet? Do you think a Tartar would use a yak only for a pet? Why do you have to be "awfully rich" to own a yak? Would *you* like to have a yak?

■ Suppose you did have a yak for a pet. Think about what you'd do with it. Then write a story about your yak.

Talking About Composition

So far, you've read a lot about composition. You've also learned how to do these things:

> Tell a story
> Write a description
> Act out a play

Writing, telling, or acting a composition is one thing. But talking about a composition is something else. It's good to make up compositions. It's also good to talk about the things you make up.

When you talk about composition, there are special words you can use. Do you remember what a *diary* is? How is it different from an *autobiography*? Which is *private* writing? How is private writing different from *public* writing?

There's one way that private writing is <u>like</u> public writing. In either kind, you can use the describers. How can Isabella Is, Harry Has, and Dudley Does help you write?

There are two other important words that people use when they talk about composition. One word is *recopy*. The other is *revise*. What do these words mean?

■ Look back over the stories you've written this year. Choose one that you think you could make more interesting. Then revise your composition.

Talking About Language

Suppose you want to study about the way ants live. You could find a real ant hill and watch the ants come and go. You could even take the ant hill apart to see inside. But the ants would probably go away while you were digging. And after you took the hill apart, you probably couldn't put it back together again. What else could you do to learn about the way ants live?

Ants are interesting to talk about. But people are much more interesting. And the most interesting person that anybody can learn about is himself.

You know a lot about yourself on the <u>outside</u>. But how much do you know about yourself on the <u>inside</u>? Suppose you want to talk about the way your heart works. You can't see your heart. So how can you talk about it? What could you use to help you learn about it?

Now suppose you want to talk about what happens when you listen, read, write, or talk. What can you use when you talk about something that happens <u>inside</u> <u>your</u> <u>head</u>?

If you never learned anything about your heart, would it still work? If you never studied anything about nominals and morphemes and where-adverbials, could you still talk? Why do you think people study language?

Purpose To review the reasons for studying language.

Preparation Suggest that the children look through the Index to find some of the special words they've already learned that help them talk about language. Then ask the children if they know more about language than a child in the first grade and what makes them think so.

Presentation Read and discuss the text with the children, encouraging a wide variety of answers and speculation. Help them relate their discussion to a range of other fields: medicine, music, carpentry, sports, auto mechanics, cooking, and so on. Stress the importance of using special words when discussing these things. Talking about something can sometimes help us <u>do</u> that thing better; equally important, talking about things can also be interesting in itself.

Evaluation As mentioned earlier, you should be observing the children's performance during each lesson in terms of the objectives listed under the Statement of Goals. Again, please note that many of the objectives stated for Chapters 1–5 and 6–9 are still applicable.

There are a few additional performance objectives stated for Chapters 13–16, and of course you should become familiar with these. However, as the year draws to a close, you should be particularly alert to the <u>many</u> different ways that children can demonstrate progress in studying the arts of English. As mentioned earlier, the guidelines included in this book do not exhaust all the possible ways that a child can demonstrate growth in a particular area.

You may also wish to use the appropriate section of the evaluation component, if it is available, at this time.

Purposes (1) To provide additional experience with the ballad as a literary form; (2) To identify some of the features of the ballad form.

Preparation If the children have learned the music to "Casey Jones," then you can sing the ballad again with them. If not, review some of the other ballads that the children may know. Focus on the fact that most ballads tell stories, and that these stories frequently describe exciting events (or, more technically, "action"). Then state that most ballads have a hero, and the hero of the ballad they'll hear today is an animal.

Presentation The comments concerning the presentation of "Casey Jones" (pages 178–179) apply with equal force here. If possible, you should sing the ballad to the children, or else invite another teacher into your class to sing it; only as a last alternative should you introduce the ballad solely through a recording.

After a musical presentation of the ballad, you can then read it to the children (which illustrates the fact that literature can frequently be enjoyed in more than one way). Try to make the reading as dramatic as possible, with stealthy movement, glee, and excitement; with changes in your voice when you switch from narration to dialogue; and with vitality as you repeat the refrain.

After first singing the ballad and then reading it, you can have the children open their books and follow along as you read it again. Encourage them to join in—

A Ballad

Some ballads are about famous people. But ballads can also be about animals. Here's one that has a fox as the main character.

The Fox

The fox went out on a chilly night,
Prayed for the moon for to give him light,
For he'd many a mile to go that night
Afore he reached the town-o, town-o, town-o,
He'd many a mile to go that night before he reached the town-o.

He ran till he came to a great big bin
The ducks and the geese were put therein,
"A couple of you will grease my chin
Before I leave this town-o, town-o, town-o,
A couple of you will grease my chin before I leave this town-o."

Daybook: Animal Metaphors, page 76

202

He grabbed the gray goose by the neck
Throwed the little ones over his back
He didn't mind their quack-quack-quack,
And the legs all dangling down-o, down-o, down-o,
He didn't mind their quack-quack-quack, and the legs all
  dangling down-o.

Then Old Mother Slipper-Slopper jumped out of bed
And out of the window she popped her head,
Crying, "John! John! the gray goose is gone,
And the fox is on the town-o, town-o, town-o,"
Crying, "John! John! the gray goose is gone, and the fox is
  on the town-o."

loudly—on the last line of each stanza (or the last two lines, if that feels more natural). Above all, the pleasure of this lesson is in participation—in sharing the pleasure of saying words such as *town-o* or *Slipper-Slopper*, or in acting out how the "little ones chewed on the bones-o."

Once the children have had a chance to get thoroughly involved in the ballad, you can discuss the action, asking for volunteers to summarize what happens in each stanza. (This will prepare for the play or puppet-show suggested in the Follow-up, below.) You can then turn to the discussion on page 204 and help the children identify the refrain at the end of each stanza. The ballad also provides an opportunity to discuss rhymes and stanzas. After a brief discussion of the technical aspects, shift to a discussion of action.

Finally, you can arrange various choral readings of the ballad: perhaps entirely in unison, perhaps with speakers for the dialogue sections, perhaps with a narrator to read the first three lines of each stanza.

Follow-up In addition to singing the ballad, some children may wish to dramatize the action in the form of a play or a puppet-show. As mentioned in the notes accompanying an earlier lesson, the puppets can be very simple cardboard cutouts. Or, if time permits, the children can make papier mâché figures to represent the fox and his family, Old Mother Slipper-Slopper, and John, as well as the ducks and the geese.

Additional Resources

Books Carmer, Carl, *America Sings,* Knopf. Lomax, John A. and Alan, *American Ballads and Folk Songs,* Macmillan. Niles, John J. and Helen L. Smith, *Folk Ballads for Young Actors,* Holt, Rinehart and Winston. Sandburg, Carl, *The American Songbag,* Harcourt. Seeger, Pete, *American Favorite Ballads,* Oak. Seeger, Ruth Crawford, *American Folk Songs for Children,* Doubleday.

Recordings *The Spoken Arts Treasury of American Ballads and Folk Songs,* 1–12″ LP, Caedmon. *Treasury of American Ballads and Folk Songs, Sung by Burl Ives,* 1–12″ LP, cassette, Miller-Brody.

Then John went up to the top of the hill
And he blew a blast both loud and shrill.
Says the fox: "The music is pretty—still
I'd rather be in my den-o, den-o, den-o,"
Says the fox: "The music is pretty—still I'd rather be in my
den-o."

He ran till he came to his cozy den
There were the little ones, eight, nine, ten,
They said, "Daddy, better go back again
Cause it must be a mighty fine town-o, town-o, town-o,"
They said, "Daddy, better go back again 'cause it must be a
mighty fine town-o."

Then the fox and his wife without any strife
Cut up the goose with a fork and knife,
They never had such a supper in their life
And the little ones chewed on the bones-o, the bones-o, the
bones-o,
They never had such a supper in their life and the little ones
chewed on the bones-o.

You already know that a *refrain* is a group of words that's repeated in a song or a poem. Many folk ballads have refrains. In this ballad, what words are repeated at the end of the first stanza? Now look at the refrain in the second stanza. Is it the same as the refrain in the first stanza? Why is it different? Why do you think the poet adds *o* to some of the words in the refrains?

Most of the time, a ballad tells a story. And so the *action* is very important. Sometimes, it's even more important than the characters.

■ Try to tell what the action in this ballad is.

More About Interviews

In an *interview,* you visit with someone and talk about something special. Once, a newspaper reporter interviewed an inventor. He asked the inventor questions and he wrote **notes** on the answers. Here's how his notebook looked.

NAME: ALLEN GRIMSHAW
ADDRESS: 90 CANAL STREET
INVENTOR OF MUSICAL JUMPROPE. HIS SECOND
INVENTION. ALSO INVENTED LEFT HANDED
PENCIL SHARPENER. "PLAYS TWO SONGS" AND
"SOUNDS LIKE A WHISTLE." COMES IN TWO
SIZES, SHORT AND LONG.

What questions do you think the reporter asked? What did he ask first? Did he remember to use all the WH questions? (Do you remember the five WH questions?) Did the reporter write down any of the exact words that the inventor said? How can you tell?

Here's how the reporter began his story.

MAN INVENTS NEW MUSICAL JUMPROPE

Allen Grimshaw said yesterday that he had invented a new kind of jumprope.

■ Copy this beginning. Now suppose that you're the newspaper reporter. Read the notes again carefully. Then write the rest of the story.

Purpose To provide additional guidelines for writing newspaper stories.

Preparation Review the five WH questions from the earlier lesson on interviews (pages 192–193), preferably by illustrating how reporters have used these questions in writing actual news stories.

Presentation Have the children read the introductory paragraph and the illustrated notes on page 205. Then have a volunteer write the five WH questions on the chalkboard, and have the class discuss which of these are answered in the notes. Be sure the children understand that "plays two songs" and "sounds like a whistle" apply to the musical jumprope. Then discuss why the reporter uses quotation marks in his notes.

The activity (■) at the bottom of the page can be done individually, in pairs, or orally with the entire class. After the writing, two children might dramatize the roles of the inventor and the reporter.

Follow-up You may want to provide an additional opportunity for the children to write newspaper stories based on a "reporter's notes." You can prepare a ditto of the following notes:

Name: Martha Cropsey
Address: 247 East 89th Street
Amateur archeologist.
Discovered dinosaur fossil on 86th Street subway platform yesterday. Was waiting for train delayed as result of construction at 86th Street Station. Believes fossil to be *tyrannosaurus rex.* Plans to "start a petition to stop construction so museum officials can search for other fossils." Expects some objections from subway riders.

After the children have finished their newspaper stories, they should write an appropriate title or headline.

Purposes (1) To provide another example of children's linguistic competence; (2) To expand the sentence-combining rules presented earlier.

[As with similar lessons, it is not the purpose of this lesson to teach children how to combine sentences. They already possess this ability as part of their linguistic competence, and in a much more complex way than the simplified rules of the sentence model indicate. Rather, the lesson demonstrates various ways of talking about these internalized rules.]

Preparation Page 206 provides a review of the earlier lessons on sentence combining, and it can serve as preparation for the new material on page 207. (By now, most children should be able to identify the two methods of combining sentences: the regular way and the special adjective way.)

Additionally, you might also review the sentence position picture, using the four sentences on page 206:

1. The boy / got / a medal.
2. The boy / won / the race.
3. The girl / sang / a song.
4. The girl / is / pretty.

Then you can ask for volunteers to provide other sentences, similar to those you've used, that can be added to the position picture.

Presentation After reading page 206 with the class, and after discussing the questions thoroughly, ask the children to suggest other sentences—using the words they know "in their heads"—which can be combined. (You can challenge them to make their sentences as interesting and imaginative as possible.)

Combining Sentences

Putting sentences together to make new sentences is very important in English. A two-year-old child almost never puts them together. A four-year-old usually puts them together using *and*. But you know lots of ways to put sentences together. And you've learned to talk about two of these ways: the *regular way* and the *special adjective way*.

Here is the regular way again.

The boy got a medal.
+ The boy won the race.
The boy who won the race got a medal.

And here's the special adjective way.

The girl sang a song.
+ The girl is pretty.
The pretty girl sang a song.

Look again at the sentences we combined the regular way. What is the matrix sentence? What is the insert sentence? What nominals are in the first position of these sentences? Where did we put the insert sentence?

Now look again at the special adjective way. Which is the matrix sentence and which is the insert sentence? What nominals are in the first position? Are they the same? How did we combine these two sentences?

In each of these examples, we added an insert sentence to the nominal in the first position of the matrix sentence. But sometimes a sentence has a nominal in the third position, too. When it does, we can add a sentence there. In fact, we can insert a sentence anywhere there's a nominal.

Daybook: Combining Sentences,
page 78

Here's a matrix sentence with a nominal in the third position.

I saw the girl.

And here's how we can add an insert sentence after the third position nominal. This is the regular way to do it.

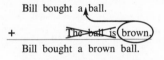

I saw the girl.

+ ~~The girl~~ has a pet monkey.

I saw the girl who has a pet monkey.

How would you add these two sentences together using the regular way?

The dog followed the boy.

+   The boy was walking home.

Here's another sentence with a nominal in the third position.

Bill bought a ball.

We can also use the special adjective way to insert a sentence with a nominal in the third position.

Bill bought a ball.

+   ~~The ball~~ is (brown).

Bill bought a brown ball.

How would you use the special adjective way to add these sentences together?

The pilot made a landing.

+   The landing was smooth.

Next, read the material on page 207 along with the children. Many children will quickly "get the feel" of the sentence-combining examples on this page. Nevertheless, you should take the time to explain each one, using the technical terms *matrix, insert, third position, special adjective way,* and so on.

You can use the following sentences as additional examples, similar to those on page 207, before asking the children to work the activity (■) on page 208.

1.   John met a man.
   + The man makes square pizzas.

2.   I have a frog.
   + The frog is purple.

3.   The man caught a fish.
   + The fish was polka-dotted.

4.   I saw a lady.
   + The lady had purple eyes.

5.   I know a boy.
   + The boy plays the flute.

Although the activity can be duplicated on ditto paper, it's probably better to have the children copy each problem, solve it, and then indicate which method they used (the regular way or the special adjective way). It's also good to have the children read the entire problem aloud, since this will give them a "feeling" for what such sentences are like in speech. You can encourage the children to express their opinions about the new sentences by asking: "Are they more interesting? Do they sound more like sentences you might use?"

Follow-up To provide additional practice, you can use the sentence-combining problems included on page 217.

Answers

1. Esther knows a man who saves string.
2. I have yellow shoes.
3. John found a broken bat.
4. Oliver knows a lady who plays the tuba.
5. I saw a man who could swallow a sword.
6. Carol likes cold spinach.

Purpose To introduce *synonym* and *antonym* as terms which can be used in talking about language.

[Children, of course, already know a great many synonyms and antonyms in their heads; what most of them probably don't know is that there are technical terms which can be used in discussing such words.]

Preparation Ask the children to compare various things: a tall child and short one, a child with blond hair and one with black hair, a shout and a whisper, a day in July and one in January, and so on. After these contrastive examples, provide some that are similar: two tall children, two black-haired children, and so on.

Presentation Suggest to the children that on page 208 they'll find two terms which describe the kinds of words they've just been using. When they've had a chance to skim page 208, write the words *synonym* and *antonym* on the chalkboard and help the children pronounce the words. Then call for volunteers to read each statement following the (•).

The activity (■) at the bottom of page 208 can be done orally. After the children have identified each pair as synonyms or antonyms, they should try to use the words in sentences.

Answers

1. antonyms	4. antonyms	7. synonyms
2. synonyms	5. antonyms	8. synonyms
3. antonyms	6. antonyms	9. synonyms

■ Here are some sentences for you to put together. But be careful. Some use the regular way. And some use the special adjective way.

1. Esther knows a man.
    + ⎯⎯⎯⎯⎯⎯⎯⎯ The man saves string. ⎯⎯⎯

2. I have shoes.
    + ⎯⎯ The shoes are yellow. ⎯⎯⎯⎯⎯⎯⎯⎯

3. John found a bat.
    + ⎯⎯⎯⎯⎯⎯⎯⎯ The bat was broken. ⎯⎯⎯

4. Oliver knows a lady.
    + ⎯⎯⎯⎯⎯⎯⎯⎯ The lady plays the tuba. ⎯⎯

5. I saw a man.
    + ⎯⎯ The man could swallow a sword. ⎯⎯

6. Carol likes spinach.
    + ⎯⎯⎯⎯⎯⎯ The spinach is cold. ⎯⎯⎯⎯⎯

Synonyms and Antonyms

There are special names for words that mean the same thing. There are also special names for words that mean opposite things.

- Words that mean the same are called **synonyms**.

- Words that mean the opposite are called **antonyms**.

■ Which of the following pairs of words are synonyms? Which are antonyms?

1. hot, cold	4. full, empty	7. certain, sure
2. almost, nearly	5. light, dark	8. help, aid
3. up, down	6. fast, slow	9. start, begin

Daybook: The Synonym-Antonym
Game, page 80

Here's a word game. Can you figure out how to play it?

First, the teacher says a sentence. Then the boy answers with a sentence that has a word which means the same thing as a word in the teacher's sentence. And the girl answers with a sentence that has a word which means the opposite of the word in the teacher's sentence.

■ Here are some sentences you can use to play the Synonym-Antonym Game. (The first one is done for you.)

1. TEACHER: Shirley lives *near* the school.
   BOY: Yes, she lives _close_ .
   GIRL: No, she lives _far_ .

2. TEACHER: The class is very *noisy* today.
   BOY: Yes, it's very _____.
   GIRL: No, it's very _____.

3. TEACHER: That jelly bean is *tiny*.
   BOY: Yes, it's very _____.
   GIRL: No, it's very _____.

4. TEACHER: George should stand *at the beginning* of the line.
   BOY: Yes, he should be _____.
   GIRL: No, he should be _____.

Then direct the children's attention to the illustration on page 209, and help them figure out how to play the game. After a brief discussion, have them check the rules in the paragraph below the illustration.

The activity (■) on page 209 can be done in groups of threes, or you can serve as the "teacher" in the game and call on volunteers for each synonym and antonym. The words which the children used during the preparation can be used again to expand the game, and then you can challenge the children to make up their own sentences for a Synonym-Antonym Game.

Follow-up The skills lessons on Synonyms (pages 319–320) and Antonyms (pages 264–265) form a natural follow-up to this lesson. Additionally, you can list a number of common words (*like, work, neat, pretty,* and so on) on the chalkboard and then ask the children to suggest a number of synonyms for each one. List these on the chalkboard, and then ask the children to suggest a number of antonyms for each, which you can list in another column. Finally, you might challenge some children by asking them to arrange the synonyms and antonyms by "degree." (For example, synonyms for *like* might be ordered as follows: *like, love, adore, idolize.* The antonyms might be ordered this way: *dislike, hate, detest, loathe.*)

Answers

The children's answers may vary somewhat for this activity.
2. loud; quiet
3. small; large
4. at the front; at the end

Purposes (1) To provide an additional example of lyric poetry; (2) To illustrate how a poem expresses a poet's feelings.

[Many earlier lessons contained lyric poems and, hopefully, you've provided the children with many others. This lesson continues the practice of introducing a technical term only after the children are familiar with what the term labels.]

Preparation Discuss with the children some things that evoke either mild or strong feelings: a child lost in the woods, a new baby in a family, a flower that's been stepped on, and so on.

Presentation Before reading the introductory material at the top of page 210, have the children read the poem silently. Then ask: "Have you ever felt the same way that the poet does? How do you think the squirrel feels?" (If the children have difficulty answering this question, you can refer them to the illustration, which is particularly good in capturing the feelings of the squirrel.) Next, read the poem to the children in a relatively soft voice.

Then read a stanza from "Casey Jones" (page 179), preferably in a rollicking voice. Suggest that "Casey Jones" sounds best when you read it with a loud voice, lots of rhythm, and accompanying body movement. Ask the children to compare this with the way you read "To a Squirrel at Kyle-Na-No." If you wish, you can then provide an additional contrast with "The Lobster Quadrille."

Next, ask the children to look through the Table of Contents to find some other poems they've read this year that sound best when read softly. You can suggest that humorous poems and ballads which tell a story generally sound best when you read them with lots of excitement. Other poems sound best when

210

A Poem

So far this year, you've read lots of poems. You've read long poems that tell a story and short poems like haiku and limericks. This is another kind of short poem. It's called a **lyric**. A lyric tells how the poet _feels_ about something. Lyrics often have words that rhyme. And they're usually quiet poems. Many years ago, the poet would read his lyric while someone played softly on a _lyre_. A lyre is an instrument like a small harp. In fact, the word _lyric_ comes from _lyre_. Try to use a soft voice when you read lyrics.

This lyric was written by an Irish poet. Kyle-Na-No is a forest in Ireland.

To a Squirrel at Kyle-Na-No

Come play with me;
Why should you run
Through the shaking tree
As though I'd a gun
To strike you dead?
When all I would do
Is to scratch your head
And let you go.

W. B. YEATS

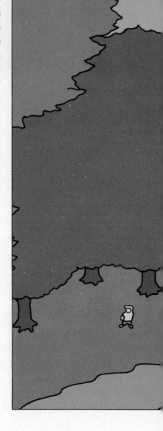

Daybook: What If . . ., page 82

you read them quietly. Then state that there's a special name—*lyric*—for the "soft" kind of poetry.

Now read the introduction at the top of page 210 to the children. This paragraph explains what the word *lyric* means. In discussing the term, it would be helpful if you drew a simplified picture of a lyre on the chalkboard. (Most dictionaries include a picture.) You can also compare a lyre to an autoharp.

This is a good poem for the children to read together, particularly if you can accompany the reading on an autoharp. Use a minor chord for each line except the last, and a major chord for it.

After this reading, you can discuss the questions at the top of page 212 with the children. During the discussion, try to emphasize feelings—those of the poet, the children, and your own.

Follow-up Under Additional Resources are listed a few other poems about animals which you may want to read to the children.

Additional Resources

Books Arbuthnot, May Hill, editor, *Time for Poetry*, Scott, Foresman, for "Night of the Wind" by Frances Frost, "Lone Dog" by Irene Rutherford McLeod, and "Little Things" and "The Snare" by James Stephens. Bogan, Louise and William Jay Smith, compilers, *The Golden Journey: Poems for Young People*, Reilly & Lee, for "The Cat and the Moon" by William Butler Yeats. Frost, Frances, *Pool in the Meadow*, Houghton Mifflin, for "White Season."

Recordings *A Gathering of Great Poetry for Children*, 4–12″ LP's, cassettes, Caedmon. Volumes 3 and 4 of this series include other poems by Yeats.

Purposes (1) To introduce pantomime as a form of communication; (2) To provide opportunities for children to create compositions in pantomime.

Preparation Arrange beforehand to have several children use pantomime to demonstrate a variety of actions (for example, writing a letter and sealing the envelope; making and eating a sandwich; putting toothpaste on a brush and then brushing one's teeth; and so on). The rest of the class can try to guess what each child is doing. Then ask the children to suggest how different people—who don't speak the same language—can communicate with each other.

Presentation Have the children open to page 212 and read the first paragraph of the lesson. Then discuss the pictures, encouraging the children to describe the signals and the motions in each one. Finally, ask a volunteer to tell—in words—the complete story.

Write the word *pantomime* on the chalkboard, help the children pronounce it, and then have them read the paragraph at the top of page 213. Stress the fact that a pantomime story is a composition, just as a written—or a spoken—story is.

In working the activity (■) on page 213, encourage the children to use their imaginations to think of a wide variety of responses (just as they use their imaginations in other kinds of compositions).

Follow-up The children might want to make up their own lists of things which can be acted out in pantomime.

Remember that a lyric tells how a poet feels. How do you think this poet feels about the squirrel? What lines in the poem give you an idea of how he feels? Have you ever had this kind of feeling toward an animal?

Quiet, Please

Long ago, there were many different tribes of Indians in North America. They spoke different languages. Often, the Indians of one tribe couldn't understand the language of another tribe. So they worked out a special way of "talking" without using words. Do you know what they did? Try to figure out what is happening in the pictures.

When people "talk" to each other without using words, it's called **pantomime.** Suppose you were in a different country, and you didn't know the language spoken there. You could use pantomime to talk to the people.

■ Try to "say" these things without using words.

1. Tell someone you are hungry.
2. Tell someone you are thirsty.
3. Tell someone you are tired.
4. Tell someone you are cold and you want a coat or a blanket to keep warm.
5. Tell someone that a dog bit your leg and you want a doctor to put a bandage on it.
6. Tell someone that you want to buy food and that you will chop wood to earn the food.
7. Tell someone that you want to wash your face and hands before eating.

What's the Idea?

Remember that a *morpheme* is a part of language that has a single meaning. All words have at least one morpheme. All prefixes and suffixes are morphemes.

Do you have an idea of what the word *clock* means? Do you have an idea of what the prefix *re-* means? You can get an idea of what *clock* and *re-* mean. You also know that *clock* and *re-* are morphemes. So we can say that a morpheme is a kind of idea.

But sometimes you can have an idea that's not a word or a prefix or a suffix. Do you remember what happens when we add a Q to a sentence? Here's an example you've seen.

Q + The chicken crossed the road.
⟹ Did the chicken cross the road?

Daybook: The Idea Is . . ., page 84

Additionally, you can suggest that they find some pictures in books and magazines which show people gesturing, making faces, and so on. After discussing how people communicate through body movements and facial expressions, the children can use the pictures as the basis for spoken or written compositions.

Additional Resources

Books Hunt, Douglas and Kari, *Pantomime: The Silent Theater*, Atheneum.

Purposes (1) To expand the concept of morpheme; (2) To illustrate that we can use the term *morpheme* when discussing ideas such as Q, Q_{tag}, and N'T.

[The usefulness of the term *morpheme* lies in the fact that it enables us to talk about any part of language that has meaning, and it thereby reminds us that complete words aren't the only meaningful units of language. Thus, this lesson provides the children with a convenient term for discussing things they already know and, in fact, have already had experience in discussing.]

Preparation The first two paragraphs on page 213 can serve as preparation for the lesson. You can use additional examples of words, prefixes, and suffixes that the children have already studied (pages 184–185 and 194–195).

Presentation After the children have had a chance to recall the term *morpheme* —and to remember that it applies to words, prefixes, and suffixes—you can suggest that there are some other things that we can also apply the term to. Call for a volunteer to read the paragraph which begins on the bottom of page 213 and continues onto page 214. Have the children study the three examples in the text, and then provide some additional ones. (Again, you can re-use earlier examples from pages 123, 153, 162–163, and 174–175.) Ask the children to explain, in their own words, what happens as you work each example.

Then read the paragraph in the middle of page 214 which contains the bold-face terms. Help the children relate the terms to the proper morphemes. Ask the children to provide examples of word morphemes as well as of prefix and suffix morphemes. Suggest that they can use the ones that you mentioned earlier in the lesson. Ask each child to write the yes-no question morpheme, then to write the tag question morpheme, and finally to write the N'T morpheme.

Continue on page 214, calling for a volunteer to read the poem. (Christina Rossetti's poem opens the third book of this series, and even children who haven't used the earlier book will generally be familiar with this classic.) Have the children give a variety of answers to the final question on the page, preferably illustrating the answers with pantomimed actions. Stress the fact that we can tell when the wind is blowing even though we can't see it.

In discussing two sentences at the top of page 215, some children might point to the question mark as representing "the idea of a question." In a way, it does perform that function, but we

And what happens when you add Q_{tag} to a sentence? Here's another example you've seen before.

Q_{tag} + The boy has eaten the pizza.
$\Longrightarrow$ The boy has eaten the pizza, hasn't he?

And do you remember what happen when we add N'T to a sentence? Here's still another example that you've already seen.

N'T + The teacher has eaten her lunch.
$\Longrightarrow$ The teacher hasn't eaten her lunch.

Q isn't a word. And Q_{tag} isn't a word. Q and Q_{tag} are both <u>ideas</u>. If they're ideas, then they must mean something. And if they mean something, then they're morphemes. We can call Q the **yes-no question morpheme**. We can call Q_{tag} the **tag question morpheme**. And we can call N'T the **N'T morpheme**.

So now we have these kinds of morphemes:

Word morphemes
Prefix and suffix morphemes
Yes-no question morphemes
Tag question morphemes
N'T morphemes

Word morphemes are easy to see in a sentence. So are prefix and suffix morphemes. But what happens to a sentence when we add a question morpheme?

Here's part of a poem you may have read.

Who has seen the wind?
  Neither you nor I:
But when the trees bow down their heads
  The wind is passing by.

If you can't see·the wind, then how do you know it's there?

Now here are two sentences. Which one of them has the idea of a question in it?

> The wind is passing by.
> Is the wind passing by?

Something happens to the trees when the wind goes through them. And something happens to a sentence that has a Q in it.

■ Here are some problems for you to try. (The first one is done for you.)

1. Q + The girl is happy.
   ⟹ *Is the girl happy?*
2. Q + The dog ate my lunch.
   ⟹
3. Q$_{tag}$ + The teacher slept all day.
   ⟹
4. N'T + The sky is blue today.
   ⟹
5. Q$_{tag}$ + Carol's dress is purple.
   ⟹
6. Q + The fish didn't swim away.
   ⟹
7. Q + You live on Jackson Street.
   ⟹
8. Q + A bird came down the walk.
   ⟹
9. N'T + The fox has eaten the goose.
   ⟹
10. Q$_{tag}$ + Jeff is going to the park.
    ⟹
11. Q$_{tag}$ + You can play with me.
    ⟹
12. N'T + The book is on the shelf.
    ⟹

don't use question marks when we speak, and, contrary to popular opinion, our voices usually don't rise at the end of a question. Our voices <u>may</u> rise at the end of a question, especially if it's a so-called echo question ("Today's Monday?"). But they may also—and generally do—fall (as in "What did you have for breakfast this morning?").

In doing the activity (■) on page 215, the children can work individually or in pairs.

Follow-up You can use a team game to review the various kinds of morphemes discussed in this lesson. First, divide the class into two teams, which can alternate turns, as in a "spelling bee." Then list the following on the chalkboard: *word morpheme, prefix morpheme, suffix morpheme, tag question morpheme, yes-no question morpheme,* and *N'T morpheme.* The child whose turn it is gives an example of one of these kinds of morphemes (for example, *dog* or *re-* or *Has the dog found the bone?*). The child whose turn it is on the opposing team must then identify the kind of morpheme exemplified. Alternatively, the child whose turn it is can suggest a kind of morpheme and the opposing team member can give an example.

Answers

2. Did the dog eat my lunch?
3. The teacher slept all day, didn't he? (or didn't she?)
4. The sky isn't blue today.
5. Carol's dress is purple, isn't it?
6. Didn't the fish swim away?
7. Do you live on Jackson Street?
8. Did a bird come down the walk?
9. The fox hasn't eaten the goose.
10. Jeff is going to the park, isn't he?
11. You can play with me, can't you?
12. The book isn't on the shelf.

Purposes (1) To review two forms of poetry—the lyric and the ballad; (2) To re-emphasize the importance of asking appropriate WH questions during an interview; (3) To review sentence combining and also the concept of morpheme as it applies to questions and negative statements.

Presentation You can extend the discussion in the Literature Review by comparing and contrasting ballads and lyrics with some of the other forms of poetry that the children have experienced. You can remind them of some of the nonsense poems and limericks that they've read, and then have the children compare these with ballads. You can also compare haiku and lyric poetry, emphasizing that it is the form of the haiku that makes this kind of poetry "special."

After discussing the Composition Review, you may also want to remind the children about the other compositional form that was introduced in this chapter: the pantomime. The children might even enjoy trying to pantomime an interview!

You can divide the class into two groups for the Language Review, with each group responsible for completing one of the activities. Then each group can present its answers to the rest of the class for discussion.

Review

Literature

In this chapter, you read a *ballad* about a fox. You also read a *lyric* about a squirrel. Do you remember what a ballad is? What kind of poem is a lyric? How were these two poems alike? How were they different? Which kind do you like better?

Now suppose we change things around a little. Suppose we change the poem about the squirrel. Then we can have the squirrel telling us what <u>he</u> thinks. What would the squirrel say? The man wants to scratch the squirrel's head. What do you feel like when some adult scratches <u>your</u> head?

■ Suppose you're a squirrel. Tell what you would do, if you saw a man. How would you feel? You can even try to write a lyric about your feelings, if you want to.

Composition

Once in a while, everyone says, "I don't know what to write about." But when you *interview* someone, you don't need to worry about what to write. If you ask the right questions, then you have lots of things to write about.

Perhaps someone in your class has been to another country or another city. (If not, then he can pretend that he's been to some special place.) What are some good questions to ask about the place? How can you learn what it looks like? How can you find out about the people who live there? How can you tell what your classmate thinks about the special place?

■ Now interview your friend. Then use your notes to write a story about him.

216

Language

In your head, you have lots of ideas. You have ideas about words and about prefixes and suffixes. You have ideas about making questions. And you have ideas about how to put two sentences together. Everything that has a single meaning is a *morpheme*.

■ Here are some morphemes. Which ones are whole words? Which are prefixes or suffixes? Which are some other kind of morpheme?

1. boy	4. un	7. N'T
2. Q	5. with	8. ness
3. pre	6. ly	9. Q_{tag}

■ Now try to put these sentences together. Some use the regular way. And some use the special adjective way.

1. I know a man.
    +   The man lives on the moon.

2. I have a yak.
    +   The yak comes from Tibet.

3. Mike saw a lady.
    +   The lady was fat.

4. George likes lemons.
    +   The lemons are sour.

 To learn more about *antonyms*, look on page 264. And for more practice using *synonyms*, turn to pages 319–320.

Here are some problems you can use to provide the children with further practice combining sentences:

1. My uncle sells balloons.
    + The balloons are yellow.

2. I know a man.
    + The man swallows swords.

3. My brother likes lollipops.
    + The lollipops are large.

4. My sister writes songs.
    + The songs are silly.

5. Mr. Golub has a gnu.
    + The gnu is tame.

6. We fed the monkeys.
    + The monkeys danced up and down.

Answers

The answers to the first activity are as follows:
1. whole word
2. yes-no question morpheme
3. prefix
4. prefix
5. whole word
6. suffix
7. N'T morpheme
8. suffix
9. tag question morpheme

The sentences in the second activity can be combined as follows:
1. I know a man who lives on the moon.
2. I have a yak who comes from Tibet.
3. Mike saw a fat lady.
4. George likes sour lemons.

Purpose To illustrate that scientific writing can sometimes be considered a form of literature.

[Some scientific writing does qualify as literature, for example, some of the writings of Newton, Darwin, and Frazer. While the selection in this lesson can't be compared with these, the author does write in a relaxed style and with a feeling for language; he also conveys a sense of real people at work.]

Preparation You can involve the children in the preparation by having them search for pictures of many different kinds of Indian houses. Some children might even make simple models of these houses. Then ask the children to describe the various kinds and to compare them with respect to materials used, shapes, sizes, suitability to the regions where the Indians lived, and so on. Then comment that today's selection describes how some Indians in California used to build houses. If you wish, you can have a volunteer locate California on a map.

Presentation Ask the children to examine the illustration of the Indian house on page 221. You can describe this as a "cut-away" picture, a kind which artists use to show both the inside and the outside of something. Point out:

1. the large (yellow) tree trunk with a fork-shape at the top
2. the pole which runs along the top
3. the smaller poles which support the twigs and branches
4. the smaller branches which support the earth and grass
5. the fire
6. the ladder which goes through the hole in the top
7. the smaller "crawl hole" at the bottom-right of the hut

Scientific Writing

You've read stories with lots of imagination. But in **scientific writing**, an author should never make things up. A scientist writes to describe or explain things, and everything he says should be true. In this story, a scientist tells how Indians in California used to build their houses.

Daybook: More Describing, page 86

218

Indian Houses in California

There are many questions to ask about the kinds of houses that Indians made in California. Why is there a center-post? Why is there a smoke hole and no chimney? How can you go in and out of the house by the smoke hole without getting burned?

You can also use the illustration to prepare the children for some of the more difficult vocabulary that they will encounter in this selection. Explain that the tree trunk acted as a *center-post*, and that a center-post was just one part of the *structure*, or way the house was put together. Another part of the structure was the *rafter*, or large pole near the roof. The rafter was sometimes called the *ridge-pole*. There were also many smaller poles, or *secondary rafters*, which *radiated* from the ridge-pole to the *rim*, something like the spokes of a wheel.

Then you can compare the hole at the top of the house to the *hatchway* on a ship, showing the children a picture of a ship's hatchway, if necessary. (Some dictionaries include a picture to illustrate the entry word *hatch*.) Also have the children compare the appearance of the smoke coming through the hole to a large feather or *plume*.

Finally, explain that such a house was usually built on a *knoll*, or small hill, and that this helped with the *drainage* of water. You can also mention that the house was really like a *cavern*, or large cave, and that it was large enough to hold a small community of people. In other words, it was a kind of *communal hall*.

After this discussion, you can have the children compare this kind of house with some of the other kinds that they've discussed during the preparation. Some children might want to consider the question of how we know that Indians actually lived in such houses many years ago. If so, you can suggest that there are some kinds of scientists who study the different ways that people lived in the past. Sometimes the scientists need to dig deep into the earth to find evidence of how people used to live. Sometimes they go to remote

219

areas where people are still living as they did long ago. You can also stress the fact that scientists like to ask questions (like those in the first paragraph of the selection itself), and then they try to find answers to their questions.

Read the introduction on page 218, as well as the selection itself, along with the children. Pause as necessary to offer brief definitions of some of the vocabulary words not already discussed, such as *process, chisels, elk antlers, patient, aeration, ranchería, ceremonies,* and *equinox.* Whenever possible, use the context to help define these words for the children.

Then have the children answer the questions on page 222 by examining the picture again and also by finding the author's answers in the selection. If the children are doing experiments in science, you can ask them to compare the author's method of asking questions and then giving answers with the methods they use in doing a scientific experiment.

Stress the two important points of the first sentence in the paragraph preceding the activity (■) on page 222. A scientific report should be truthful and should also be as complete as possible. The "list-making" suggestion is one way to determine completeness. You can get the children started by making two columns on the chalkboard: one for things the Indians used and another for things the Indians did. Direct the children to reread the second paragraph on page 220 to find the first thing that the Indians did. When someone suggests "dug the ground," you can write this in the second column on the chalkboard. Then ask: "What did the Indians use to dig the ground?" When the children have located the answer, you can write *digging-sticks* in the first column.

In the first place, the fire is a small fire, just about the size of the campfire you build in the country when you are on a picnic. The Indian house is a pretty large affair. There is no chimney, but there is a large hole in the roof. That hole is part of the structure when you build the house. It is something like a hatchway on the deck of a ship. It is the main door of the house, as well as the way out for the smoke. At that height, the little bit of smoke and the heat from the fire are not enough to bother anyone going up or down the ladder. Anyway, the fire was always a small one. A big fire would make the house unbearably hot, since it was like a sort of cellar or cavern dug into the ground, and covered over with earth.

In making an Indian house, the first thing was to dig the ground. Everybody got together (a house like that was a kind of communal hall, and held from twenty to fifty, and even sixty people, sometimes) and dug into the ground with digging-sticks, scooped the earth into baskets with their hands, and piled it outside like a rim or round wall. The site of the house was always chosen on a knoll, for good drainage.

The next thing was to erect the center-post. That was the main thing. The center-post was a tree, sometimes as large around as a fat man, with a fork three or four times a man's height. It had to be felled in the woods (which was a long process, since the Indians had no metals, no axes—they cut the wood of the trunk with chisels made out of elk antlers and rocks for hammers; after a day or two, the shreds of wood would be dry enough to burn, then you started to chip the next two or three inches of wood around the trunk; it was a slow business, but the Indians were patient).

When the center-post was ready, it had to be dragged to the site of the house, everybody pulling, and then set up. That's when all those who thought they were chiefs gave advice, and the old fellows who really were chiefs kept silent and waited to say the last word.

Then you dragged the main rafter, or ridge-pole, which was a long, straight pine tree. The butt was laid on the rim of the house site, and the other end lifted, raised, and laid to rest into the fork of the center-post. And that took more shouting.

Then you laid the secondary rafters, with one end resting on the ridge-pole, and the other end more or less radiating and resting on the rim. After that came a lot of small, short poles, like the ceilings in our frame houses. Then more branches and twigs. On top of that, large slabs of pine bark. Then, on top of it all, a layer of earth.

From the outside, at a distance, the whole thing was hardly visible. It was just a large mound of earth with grass growing over it; except that you might notice a plume of smoke coming out of it, and the ladder sticking out. You walked to the top, and peered down the hatchway, and it was

Continue in this manner until you think the children are ready to complete the list on their own. (Included in the first column—under things the Indians used —should be such things as the following: baskets; a forked tree; elk antlers and rocks; a straight pine tree; secondary rafters; small, short poles; branches and twigs; a layer of earth; and a ladder. The second column—things the Indians did —should include the following: dug the ground; scooped earth with hands; piled dirt outside; felled a large tree; dragged the center-post and the ridge-pole to the site; erected the center-post; lifted, raised, and laid the ridge-pole into position; laid the secondary rafters; added poles, branches, and twigs; added slabs of pine bark; added a layer of earth.)

When the children have finished their lists, they can compare them to try to discover omissions and inaccuracies.

Follow-up If the children have not already looked into some of the methods other Indians used to build houses, then you can suggest that they do so now. *The New Book of Knowledge, Volume 9,* contains brief descriptions of the different houses used by a number of North American tribes. *The World Book Encyclopedia, Volume 10,* includes illustrations of a variety of Indian houses, from simple tepees and wickiups to elaborate temples and ceremonial buildings. Your library probably contains a number of other helpful resource books.

In addition to making models of some of these houses, the children might want to construct a model of the dwelling described in the selection in the text. It would probably be helpful to have on hand a copy of the book *Indian Tales,* from which the selection was excerpted.

Additional Resources

Books Berke, Ernest, *The North American Indians,* Doubleday. Bleeker, Sonia, *The Apache Indians: Raiders of the Southwest; The Crow Indians: Hunters of the Northern Plains; Horsemen of the Western Plateaus: The Nez Percé Indians; The Inca: Indians of the Andes; Indians of the Longhouse: The Story of the Iroquois;* and *The Pueblo Indians,* Morrow. Clark, Ann N., *In My Mother's House* and *Little Navajo Bluebird,* Viking. de Angulo, Jaime, *Indian Tales,* Hill and Wang. La Farge, Oliver, *The American Indian,* Golden. Scheele, William E., *The Mound Builders,* World. Silverburg, Robert, *Home of the Red Man, Indian North America before Columbus,* Graphic. Tunis, Edwin, *Indians,* World. Williams, Barbara, *Let's Go to an Indian Cliff Dwelling,* Putnam.

like looking down into a cavern. You saw the fire, and then you could make out the shapes of people sitting around against the wall, or walking about, stepping over people lying down.

The aeration was fairly good, because there was a sort of tunnel running out. That provided a draft; the outside air was sucked in down through that tunnel and went out through the smoke-hole. And the dogs, and the little children big enough to crawl, but not big enough to climb the ladder, also used that runway or tunnel.

That was the old-time Indian house. It would last for ten or twenty years, until the timbers rotted. There may be a few of them yet, or their remains. But they are seldom built nowadays. Yet every once in the while a small community of Indians living on a "ranchería" will get together and put up an old-time communal house for their dances and ceremonies of spring and autumn, at the time of the equinoxes. I myself helped build such a house (although of a slightly different type, with four center-posts and a door) at a ranchería near Ione, not so very far from San Francisco.

JAIME DE ANGULO

The scientist who wrote this story begins by asking questions. Why do the houses have a center-post? Why is there a smoke-hole but no chimney? How do you get in and out without getting burned? Scientists often begin by asking questions. How did this scientist find the answers?

The important thing in scientific writing is to tell the truth—and to tell it as completely as possible. One way to check if something is complete is to make a list. Then you can see if the author has left anything out.

■ First, make a list of all the things the Indians used when they built their houses. Then make a list of all the things they did. Has anything important been left out?

Acting Without Talking

There are many different kinds of *pantomime*. Sign language is one kind. Dances are another. Whenever people talk without using words, that's pantomime.

You can use these pictures to make a play without words. Suppose the title is "The Magic Shoes."

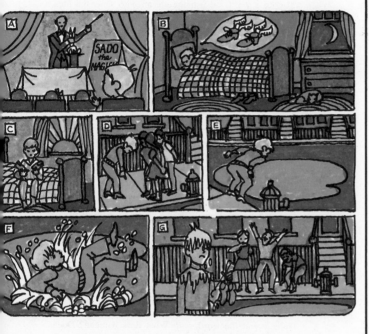

How many characters will you need? What are some things you can have each character doing? Remember, you must "tell the story" without really talking.

Purposes (1) To develop further the children's understanding of pantomime; (2) To provide an additional opportunity for children to create compositions in pantomime.

Preparation If you have Scouts in the class, they might demonstrate such things as flag signals, sign language of the deaf and dumb, and so on. Children studying modern dance or ballet might also describe its symbolism. Alternatively, you could have the children repeat the activity from the earlier lesson on pantomime (page 213).

Presentation Ask the children to read the two introductory paragraphs on page 223 and then to examine the pictures. It might be best not to have an oral discussion of the pictures before the children plan the play. Instead, you can ask the children to suggest names for the characters and make a list on the chalkboard; they can also suggest the properties they'll need (for example, the shoes, a table for a bed, and so on). Then you might divide the class into groups, each with a cast, a director, and a property committee. The director can lead a discussion of what the children are to do as they pantomime each part.

Follow-up The children can suggest other stories, either ones they've read or others they've made up themselves, that they can act out in pantomime.

Some children might be interested in finding out more about the sign language used by the North American Indians. For information the children can consult encyclopedias or the well-illustrated handbook of Indian sign language by Robert Hofsinde, listed below.

Additional Resources
Books Hofsinde, Robert, *Indian Sign Language*, Morrow.

Purpose To increase the children's understanding of their linguistic competence by expanding the concept of morpheme to include plural and past tense forms.

[If the spoken usage of some children in your class is markedly different from standard English, particularly in the formation of plural and past tense forms, then you may want to forgo presenting this lesson. The purpose of the lesson is not to instruct children in standard forms; rather, the lesson is similar to earlier lessons which use some fact of language to demonstrate the nature of linguistic competence. Speakers of non-standard English have internalized rules for forming plural and past tense forms, but these rules are sometimes different from those of standard English.]

Preparation Write several pairs of singular and plural nouns on the chalkboard, beginning with those that have regular plurals (*cat, boy, school, pencil,* and so on) and then adding some with irregular plurals (*goose, foot, mouse, child, man, woman,* and *moose*). Unless most of the children are already familiar with the word *plural,* avoid using it at this time.

Presentation Read the first half of page 224 with the children. Then, before continuing with the paragraph which begins "In your head," write the words *girl, foot, dish,* and *house* on the chalkboard. Call for volunteers to supply the correct plural form of these words, but do not yet write the plural forms on the chalkboard. First, read the two paragraphs in the middle of page 224, which explain *plural morpheme* and the meaning of *Pl.* Once the children understand this terminology, you can write + *Pl* after each word on the chalkboard. Then add a double arrow (⇒) and the correct plural form.

More Morphemes

Suppose you add the suffix -*s* to a word like *boy* or *girl* or *frog.* What does the -*s* mean? There's a special word for "more than one." You probably already know it. The special word is **plural.** How do you make these words plural?

dog　　　　lion　　　　zebra　　　　cat

When we write a word, we usually add an -*s* to show the idea of plural. This is the *regular* way. But the plurals of some words are *irregular.* How do you make these words plural?

child　　　　dress　　　　man　　　　mouse

With some words—like *child* and *dress*—we add a special suffix to show the idea of plural. And with other words—like *man* and *mouse*—we change the spelling to show the idea of plural.

In your head, you have an idea of what *plural* means. And if plural is an idea, then it's also a morpheme. We can show the "idea of plural" this way: **Pl.** *Pl* stands for the **plural morpheme.**

What happens when you add the plural morpheme to these words?

| girl + Pl | dish + Pl |
| foot + Pl | house + Pl |

The idea of plural is something we add to nouns. There's also a special idea that we can add to verbs: **tense.** In English, we use tense to keep time straight in sentences. We'll talk about two kinds of tense: **present tense** and **past tense.**

Think about the word *visit.* What does it mean? Does *visit*—all by itself—show <u>when</u> you go to see someone? What can you add to *visit* to show that you have already gone to see someone?

Daybook: Plural and Tense, page 88

224

You already have the idea of past tense in your head. So past tense must also be a morpheme. We can show that something has already happened by adding the **past tense morpheme** to a verb.

visit + Past tense $\Longrightarrow$ visited
walk + Past tense $\Longrightarrow$ walked

How would you show the past tense of these verbs?

laugh   help   play   dance

There's more than one way to show the idea of plural. And there's more than one way to show the idea of past tense. The *regular* way is to add *-ed* to the verb. But for some verbs we form the past tense in an *irregular* way.

run + Past tense $\Longrightarrow$ ran
eat + Past tense $\Longrightarrow$ ate

Have you ever heard a baby learning to talk? How might he say the plural of *man* or *foot*? How might he say the past tense of *run* or *eat*?

A baby knows the idea of plural. He also knows the idea of past tense. But he doesn't know how to say them correctly. Everybody—even a baby—has a lot of ideas in his head. And a sentence model helps you talk about them.

■ Here's something for you to try. First, give the answer the way that a very young child would. Then, give the answer the way that an adult would.

1. woman + Pl $\Longrightarrow$
2. eat + Past tense $\Longrightarrow$
3. child + Pl $\Longrightarrow$
4. goose + Pl $\Longrightarrow$
5. swim + Past tense $\Longrightarrow$
6. ride + Past tense $\Longrightarrow$
7. foot + Pl $\Longrightarrow$
8. mouse + Pl $\Longrightarrow$
9. run + Past tense $\Longrightarrow$
10. write + Past tense $\Longrightarrow$

Answers

1. womans; women
2. eated; ate
3. childs; children
4. gooses; geese
5. swimmed; swam
6. rided; rode
7. foots; feet
8. mouses; mice
9. runned; ran
10. writed; wrote

The discussion of tense, which follows, may be more difficult for some children than the discussion of plural. You should read the final two paragraphs on page 224 as the children follow along. The key sentence is: "In English, we use tense to keep time straight in sentences." (In other words, *tense* and *time* are different things. Thus, verbs only convey a sense of time when they are used in sentences. However, don't be concerned if this concept eludes some children; it's repeated in later books in the series.)

Continue to read the material on page 225 of the text with the children, calling attention to the use of the "+ sign" and the double arrow in the examples. You can work the examples on the chalkboard, calling for volunteers to supply the past tense forms. Then have the children use both the present tense and past tense forms of each verb in sentences.

Then read the rest of the lesson with the class. Most children will imitate the "baby talk" readily (*mans, foots, runned, eated*); if they don't, you can supply the forms and ask for reasons why a baby might say them. The last paragraph on page 225 re-emphasizes the major point of the lesson: All children—even very young ones—have rules in their heads. But young children can't talk about these rules. Studying English means—among other things—learning to talk about rules you have in your head.

Since the activity (■) is partly humorous, it's probably best done orally with the entire class.

Follow-up   For additional practice exercises, see page 237 of this guide. Also, you may wish to teach the Usage lesson Adding *-ed* and *-d* to Verbs on pages 328–329 at this time.

Purposes (1) To provide additional information about the nature of language; (2) To illustrate how English has borrowed words from other languages; (3) To suggest that words have interesting histories.

[For some literal-minded children, the word *borrow* may seem a strange choice, since we don't "use it and then give it back." If someone raises this objection, you can certainly agree—it i<u>s</u> strange; then add that people have used the word this way for a very long time.]

Preparation If possible, have someone address the class in a foreign language, and ask the children to listen for words that sound like English words. Alternatively, you can discuss various foods—pizza, hamburger, bananas, tacos, sukiyaki, and so on. Have the children try to guess where these foods came from originally and to speculate on why we eat them in this country. Then suggest that people can share words as well as foods.

Presentation Ask the children to skim pages 226 and 227 and to make lists of the names of countries from which we've borrowed words. You might want to ask how many children are descended from the people of these countries. Then ask the children to skim page 226 again to find a name for a person who studies words and where they come from. You will probably need to help them with the pronunciation of the word *etymologist*. Then ask: "Do you think you would enjoy such work? Why?"

Next, have the children relate the six words at the bottom of page 226 to the illustration on page 227. You can also have them use these words in sentences that illustrate their meanings.

Borrowed Words

A dictionary is like the lexicon in your head. You know thousands of words. Do you remember how many? Can you guess how many more words there are in the dictionary?

Besides all the words in the English language, there are lots of words in other languages. And there are probably more than three thousand different languages.

Sometimes, you may wonder where all these words come from. In fact, some people spend years studying where words come from. These people are called **etymologists.** Etymologists try to find out where words come from and how they change over the years. They study the *history* of words.

The history of English words can be interesting. We've borrowed words from people all over the world. We've borrowed some of our simplest words from the Vikings. The Vikings were daring pirates from Norway who raided the coast of Europe hundreds of years ago. They gave us these words.

gate	bull	take	ugly	old

But most of our borrowed words come from two very old languages: Greek and Latin. In fact, the word *etymologist* comes from two Greek words *etymon* and *logos*. In Greek, *etymon* means "true" and *logos* means "word." Another Greek word that we've used a lot is *auto*, which means "self." Here are some words we've made using *auto*.

autobiography	automobile	autograph

When the English came to America, they saw many things that they had no words for. So they borrowed words from the Indians. Can you find these things in the picture?

papoose	squaw	tobaggan
wigwam	skunk	chipmunk

And we haven't stopped borrowing. Many people who speak English travel and learn words from other languages. And many people from other countries come to America, bringing words with them. Some of these words become part of our language.

Here's a list of some words from other languages and the names of the countries where these languages are spoken.

1. slaugh gairm (Ireland)
2. blitzen (Germany)
3. el lazo (Mexico)
4. beddesprei (Holland)
5. t'e (China)
6. galoche (France)
7. tun (Denmark)
8. atomos (Greece)

People who speak English borrowed these words from other languages. But they changed the words a little first.

■ Now here are some English words. Try to match each English word with one of the words from the list above.

1. bedspread
2. tea
3. slogan
4. atom
5. lasso
6. galoshes
7. blizzard
8. town

Answers

1. beddesprei
2. t'e
3. slaugh gairm
4. atomos
5. el lazo
6. galoche
7. blitzen
8. tun

You can then read over page 226 more leisurely. Help the children see how *etymon* and *logos* fit together to form part of the word *etymologist*. The *-ist* suffix refers to a person who does a certain thing (scientist, artist, and so on). Have a volunteer check a dictionary for other words beginning with *auto-*. If possible, exhibit an unabridged dictionary and demonstrate how it indicates etymologies.

If it seems appropriate, you can use the second paragraph on page 227 to suggest that languages are constantly changing. Borrowing is one way languages change; spelling is another.

Have the children do the matching suggested in the activity (■) on page 227. They can then use the words in sentences, or check an unabridged dictionary to see how the etymologies are indicated.

Follow-up You can challenge some children to find examples of other English words that have been borrowed from different languages. (See Additional Resources below.) Perhaps, after doing some research, these children can make a bulletin board display of the "borrowed words," illustrated with pictures cut out of magazines or newspapers.

Other children might want to consider how foreign languages also borrow English words. Here are some typical examples of words that have been borrowed: *baseball, bridge, chewing gum, cold cream, hot dog, living room, rock and roll, shampoo, supermarket, and television.*

Additional Resources

Books Lambert, Eloise, *Our Language: The Story of the Words We Use*, Lothrop, Lee & Shepard. Mathews, Mitford M., *American Words*, World. Ludovici, L. James, *Origins of Language*, Putnam.

Purposes (1) To introduce the tall tale as a literary form; (2) To illustrate how a tall tale uses exaggeration to achieve its humorous effect.

Preparation Many children's magazines contain jokes, as do the magazine sections of some Sunday newspapers. A few days before teaching this lesson, you can ask the children to clip or copy some jokes they like particularly well to bring to class. (You might also do this yourself.) Have the children take turns telling the jokes, and, after several have done this, you can compare the different ways of telling jokes. Then ask the children when they think the listeners should laugh, and also if a joke teller should try to keep "a straight face." If necessary, have someone demonstrate what this means. Then you can tell the children that in today's lesson they'll have a chance to read a very long joke.

Presentation Ask a volunteer to read the first paragraph of the introduction on page 228, and then relate this paragraph to the discussion which occurred during the preparation. Then discuss the second paragraph, giving brief definitions of *trapper, trailbreaker,* and *tenderfoot* if the children can't supply explanations themselves.

A Tall Tale

Many people have favorite myths and folk tales. There's a special kind of folk tale that's very popular in our country. It's called a **tall tale**. A tall tale is really impossible. But the person who tells the tale pretends that it's true. And he never laughs at his own story.

There are thousands of tall tales about American heroes. Here's one about Jim Bridger. He was a trapper, a trailbreaker, and a scientist. In this tale, Jim is telling a tale to a *tenderfoot*.

Jim Bridger was sitting with his friend Jack, and both of them were telling stories to a tenderfoot. Jack was talking, and he was telling about a camp where he and Jim had once spent the night.

"In this camp we had, just before we turned in for the night, Jim would holler out, 'Time to git up!' Six hours later—"

"Six hours and seven minutes." Jim Bridger cut in.

"Six hours and seven minutes later, the echo would come back and wake us for breakfast," Jack said. "Jim knew, by testing it out, about acoustics and such —knew how long it took for a medium-sized echo to travel. After we'd been woke that way, we'd catch our breakfast in

Daybook: Tall Tales and Taller Tales, page 90

228

You might also want to explain to the children that Jim Bridger was a <u>real</u> hero—one of America's great frontiersmen—who lived over a hundred years ago. He was a tall and grizzled man, whom friends called "Old Gabe." Even though he never learned to read, he knew more than most men about the Rocky Mountain wilderness, where for many years he searched for furs. He also knew a lot about the Indians who lived in this part of the country. After the fur trading business died down, Jim Bridger became a scout for exploring parties and also a government guide. But he is perhaps most famous today for his ability as a storyteller.

Then have the children follow along in the book as you read the story to them. Or you can give them the option of just listening to the story, at least during the first reading. As you read, try to assume a conversational style, as if you were telling the story rather than reading it. (And don't forget to keep a straight face!) If a few of the vocabulary words require an explanation not provided in the story (for example, *acoustics, logical, sage, varmints, spurred, gravity, smug, loco, cartridge,* or *ruckus*), then you can use the same conversational tone in offering a definition.

The story gets quite exciting at the end. Because the "punch line" comes so quickly, many children will still be excited at the end of the story. For this reason, it's good to have a break of some kind before discussing the questions at the bottom of page 232. You might ask the children to make a face like Jim Bridger must have made when he was telling the story, and then to make a face like the tenderfoot must have made at the end of the story—when he realized it was a joke. Perhaps you could ask for two volunteers to read the last part of the story (page 232), beginning with the tenderfoot's words: "Please tell me about it." Encourage them to make the appropriate kinds of faces. Two other children could then repeat the reading.

After the initial excitement has abated, you can discuss the questions at the bottom of page 232. Have the children refer to the story in answering the questions about the true—and not true —events. After this, you can call on other volunteers to read various parts of the story again.

Fire Hole River—just pulled our trouts out, took off the hooks, and ate them, then and there."

"Ate them?" says the tenderfoot, looking sickish. "Raw?"

"Course not," Jack told him. "Fire Hole River's a body of water Jim went and discovered. It's cold on the bottom, so trouts live there, but it's hot on top. These trouts would be cooked beautiful by the time they'd been landed— all except the seasoning, which we'd take along with us when we fished."

The tenderfoot didn't look so sick any more, but by now he looked more or less like a little boy that had gone to bed at home in the usual way, and then had wakened up on the moon—a mite astonished and puzzled.

Jim thought a minute, then said, "It wasn't far from Fire Hole River, as I remember it, that my pony got some ideas—logical ideas, too—that in the end went and killed him. He was a right fine pony, too, and I hated to lose him."

Jim thought for a while, and then he went on. "It was along toward sundown, and I wanted to get to a camping place I was fond of before dark. Well, I tried a short cut. And that's the way I happened to get into this here peetrified forest."

"Peetrified?" the tenderfoot said.

"Sure. Everything was turned plumb to stone—the green grass, the trees—"

"Pardon me," says the tenderfoot. "I presume that you mean petrified."

"I presume I don't," says Jim, sort of sharp. "Maybe forests get petrified back east in New York, but out here in this man's country, where everything's on a big scale, they get peetrified. Everything there, like I said, was peetrified— the sage, the spruce, the varmints. In the air was the peetrified perfume of the stone flowers and the songs of the stone birds. The fruit was turned to stone, too, and I picked me a pocketful of rubies, emeralds, and such stuff without bothering to get off my pony. But I had to hurry, so I spurred the critter along.

"What we did, finally, was come to a great wide canyon that appeared to cut me off from where I was going. At first, I was worried, but then I got an idea, drove my pony to the edge of the canyon, and says 'Git up!' He turned around for a look at my face, naturally, to see if I was joking, the way I sometimes did with him, for we were old friends, you see. When he saw I wasn't, of course he stepped right ahead. He pranced right across the air in the canyon, the way I knowed he would. And well before sundown—"

"Wait a minute!" the tenderfoot said. "That's going too far! That's impossible!"

"Not there," Jim told him. "You're educated and can see why, too, soon as I tell you. You see, *there, even the law of gravity was peetrified.* That's what I'd figured would be the case—and well before sundown, we got to that camp."

"Sounds logical," the tenderfoot had to admit. "Have you any additional proof, however?"

"Well, lemme see—Oh yes, Jack saw what happened to that pony later, didn't you, Jack?"

Jack took his pipe out of his mouth to answer. "Sure did. Some time later, that pony got together three or four other ponies on the edge of Wildcat Bluff—lined them up to watch him, you know. Then, with a smug smile on his face, he pranced out over the edge of that bluff. I never saw a horse look as surprised as that pony did when, all of a sudden, he started to fall. We figured he was loco till Jim here told us why he went and done it."

"He was a good pony," Jim said, looking sad. "Logical, too. Only thing he didn't know, you see, was that in most places—like Wildcat Bluff, say—the law of gravity *isn't* peetrified. A while back I myself had good reason to wish

Follow-up Listed under Additional Resources are a number of other tall tales which the children might enjoy reading. You can suggest that interested children begin a collection of tall tales, which they can illustrate and share with other members of the class. Some children might even want to try writing tall tales of their own.

A group of children can work together creating a "chain tale," perhaps using some recent happening as the basis for the story. Starting with a few "facts," one child can begin the tale, elaborating on or exaggerating the actual fact. Another child can continue the story, adding exaggerations of his own, and so on. If you decide to have the children do this as an oral activity, then you may want to tape the story so the children involved can "hear it grow."

Additional Resources

Books Blair, Walter, *Tall Tale America*, Coward-McCann. This book, from which the selection in the text was taken, also includes tall tales about other heroes, such as Pecos Bill, Davy Crockett, and Windwagon Smith. Chase, Richard, editor, *Grandfather Tales*, Houghton Mifflin. Children living in the South might enjoy reading some of the tales told in their own part of the country. Cothran, Jean, editor, *With a Wig, With a Wag*, McKay. This is another book of regional folktales for children. Crane, Lucy, translator, *Household Stories*, Macmillan. Credle, Ellis, *Tall Tales from the High Hills*, Nelson. Felton, Harold, *New Tall Tales of Pecos Bill*, Prentice-Hall. Finger, Charles J., *Tales from Silver Lands*, Doubleday. This Newbery winner is a collection of tales from South America. Jagendorf, Moritz A., *Marvelous Adventures of Johnny Caesar Cicero Darling*, Vanguard. This book contains tall tales about a folk hero from the Catskill Mountains. Leach, Marie, *The Rainbow Book of American Folk Tales and Legends*, World. This book includes folklore originating in all fifty states. Reinfeld, Fred, *Trappers of the West*, Dell. Jim Bridger is one of the tall tale heros whose adventures are recounted in this collection. Shippen, Katherine B., *Big Moose*, Harper & Row. Urban children in particular might enjoy reading these tall tales about a New York City fireman. Steele, William O., *Andy Jackson's Water Well*, Harcourt. This book tells a tall tale about one of our early Presidents.

Filmstrips *American Folklore Series*, Holt, Rinehart and Winston.

he'd been right instead of wrong. If the law of gravity had been peetrified everywhere, I'd have been saved from what was just about the most horrible thing ever happened to me."

"Please tell me about it, Mr. Bridger," the tenderfoot said.

"It was when six grizzly bears saw me and started to chase me. I was on my pony, not this one but another, and naturally, I kept a-twisting around in my saddle, and picking off the lead grizzly. Got five that way, so there was only one left—and I had only one cartridge in my gun.

"He was coming fast at me, this last one, just as we came up to the edge of the Grand Canyon. No horse on earth could jump across a ditch that size, and a fall to the bottom meant sure death. I turned my horse sudden, and the bear was upon me, roaring like mad. My horse got scared and leaped over the side, but I managed to jump off. The bear and me got into a hand-to-hand ruckus. He was a powerful bear, big too—about nine feet tall. It was a long fight, with one on top, then the other. Finally, though, I began to tire. He edged me over to the edge, and howling like a panther, he gave me a horrible hard push. I couldn't grab hold of anything—started to fall—"

"Good heavens!" said the tenderfoot, standing up in his excitement. "I do not see how you survived!"

Jim looked at him, even sadder than before. "I didn't" he said. "That dratted bear killed me. Time to turn in."

WALTER BLAIR

Remember, a tall tale really isn't true. But the storyteller pretends that it's true. What things in this tale could never be true? What things could be true?

Why doesn't the storyteller laugh while's he's telling a tall tale? Try reading aloud some parts of this tale. But don't laugh. Try to sound very, very serious.

Revising a Play

Do you remember the play about the magic shoes? Suppose the artist decided to revise his pictures this way.

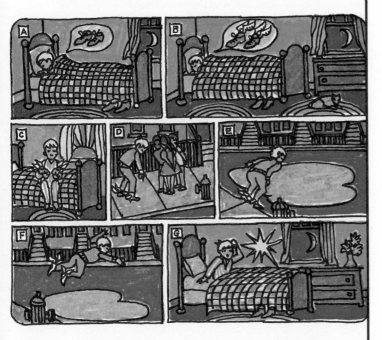

One way we can revise the play is to change the way of telling the story. How are these pictures different from the ones on page 223? How has the story changed?

Another way to revise the story is to change the way it's told. Try to make the story into a play where the characters really talk. What could you have them say?

Purposes (1) To emphasize the importance of revising compositions; (2) To provide an opportunity for revising an earlier composition.

[This lesson also prepares the children for a discussion of revision in the final lesson on composition (page 241), where they'll have the opportunity to revise an earlier, written composition.]

Preparation Have the original cast repeat the pantomimed play from the first composition lesson in this chapter.

Presentation Ask the children to compare the pictures on page 233 with those on page 223. If an overhead projector is available, you can project the first set of pictures while the children look at the revised set in their books. Then ask: "Which pictures are the same? Which ones are different?"

After the children have discussed the artist's revision, remind them that, in the last composition lesson, they presented the play in pantomime. Ask how they might revise the <u>way</u> of presenting the play, as well as <u>the</u> story of the play. Elicit the fact that one way to do this would be to have the characters speaking, and then have the class suggest things for these characters to say. Suggest also that there are several ways to end the new play: The boy might be glad to wake up —because he thought he was falling—or he might be sad—because he knew he could fly across the puddle.

Follow-up The children might also like to dramatize the tall tale about Jim Bridger (pages 228–232), or perhaps some of the other stories that they read as a follow-up to that lesson. Encourage them to think about how they might revise the story before they actually act it out.

Purposes (1) To illustrate again that children possess sentence-combining rules as part of their linguistic competence; (2) To demonstrate the use of *who, whom, which,* and *that* in combining certain kinds of sentences.

Preparation Have the children consult the Index to locate previous lessons on combining sentences (pages 38–41, 50–52, 102–103, and 206–208). They should find and read aloud the different forms which the sentence-combining rule may take. (You can also suggest that there are other ways of combining sentences in addition to those given in this book.) For each type of sentence combining, provide examples as illustrations.

Presentation Have the children solve the two problems at the top of page 234 individually. Then call on two volunteers to write their solutions on the chalkboard and also to explain the steps they followed.

Then read the material on page 234 with the children, calling special attention to the sentence after the (●). Provide whatever help is necessary in using terms such as *nominal, adjective, matrix,* and *insert.* Help the children see that the "parentheses problems" on the bottom half of page 234 are simply another way of doing the same thing as the addition problems. (You might want to do each of the examples first as an addition problem and then as a parentheses problem.) Call on volunteers to explain what happens at each step.

Answers

1. Arthur saw a clown who walks on his hands.
2. The lady who lives next door likes to jump rope.
3. Fred found a funny frog.

234

Combining Sentences

Here are two sentence problems. They're like some that you've seen before. How do you solve them?

> The boy bought a pizza.
> + The boy found a dollar.

> Edna made a cake.
> +   The cake was square.

Combining sentences is a very important part of English. That's why we put the sentence-combining rule in the sentence model.

● Wherever you have a nominal in a sentence, you can always insert another sentence.

We can use a sentence problem to show how the rule works. We can also use parentheses, like this.

The mailman (~~the mailman~~ *who* rescued the cat) got a medal.
⟹ The mailman who rescued the cat got a medal.

■ Now show how you would combine these sentences.

1. Arthur saw a clown (the clown walks on his hands).
⟹
2. The lady (the lady lives next door) likes to jump rope.
⟹
3. Fred found a frog (the frog was funny).
⟹

You already know one important thing about combining sentences. The noun in the insert sentence must be the same as a noun in the matrix sentence.

Daybook: Combining Sentences Again,
page 92

There's another important thing to know. It's about combining sentences in the regular way. If the noun is a person, then you use *who* (or sometimes *whom*). If the noun is a thing, then you use *which* (or sometimes *that*).

- With people, use *who* (or sometimes *whom*).

- With things, use *which* (or sometimes *that*).

(If you combine sentences in the special adjective way, then you don't need *who* or *whom* or *which* or *that*.)

■ Here are some sentence problems for you to solve. Some of the nouns refer to things. Remember, you need to use *which* or *that* instead of *who*. (The first one is done for you.)

1. I saw a bird
   + *which*
     The bird lives in a hat.
   I saw a bird which lives in a hat.

2. Ruth bought a pizza.
   +   The pizza cost a dollar.

3. The frog frightened me.
   + The frog croaked loudly.

4. I painted a picture.
   +   The picture won a prize.

5. Phil likes clocks.
   +   The clocks go "tock-tick."

6. The paint fell on the floor.
   + The paint filled up the can.

7. Sue climbed the tree.
   +   The tree is in our backyard.

Next, point out—on the chalkboard—those problems that use *who* in the final sentence and ask if anyone knows why *who* was used. Then suggest that, on the top part of page 235, they can read about the rules for using *who* and some other words when they combine sentences.

The sentence problems in the activity (■) can be done orally as an entire class. You should ask for complete explanations of each step in all the problems, involving as many children as possible. (You might want to use an opaque projector for this, or perhaps large sheets of paper and Magic Marker.) After completing the activity, you might redo two or three problems as parentheses problems.

Follow-up Here are some additional sentence-combining problems which you can use as an individual assignment.

1. John caught a tadpole.
   + The tadpole was sitting on a log.

2. The man told a tall tale.
   + The man was short.

3. I met a lady.
   + The lady trained canaries.

4. Dick collects coins.
   + The coins are old.

5. The piano was out of tune.
   + The piano sounded strange.

Answers

In all of these sentences, either *which* or *that* may be used.

2. Ruth bought a pizza which cost a dollar.
3. The frog which croaked loudly frightened me.
4. I painted a picture which won a prize.
5. Phil likes clocks which go "tock-tick."
6. The paint which filled up the can fell on the floor.
7. Sue climbed the tree which is in our backyard.

Purposes (1) To reinforce the distinction between literature which is purely factual and that which is fanciful; (2) To re-emphasize that pantomime is one possible form of composition; (3) To review the sentence-combining rule.

Presentation This is another lesson that can be done effectively with the class divided into three groups. Each child can choose the section—Literature, Composition, or Language—that he wishes to complete, and then each group can present its work to the rest of the class.

Those children who choose to do the Literature Review may need some help getting started on the tall tale. You can offer suggestions or ask leading questions, such as "Where do you think the tale should begin? Where should it end? Is there anything in the story that you can use for a 'punch line'? What could you say at the end to surprise your listeners?" You might also suggest that, before the children actually begin to adapt the story into a tall tale, they practice reading it aloud a few times. Encourage them to use a conversational tone as they do so. Then suggest that they choose a few words to "define," just as Jim Bridger did. Ask the children if they want to have someone "interrupt," as the tenderfoot did. Finally, suggest that they tape the tall tale which they made up so they can hear it before they present it to the rest of the class.

Review

Literature

In *scientific writing,* everything the author says should be true. But when someone is telling a *tall tale,* then he only pretends that the story is true. He tries—for as long as he can —to make people think that the tale is true.

Suppose the scientist who wrote about Indian houses in California wanted to play a joke. Suppose that—one time when he was telling about the houses—he made the story into a tall tale. What are some of the things he could say? How would he sound while he was telling the story?

■ Try to make the story about the Indian houses into a tall tale. You can change the story a little. But be careful not to change it too much, or you won't trick anybody.

Composition

Acting without talking is *pantomime.* Pantomime is one good way to make a composition. You can also make a game out of pantomime. Here's how to do it.

First, you think of some ideas to act out. (Someone could be a balloon blowing up or a bird building a nest.) Then someone in the class acts out one of the ideas. The rest of the class watches. And then everybody writes down what they think the person is doing.

When everyone is done writing, you can take turns reading what you wrote. The one who does the best job of describing what the actor was doing is the winner.

Then someone else can have a turn acting out one of the other ideas.

Language

Do you remember the sentence-combining rule? It says that, whenever you have a nominal in a sentence, you can always insert another sentence. This is one of the most important rules in the sentence model.

■ Here are some problems you can do for practice.

1.   I can play the piano.
   +   The piano is in the auditorium.

2.   Mother called for the plumber.
   +   The plumber lives down the block.

3.   My bike has five gears.
   + My bike is orange.

4.   Bob has a book.
   +   The book is about snakes.

5.   My uncle lives in a castle.
   + My uncle is rich.

6.   I can't open my locker.
   +   My locker is broken.

In this chapter, you learned about the *past tense morpheme.* You know that there's more than one way to show the idea of past tense. If you turn to page 328, then you'll find out how to form the past of some verbs you use all the time.

In addition to the language activity suggested in the text, you might also want to review the concept of morpheme as it applies to plural and past tense forms. Here are two exercises you can use:

A. List the following words on the chalkboard:

1. tooth	6. fish
2. pancake	7. crayon
3. shrimp	8. half
4. feather	9. zebra
5. matchbox	10. sheep

Call for a volunteer to use one of the words in a sentence (for example, "I lost a tooth."). Then call for another volunteer to use the plural form of that word in a similar sentence (for example, "I lost two teeth.").

B. Have the children give the past tense forms of these verbs and then use each one in a sentence.

1. like	6. come
2. know	7. swallow
3. tickle	8. climb
4. go	9. paint
5. see	10. take

Answers

For sentences 1 and 4, either *which* or *that* may be used.
1. I can play the piano which is in the auditorium.
2. Mother called for the plumber who lives down the block.
3. My orange bike has five gears.
4. Bob has a book which is about snakes.
5. My rich uncle lives in a castle.
6. I can't open my broken locker.

Purposes (1) To review some of the major concepts presented in the earlier lessons on literature, particularly those on poetry; (2) To provide an occasion for discussing some things the children have learned about literature during the year.

Preparation Have a few children read their favorite poems, selected from those in this text or any other books the children have used. If you've made tape recordings of the class reading poems, you can play these again. Or you can have the children request poems for you to reread to them. If you read to the children, you can encourage them to join in whenever they feel like doing so. After each reading, the children can briefly discuss some of the things they like about the poem.

Presentation Remind the children of the lesson on etymologies (pages 226–227) and then have them read the first paragraph on page 238 to discover the history of the word *poet*.

Then read the second paragraph with the children, pausing to discuss the points that are made. (You might use *tintinnabulation* as an example of a word which a poet made. You can also use Cummings' poem on page 141 to illustrate old words used in new ways.)

If the discussion is going well, you can continue it by turning immediately

Talking About Literature

The word *poet* is very old. We borrowed it from the French language. But the French got the word from the Latin language. And the people who spoke Latin got the word from the Greek language. In Greek, the word means "maker." We can think of a poet as a "maker." And we can think of a poem as "the thing a poet makes."

Sometimes, a poet really does make language. He may invent a new word. He may use an old word in a new way. But mostly a poet makes us see things and feel things and think about things in a new way.

Here's a poem for you to think about. It tells how one poet felt when a friend moved away.

I Loved My Friend

I loved my friend.
He went away from me.
There's nothing more to say.
The poem ends,
Soft as it began—
I loved my friend.

LANGSTON HUGHES

238

to page 240 (and save the poem on page 238 for later in the lesson). Beginning in the third paragraph and continuing to the bottom of the page are many questions that will stimulate an interesting discussion.

As the discussion begins to wind down, you can turn back to page 238 and read the poem by Langston Hughes to the class. Ask the children what the poet makes them think of as they listen. You might ask: "Do you see any special pictures in your heads? How do you feel when you listen to the poem?"

Read the poem a second time and ask the children if the poet makes them think (as the text says at the bottom of page 240). Encourage a wide variety of answers; it would also be good if you could contribute some thoughts of your own. Finally, have the children complete the activity (■) on page 240.

Follow-up While it is certainly not necessary, or in many cases even desirable, to supply the children with biographical information regarding the authors whose works are contained in the text, Langston Hughes is one poet whom the children might be interested in learning more about. (See Additional Resources.) Also listed under Additional Resources are a few other poems by Langston Hughes that you may want to read to the children.

Additional Resources

Books Hughes, Langston, *The Dream Keeper and Other Poems for Young People*, Knopf. Larrick, Nancy, compiler, *On City Streets*, Evans. This anthology contains a number of poems by Langston Hughes, including "Could Be," "Dream Deferred," and "Stars." Meltzer, Milton, *Langston Hughes: A Biography*, Crowell. You may want to select parts of this book to read to the children. Myers, Elizabeth I., *Langston Hughes, Poet of His People*, Garrard. Many of the children in your class will be able to read this biography on their own.

Recordings *An Anthology of Negro Poetry for Young People*, 1–10″ LP, Folkways. On this recording, Arna Bontemps reads some of Langston Hughes poetry. *The Dream Keeper*, 1–10″ LP, Folkways. This recording includes a number of Langston Hughes' poems that are particularly appropriate for elementary school children. *The Rhythms of the World,* 1–10″ LP, Folkways. Langston Hughes uses everyday sounds and rhythms to explain how all the world's rhythms are related.

Have you ever had a friend who moved away? How did you feel? Does this poem make you think about a friend?

■ Have you ever had a dream you wish would come true? Try to write a poem or a story about a dream you liked. If you want, you can tell why you like it.

Poets help us think about things. They make *metaphors* to help us see things in a new way. Poets also help us hear things. They use *rhyme* and *rhythm* so we hear language in a special way.

Do you remember the poem about the Christmas tree? Did you ever think a Christmas tree was like a flower? Did you think a Christmas tree could be sorry to leave the forest? Did you ever think that Christmas tree decorations would "sleep all the year"? One poet thought these things. He made up a poem so we could think them, too.

Do you remember "The Lobster Quadrille"? Did it make you think of a square dance? Do you remember "Casey Jones"? When you read the poem about Casey, did it sound something like the music a train makes?

When we say a poet is a "maker," we can also mean that he makes things up in his head. Sometimes a poet makes up funny things. He may write a poem about a yak. And sometimes a poet makes believe that an animal can use a typewriter. Then he writes a poem like "pete at the seashore."

Here are some of the things a poet makes:

A poet makes metaphors.
A poet makes music.
A poet makes jokes.
A poet makes stories.

But here's the most important thing a poet makes us do:

A poet makes us <u>think</u>.

Talking About Composition

This is the last section on composition. It's a good time to stop for a few minutes so you can think about some of the things you've done. You've written lots of compositions this year.

You started a diary.
You wrote some poetry.
You made up stories.

You've also made up compositions that you didn't write down.

You acted out plays.
You played "Someplace Else."
You interviewed people.

You even told a story without using words at all. You used *pantomime*.

What do you like about the compositions that you don't write down? When you write a composition, then you get to keep it. And you can keep it as long as you want. You can read it again any time you want to, even years later. What else is good about compositions you do write down?

Now is a good time to look again at the compositions you've written. Which ones do you like best? What do you like about them?

■ Now choose one of your compositions. Think how you could make it more interesting. Then revise your composition to make it better. (If you don't want to revise any of your compositions, then you can choose one to recopy neatly.)

■ If you want to, you can choose a composition that you like. Then you can write another composition of the same kind.

Purposes (1) To review some of the major concepts presented in the earlier lessons on composition; (2) To provide an occasion for discussing, revising, and recopying earlier compositions.

Preparation Have the children discuss their feelings about the kinds of compositions they've written this year. (You'll find a complete list in the Index.) You might ask questions such as these: "Which kind is your favorite? Which is the hardest to write? What are some of the problems you have in writing compositions? Is it easy to write at certain times and hard at other times? Can you explain why?" During the discussion, remind the children that, in answering these questions, they're talking about compositions. Then state that the last lesson on composition has the title: Talking About Composition.

Presentation Have the children read the first half of the lesson and then answer the questions in the second paragraph. Encourage as many children as possible to respond.

As you read the last paragraph of the lesson, provide ample time for the children to look through their earlier compositions. Have them select two or three (or four) that they really like. Again, encourage a wide variety of responses as they state what they like about particular ones. The activities (■) should be done on an individual basis. You should probably extend work on the activities over several days so that you have time to consult with each child.

Follow-up As a final review, you might want to reread the lesson on Proofreading on pages 302–305 of the Skills Section.

Purposes (1) To review some of the major concepts presented in the earlier lessons on language; (2) To demonstrate, again, that we can use a sentence model to discuss some of the things we know about language.

Preparation Assign volunteers to check the following topics in the Index, and then to summarize the pages referred to:

Adjectives
Adverbials
Auxiliaries
"Be" words
Derived sentence
Insert sentence
Lexicon
Matrix sentence
Morphemes
Nominals
N'T
Position picture of a sentence
Q
Q$_{tag}$
Verb phrases

You can also have children demonstrate how to make a sentence with a nominal and a verb phrase, how to add Q to a sentence, how to add Q$_{tag}$ to another sentence, and how to add N'T to still another sentence.

Presentation Read pages 242 and 243 with the children, providing ample time to answer (and—when necessary—discuss) the questions. Whenever possible, re-emphasize that the children know the

The Sentence Model

What state do you live in? Can you name three big cities in your state? Can you name every city in your state? Where could you look to find out the names of all the cities in your state?

Suppose you have a map of your state. Does it show the important cities? Does it show every little town? Does it show every street—and every house—in every city and town? Why not?

A map is a kind of model. And no model shows everything. There are too many things—streets and apartment buildings and stores and traffic lights—to show on any map. And there are too many things in your head—ideas and words and rules—to show in a sentence model.

You probably know about forty thousand morphemes in your head. You can use them to make nouns and verbs and adjectives. You can make when-adverbials, where-adverbials, and how-adverbials. You can even make lots of other adverbials that you haven't studied about yet. You can use all these different kinds of words to make sentences. And you can make basic and derived sentences.

Suppose you had a piece of paper big enough. Then maybe you could make a map of all the houses and buildings and streets and roads and towns and cities in your state. But how big would the paper have to be? Why would you want to make such a map? Do you think anyone has ever made one? Do you need such a big map to talk about your state?

If a scientist really wanted to, he might be able to make a sentence model that shows everything in your head. He might be able to show everything you know about sentences. But such a sentence model would be much bigger than this book. It would even be much bigger than an encyclopedia.

Nobody really needs such a big sentence model. We can talk about English—about what you know in your head—just by using a small model. We can use one which shows the most important things that you know.

One of the most important things you know is the first rule.

● A sentence has a nominal and a verb phrase.

This is the rule you use to make basic sentences. You also know rules for adding a Q or a Q_{tag} or an N'T to a sentence. And you know lots of rules for combining sentences.

Here's a picture that you've already seen in this book.

Of course everyone can talk. But not everyone can "talk about talking." This year, you've learned lots of things to help you talk about the way you talk!

rules of language in their heads. The sentence model is only a device for talking about things they know.

The sentences below the illustration on page 243 deliberately use the word *talk* several times. After reading them, ask the children how they can talk about the illustration. What are some things in language that they've learned to talk about since they first saw the illustration (page 29)? Do they think that learning to talk about language will help them use language better—in speaking, writing, reading, and listening? (No one knows the answer to this question, but it will be interesting to learn what the children think.)

Evaluation As a final evaluation, you should think about each child in terms of all of the objectives listed under the Statement of Goals, and not merely those which apply to Chapters 13–16. Some children may have exhibited a number of these objectives at different times throughout the year. Other children may be just beginning to demonstrate an understanding of certain basic concepts. In other words, what is important is not so much when an individual child shows that he has acquired a new learning, but that he shows it. And there is no end to the many ways in which he may show it.

If the evaluation component is available, you may also wish to use it to help you determine an individual child's progress over the course of the year.

Introduction: The Skills of English

The skills of English are primarily social in contrast to the arts which are primarily humanistic. The skills section focuses on skills of written composition. It includes suggestions for locating information and for selecting and ordering ideas. It comprises about 25% of the text in contrast to 75% comprised by the arts. (Class time may be divided in about the same ratio.) Moreover, many of the skills are unrelated to other skills and generally can be presented in random order.

Since the skills are different in kind from the arts, they are presented differently. It is possible to omit lessons for some children and use lessons with only those children who need them. In short, you can be quite flexible in presenting the skills.

Each book in the series presents in alphabetical order the skills that are appropriate for that level. In some instances, the children at a particular level will have had considerable experience with a specific skill. In these cases, the text simply notes the skill and provides examples of its application. Other skills are presented with more explanation. Generally, each skill presented at one level is repeated and extended at the next level.

A series of diagnostic exercises, a part of the evaluation package available from the publisher for duplication, can be used to determine whether or not each child has command of the skills at each level. When the diagnostic exercises reveal a weakness in a specific skill, the child is referred to the text. The performance objectives in the teacher's edition tell what he should be able to do after reading the text, participating in the discussion, and completing the exercises.

Individualized Instruction

Any individualized approach to instruction should help each child achieve maximum growth in a given instructional area. A basic premise of individualized instruction is that each child should receive instruction in that specific area in which we know he needs instruction. Specific interests of each child are also accommodated.

Once weaknesses in the skills have been determined through the use of the diagnostic exercises, the child with weaknesses can be directed to specific skills lessons. He may study the lessons independently. Or those children who have the same skill needs may be grouped for discussion of a skills lesson. After the skills discussion, each child may apply the skill to one of the two sets of exercises that follow. The child who demonstrates that he has not yet fully mastered the skill will need additional help before attempting the second set of exercises. Achievement exercises, also a part of the evaluation package, may be administered to help determine mastery of the skill. For further proof of mastery, notice how well the child applies the skill in subsequent compositions.

Another approach might be interest-oriented. The entire class might examine and discuss the various skills entries in the table of contents. Allow the children to select and examine the skills that interest them. Then, about one class period a week, they can report to the class what they learn about skills.

Large-Group Instruction

Group instruction of the skills may be initiated through the references to skills lessons in the arts section. Or time may be set aside after the completion of two or three chapters in the arts section for skills lessons. Either way, you might have all the children do one set of exercises together, and then have them complete the other exercise independently.

The skills section is organized for use as a reference tool. When the children are working in other subject areas, they can use the skills text as a reference for writing reports.

The Skills of English

Usage Instruction

A usage section, which warrants special consideration, follows the skills lessons. It's important that you understand what these lessons do and don't do.

First, the negative: the usage section does not contain lengthy drills on correct usage. While there are exercises in this section, they are not intended to teach standard forms but only to indicate where a student may habitually use non-standard forms. Even given a student who wishes (for whatever reasons) to learn the standard written forms, the use of lengthy written drills is not pedagogically effective.

Now, the positive: the usage material provides an objective discussion of both historical and current language concerns. Specifically, the section includes a discussion of the distinctions between formal and informal, standard and non-standard, and spoken and written usage. The discussion material demonstrates that correct English is frequently relative and generally a function of many factors that are social as well as linguistic.

The opening discussion on usage should be studied in a total class situation. Even the children whose usage is consistently standard have much to learn from this material. The children should not only be aware that they have "knowledge in their heads," they should also be aware that there are levels of appropriateness which depend upon social situations. The exercises which follow the general discussion are designed to strengthen a child's sensitivity to language differences as well as to levels of usage.

Abbreviations (Pages 246–254)

These abbreviations are presented:

1. Titles of respect (Mr., Rev., Dr., Mrs., Gov.)
2. Days and months (Sun., Mon., Tues., Wed., Thurs., Fri., Sat., Jan., Feb., Mar., Apr., Aug., Sept., Oct., Nov., Dec.)
3. States of the United States (expect mastery only of abbreviation for local state)
4. Abbreviations used in addresses (N., S., E., W., Rd., St., Dr., Ave., Blvd., Apt., P.O., R.F.D.)
5. Units of measure (oz., lb., in., ft., yd., mi., pt., qt., gal., t.)

These generalizations are presented:

1. When the word you are abbreviating begins with a capital letter, the abbreviation also begins with a capital letter. When the word begins with a small letter, the abbreviation begins with a small letter.
2. You usually end an abbreviation with a period.

Call attention to the illustration. Note that each abbreviation ends with a period; that each abbreviation begins with a capital letter only when the word or words it stands for begin with capital letters.

Call attention to the meaning of the titles of respect in the display. Note that there is no abbreviation for *Miss.*

Abbreviations

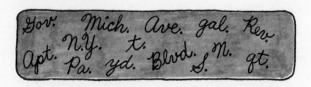

An **abbreviation** is a short way of writing a word. Here are some abbreviations and the words they stand for.

Thurs.	Thursday	oz.	ounce
Mr.	Mister	Dr.	Doctor
Sept.	September	Ave.	Avenue
Apt.	Apartment	N.	North
Calif.	California	N.Y.	New York

How can you tell when to begin an abbreviation with a capital letter? How do most abbreviations end?

Titles of Respect

Most titles which go before the names of people are written as abbreviations.

Mr. Joseph Barnes	Dr. Ricardo Jimenez
Rev. Joshua Moore	Mrs. Miriam McLaughlin
Miss Theresa Poli	Gov. Charles Brown

Mr. stands for the title *Mister.*
Rev. stands for *Reverend*, a title for a minister.
Miss is the title for an unmarried woman. It has no abbreviation.
Dr. stands for the title *Doctor.*

Objectives: Abbreviations
1. Name and describe the titles for married women, unmarried women, men, doctors, ministers, and governors.
2. Demonstrate the use of the abbreviations *Mrs., Mr., Dr., Rev.,* and *Gov.*
3. Demonstrate the use of abbreviations for days and months.
4. Demonstrate the use of abbreviations in addresses.

Mrs. stands for *Mistress*. *Mistress* is an old title, that we no longer use, for a married woman.

Gov. stands for the title *Governor*.

Exercises

A. Write titles to complete these sentences. You may use *Miss, Mr., Mrs., Dr., Gov.,* or *Rev.* (More than one title may fit the meaning of the sentence.)

1. _____ and _____ Klugman went to Washington, D. C.
2. _____ Fadiman, a pediatrician, is moving to town.
3. _____ Priscilla Guzman entertained a group of her friends at her ninth birthday party last Sunday.
4. _____ Denise Patchen and _____ Norman Marcus are opening a clinic to treat minor illnesses.
5. _____ Andrea Vincent just returned from a trip around the world with her five children.
6. _____ Thomas Hoover of the Methodist Church will offer the prayer at the ceremony.
7. _____ Nelson Rockefeller was the governor of New York state in 1970.
8. _____ and _____ Parker live in the green house.
9. _____ Jane Daw and _____ Dale Segal will be married in the Grace Episcopal Church by _____ Phillip Shaw.
10. _____ Kelly and _____ Smith are secretaries.

B. Suppose that you are writing a column of a newspaper which announces important events in your city or town. They may be births, marriages, trips, parties, or coming events. Make up and write five different announcements. Try to use each of these abbreviations for titles at least once: *Mr., Mrs., Miss, Dr., Gov.,* and *Rev.*

Answers

EXERCISE A
1. Mr., Mrs.
2. Dr.
3. Miss
4. Dr., Dr.
5. Mrs.
6. Rev.
7. Gov.
8. Mr., Mrs.
9. Miss, Mr., Rev.
10. Miss, Miss

Accept any other answers that are reasonable.

EXERCISE B
Accept any reasonable announcement that uses abbreviations correctly.

5. Construct abbreviations for given units of measure.
6. Construct words for given abbreviations of units of measure.

The abbreviations for days of the week are:

Sun.—Sunday Thurs.—Thursday
Mon.—Monday Fri.—Friday
Tues.—Tuesday Sat.—Saturday
Wed.—Wednesday

Tues. and Thurs. use more than the first three letters of the day.

Abbreviations for months:

Jan.—January Sept.—September
Feb.—February Oct.—October
Mar.—March Nov.—November
Apr.—April Dec.—December
Aug.—August

There are no abbreviations for *May*, *June*, or *July* because they are short words. Most of the abbreviations use the first three letters of the name—except for Sept.

Call attention to the illustration at the bottom of the page. Have the children identify the abbreviations. Discuss other abbreviations that could be used to tell about the scene, such as the time, and the address of the place where the party is held.

Days and Months

All the days of the week have abbreviations.

Sun.	Tues.	Thurs.	Sat.
Mon.	Wed.	Fri.	

Which day of the week does each abbreviation stand for? Which of these abbreviations are made from the first three letters of the day? Which abbreviations use more than the first three letters of the day?

Only nine of the months have abbreviations.

Jan.	Apr.	Oct.
Feb.	Aug.	Nov.
Mar.	Sept.	Dec.

Which month of the year does each abbreviation stand for? Which months of the year don't have abbreviations? Why do you think they don't? Which letters are taken from the names of the months to make these abbreviations? How many of the abbreviations have more than three letters?

248

Exercises

A. The names of the days of the week came from myths. The myths explain the beginnings of a part of nature or tell how a god received power over a part of nature.

Read this list that tells the part of nature or the god each day was named after. Then write the name of the day as we know it, with its abbreviation.

1. the sun's day
2. Woden's day (Woden was a king of the gods in the old Norse myths.)
3. Frigga's day (Frigga was the goddess of love and beauty in Norse myths.)
4. the moon's day
5. Saturn's day (Saturn was a Roman god of the harvest.)
6. Thor's day (Thor was a Norse god of thunder.)
7. Tyr's day (Tyr was the Norse god of war.)

B. Now see if you can write the dates for these days. Use abbreviations for the months—wherever possible. If you don't know these dates, look them up on a calendar, or ask your teacher.

1. Christmas
2. Halloween
3. Thanksgiving Day
4. Valentine's Day
5. Independence Day
6. Easter Sunday
7. Hanukkah
8. New Year's Day
9. May Day
10. April Fool's Day
11. your birthday
12. Washington's birthday
13. your friend's birthday
14. another friend's birthday
15. your teacher's birthday
16. your mother's birthday
17. Lincoln's birthday
18. today's date
19. last Monday's date
20. next Friday's date

Answers

EXERCISE A
1. Sunday
2. Wednesday
3. Friday
4. Monday
5. Saturday
6. Thursday
7. Tuesday

EXERCISE B
1. December 25
2. October 31
3. See calendar for the fourth Thursday in November
4. February 14
5. July 4
6. March or April: see calendar (the first Sunday after the first full moon after the vernal equinox which occurs on or shortly after March 21)
7. December: see calendar (the 25th day of Kislev which is the third month of the Jewish calendar)
8. January 1
9. May 1
10. April 1
11. Answers will vary.
12. February 22, but may be celebrated at other times in February
13–16. Answers will vary.
17. February 12
18–20. Answers will vary with day exercise is done.

249

Call attention to the illustration. Have the children identify the abbreviations on the envelope.

Abbreviations for the names of states may vary. The abbreviations used in this text are taken from *The Winston Dictionary for Schools*, published by Holt, Rinehart and Winston, Inc. Copyright 1967.

Other abbreviations may be used. For example, the Post Office Department uses these abbreviations in the *National Zip Code Directory*. These abbreviations all have two capital letters and no periods.

Alabama	AL	Nebraska	NB
Alaska	AK	Nevada	NV
Arizona	AZ	New	
Arkansas	AR	Hampshire	NH
California	CA	New Jersey	NJ
Colorado	CO	New Mexico	NM
Connecticut	CT	New York	NY
Delaware	DE	North Carolina	NC
Florida	FL	North Dakota	ND
Georgia	GA	Ohio	OH
Hawaii	HI	Oklahoma	OK
Idaho	ID	Oregon	OR
Illinois	IL	Pennsylvania	PA
Indiana	IN	Rhode Island	RI
Iowa	IA	South Carolina	SC
Kansas	KS	South Dakota	SD
Kentucky	KY	Tennessee	TN
Louisiana	LA	Texas	TX
Maine	ME	Utah	UT
Maryland	MD	Vermont	VT
Massachusetts	MA	Virginia	VA
Michigan	MI	Washington	WA
Minnesota	MN	West Virginia	WV
Mississippi	MS	Wisconsin	WI
Missouri	MO	Wyoming	WY
Montana	MT		

More activities on writing addresses are given on page 255.

Addresses

When you mail a letter to someone, his address and your address are written on the envelope. Sometimes you use abbreviations to write both addresses.

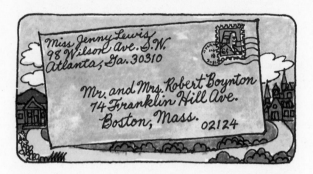

Miss Jenny Lewis
98 Wilson Ave. S.W.
Atlanta, Ga. 30310

Mr. and Mrs. Robert Boynton
74 Franklin Hill Ave.
Boston, Mass. 02124

You can use abbreviations to write the names of all states—except Alaska and Hawaii. Here are some of them.

Ariz.	Arizona	N. Y.	New York
Pa.	Pennsylvania	Ga.	Georgia
Calif.	California	Mich.	Michigan

What is the abbreviation for your state?

You can use other abbreviations in addresses, too. Here are some of them.

N.	North	Dr.	Drive
S.	South	Ave.	Avenue
E.	East	Blvd.	Boulevard
W.	West	Apt.	Apartment
Rd.	Road	P.O.	Post Office
St.	Street	R.F.D.	Rural Free Delivery

Which abbreviations can you use in these addresses?

1. Miss Barbara Kelly
   282 South River Street
   Wilkes Barre, Pennsylvania   18702

2. Mister Ralph Poindexter
   251 Brown Boulevard North West
   Warren, Ohio   44483

Exercises

A. Try to use abbreviations to write these addresses.

1. Mister and Mrs. Joseph Radigan
   302 East Royal Palm Road
   Phoenix, Arizona   85020

2. Mister and Mrs. William Kelley
   75 183rd Street, Apartment 4B
   Flushing, New York   11366

3. Mister and Mrs. Ole Larsen
   2121 Lawson Avenue
   Springfield, Illinois   62704

B. Now use abbreviations to write these addresses.

1. Mrs. John D. Ewing
   3431 Esperanza Drive
   Concord, California   94520

2. Mister and Mrs. Samuel Bunker
   Rural Free Delivery
   Monroeton, Pennsylvania   18832

3. Miss Louise Seelinger
   2306 Sloping Hill Boulevard
   Austin, Texas   78703

The abbreviations that can be used in the addresses:

1. Miss Barbara Kelly
   282 S. River St.
   Wilkes Barre, Pa. 18702
2. Mr. Ralph Poindexter
   251 Brown Blvd. N.W.
   Warren, O. 44483

Note that the abbreviation for Ohio is not given in the text. It must be found in another source, such as a dictionary. Expect the children to identify and write the abbreviation for the state in which they live.

Answers

EXERCISE A

1. Mr. and Mrs. Joseph Radigan
   302 E. Royal Palm Rd.
   Phoenix, Ariz. 85020
2. Mr. and Mrs. William Kelly
   75 183rd St., Apt. 4B
   Flushing, N.Y. 11366
3. Mr. and Mrs. Ole Larson
   2121 Lawson Ave.
   Springfield, Ill. 62704

EXERCISE B

1. Mrs. John D. Ewing
   3431 Esperanza Dr.
   Concord, Calif. 94520
2. Mr. and Mrs. Samuel Bunker
   R.F.D.
   Monroeton, Pa. 18832
3. Miss Louise Seelinger
   2306 Sloping Hill Blvd.
   Austin, Tex. 78703

Note that the abbreviation for *Illinois* and *Texas* are not given in the text. They must be found in another source.

Note that the abbreviations for the singular form and for the plural form of each unit of measure are the same; that in recipes *t.* is sometimes used as the abbreviation for teaspoon and *T.* is used for tablespoon.

Answers

Sally's Sewing Shop
(2 mi. e. of town)
18 in. zipper
4 ft. ribbon
2 yd. yellow cotton

Grocery Store
2 gal. milk
8 oz. heavy cream
1 pt. light cream
5 lb. sugar

Units of Measure

Many words for measurements have abbreviations. Most of these abbreviations can be used for both the singular and the plural form of the words they stand for. You don't have to put an *s* on the abbreviation, although some people do.

oz.	ounce	mi.	mile
lb.	pound	pt.	pint
in.	inch	qt.	quart
ft.	foot	gal.	gallon
yd.	yard	t.	ton

Exercises

A. Now write these shopping lists using abbreviations. Remember to put periods where they are needed.

Sally's Sewing Shop

(2 miles east of town)
18 inch zipper
4 feet ribbon
2 yards yellow cotton

Grocery Store

2 gallons milk
8 ounces heavy cream
1 pint light cream
5 pounds sugar

B. What do the abbreviations in these lists stand for? Write the lists without abbreviations.

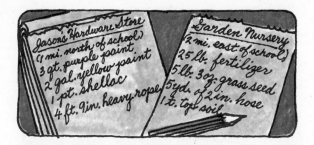

Summary

Here are some rules about abbreviations.

● When the word you are abbreviating begins with a capital letter, the abbreviation also begins with a capital letter. When the word begins with a small letter, the abbreviation begins with a small letter.

● You usually end an abbreviation with a period.

Exercises

A. See how many of these abbreviations you can remember. Write the word for each abbreviation.

1. Rev.	6. lb.	11. R.F.D.
2. Sat.	7. S.	12. Apr.
3. Aug.	8. Fri.	13. St.
4. P.O.	9. Pa.	14. qt.
5. Mich.	10. pt.	15. Dr.

Skillsbook: Abbreviations, page 1

1. Mr.   9. Gov.
2. Thurs.   10. mi.
3. Dec.   11. Apt.
4. Blvd.   12. gal.
5. N.Y.   13. E.
6. Calif.   14. Feb.
7. Sept.   15. oz.
8. t.

Addresses (Pages 254–255)

The forms for addresses used in social letters and in business letters are presented:

1. Address of person or company that the letter is sent to
2. Return address

Call attention to the illustration. Have the children read the addresses, identify the person who sent the letter, identify the person to whom the letter was sent, and give the street, the house number, the city, the state, and the zip code in both addresses.

Note that mailmen return letters when the person to whom the letter is sent is not at the address on the envelope.

B. Now write the abbreviations for these words.

1. Mister	6. California	11. Apartment
2. Thursday	7. September	12. gallon
3. December	8. ton	13. East
4. Boulevard	9. Governor	14. February
5. New York	10. mile	15. ounce

Addresses

When you write a friendly letter to someone, you write his address in the center of the envelope as shown above. You also write your address in the upper left-hand corner. The addresses tell the mailmen where to deliver or return your letter. When would the mailmen return your letter to you?

The zip code number tells the mailmen which post office should get your letter. The number helps make sure that your mail will be delivered quickly to the right place.

Objectives: Addresses
Demonstrate how to address an envelope by placing the elements in proper position.

When you write a business letter, you write the name of the company or the government office under the name of the person you are writing to. Look at the sample below.

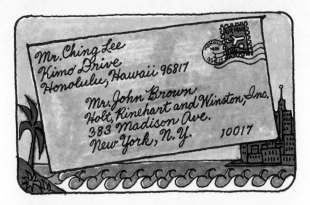

Mr. Ching Lee
Kimo Drive
Honolulu, Hawaii 96817

Mr. John Brown
Holt, Rinehart and Winston, Inc.
383 Madison Ave.
New York, N.Y.   10017

Exercises

A. Suppose that you want to write a letter to a company or a government office to ask for information. On a piece of paper, show what the addressed envelope would look like. Be sure to write your name and address as well as the name and address of the company or government office.

B. Follow these directions.

1. Use a piece of paper to show how you would address an envelope to a friend.

2. Now suppose that your friend grows up to be the president of a company or the owner of a business. Make up the name of a company and an address for it. Then show how you would address an envelope to him.

Call attention to the illustration. Note that the address on the envelope shows the name of the person who is to receive the letter and the name of the company in which he works.

You may want to refer to the uses of abbreviations in writing addresses. See page 250. You may also want to coordinate Addresses with Letters, pages 290–291.

Answers

EXERCISES A AND B

Accept any reasonable addresses. Call attention to errors made in abbreviations and encourage the children to check the abbreviation in a dictionary or some other source.

Alphabetical Order (Pages 256–262)

Alphabetical order is developed by:

1. reviewing the order of the twenty-six letters in the English alphabet.
2. demonstrating how words with as many as six of the same initial letters are alphabetized.
3. demonstrating how words with endings are alphabetized.
4. demonstrating how words that are made up of two or more words are alphabetized.

Call attention to the letters of the alphabet in alphabetical order at the top of the page. Ask the children to tell what letter comes before or after a given letter.

Missing letters in the display:

1. <u>c</u> d e <u>f</u>
2. <u>w</u> x <u>y</u> z
3. <u>m</u> n <u>o</u> p
4. <u>g</u> <u>h</u> i <u>j</u>
5. <u>r</u> s t <u>u</u>
6. <u>a</u> b c <u>d</u>
7. t <u>u</u> v w
8. j <u>k</u> <u>l</u> m
9. o <u>p</u> q r
10. e <u>f</u> <u>g</u> h
11. <u>i</u> j k <u>l</u>
12. <u>u</u> v w x
13. n <u>o</u> p q
14. f <u>g</u> <u>h</u> i
15. <u>b</u> <u>c</u> d e

Alphabetical order of words in display: <u>a</u>sparagus, <u>b</u>eets, <u>c</u>auliflower, <u>s</u>quash, <u>z</u>ucchini

Alphabetical Order

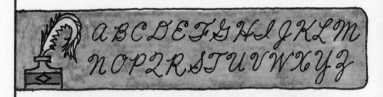

Alphabetical order is the order of the letters in the alphabet, as shown above. See if you can tell which letters are missing in each group of letters below.

1. __ d e __
2. __ x __ z
3. __ n __ p
4. g __ __ j
5. __ s t __
6. __ __ c d
7. t __ __ w
8. __ k __ m
9. __ __ q r
10. __ f __ h
11. __ j k __
12. __ __ w x
13. n __ __ q
14. f __ __ i
15. __ __ d e

Using the First Letter

If you know the alphabet, it is easy to put words in alphabetical order. Read this list of vegetables.

cauliflower, beets, asparagus, zucchini, squash

Look at the first letter in each word. Do any of the words start with <u>a</u>? Do any of them start with <u>b</u>? with <u>c</u>? Suppose the first three words are listed in alphabetical order.

asparagus, beets, cauliflower, _____, _____

What two words are missing from the list? What's the first letter in each missing word? Which word comes next in the list? Which word comes last?

Objectives: Alphabetical Order
1. Identify the letters omitted from a group of letters in an alphabetical list.
2. Order alphabetically a given list of words by first, second, third, fourth, fifth, and sixth letters.

Exercises

A. Try to put each group of words in alphabetical order.

1. lemon
   cantaloupe
   orange
   grapefruit
   tangerine
   melon

2. mailman
   fireman
   policeman
   teacher
   pilot
   carpenter

3. shirt
   tie
   coat
   hat
   belt
   pants

B. Now put these groups of words in alphabetical order.

1. plant
   flower
   tree
   vine
   bush
   shrub

2. diamond
   ruby
   onyx
   emerald
   sapphire
   topaz

3. lake
   river
   pond
   ocean
   stream
   brook

Using the Second Letter

Read this list of vegetables in alphabetical order.

asparagus, beets, cauliflower, squash, zucchini

Suppose you want to add *spinach* to this list of vegetables. Where would you put it? What other word on the list begins with *s*? What's the second letter in this word? Does *spinach* come before or after *squash*?

Where would you add *Brussels sprouts* to this list of vegetables? When a name is made up of two words, you put the name in alphabetical order by the letters in the first word. Does *Brussels sprouts* come before or after *beets*?

Answers

Answers

EXERCISE A

1. cup
   glass
   napkin
   plate
   saucer
   silverware
   soup bowl

2. dragon
   dwarf
   elf
   ghost
   goblin
   troll
   witch

3. chocolate
   mocha
   peach
   pineapple
   pistachio
   strawberry
   vanilla

4. Peter
   Philip
   Ralph
   Simon
   Steve
   Walter
   William

5. sandals
   shirt
   skirt
   slacks
   socks
   stockings
   sweater

6. boil
   braise
   broil
   burn
   fry
   heat
   roast

EXERCISE B

Answers will vary. Check classification as well as alphabetical order.

Exercises

A. Try to put each group of words in alphabetical order.

1. plate	2. ghost	3. pistachio
cup	dwarf	strawberry
saucer	witch	pineapple
soup bowl	dragon	peach
silverware	goblin	mocha
napkin	troll	chocolate
glass	elf	vanilla

4. Walter	5. shirt	6. heat
Steve	skirt	burn
Peter	sweater	broil
William	socks	roast
Philip	sandals	boil
Simon	stockings	fry
Ralph	slacks	braise

B. Follow these directions.

1. Make a list of five different kinds of meat. Then put the words in alphabetical order.
2. Make a list of five kinds of things people wear on their feet. Put these words in alphabetical order.
3. Make a list of the names of five games. Put the names of the games in alphabetical order. Now don't forget, when a name has more than one word, you put it in order by the first letters in the first word.
4. Make a list of five colors. Put the words for the colors in alphabetical order.
5. Make a list of five people in your class. Write their last names first, then a comma and their first names. Put the list of names in alphabetical order.

Using More Than Two Letters

Look at these pictures and the words under them.

log   lobster   locks

The first two letters in each of these words are the same. What are these letters? What is the third letter in each word? Which letter comes first in the alphabet? Which word comes first in alphabetical order? Which word would be next? And which one is last?

Now read these words under the pictures.

chimpanzee   chickens   chipmunk

How would you put these words in alphabetical order?

Call attention to the labelled illustrations.

Alphabetical order of words that are labels:

lobster, locks, log

chickens, chimpanzee, chipmunk

Alphabetical order of words in display:

ruled, ruler, rules, ruling

counterclockwise, counterfeit, countess, country

overthrow, overtime, overtook, overturn

Answers

EXERCISE A

1. Albert
   Alex
   Alvin
   Michael
   Michele
   Roger
   Steve
   Susan

2. backyard
   badminton
   bagpipe
   barn
   barnacle
   barnyard
   baseball
   bat

3. daddy-longlegs
   daffodil
   daffy
   dahlia
   dairy
   daisy
   damsel
   dandelion

4. jack rabbit
   jade
   jaguar
   laboratory
   lamb
   lament
   llama
   lobster

5. polar bear
   poodle
   porcupine
   porpoise
   raccoon
   rat
   rattlesnake
   reindeer

6. fact
   factory
   fall
   fan
   farm
   fashion plate
   fast
   fatty

Here is a group of words that have the same root word but different endings. See if you can put these words into a list alphabetically.

rules, ruled, ruling, ruler

Now see if you can tell how to put these groups of words in alphabetical order.

counterclockwise, country, counterfeit, countess
overtook, overtime, overthrow, overturn

Exercises

A. Here are some lists of words for you to alphabetize. Be sure to remember that sometimes you have to look at more than the first and second letters of the words.

1. Susan
   Steve
   Alex
   Michele
   Alvin
   Roger
   Michael
   Albert

2. bat
   barn
   bagpipe
   backyard
   badminton
   baseball
   barnacle
   barnyard

3. daisy
   daffy
   dahlia
   dairy
   damsel
   daffodil
   dandelion
   daddy-longlegs

4. jaguar
   lament
   jack rabbit
   lamb
   llama
   jade
   lobster
   laboratory

5. polar bear
   rattlesnake
   porcupine
   reindeer
   porpoise
   rat
   poodle
   raccoon

6. fan
   fast
   fall
   fact
   farm
   fatty
   factory
   fashion plate

B. Follow these directions.

1. Make a list of five words that begin with <u>r</u>. Then put the words in alphabetical order.
2. Make a list of five words that begin with <u>ch</u>. Put the words in alphabetical order.
3. Make a list of five words that begin with <u>pr</u>. Put the words in alphabetical order.
4. Write the names of five different languages. Put the names in alphabetical order.
5. Write the names of five comic strip characters. Put the names in alphabetical order.

Summary

Here are some rules about alphabetical order.

● You put words in alphabetical order by using the first letter in each word.

● When you have words that begin with one or more of the same letters, you put them in alphabetical order by using the next letters.

Exercises

A. Now put each group of words in alphabetical order.

1. outcome, ourself, outfield, ourselves, out, our
2. mistake, misplace, mischief, mispronounce, misfortune
3. overshoe, overhear, overhand, oversleep, overalls
4. playwright, player, playground, playful, playhouse
5. friend, friendly, friendship, friendless, friendliness
6. downtown, downy, downhill, downpour, downstairs

EXERCISE B

Answers will vary. Check to see that the answers fit the classification as well as alphabetical order.

Note the summary about putting words in alphabetical order. Have the children give examples of the application of each "rule."

Answers

EXERCISE A

1. our
   ourself
   ourselves
   out
   outcome
   outfield

2. mischief
   misfortune
   misplace
   mispronounce
   mistake

3. overalls
   overhand
   overhear
   overshoe
   oversleep

4. player
   playful
   playground
   playhouse
   playwright

5. friend
   friendless
   friendliness
   friendly
   friendship

6. downhill
   downpour
   downstairs
   downtown
   downy

Skillsbook: Alphabetical Order, page 2

EXERCISE B
Answers will vary.

Announcements (Pages 262–263)

An announcement about an event should include the following information:

1. <u>Who</u> is presenting the event
2. <u>What</u> the event is
3. <u>When</u> the event will take place
4. <u>Where</u> the event will take place
5. <u>Why</u> the event is taking place

Call attention to the announcement in the illustration. Ask questions, such as these:

1. What is announced?
2. What is a rummage sale?
3. Who is sponsoring the rummage sale?
4. Where will they sell the rummage?
5. When is the sale?
6. What will the children do with the money they get from this sale?

B. Think of a word you could find in the dictionary between each of these pairs of words.

1. almond _____ tadpole
2. knot _____ lock
3. relax _____ sleep
4. park _____ party
5. trace _____ travel
6. strange _____ struggle
7. reach _____ reason
8. sand _____ subway
9. boo _____ boot
10. ear _____ eat

Announcements

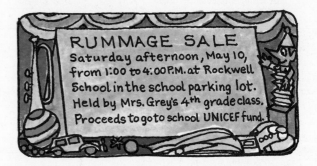

An **announcement** is a way of telling about something that has happened or is going to happen. It may be written and sent to people, advertised on a poster, or printed in a newspaper. It may also be spoken directly to people. Every announcement should include the following information:

1. <u>who</u> is presenting the event
2. <u>what</u> the event is
3. <u>when</u> the event will be presented
4. <u>where</u> the event will take place
5. <u>why</u> the event is taking place

Objectives: Announcements
Construct an announcement that contains given "who, what, when, and where" information.

An announcement should catch the attention of those who hear it or see it. It should try to interest them in the event it tells about. Usually an announcement should tell the most important thing first. If it's on a poster, the most important thing should stand out from the other information on it. The most important information may be written larger, with capital letters, or with brighter colors.

Look at the poster on page 262. What is the most important information in this announcement? How is it written to make it stand out from the other information? Try to tell from this announcement who is presenting the event, what it is, and where, when, and why it will take place.

Exercises

A. Write an announcement with the following information. If you want to, you can make it into a poster. You can draw pictures or designs to go with it.

Who: Mr. Pratt's art class
What: display of their weaving projects
When: Saturday, November 15, 7:00–9:00 PM
Where: Fairview School art room
Why: to show projects to parents and friends

B. Now put this information on a poster. Remember to put the most important information in large letters. You can draw pictures or designs to go with it, too.

Who: The Punch and Judy Puppet Club
What: a musical of *Hansel and Gretel*
When: Friday, February 16, 7:00 PM
Where: Bedford Road School Auditorium
Why: To entertain you

Note that the most important information in the announcement on the preceding page is <u>what</u> is going to take place—a rummage sale. This information is written in larger letters than the rest of the announcement and it is written with all capital letters. Information presented:

Who—Mrs. Grey's 4th grade class
What—rummage sale
When—May 10 from 1:00 to 4:00 P.M.
Where—Rockwell School parking lot
Why—to raise money for UNICEF

Answers

EXERCISES A AND B
Accept any announcement that contains the information requested.

Skillsbook: Announcements, page 4

Antonyms (Pages 264–265)

Antonyms are presented as words that have opposite meanings.

Call attention to the illustration. Ask the children to describe the scene and what is happening. Then ask them to list all the words with opposite meanings that the illustration calls to mind, such as:

front—back   tall—short
young—old   old—new
child—adult   light—dark
big—little   up—down

Pairs of antonyms in the display:

large—small
yes—no
come—go

Other antonyms for these words:

large—little, tiny
yes—never, nay
come—leave, depart, exit
small—huge, big, gigantic, mammoth
go—arrive, enter, appear
no—yea, aye

Antonyms

old car   young boy   old man   new car

Antonyms are words that have opposite meanings. An antonym for *big* is *little*. An antonym for *light* is *dark*.

Now read these words and find three pairs of words that are antonyms.

large, yes, come, small, go, no

Try to think of other antonyms for each word.

Objectives: Antonyms
1. Describe antonyms in operational terms.
2. Demonstrate the use of antonyms in context.

Skillsbook: Antonyms, page 5

Exercises

A. Think of an antonym for the underlined word in each of these sentences. Then copy each sentence and complete it by writing the antonym. (The first one is done for you.)

1. Bob is <u>tall</u>, but Bill is _____.
   Bob is <u>tall</u>, but Bill is <u>short</u>.

2. Tommy <u>opened</u> the door, and Sally _____ it.

3. I wanted to <u>work</u>, but my brother just wanted to _____.

4. Tom <u>finished</u> his work before I _____ mine.

5. I like to sleep on a <u>soft</u> mattress, but my Dad likes one that is _____.

6. I am the <u>girl</u> in the family. My brother is the _____.

7. Dick is the <u>first</u> one in line, and Bill is _____.

8. The <u>old</u> man told tales about his life as a _____ man.

B. Copy these words. Then write as many antonyms for each word as you can think of.

1. fat	5. cold	9. good
2. in	6. down	10. work
3. unhappy	7. empty	11. push
4. fast	8. high	12. awake

Capital Letters

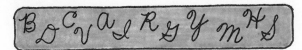

Capital letters and punctuation marks are used to help a reader understand what a writer wants to say.

Objectives: Capital Letters
Demonstrate the use of capital letters:
a. to begin sentences.
b. in proper nouns.
c. in the pronoun I.
d. in titles.
e. in the greeting and the closing of letters.

Answers

EXERCISE A
1. Bob is *tall*, but Bill is <u>short</u>.
2. Tommy *opened* the door, and Sally <u>closed</u> it.
3. I wanted to *work*, but my brother just wanted to <u>play</u>.
4. Tom *finished* his work before I <u>started</u> mine.
5. I like to sleep on a *soft* mattress, but my Dad likes one that is <u>hard</u>.
6. I am the *girl* in the family. My brother is the <u>boy</u>.
7. Dick is the *first* one in line, and Bill is <u>last</u>.
8. The *old* man told tales about his life as a <u>young</u> man.

EXERCISE B
Accept any reasonable answers. Possible answers are:
1. fat—thin, slender, skinny, underweight, scrawny, slim, bony, lanky
2. in—out, outside, outdoors
3. unhappy—happy, glad, joyous, gay, contented, cheerful
4. fast—slow, leisurely, sluggish
5. cold—hot, heated, warm, fiery
6. down—up, upward, above, aloft
7. empty—full, filled, brimming
8. high—low, sunken, squat, deep
9. good—bad, unworthy, evil, wicked, sinful, harmful, impure, unfortunate, unpleasant, horrible
10. work—play, idle, rest, relax, nap, loaf, lounge, inactive
11. push—pull, haul, drag, draw, tug, tow
12. awake—asleep, numb

Capital Letters (Pages 265–271)

These uses of capital letters are presented:

1. The first word in a sentence
2. The first letter in each word that makes up a proper noun
3. The pronoun *I*
4. The first letter in titles of respect
5. The first word and other important words in a title
6. The first word in the greeting and the first word in the closing of a letter

Have the children tell where capital letters and punctuation marks are needed in the sample paragraph. Reading the paragraph aloud will help supply sound clues for sentence endings.

There is an old saying that people who live in glass houses shouldn't throw stones. The saying catches your attention because it is silly. Did you ever hear of anyone living in a glass house? This saying makes sense only when you think of another saying, "Do unto others as you would have them do unto you."

You may wish to refer to Punctuation Marks, pages 306–315.

Answers

EXERCISE A

Can you tell the difference between moths and butterflies? Butterflies have knobs on the tips of their antennae. The antennae of moths are shorter and often feathery. Most butterflies have long, thin bodies. Most moths' bodies are short and thick. Butterflies hold their wings straight up over their backs when resting. Moths rest with their wings flat at their sides. When you know how moths and butterflies are different, then it's easy to tell one from the other.

The First Word in a Sentence

When a person talks, his voice tells when he stops one sentence and starts another. When a person writes, he uses capital letters and punctuation marks to show where the sentences begin and end. Where do sentences in the paragraph below begin and end? What words should have capital letters?

there is an old saying that people who live in glass houses shouldn't throw stones the saying catches your attention because it is silly did you ever hear of anyone living in a glass house this saying makes sense only when you think of another saying, "do unto others as you would have them do unto you"

Exercises

A. Now copy this paragraph. Put capital letters and marks of punctuation where they are needed.

can you tell the difference between moths and butterflies butterflies have knobs on the tips of their antennae the antennae of moths are shorter and often feathery most butterflies have long, thin bodies most moths' bodies are short and thick butterflies hold their wings straight up over their backs when resting moths rest with their wings flat at their sides when you know how moths and butterflies are different then it's easy to tell one from the other

B. Copy and complete these sentences. You can use any words you want. Don't forget to use capital letters.

1. _____ is lighter than a rock.
2. _____ is thicker than a pencil.
3. _____ goes faster than a turtle.
4. _____ goes well with milk.
5. _____ is more fun than playing a game.
6. _____ takes longer than eating breakfast.
7. _____ is taller than I am.
8. _____ floats better than a board.

Proper Nouns and the Pronoun "I"

Proper nouns and the pronoun "I" begin with capital letters. Proper nouns are names of people, days of the week, months, cities, states, countries, streets, and holidays.

People: Miss Sarah Stine	Months: November
Streets: Woodland Drive	States: New Mexico
Holidays: Thanksgiving	Cities: Charleston
Days of the week: Friday	Countries: France

Exercises

A. Now write these sentences. Put capital letters where they are needed.

1. my birthday is august 15, and my sister's is january 2.
2. did cindy tell you about the meeting on friday?
3. i'm going to see mr. schneider on monday.
4. rosa's mother and i were born in puerto rico.
5. christi lives on lincoln street in new york city.
6. tom's father is in the united states air force.

EXERCISE B

1. Mabel, James, Peru, France
2. Fifth Avenue, New London, Cortland, Lincoln
3. June, Martha's Beauty Salon, England
4. December, Timothy, Long Island, Nigeria
5. Chicago, Rocky Mountains, Aunt Polly, Canada
6. Uncle Ben, Maryland

Call attention to the book titles in the illustration of books. Note that small words, such as *in, of, and,* and *the,* do not begin with a capital letter in a title unless they are the first word in the title.

Note that titles of respect, such as *Mr., Mrs., Dr.,* and *Miss* begin with capital letters. If the section about abbreviations hasn't been studied, this might be a good time to study at least the part about titles of respect—page 246.

B. Some of the words in each list below are proper nouns and some are not. Write the number of each list and copy just the proper nouns. Remember to use capital letters.

1. mabel, james, store, peru, hat, france
2. fifth avenue, new london, cortland, lincoln, street
3. horse, june, martha's beauty salon, table, england
4. december, timothy, long island, day, avenue, nigeria
5. chicago, rocky mountains, city, aunt polly, canada
6. car, sister, uncle ben, bus, maryland

Titles and Parts of a Letter

Capital letters are used in titles.

Read the titles of the books in this picture. Which words in each title begin with capital letters? What words do not begin with capital letters?

Titles of respect begin with capital letters—even if the titles are abbreviations. (See the section about Abbreviations on page 246.)

The first word in a title always begins with a capital letter. If the title has more than one word, then <u>all</u> the words begin with capital letters—except for short words like *in* and *the.*

When you write a letter, the first word of both the greeting and the closing begins with a capital letter, as shown below. (See the section about Letters, page 290.)

Exercises

A. Follow these directions.

1. Write three names with three different titles of respect.
2. Write just the greeting and the closing that you would use in a letter to each of these people.

  a. your teacher
  b. someone in your family
  c. a famous singer or actor

3. Write the titles of three poems in this book.
4. Write the titles of three of your favorite TV shows.
5. What would be a good title for a book about your school?

Call attention to the illustrated letter. Have the children use the letter to describe the uses of capital letters. Encourage the children to identify the letter parts as they talk about capital letters. The letter parts are the heading, the inside address, the greeting, the body, the closing, and the signature. If there is difficulty recognizing any of the letter parts, turn to Letters, pages 290–291, to review the parts of a letter.

EXERCISE A
Accept any reasonable answers that belong to the category asked for.

Accept any reasonable answers that belong to the category asked for.

Note the summary about the uses of capital letters. Have the children give examples of the application of each "rule."

B. Follow these directions.

1. Write a sentence with three names that have different titles of respect.
2. Write just the greeting and the closing that you would use in a letter to each of these people.

   a. the governor of your state
   b. a good friend
   c. someone who lives near you

3. Write titles for these things.

   a. three books that you like
   b. three stories that you like
   c. three poems that you like

4. What would be a good title for a book about dinosaurs? For a book about climbing a mountain?
5. Draw a picture about building a sailboat. Then write a title under it.

Summary

Here are some rules about capital letters.

● The first word in a sentence always begins with a capital letter.

● The names of days, months, and holidays always begin with capital letters.

● The names of people, streets, cities, states, and countries always begin with capital letters.

● The words in a title, except for words like *the* and *in,* always begin with capital letters.

Exercises

A. Copy this letter and put capital letters where they are needed. (Twenty-six capital letters are needed.)

> 34 pine street
> miami, florida 33146
> february 29, 1972
>
> dear roger,
>
>   so far, so good. my uncle ralph took me to work with him, and i have seen three movies.
>
>   did you ever see king kong? it's an old movie about a giant gorilla who ends up climbing the empire state building in new york.
>
>   i'll be home monday. see you then.
>
>   your friend,
>   van

B. Follow these directions.

1. Write two book titles.
2. Write two story titles.
3. Write two titles of poems.
4. Write the names of three states.
5. Write the names of two countries.
6. Write the names of two people with titles of respect.
7. Write the names of two days of the week.
8. Write the names of three months of the year.
9. Write a closing for a letter to a friend.
10. Write the names of two holidays.

Skillsbook: Capital Letters, page 6

Answers

EXERCISE A

34 Pine Street
Miami, Florida 33146
February 29, 1972

Dear Roger,

    So far, so good. My Uncle Ralph took me to work with him, and I have seen three movies.

    Did you ever see King Kong? It's an old movie about a giant gorilla who ends up climbing the Empire State Building in New York.

    I'll be home Monday. See you then.

            Your friend,
            Van

You may wish to call attention to *King Kong* as the title of a movie and to mention that titles are printed in italics in a book. Show examples of italics in the text. Italics are presented in Book Five of this series.

EXERCISE B

Accept any reasonable answers. Call attention to errors in the use of capital letters. Note any other errors for future skills teaching and reinforcement.

Contractions (Pages 272–274)

These contractions are developed:

1. Contractions using *will* (I'll, he'll, she'll, we'll, you'll, they'll)
2. Contractions using *would* (I'd, he'd, she'd, we'd, you'd, they'd)
3. Contractions using *am, are,* and *is* (I'm, we're, you're, he's, she's, there's)
4. Contractions using *not* (don't, doesn't, isn't, aren't, haven't, hasn't, wouldn't, couldn't, can't, won't)

Contractions are presented as two words that are made into one word by leaving out part of the second word. An apostrophe is used to show where part of a word has been left out. The lessons are carefully structured to help the child "discover" for himself how to form contractions.

Call attention to the word-pairs and the corresponding contractions in the illustration and in the display.

Making contractions with *will*.

I will—I'll

he will—he'll

she will—she'll

we will—we'll

you will—you'll

they will—they'll

Contractions

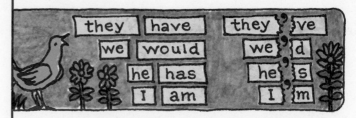

Sometimes when people write, and even more often when they speak, they make two words into one by leaving out part of the second word. The new word is called a **contraction.**

When you "contract" words, you make them shorter. You always use an apostrophe in a contraction to show that something in a word has been left out. Read these words and the contractions made from them.

I am	I'm	he is	he's
she will	she'll	is not	isn't
they have	they've	do not	don't

Try to make contractions with the word **will.** Follow these directions.

1. Write these words. Put one word under the other.

I	we
he	you
she	they

2. Write the word <u>will</u> after each word on your paper.
3. Cross out the letters <u>wi</u> in each <u>will</u> you wrote.
4. Put an apostrophe above the letters you crossed out.
5. Rewrite the contractions and use them in sentences.

Objectives: Contractions

Demonstrate how to write contractions for these given pairs of words: I-will, he-will, she-will, we-will, you-will, they-will, I-would, he-would, she-would, we-would, you-would, they-would, I-am, we-are, you-are, he-is, she-is, there-is, do-not, does-not, is-not, are-not, have-not, has-not, would-not, could-not, can-not, will-not, they-have.

Try to follow these directions to make contractions with the word **would.**

1. Write these words. Put one word under the other.

I	we
he	you
she	they

2. Write the word <u>would</u> after each word on your paper.
3. Cross out all of the letters in <u>would</u> except the <u>d</u>.
4. Put an apostrophe above the letters you crossed out.
5. Rewrite the contractions and use them in sentences.

Now follow these directions to make contractions with **am, are,** and **is.**

1. Write these words. Put one word under the other.

I am	he is
we are	she is
you are	there is

2. Put a line under the words <u>am</u>, <u>are</u>, and <u>is</u>.
3. Cross out the first letter in each of these words.
4. Put an apostrophe above the letters you crossed out.
5. Rewrite the contractions and use them in sentences.

Follow these directions to make contractions with **not.**

1. Write these words in a list.

do	have
does	has
is	would
are	could

2. Write <u>not</u> very close to each word on the list.

Making contractions with *would.*

I would	I'd
he would	he'd
she would	she'd
we would	we'd
you would	you'd
they would	they'd

Making contractions with *am, are,* and *is.*

I am	I'm
we are	we're
you are	you're
he is	he's
she is	she's
there is	there's

Making contractions with *not.*

do not	don't
does not	doesn't
is not	isn't
are not	aren't
have not	haven't
has not	hasn't
would not	wouldn't
could not	couldn't

Call attention to the underlined words and contractions in the displayed sentences. Note that these contractions with *not* are formed in an irregular way.

Making contractions from words in the display:

He won't tell me anything.

The baby can't walk, but she can talk.

I won't be unhappy if I can't see the show.

More work with contractions can be found under Punctuation Marks, Apostrophes, pages 306–307.

Answers

EXERCISE A
1. it'll
2. won't
3. shouldn't
4. they're
5. there's
6. I'm
7. you'd
8. haven't
9. you've

EXERCISE B
1. I'd be happy if you'd call my mother for me.
2. I'm so tired that it's not (it isn't) easy to stay awake.
3. Ted'll go shopping if you'll tell him what to buy.
4. Sally doesn't have boots, so she can't go outside.
5. The boys aren't home because they're outside playing.
6. Where there's a will there's a way.

3. Cross out the o in each not you wrote.
4. Put an apostrophe over each letter you crossed out.
5. Now rewrite the contractions and use them in sentences.

The contractions **can't** and **won't** are also made with not, but not in the same way as most contractions. The words that are underlined in the sentences below show you these contractions and the words they are made from.

I cannot play.	She will not sing.
I can't play.	She won't sing.

Now read these sentences with contractions.

He will not tell me anything.
The baby cannot walk, but she can talk.
I will not be unhappy if I cannot see the show.

Exercises

A. Change these words to contractions.

1. it will
2. will not
3. should not
4. they are
5. there is
6. I am
7. you would
8. have not
9. you have

B. These sentences don't have contractions in them. Copy the sentences with as many contractions as possible.

1. I would be happy if you would call my mother for me.
2. I am so tired that it is not easy to stay awake.
3. Ted will go shopping if you will tell him what to buy.
4. Sally does not have boots, so she cannot go outside.
5. The boys are not home because they are outside playing.
6. Where there is a will there is a way.

Skillsbook: Contractions, page 7

274

The Dictionary

You use a dictionary to find out what a word means, how to spell a word, or how to say a word.

Entry Words

Every word "entered" in a dictionary is called an **entry word.** The words are "entered" in alphabetical order. If you need help with alphabetical order, turn to page 256.

Look at the dictionary page shown on page 283. What is the first entry word on this page? What is the last entry word on this page?

Words that look like the same word may be entered in a dictionary more than once. These words are called **double entry words.** *Double entry words* may be pronounced in the same way or in a different way. Yet, they have different meanings and origins. By origin, we mean the place that they came from or the time that they became part of our language. There are some words of this kind in the section about homographs that you can find by turning to page 284.

The Dictionary (Pages 275–283)

These features of a dictionary are presented:

1. Entry words
2. Double entry words
3. Guide words
4. Definitions
5. Pronunciation key
6. Syllables and accent marks

Call attention to the illustration. Have the children identify the book as a dictionary and discuss its use.

Call attention to the illustrated dictionary page on page 283 of the text. Note that the first entry word on the page is *mill* and the last entry word is *mindful*.

Call special attention to double entry words. Note that all double entry words are homographs. Refer to the homographs on pages 284–285.

Objectives: The Dictionary
1. Identify the entry words and double entry words on a given dictionary page.
2. Identify the guide words on a given dictionary page.
3. Demonstrate how to use guide words in a dictionary.
4. Identify the appropriate dictionary definition of a word used in context.
5. Identify or construct sentences with a word that has multiple meanings.
6. Demonstrate how to use diacritical marks, syllables, and accent marks to pronounce words.

Entry words used in sentences:

1. Tall buildings <u>loom</u> over you on a city street. (loom²)
2. This rug was made on a <u>loom</u>. (loom¹)

1. The clerk will <u>present</u> Sue with the bill. (present²)
2. All the children in my class are <u>present</u> today. (present¹)

If children have trouble finding words ordered alphabetically in the dictionary, refer them to the section on Alphabetical Order, pages 256–262.

Answers

EXERCISES A AND B
Answers will vary with the dictionary used.

Read these double entries as they might be seen in a dictionary. Then read the sentences and tell which entry word is used in each one.

loom¹ (lüm), machine for weaving cloth.

loom² (lüm), seen dimly, not easily seen; look very large, threatening, or dangerous.

1. Tall buildings <u>loom</u> over you on a city street.
2. This rug was made on a <u>loom</u>.

present¹ (prez′nt), **1** at hand; not absent. **2** living or happening now: *the present ruler.* **3** the time being: *That is all for the present.*

present² (pri zent′), **1** give: *We present flowers.* **2** make acquainted; introduce: *Miss Jones, may I present Miss Keller?* **3** bring before the public: *We present a show.* **4** hand in; send in: *He will present his bill.*

1. The clerk will <u>present</u> Sue with the bill.
2. All the children in my class are <u>present</u> today.

Exercises

A. Turn to page 94 in your classroom dictionary. Then find the first entry word on this page. Now write the word and put a line under the first two letters. How many other words on the page begin with these two letters? If you see any double entry words on this page, write them.

B. Use your dictionary to find out how many entry words begin with <u>dw</u>, with <u>cy</u>, with <u>ug</u>, and with <u>tw</u>.

Guide Words

At the top of most dictionary pages, there are two words called **guide words.** What are the guide words on page 283? Where do you see the first word again on the page? Where do you see the second guide word again? The guide words tell you the first and last words on each page.

Now look at these page numbers and guide words.

page 526	page 527	page 528
rascal ravage	rave read	read reason

On which page of this dictionary would you find the word **react**? The word **raspberry**? **realize**? **ready**? **rattle**?

Exercises

A. Use your classroom dictionary. Copy the guide words from each of these pages.

1. page 165
2. page 220
3. page 89
4. page 426
5. page 51
6. page 354
7. page 274
8. page 300

B. Use these page numbers and guide words to tell where you would find these words in a dictionary.

page 308	page 309	page 310
ginger gladden	glade gloomily	gloomy goat

1. glance
2. giraffe
3. girl scout
4. gnarl
5. glue
6. globe
7. glimmer
8. goal

Note that the guide words on page 283 are the first and the last entry words —*mill* and *mindful.*

Matching the page numbers and guide words in the display:

react—527
raspberry—526
realize—528
ready—528
rattle—526

Answers

EXERCISE A
Answers will vary with the dictionary used.

EXERCISE B
1. glance—309
2. giraffe—308
3. girl scout—308
4. gnarl—310
5. glue—310
6. globe—309
7. glimmer—309
8. goal—310

Call attention to the definition of *hare*. Stress that a definition states the genus and species of each noun.

Definitions of *line* used in sentences:

1. Put a <u>line</u> under each of the words that are antonyms. (2)
2. The last <u>line</u> of the story tells who fixed the car. (5)
3. Write between the <u>lines</u> on your paper. (2)
4. Now <u>line</u> your paper and write these words. (4)
5. We get into a <u>line</u> to get our lunch in the cafeteria. (3)

Definitions

You can use a dictionary to learn what a word means. The meaning of a word is called its **definition.**

 hare (hãr), an animal with long ears, a divided upper lip, a short tail, and long hind legs. A hare is very much like a rabbit, but larger.

The first few words of any definition tell the group something belongs to. The rest of the definition tells what's different about this special part of the group. What group of things does a hare belong to? What's different about a *hare*?

Many times a word has more than one definition. Each definition of a word is numbered in a dictionary. Read these definitions for the word *line*.

line (līn), **1** a thin rope, cord, or wire: *a fishing line, a telephone line.* **2** a long narrow mark: *Draw a line.* **3** a row of persons or things: *a line of people, a line of chairs.* **4** mark with lines: *Use a ruler to line your paper.* **5** a line of writing or printing: *Read the first line in the paragraph.*

Now try to tell which one of these definitions of line is used in each of the following sentences.

1. Put a <u>line</u> under each of the words that are antonyms.
2. The last <u>line</u> of the story tells who fixed the car.
3. Write between the <u>lines</u> on your paper.
4. Now <u>line</u> your paper and write these words.
5. We get into a <u>line</u> to get our lunch in the cafeteria.

Exercises

A. Here are definitions for the word *stream* and sentences with the word. Copy each sentence and write the number of the definition of *stream* used in the sentence.

> **stream** (strēm), **1** running water: *Small rivers, creeks, and brooks are all streams.* **2** anything with a steady flow: *a stream of lava, a stream of light, a stream of words.* **3** flow or drip: *Tears streamed down the baby's face.* **4** move swiftly; move in a steady, continuous manner: *The children streamed out of the school building.* **5** float or wave. *Flags stream in the wind.*

1. A <u>stream</u> of milk flowed from the overturned bottle.
2. Droplets of milk <u>streamed</u> onto the floor.
3. Children enjoy wading in a cool <u>stream</u> on a warm day.
4. The clothes on the clothesline <u>streamed</u> out to greet us.
5. People <u>streamed</u> out of the train and onto the street.
6. We enjoyed walking along the <u>stream</u> in the forest.
7. The <u>stream</u> of people moved quickly down the street.

B. Look through your classroom dictionary for two words you know that have more than one definition. Copy several of the definitions for each word. Then write at least six sentences in which you use words with each of these meanings.

Pronunciation Key

Dictionaries show you how to pronounce a word. The pronunciation is shown between parentheses ( ) or slashes / / after each entry word.

Answers

EXERCISE A

Definitions of *stream* that are used in sentences:

1. A <u>stream</u> of milk flowed from the overturned bottle. (2)
2. Droplets of milk <u>streamed</u> onto the floor. (3)
3. Children enjoy wading in a cool <u>stream</u> on a warm day. (1)
4. The clothes on the clothesline <u>streamed</u> out to greet us. (5)
5. People <u>streamed</u> out of the train and onto the street. (4)
6. We enjoyed walking along the <u>stream</u> in the forest. (1)
7. The <u>stream</u> of people moved quickly down the street. (2)

EXERCISE B

Answers will vary with the dictionary used.

Ask for additional examples of words that have the same sound as the one shown for each symbol in the pronunciation key. Then look up the word in a dictionary to verify the similarity in sound. If the Thorndike Barnhart Beginning Dictionary is not available, compare the sound symbols in the text to the symbols used in the pronunciation key of another dictionary.

You may want to refer to Sounds and Letters, pages 316–318, as you go through the pronunciation key.

Some of the letters in our alphabet stand for more than one sound. But a dictionary uses only one letter to stand for each sound.

The c in cat and the k in kid sound alike.
cat (kat)   kid (kid)
The c in cell and the s in sat sound alike.
cell (sell)   sat (sat)
The j in jet and the g in gem sound alike.
jet (jet)   gem (jem)

Our language has more sounds than letters. We use marks with letters in dictionaries to show how to pronounce the words. Every dictionary has a pronunciation key. The key tells which letters and marks stand for each sound. If you need more help with sounds, look at the section about Sounds and Letters, page 316.

Here is the pronunciation key used in the *Thorndike Barnhart Beginning Dictionary*. Look at each letter and mark that shows how to say the underlined letter in each word. (A page from this dictionary is shown on page 283.)

a as in hat	e as in best	o as in hot
ā as in face	ē as in be	ō as in go
ã as in care	ėr as in learn	ô as in all
ä as in father		

i as in pin	u as in cup	ü as in rule
ī as in ice	ủ as in put	ū as in use
oi as in oil	th as in thin	ng as in long
ou as in out	ŦH as in then	zh as in measure

ə stands for these sounds:

a as in about	e as in taken	i as in April
o as in lemon	u as in circus	

We use spaces between letters and symbols to show the syllables in a word. (mil′ ər) Each **syllable** is made up of consonant sounds and a vowel sound or just a vowel sound. (ə go′) One of the syllables in a word is always stressed or said louder than the others. An **accent mark** (′) is used to show the **accented syllable.**

Use the letters and symbols to help you say these words on the right. Spell the word they tell you how to say.

(bā′ bē)	hamburger
(ə lōn′)	baby
(ham′ bėr gər)	alcove
(bag′ ē)	baggy
(al′ kōv)	alone

Exercises: 1

A. Now copy each word on the left. Draw a line after it. Then find the letters and symbols in parentheses that go with each word. (The first one is done for you.)

able—*c.*	a. (ə buv′)
above—	b. (bi twēn′)
abscess—	c. (ā′ bl)
between—	d. (bev′ l)
bevel—	e. (ab′ ses)
better—	f. (bet′ ər)

B. Now see if you can divide these words into syllables. Show where the accent marks should be. Use a dictionary to check your work. (The first one is done for you.)

fable—fa′ ble	creamy—	destroy—
about—	radio—	deputy—
basket—	native—	flaming—

Note that each syllable contains just one vowel sound and that words of more than one syllable have one syllable stressed more than the others. Note that the schwa sound is presented but not identified as schwa. The schwa is developed in the lessons on Sounds and Letters, pages 316–318.

Matching letters and symbols with words:

(bā′bē)—baby
(əlōn′)—alone
(ham′bėr ger)—hamburger
(bag′ē)—baggy
(al′kōv)—alcove

Answers

EXERCISE 1A
able—c.
above—a.
abscess—e.
between—b.
bevel—d.
better—f.

EXERCISE 1B
fable—fa′ble
about—a bout′
basket—bas′ket
creamy—cream′y
radio—ra′di o
native—na′tive
destroy—de stroy′
deputy—dep′u ty
flaming—flam′ing

Syllables and accent marks are all that are asked for, but accept diacritical marks if they are given.

EXERCISE 2A

EXERCISE 2A

1. mill, mindful
2. eleven, six
3. mill, mindful
4. mile—no
   mixer—no
   mimic—yes
5. Accept any reasonable sentence that uses the word with the given definition correctly.
6. (mil'yənth) millionth
   (mins'mēt) mincemeat
   (mim'ik) mimic

EXERCISE 2B

Answers will vary with the dictionary used.

Exercises: 2

A. Use the page of the dictionary shown on page 283 of this book. Answer these questions and follow these directions.

1. What are the first and last entry words on this page?
2. How many entry words begin with <u>mil</u>? with <u>min</u>?
3. What are the guide words on this page?
4. Would you find these words on this page?

   mile   mixer   mimic

5. Read the numbered definitions of these words. Then use each word with this meaning in a sentence. (The first one is done for you.)

   millionaire 1   miller 2   mind 3, 10

   A millionaire has a million or more dollars.

6. Study these letters and marks that show how to say words. Then find and write the word they show you how to say. (The first one is done for you.)

   (mil' yənth) *millionth*   (mins' mēt)   (mim' ik)

B. In your classroom dictionary, choose a page of words that start with <u>m</u>. Then answer these questions.

1. What are the guide words on this page?
2. How many entry words have the same first two letters as the first entry word on the page?
3. How many entry words have the same first two letters as the last entry word on the page?
4. Are there two words that have more than one definition? Write sentences that use each meaning of the word.
5. Are there four words that have the same vowel sound? Write the words in sentences.

Skillsbook: The Dictionary, page 8

MILL WHEEL

mill (mil), **1** a building where manufacturing is done: *A cotton mill makes thread from cotton.* **2** the building containing a machine for grinding corn, wheat, or other substances into flour or meal. **3** such a machine. **4** grind (grain) into flour or meal. **5** grind very fine. **6** move about in a circle in a confused way: *Cattle sometimes mill around when they are frightened.*

mill er (mil′ər), **1** one who owns or runs a mill, especially a flour mill. **2** a moth whose wings look as if they were powdered with flour. See the picture.

mil let (mil′it), a grain used for food in Asia and Africa. In the United States and Europe, millet is grown chiefly for hay.

mil li ner (mil′ə nər), person who makes, trims, or sells women's hats.

mil li nery (mil′ə nər/ē), **1** women's hats. **2** the business of making, trimming, or selling women's hats.

mil lion (mil′yən), one thousand thousand; 1,000,000.

mil lion aire (mil′yən âr′), **1** person who has a million or more dollars, pounds, francs, etc. **2** very wealthy person.

mil lionth (mil′yənth), **1** last in a series of a million. **2** one of a million equal parts.

mill race, **1** the current of water that drives a mill wheel. **2** the trough through which the water flows to the mill.

mill stone (mil′stōn′), **1** one of a pair of round flat stones for grinding corn,

millstone (definition 1)
women using millstones to grind corn

wheat, etc. See the picture. **2** heavy burden. **3** anything that grinds or crushes.

mill wheel, a wheel that is turned by water and supplies power for a mill. See the picture.

mim ic (mim′ik), **1** make fun of by imitating: *We like to get him to mimic our old music teacher.* **2** person or thing that imitates. **3** copy closely; imitate: *A parrot can mimic a person's voice.* **4** resemble closely: *Some insects mimic leaves.* See the picture. **5** not real, but imitated or pretended for some purpose: *The soldiers staged a mimic battle for the visiting general.* **mim icked, mim ick ing.**

min., minute; minutes.

min a ret (min′ə ret′), a slender high tower attached to a Moslem mosque with one or more projecting balconies, from which a crier calls the people to prayer. See the picture.

mince (mins), **1** chop up into very small pieces. **2** put on fine airs in speaking or walking. **3** walk with little short steps. **minced, minc ing.**

mince meat (mins′mēt′), mixture of chopped meat, suet, apples, raisins, currants, spices, etc., used as a filling for pies.

mind (mīnd), **1** the part of a person that knows and thinks and feels and wishes and chooses. **2** intelligence; mental ability; intellect: *To learn arithmetic easily, you must have a good mind.* **3** what one thinks or feels: *Speak your mind freely.* **4** notice; observe. **5** be careful concerning: *Mind the step.* **6** take care: *Mind that you come on time.* **7** attend to; take care of: *Please mind the baby.* **8** obey: *Mind your father and mother.* **9** memory: *Keep the rules in mind.* **10** feel bad about; object to: *I minded parting from my friends. Some people don't mind cold weather.* **11** Some special meanings are:
be of one mind, have the same opinion; agree.
have a mind to, intend to; think of doing.
make up one's mind, make a choice; think fit; choose; decide: *I made up my mind to study harder and get better grades.*
on one's mind, in one's mind; in one's thoughts.
put in mind, remind.
set one's mind on, want very much.
to one's mind, to one's way of thinking; in one's opinion.

mind ful (mīnd′fəl), **1** having in mind; thinking; be aware: *Mindful of your advice, I went slowly.* **2** taking thought; careful:

mill
────────────
mindful
────────────

miller (definition 2)
(about actual size)

mimic (definition 4)
Butterfly that mimics
dead leaves. Its shape,
markings, and brown color
make it look very much
like the leaf at left.

minaret

Homographs (Pages 284–285)

Homographs are presented as words that have the same letters but different meanings and origins. They may sound the same or differently.

Call attention to the illustration at the top of the page. Have the children discuss the scene. Then have them read the sentences under the picture and note the homographs (record) in them.

Help the children understand the meaning of *word origins* as they read about the origins of these three homographs.

You may want to refer to the pronunciation key on page 280 or to Sounds and Letters, pages 316–318, as you go through this lesson.

These homographs are presented:

record—(rek'ərd) (ri kôrd') (rek'ərd)
close—(klōs) (klōz)

Homographs

Linda is listening to a <u>record</u>.　(**rek'ərd**)
She wants to <u>record</u> the words of the song.　(**ri kôrd'**)
The song set a <u>record</u> for sales.　(**rek'ərd**)

These three words are written as *record,* but they have different meanings. What does each word mean?

Homographs are words that have the same letters but different meanings and different word origins. They may sound the same or differently.

The word (**ri kôrd'**) found its way into the English language from an old French word. Over the years, its meaning and pronunciation changed to make another word— (**rek'ərd**). In more modern times, another new meaning was added—the one used in (rek'ərd) sales.

Use these pronunciation marks to read these homographs and then read the sentences in which they are used.

close (klōs)　　　close (klōz)

Please <u>close</u> the window.
Little Billy stood <u>close</u> to his big brother.

What sounds are different in these homographs? What letter stands for each of these sounds? What does each word mean?

Objectives: Homographs
1. Describe homographs in operational terms.
2. Demonstrate the use of homographs in context.

Exercises

A. Read how to say these homographs and their meanings. Then copy the number of the sentence and the letter that shows the meaning of the homograph used in the sentence. Write a sentence with the other homograph in it, too.

> a. excuse (eks kūs′) a reason or explanation
> b. excuse (eks kūz′) let off; free from duty

1. The teacher will *excuse* Mike from taking the test.

> a. desert (dez′ ərt) sandy land without water
> b. desert (di zert′) go away and leave

2. A boy shouldn't *desert* his friends.

> a. object (ob′ jikt) a thing seen or touched
> b. object (əb jekt′) protest; be against

3. I *object* to going to bed before nine o' clock.

> a. content (kon′ tent) that which is inside
> b. content (kən tent′) satisfy; please

4. The cat was *content* after eating dinner.

> a. cape (kāp) a coat without sleeves
> b. cape (kāp) a point of land extending into water

5. The girl's *cape* had a hood on it.

B. Now read how to say each word and its meaning. Then write the word in a sentence. Finally, write a homograph for each word and use it in a sentence. (Use a dictionary if you need help.)

1. live (līv)   alive; having life
2. lead (led)   a bluish-gray metal
3. read (rēd)   get the meaning of someone's composition
4. house (houz)   give shelter to
5. wind (wīnd)   twist around something

Answers

EXERCISE A
Accept any sentence that uses the other homograph correctly and makes sense.

1. The teacher will <u>excuse</u> Mike from taking the test. (b)
2. A boy shouldn't <u>desert</u> his friends. (b)
3. I <u>object</u> to going to bed before nine o'clock. (b)
4. The cat was <u>content</u> after eating dinner. (b)
5. The girl's <u>cape</u> had a hood on it. (a)

EXERCISE B
Accept any reasonable sentences that use the homograph given and another homograph. Check pronunciation by having sentences read aloud. Ask which letter or letters stand for different sounds in the homographs.

1. l<u>i</u>ve (liv) be alive; dwell
2. l<u>ea</u>d (lēd) go first to show the way
3. r<u>ea</u>d (red) learned from reading
4. h<u>ou</u>se (hous) a building
5. w<u>i</u>nd (wind) moving air

Skillsbook: Homographs, page 10

Homophones (Pages 286–287)

Homophones are presented as words that are spoken the same way but written differently and have different meanings.

Call attention to the illustration at the top of the page. Have the children discuss the scene. Then have them read the sentences below the picture and note the homophones in them:

blew—blue
close—clothes

These homophones are presented:

blew meaning <u>to blow</u>
blue meaning <u>a particular color</u>
  /ü/ spelled *ew* and *ue*

close meaning <u>to shut</u>
clothes meaning <u>garments for the body</u>
  /ōz/ spelled *ose* and *othes*

stairs meaning <u>steps</u>
stares meaning <u>look without blinking</u>
  /ãr/ spelled *air* and *are*

sew meaning <u>fasten with needle and thread</u>
sow meaning <u>plant</u>
  /ō/ spelled *ew* and *ow*

You may wish to refer to the pronunciation key on page 280 and to Sounds and Letters, pages 316–318, for identification of sounds and variant spellings of the sounds.

Homophones

The wind <u>blew</u>.   Joe has a new <u>blue</u> suit.
The door will <u>close</u>. He likes new <u>clothes</u>.

Homophones are words that are spoken the same way but written differently. They also have different meanings.

The underlined words in the sentences under the picture are homophones. What sound in each pair of homophones has been written differently? What different letters stand for this sound? Tell the meaning of each homophone.

Now read these pairs of sentences and tell which words in them are homophones.

The boy sat on the stairs.
He just sits there and stares at nothing.

I must sew the hem in my new dress.
Farmers sow seeds in the spring.

Tell the different meaning of each homophone in the sentences. What sound in the homophones is spelled in a different way? What letters stand for this sound in each homophone?

Answers

EXERCISE A

1. When my sister is away, our bedroom is *wholly* mine.
   The Bible is a <u>holy</u> book.
2. King George *reigned* over England at that time.
   It <u>rained</u> all day Saturday.

Objectives: Homophones
1. Describe homophones in operational terms.
2. Demonstrate the use of homophones in context.

Exercises

A. Read each pair of sentences. Think of a homophone for the underlined word in the first sentence. Then copy the second sentence and complete it by writing the homophone. (The first one is done for you.)

1. When my sister is away, our bedroom is <u>wholly</u> mine.
   The Bible is a <u>holy</u> book.

2. King George <u>reigned</u> over England at that time.
   It _____ all day Saturday.

3. Use your bike to <u>tow</u> the wagon.
   Bob yelled when he stubbed his _____ on the rock.

4. He hoisted the <u>sail</u> on our boat and drifted out to sea.
   Barney's Store is having a _____ on dresses today.

5. What kind of <u>meat</u> did you have for dinner last night?
   I will _____ you in front of the fountain.

6. The little deer's mother was a beautiful <u>doe</u>.
   The baker popped the _____ into a pan and baked it.

7. Dip the fish in <u>flour</u> and milk before you fry it.
   We picked a _____ from the garden for Mother.

8. We <u>rode</u> to school in the bus this morning.
   There are too many cars on the _____ today.

9. I <u>would</u> not like to go swimming on such a cold day.
   We cut some _____ to build a fire.

10. I <u>read</u> that story last year.
    Most fire engines are _____.

B. Copy these words and write a homophone for each one. Then use each pair of homophones in sentences.

1. too	4. knight	7. right
2. sun	5. dew	8. wait
3. pail	6. buy	9. hare

Skillsbook: Homophones, page 11

3. Use your bike to *tow* the wagon.
Bob yelled when he stubbed his <u>toe</u> on the rock.

4. He hoisted the *sail* on our boat and drifted out to sea.
Barney's Store is having a <u>sale</u> on dresses today.

5. What kind of *meat* did you have for dinner last night?
I will <u>meet</u> you in front of the fountain.

6. The little deer's mother was a beautiful *doe*.
The baker popped the <u>dough</u> into a pan and baked it.

7. Dip the fish in *flour* and milk before you fry it.
We picked a <u>flower</u> from the garden for Mother.

8. We *rode* to school in the bus this morning.
There are too many cars on the <u>road</u> today.

9. I *would* not like to go swimming on such a cold day.
We cut some <u>wood</u> to build a fire.

10. I *read* that story last year.
Most fire engines are <u>red</u>.

EXERCISE B
Accept any reasonable sentence that uses a correct homophone. The homophones are:

1. too—two, to	6. buy—by, bye
2. sun—son	7. right—write, rite
3. pail—pale	
4. knight—night	8. wait—weight
5. dew—due, do	9. hare—hair

Initials (Pages 288–289)

Initials are presented as the first letters in each word in a proper noun.

Call attention to the initials in the illustration. Note that initials may be written without periods and that small, unimportant words aren't used in the initials.

More work with initials can be found in the lessons on Periods, pages 312–313.

Initials

Initials are the first letters of names. Periods are used after initials to show that they are initials.

Sometimes people use only one initial to write their names. Here are the names of some of our presidents and the initials by which they sometimes were known.

Abraham Lincoln	A. Lincoln
Dwight David Eisenhower	Dwight D. Eisenhower
Ulysses Simpson Grant	U. S. Grant
Franklin Delano Roosevelt	F.D.R.

Which part of each name is written with initials? What do the initials stand for in each name?

Initials are used to write the names of organizations as well as the names of people. When initials stand for well-known organizations, they aren't usually followed by periods. Read the names of these organizations and initials for them.

Parent-Teacher Association	PTA
Federal Bureau of Investigation	FBI
The American Society for the Prevention of Cruelty to Animals	ASPCA

What words in each name are written with initials? Little words like *the* and *for* aren't usually used in initials.

What is the name of the principal of your school? How could the principal's name be written with initials?

Objectives: Initials
Construct initials for the names of given people and companies.

Now what would the initials for these names be?

Associated Press   United States of America
Trans World Airlines   Office of Civil Defense
National Association for the Advancement of Colored
People
American Association for the United Nations

Exercises: 1

A. Write any—but the last—part of these names with initials.

1. Gerard Manley Hopkins
2. Paul Laurence Dunbar
3. Edward Estlin Cummings
4. James Weldon Johnson
5. Thomas Stearns Eliot
6. Albert Edward Hough
7. John Edgar Davis
8. Agnes Scott Anthony

B. Now use initials to write these names.

1. National Aeronautics and Space Administration
2. United Nations International Children's Emergency Fund
3. Organization of American States
4. Southern Christian Leadership Conference
5. Daughters of the American Revolution
6. United Press International

Exercises: 2

A. Write six names of people. Use initials for the first names of two people. Use initials for the middle names of two people. Write initials for the first and middle names of two of the people.

B. Use initials to write the names of six organizations. If you can't think of any organization, make up names for some.

Note the initials for the names of organizations in the display:

Associated Press—AP

United States of America—USA

Trans World Airlines—TWA

Office of Civil Defense—OCD

National Association for the Advancement of Colored People—NAACP

American Association for the United Nations—AAUN

Answers

EXERCISE 1A
1. Gerard M. Hopkins or G.M. Hopkins
2. Paul L. Dunbar or P.L. Dunbar
3. Edward E. Cummings or E.E. Cummings
4. James W. Johnson or J.W. Johnson
5. Thomas S. Eliot or T.S. Eliot
6. Albert E. Hough or A.E. Hough
7. John E. Davis or J.E. Davis
8. Agnes S. Anthony or A.S. Anthony

EXERCISE 1B
1. NASA
2. UNICEF
3. OAS
4. SCLC
5. DAR
6. UPI

EXERCISES 2A AND 2B
Accept any names written with initials. Check to see that child has a name in mind.

Letters (Pages 290–292)

The five parts of a friendly letter are presented:

1. Heading
2. Greeting
3. Body
4. Closing
5. Signature

The six parts of a business letter are presented:

1. Heading
2. Inside address
3. Greeting
4. Body
5. Closing
6. Signature

Call attention to the illustrated letter. Have the children identify and describe the five parts of a friendly letter.

Note that the letter in the sample was written by Charlie at 178 Colonial Road, Harrisburg, Pennsylvania (zip code number 17113), on January 1, 1972. He wanted to tell Steve that everyone at the New Year's Eve party thought of him. He said "hello" by writing Dear Steve and "good-by" by writing Your cousin. If the children have any difficulty reading abbreviations in the letter, refer to Abbreviations, pages 246–253.

Letters

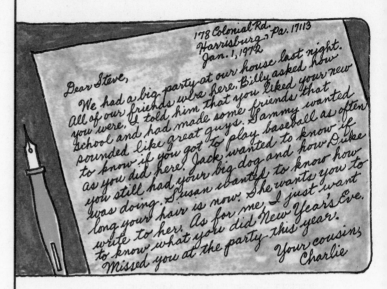

The five parts of a friendly letter are shown on this letter. Each part of the letter tells you something.

1. The heading tells the address of the writer and when the letter was written.
2. The greeting is like saying "hello."
3. The body tells what the writer wants to say.
4. The closing is like saying "good-by."
5. The signature tells who wrote the letter.

Who wrote the above letter? Where and when was the letter written? What did the writer want to say to Steve? How did he say "hello" and "good-by"?

A business letter has one more part than a friendly letter. After the heading and before the salutation, the **inside address** is written. The *inside address* tells the name and address of the person the letter is written to. It is the same address as the address written on the outside of the envelope. In a large company, the envelopes get lost and then no one can tell whom the letter was written to.

There is another difference between a friendly letter and a business letter. In a business letter a colon (:) comes after the greeting instead of a comma.

Read this business letter and tell what each part does. Then address an envelope for it.

34 Rhodes Avenue
Austin, Texas 78745
March 5, 1973

Mr. John Rand
Dobbs Corporation
1326 Third Street
Lima, Ohio 45804

Dear Mr. Rand:

Please send me information on the uses of the new fluorescent light your company has developed. I am writing a report for school on fluorescent lights. I would appreciate any information you might be able to send me.

Sincerely yours,

Cindy Louis

Call attention to the sample business letter. Have the children identify and describe the six parts of a business letter. Then have them compare a business letter to a friendly letter.

The addressed envelope for the sample business letter:

Miss Cindy Louis
34 Rhodes Avenue
Austin, Texas 78745

Mr. John Rand
Dobbs Corporation
1326 Third Street
Lima, Ohio 45804

Skillsbook: Letters and Addresses, page 12

Answers

EXERCISES A AND B

Accept any content in the body of the letters, but call attention to all the parts of each letter. Check to see that the friendly letter has five parts and that the business letter has six parts.

Plural Words (Pages 292–296)

These rules for changing a singular word to a plural word are presented:

1. Most of the time, you just add *s* to a singular word to make the plural form of the word.
2. If a singular word ends in *ch, sh, s, x,* or *z,* you generally add *es* to make the plural form of the word.
3. If a singular word ends in a consonant and *y,* you change the *y* to *i* and add *es* to make its plural form.
4. Some plural words are made by changing the vowel sound in the singular word.
5. Some plural words are the same as the singular words.
6. Some plural words that end in *f* or *fe* form plural words by changing the *f* to *v* and adding *s* or *es.*

Call attention to the illustration and to the singular and plural forms of the words in the illustration.

Note that all the plural forms in the display are made from the singular word by just adding *s* to the singular form—even if *s* stands for /z/.

Exercises

A. Suppose that you went away. Write a friendly letter to someone in your home. Tell him where you are and what you are doing there.

B. Suppose that you are planning a trip somewhere. Write a business letter to a travel agency for information. You may want to know how to get there or something about the place.

Plural Words

Words that mean "just one" are called **singular** words. Words that mean "more than one" are called **plural** words.

Adding *s* or *es* to Form Plurals

Read these singular and plural words.

dog	dogs	boy	boys
shell	shells	lake	lakes
trick	tricks	sea	seas
lion	lions	cape	capes

How are these plural words different from the singular words? Most of the time, you just add an *s* to a singular word to make a plural word.

Objectives: Plural Words
Demonstrate how to form plural words:
a. by adding s to a singular word.
b. by adding es to a singular word that ends in *ch, sh, s, x,* or *z.*
c. by changing the final *y* to *i* and adding es to a singular word that ends in a consonant and *y.*

Now read these singular and plural words.

branch	branches	dress	dresses
flash	flashes	ax	axes
gas	gases	waltz	waltzes

How are these plural forms different from the singular forms? When a word ends in *ch, sh, s, x,* or *z,* you add *es* to the singular word to make it a plural word.

Exercises

A. Copy these sentences. Use the plural form of the word at the end of the sentence to complete the sentence. (The first one is done for you.)

1. Kangaroos carry their babies in _____. (pouch)
   Kangaroos carry their babies in pouches.

2. Can you start a fire without _____? (match)
3. Let's walk along the railroad _____. (track)
4. My dog doesn't like _____. (leash)
5. We're going to have cheese _____ for lunch. (blintz)
6. We use _____ to carry our food to the table. (tray)

B. Now copy these sentences. Complete them in the same way. (The first one is done for you.)

1. _____ have a yellowish color. (topaz)
   Topazes have a yellowish color.

2. The soldiers built _____ to hide in. (trench)
3. Ted can't see a thing without his _____. (glass)
4. I like to hear the _____ that sailors sing. (chant)
5. I don't like _____ in my salad. (radish)
6. There are two _____ in the numeral. (six)

Note that all the plural words in the display are formed from the singular words by adding *es* for /əs/ or /əz/ to the singular words. Also note that each singular word ends in *ch, sh, s, x,* or *z.*

Answers

EXERCISE A

1. Kangaroos carry their babies in <u>pouches</u>.
2. Can you start a fire without <u>matches</u>?
3. Let's walk along the railroad <u>tracks</u>.
4. My dog doesn't like <u>leashes</u>.
5. We're going to have cheese <u>blintzes</u> for lunch.
6. We use <u>trays</u> to carry our food to the table.

EXERCISE B

1. <u>Topazes</u> have a yellowish color.
2. The soldiers built <u>trenches</u> to hide in.
3. Ted can't see a thing without his <u>glasses</u>.
4. I like to hear the <u>chants</u> that sailors sing.
5. I don't like <u>radishes</u> in my salad.
6. There are two <u>sixes</u> in the numeral.

d. by changing the letters that stand for the vowel sound in a singular word.

e. by using the same form for both singular and plural forms of a word.

f. by changing the f to v and adding s or es to a singular word that ends in f or fe.

Note that the plural words in the display are made from the words that end in a vowel and *y* (*key, bay, joy*) by adding *s*; from the words that end in a consonant and *y* (*city, sky, story*) by changing the *y* to *i* and adding *es*.

Answers

EXERCISE A

Accept any reasonable sentence that uses the plural form of each word correctly.

1. boys
2. toys
3. bunnies
4. monkeys
5. countries
6. diaries
7. guys
8. valleys
9. daisies

EXERCISE B

1. Flashlights won't work if the <u>batteries</u> are dead.
2. <u>All</u> the classes in our school present <u>plays</u>.
3. Forty <u>families</u> live in that apartment building.
4. The <u>cherries</u> on the cherry tree were not ripe.
5. The glass turned the sun's <u>rays</u> into a rainbow.

Words Ending in *y*

Each of these singular words ends in *y*. But not all the plural words are made by adding just an *s*.

key	keys	city	cities
bay	bays	sky	skies
joy	joys	story	stories

How are plural words made from the singular words like *key, bay,* and *joy*? How are plural words made from singular words like *city, sky,* and *story*?

When a singular word ends in a vowel and *y*, you just add *s* to make the plural word. When the singular word ends with a consonant and *y*, you must change the *y* to *i* and add *es* to make the plural word.

Exercises

A. Write the plural form of each word. Then use the word in a sentence.

1. boy
2. toy
3. bunny
4. monkey
5. country
6. diary
7. guy
8. valley
9. daisy

B. Copy and complete each sentence. Use the plural form of the word in parentheses ( ). (The first one is done for you.)

1. Flashlights won't work if the _____ are dead. (battery)
Flashlights won't work if the <u>batteries</u> are dead.

2. All the classes in our school present _____. (play)
3. Forty _____ live in that apartment building. (family)
4. The _____ on the cherry tree were not ripe. (cherry)
5. The glass turned the sun's _____ into a rainbow. (ray)

6. Mother closed her ears to my _____ of protest. (outcry)
7. How many milk chocolate _____ are in that box? (candy)
8. The most difficult animals to train are _____. (donkey)
9. Did you know that _____ have two pairs of wings? (fly)

Words with Special Plural Forms

What are the singular and plural words for the things in these pictures?

Some plural forms of words aren't made by adding *s* or *es* to singular words. Read these singular and plural words and see if you can tell how the plural words are formed.

tooth	teeth	fish	fish
woman	women	half	halves
sheep	sheep	knife	knives

● Some plural words are made by changing the vowel sound in the singular words.

● Some plural words are the same as singular words.

● When singular words end in *f* or *fe*, plural words are sometimes made by changing *f* to *v* and adding *s* or *es*.

6. Mother closed her ears to my <u>outcries</u> of protest.

7. How many milk chocolate <u>candies</u> are in that box?

8. The most difficult animals to train are <u>donkeys</u>.

9. Did you know that <u>flies</u> have two pairs of wings?

Note the singular and plural words for things in the picture:

tooth—teeth	apple—apples
woman—women	fruit—fruit
sheep—sheep	bead—beads
fish—fish	scarf—scarves
half—halves	tree—trees
knife—knives	grass—grass
coconut—coconuts	sky—skies
eye—eyes	mouth—mouths
face—faces	head—heads

List the words on the chalkboard and discuss how the plural word is formed from the singular word.

Note the rules for forming special plural forms. Have the children give examples of the application of each rule.

Answers

1. leaf—leaves   6. shelf—shelves
2. half—halves   7. man—men
3. wolf—wolves   8. wife—wives
4. deer—deer   9. trout—trout
5. goose—geese

Accept any reasonable sentence that uses the plural form of each word correctly.

EXERCISE B
1. loaf—loaves   7. fish—fish
2. foot—feet   (fishes may
3. calf—calves   be used)
4. life—lives   8. knife—knives
5. tooth—teeth   9. starfish—
6. mouse—mice   starfish

Note the summary about forming plural words. Have the children give examples of the application of each "rule."

Exercises

A. Write the plural for each singular word. Then write each word in a sentence. (Use your dictionary if you need help.)

1. leaf   4. deer   7. man
2. half   5. goose   8. wife
3. wolf   6. shelf   9. trout

B. Now write the plurals for these singular words. Then write each word in a sentence. (Use your dictionary for help.)

1. loaf   4. life   7. fish
2. foot   5. tooth   8. knife
3. calf   6. mouse   9. starfish

Summary

Here are some rules about plural words.

- Most of the time, you just add *s* to a singular word to make a plural word.

- If a singular word ends in *ch, sh, s, x,* or *z,* you add *es* to make the plural word.

- If a singular word ends in a consonant and *y,* you change the *y* to *i* and add *es* to make the plural word.

- Some plural words are made by changing the vowel sound in the singular word.

- Some plural words and singular words are the same.

- Some singular words that end in *f* or *fe* form plural words by changing the *f* to *v* and adding *s* or *es*.

Skillsbook: Plural Words, page 13
Skillsbook: More Plurals, page 14

Possessive Nominals

the bird's feather   the birds' feathers

Possessive nominals are used to show several things. Some show that something belongs to someone.

the book belongs to Sam   Sam's book
the games belong to the boys   the boys' games

Some possessive nominals show that people are related to each other.

the aunt of Nathan   Nathan's aunt
the mother of the girls   the girls' mother

Some possessive nominals show that people are related in other ways, too.

the neighbor of Saul   Saul's neighbor
the friend of my parents   my parents' friend

Singular Words

Read each phrase and possessive nominal and tell what was added to each singular word to make a possessive nominal.

the toy that belongs to Amy   Amy's toy
the beard of the goat   the goat's beard

Possessive Nominals (Pages 297–301)

Possessive nominals are presented as ways of showing ownership or relationship. These rules for forming possessive nominals are presented:

1. You usually add an apostrophe and an *s* to write a possessive word for a singular word.
2. You add just an apostrophe to make a possessive word for a plural word that ends in *s*.
3. You add an apostrophe and an *s* to a plural word that doesn't end in *s* to make a possessive word.

Call attention to the illustrations and to the possessive nominals written under them.

Note that possessive nominals show relationships as well as possession. Also note that some possessive nominals are formed by adding *'s* and others are formed by adding just an apostrophe.

Answers

EXERCISE A

1. Charlene's umbrella
2. Dad's chair
3. Pam's skirt
4. Danny's dime
5. my brother's bedroom
6. Mrs. Zink's pen
7. my grandmother's neighbors
8. my father's ties
9. my mother's grocery cart
10. Paula's play

EXERCISE B

1. Joe's house is white.
2. Mrs. Baroni's class went on a picnic.
3. The earth's orbit is around the sun.
4. Anita's purse is red.
5. The dog's collar is new.
6. The crowd's noise was so loud I didn't hear you.
7. The guppy's tail gradually disappeared.
8. The sun's rays broke through the clouds.
9. The boys use Corey's bat to play ball.
10. Pat's kite soared above the treetops.

When you want to write a possessive nominal for a singular word, you add an apostrophe and an *s*.

Exercises

A. Change these phrases to possessive nominals. (The first one is done for you.)

1. the umbrella which belongs to Charlene
   Charlene's umbrella

2. the chair which belongs to Dad
3. the skirt which Pam wears
4. the dime which belongs to Danny
5. the room in which my brother sleeps
6. the pen which belongs to Mrs. Zink
7. the neighbors of my grandmother
8. the ties my father has
9. the grocery cart which belongs to my mother
10. the play written by Paula

B. Now change these sentences so that they have possessive nominals. (The first one is done for you.)

1. The house that Joe lives in is white.
   Joe's house is white.

2. The class taught by Mrs. Baroni went on a picnic.
3. The orbit of the earth is around the sun.
4. The purse which belongs to Anita is red.
5. The collar of the dog is new.
6. The noise of the crowd was so loud I didn't hear you.
7. The tail of the guppy gradually disappeared.
8. The rays of the sun broke through the clouds.
9. The boys use the bat that belongs to Corey to play ball.
10. The kite that belonged to Pat soared above the treetops.

Plural Words

Look at this picture and the phrases below it.

the capes of the <u>goblins</u>   the goblins' capes

Is the underlined word singular or plural? Does it end in *s*?
What was added to the plural word to make a possessive
word?

When you write possessive words for plural words
that end in *s*, you just add an apostrophe. Now tell how you
would write possessive nominals for these phrases.

the pie of the girls
the papers of the students
the stalls of the horses

Sometimes you want to write possessive nominals
with plural words that don't end in *s*. You write possessives
for these words in the same way that you write possessives
for singular words. You just add an apostrophe and an *s*.

Tell how you would write possessive nominals for
these phrases.

the skirts of the women
the boots of the firemen
the wool of the sheep

Call attention to the illustration and
to the phrase and the possessive nominal
written under it.

Note that possessive words for plural
words that end in *s* are formed by adding
just an apostrophe.

Possessive nominals for phrases in
the display:

the girls' pie
the students' papers
the horses' stalls

the women's skirts
the firemen's boots
the sheep's wool

For more work with possessive nomi-
nals, see Apostrophes, pages 306–307.
You also may want to refer to Plural
Words, pages 292–296.

Answers

EXERCISE A

1. the peacocks' tails
2. my uncle's house
3. the children's playground
4. the men's cars
5. the babies' rattles
6. the birds' nests
7. the shepherds' dreams
8. a doctors' meeting
9. the snails' tracks
10. the women's rights
11. the wizards' hats
12. the girls' friend

EXERCISE B

1. The girls' coats are in the closet.
2. The teachers' lounge isn't very big.
3. The carpenters' tools are in the basement.
4. His parents' canes have carved handles.
5. The boys' team is playing ball on Saturday.
6. The children's laughter made them happy.
7. My cousins' apartment is on the fifteenth floor.
8. The teachers' meeting is after school.
9. The flowers' nectar is gathered by the bees.
10. The men's jackets are red.

Exercises

A. Change these phrases to possessive nominals. (The first one is done for you.)

1. the tails of the peacocks
   the peacocks' tails

2. the house which belongs to my uncle
3. the playground for the children
4. the cars of the men
5. the rattles of the babies
6. the nests of the birds
7. the dreams the shepherds had
8. a meeting for doctors
9. the tracks of the snails
10. the rights of women
11. the hats of the wizards
12. the friend of the girls

B. Now rewrite these sentences with possessive nominals. (The first one is done for you.)

1. The coats which belong to the girls are in the closet.
   The girls' coats are in the closet.

2. The lounge for the teachers isn't very big.
3. The tools of the carpenters are in the basement.
4. The canes which belong to his parents have carved handles.
5. The team the boys belong to is playing ball on Saturday.
6. The laughter of the children made them happy.
7. The apartment of my cousins is on the fifteenth floor.
8. The meeting of the teachers is after school.
9. The nectar of the flowers is gathered by the bees.
10. The jackets of the men are red.

Summary

Here are some rules about possessive words.

● Most of the time, you just add an apostrophe and an *s* to make possessive words for singular words.

● You add just an apostrophe to make possessive words for plural words that end in *s*.

● You add an apostrophe and an *s* to plural words that don't end in *s* to make possessive words.

Exercises

A. Change these phrases to possessive nominals.

1. the wings of a bat
2. the cries of owls
3. the mouths of the boys
4. the voice of his friend
5. the castles of kings

6. the wings of bats
7. the cries of an owl
8. the books of the boy
9. the voices of children
10. the eyes of kittens

B. Now write these sentences with possessive nominals. (The first one is done for you.)

1. I saw the tail of a chipmunk. *I saw a chipmunk's tail.*
2. Jack watched the tails of the chipmunks bob up and down.
3. Mary took a long drink from the canteen that belonged to her brother.
4. She was glad that she took the biggest of the canteens that belonged to her brothers.
5. Then she walked downhill to the house of her aunt.
6. The sun set as Sue reached the house of her aunts.
7. The wagon of the boy rolled quickly down the hill.
8. The wagons of the boys raced down the hill together.

Skillsbook: Possessive Nominals, page 15

Note the summary about possessive words. Have the children give examples of each "rule."

Answers

EXERCISE A

1. a bat's wings
2. the owls' cries
3. the boys' mouths
4. his friend's voice
5. the kings' castles
6. the bats' wings
7. an owl's cries
8. the boy's books
9. the children's voices
10. the kittens' eyes

EXERCISE B

1. I saw a chipmunk's tail.
2. Jack watched the chipmunks' tails bob up and down.
3. Mary took a long drink from her brother's canteen.
4. She was glad that she took the biggest of her brothers' canteens.
5. Then she walked downhill to her aunt's house.
6. The sun set as Sue reached her aunts' house.
7. The boy's wagon rolled quickly down the hill.
8. The boys' wagons raced down the hill together.

Proofreading (Pages 302–305)

Sample compositions are presented for the children to proofread for:

1. Misspelled words
2. Use of capital letters
3. Use of punctuation marks
4. Neatness and margins

Call attention to the illustration. Note the mistakes in the sample letter:

Spelling—birds, like, bird, skin, feathers, hatch, mammals

Apostrophe in possessive forms—bat's, mother's

Apostrophe in contractions—they're

Periods at the end of sentences

The child who wrote the letter should recopy the letter neatly to make it easier to read.

You may want to refer to Sounds and Letters, pages 316–318, Punctuation Marks, pages 306–315, Capital Letters, pages 265–271, Contractions, pages 272–274, or Possessive Nominals, pages 297–301, or Plural Words, pages 292–296, as you go through the exercises on proofreading.

Proofreading

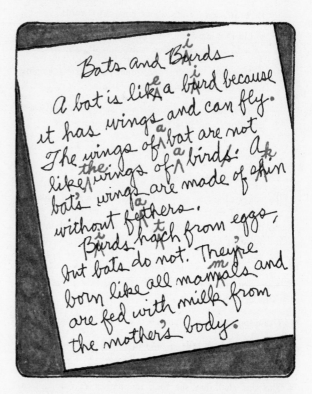

The boy who wrote this composition was **proofreading** it. He read it carefully for mistakes and corrected them. What kind of mistakes did he make? Is his composition easy to read with the corrections? What should he do to make it easier for people to read?

Objectives: Proofreading

1. Demonstrate the use of capital letters by correcting errors in a given composition.
2. Demonstrate the use of punctuation marks by correcting errors in a given composition.
3. Demonstrate phoneme-grapheme relationships by correcting spelling errors in a given composition.

After you have completed a composition, you should proofread it to be sure you have said all you wanted to say. You should check it for mistakes and to see if it is easy to read and understand. If you have too many mistakes to correct neatly, you should recopy your composition.

Here are some questions to remind you what to check when you proofread a composition.

1. Are all the words spelled correctly? Did you check words you weren't sure how to spell in a dictionary?
2. Did you use capital letters correctly? If you aren't sure where to use capital letters, turn to page 265 for help.
3. Did you use punctuation marks correctly? If you need help with the use of punctuation marks, turn to page 306.
4. Did you leave good margins? Is your paper neat?
5. Do your paragraphs start about an inch inside the margins?

Exercises: 1

A. Read this composition to find twenty-five words that are spelled wrong. Then copy and correct the composition.

The Fare Princes

Onse upon a time thier was a fare princes who lived in the wods. She had allways herd storys about humans and how big they wer. She thot they must be very beautiful. Ome day wile she lay sleping under an oke leef, she was awakened by the loud sond of voices. She peeped out and saw a human family haveing a picnic. They were jus as large as she had hard, but they wer not as beautiful as the fares she new.

Call attention to the check list of things to think about as you proofread a composition. You might suggest that each composition be read through once for sense, then read again for mistakes in punctuation, and again for mistakes in spelling.

Answers

EXERCISE 1A

The <u>Fairy</u> <u>Princess</u>

<u>Once</u> upon a time <u>there</u> was a <u>fairy</u> <u>princess</u> who lived in the <u>woods</u>. She had <u>always</u> <u>heard</u> <u>stories</u> about humans and how big they <u>were</u>. She <u>thought</u> they must be very beautiful. <u>One</u> day <u>while</u> she lay <u>sleeping</u> under an <u>oak</u> <u>leaf</u>, she was <u>awakened</u> by the loud <u>sound</u> of voices. She peeped out and saw a human family <u>having</u> a picnic. They were <u>just</u> as large as she had <u>heard</u>, but they <u>were</u> not as beautiful as the <u>fairies</u> she <u>knew</u>.

Note the kind of spelling errors made or omitted in each child's copy to determine which sound-letter relationships or plural forms to introduce or reinforce in another skills lesson.

EXERCISE 1B

Many words in the English language come from ancient Greek. For example, the word "geography" comes from the Greek words "gē," which means "earth," and "graphein," which means "to write." When these two words are put together, you can see that the word "geography" used to mean "to write about the earth." Over many years, the word has come to mean "the study of the earth."

EXERCISE 2A

Krakatoa

On August 27, 1883, the volcano on the island of Krakatoa blew up with a tremendous explosion. Two thirds of the island disappeared. The volcano threw out enough rock to fill a box a mile long, a mile wide, and a mile deep. The sound of this explosion was so great that it could be heard in Japan, which is about the same distance from the island of Krakatoa as New York is from California. It also created enormous waves a hundred feet high which smashed against the coasts of nearby Java and Sumatra, killing 36,000 people.

Note that sentences may vary. Accept any reasonable sentences. Make a note of the kinds of errors that are missed for future skills work.

B. Now read this composition to find fourteen mistakes in spelling. Then recopy it correctly. (The Greek words in this composition are spelled correctly.)

Meny werds in the English language com from ancient Greek. For example, the word "geography" coms from the Greek words "gē," wich means "earth," and "graphein," wich means "to write." Wen thes too words are put together, you can see that the word "geography" used to mean "to right about the eath." Over many years, the wurd has com to meen "the study of the earth."

Exercises: 2

A. Read this composition for missing capital letters and periods. Then copy and correct the composition.

krakatoa

on august 27, 1883, the volcano on the island of krakatoa blew up with a tremendous explosion two thirds of the island disappeared the volcano threw out enough rock to fill a box a mile long, a mile wide, and a mile deep the sound of this explosion was so great that it could be heard in Japan, which is about the same distance from the island of krakatoa as new york is from california it also created enormous waves a hundred feet high which smashed against the coasts of nearby java and sumatra, killing 36,000 people

B. Proofread this composition for mistakes in the use of apostrophes. Three apostrophes should be taken out and five should be put in. Copy and correct the composition.

> All the animals' near Oppermans Pond were invited to a Halloween Party at Maxwells Swamp. The cow came as Babe, Paul Bunyans blue ox. Some of the mice came in capes as bat's. A beaver, who wanted to look like a turtle, carried a squirrels nest on his back. When some wolve's showed up in sheeps clothing, the other animals went home.

Exercises: 3

A. Now copy and correct mistakes in spelling, in the use of capital letters, and in punctuation in this composition.

> robbins are broun birds' with red breasts they are sad to be one of the frist signs of spring the robbins red breasts make them easy to see?

B. Proofread this composition. Then copy and correct it.

> John and mike fond a babe robin wich fell out of its nast they took it home and put in in a box they dug up worms and fed it every day wen the robins body was strong, the boys' carried it to the childrens park and set it fre

Skillsbook: Proofreading, page 17

EXERCISE 2B

All the animals near Opperman's Pond were invited to a Halloween Party at Maxwell's Swamp. The cow came as Babe, Paul Bunyan's blue ox. Some of the mice came in capes as bats. A beaver, who wanted to look like a turtle, carried a squirrel's nest on his back. When some wolves showed up in sheep's clothing, the other animals went home.

EXERCISE 3A

Robins are brown birds with red breasts. They are said to be one of the first signs of spring. The robins' red breasts make them easy to see.

Note that an apostrophe is deleted in *birds* in the first sentence and inserted in *robins* in the last sentence.

EXERCISE 3B

John and Mike found a baby robin which fell out of its nest. They took it home and put it in a box. They dug up worms and fed it every day. When the robin's body was strong, the boys carried it to the children's park and set it free.

Punctuation Marks (Pages 306–315)

The punctuation marks presented are:

1. The apostrophe (pages 306–307)
2. The colon (pages 308–309)
3. The comma (pages 310–311)
4. The exclamation mark (pages 311–312)
5. The period (pages 312–313)
6. The question mark (pages 313–314)
7. Quotation marks (pages 314–315)

Call attention to the illustrated punctuation marks at the top of the page. Have the children identify each mark.

The apostrophe is presented as a mark of punctuation that is used:

1. in a contraction to show where letters have been left out when two words are contracted.
2. in possessive nominals—an 's is added to most words to make possessive words; only an apostrophe is added to a plural word that ends in s to make a possessive word.

The words that are contracted to form the contractions in the display are:

they're—they are   they'd—they would
can't—can not   he's—he is
we've—we have   I'm—I am
she'll—she will   he'd—he would
aren't—are not

For more work with contractions, see pages 272–274.

Possessive words in the display:

Singular words	Plural words	
Fred's	women's	boys'
girl's	horses'	children's
sheep's	sheep's	girls'

For more work with possessive nominals, see pages 297–301.

306

Punctuation Marks

Punctuation marks and capital letters are used to help a reader understand what a writer wants to say.

Apostrophes

An **apostrophe** (') is used in contractions to show where letters have been left out when two words are put together and shortened. Read these contractions.

they're	she'll	he's
can't	aren't	I'm
we've	they'd	he'd

Tell what words were put together to make each contraction. Then tell what letters in the words were left out. (If you need help understanding contractions, turn to page 272.)

An apostrophe is also used to make a possessive word in a possessive nominal. Most of the time, an apostrophe and an s are added to a singular word and just an apostrophe is added to a plural word that ends in s to make a possessive word. Read the possessive words in these nominals.

Fred's jar	boys' house
women's shop	girl's bike
horses' manes	children's park
sheep's wool	girls' shoes

Tell what was added to each underlined word to make it a possessive word. Is it a singular or a plural word?

Objectives: Punctuation Marks
Demonstrate the use of apostrophes:
a. in writing contractions for given words.
b. in writing possessive nominals.

Exercises

A. Try to write these words and phrases without apostrophes. For example: Abby's dress; *the dress that belongs to Abby.*

1. Alice's restaurant
2. Gabriel's car
3. hadn't seen Joe
4. he'd like
5. the boys' skates
6. they're here
7. wouldn't we
8. don't they
9. Paul's pajamas
10. Aunt Anna's pies
11. it's here
12. there's John
13. Harry's family
14. she's gone
15. Sonny's friends
16. the Allens' house
17. Linda's brother
18. I'll see

B. Copy these sentences and use apostrophes where they are needed in contractions and in possessive nominals. (The first one is done for you.)

1. Mothers new dishes arent in the cupboard.
   Mother's new dishes aren't in the cupboard.

2. Mothers dont like to use their new dishes every day.
3. I just cant believe thats Martins new car.
4. Hes been working all night at Joes Garage.
5. Mary Anns paper is on the teachers desk, isnt it?
6. Lees letter wasnt mailed until Saturday morning.
7. Weve met Gabriels family. Theyre very nice people.
8. Wasnt that one of your aunts that just drove by?
9. Ednas mother and my mother cant go to PTA tonight.
10. They wouldve liked to go, but theyre sick with the "flu."
11. We havent been to the Spocks house this year.
12. Well go visit them when we visit Rays family.
13. Isnt that Johns cat on our front porch?
14. We arent going to Grandmothers house until next week.

Skillsbook: Apostrophes, page 20

Answers

EXERCISE A

Accept any reasonable responses.

1. the restaurant that belongs to Alice
2. the car that belongs to Gabriel
3. had not seen Joe
4. he would like
5. the skates that belong to the boys
6. they are here
7. would we not
8. do they not
9. the pajamas that belong to Paul
10. the pies that Aunt Anna baked
11. it is here
12. there is John
13. the family that Harry belongs to
14. she is/has gone
15. the friends that Sonny has
16. the house that belongs to the Allens
17. the brother of Linda
18. I will see

EXERCISE B

1. Mother's new dishes aren't in the cupboard.
2. Mothers don't like to use their new dishes every day.
3. I just can't believe that's Martin's new car.
4. He's been working all night at Joe's garage.
5. Mary Ann's paper is on the teacher's desk, isn't it?
6. Lee's letter wasn't mailed until Saturday morning.
7. We've met Gabriel's family. They're very nice people.
8. Wasn't that one of your aunts that just drove by?
9. Edna's mother and my mother can't go to PTA tonight.
10. They would've liked to go, but they're sick with the "flu."

(Continued)

11. We haven't been to the Spock's house this year.

12. We'll go visit them when we visit Ray's family.

13. Isn't that John's cat on our front porch?

14. We aren't going to Grandmother's house until next week.

The colon is presented as a mark of punctuation that is used:

1. after the greeting of a business letter.
2. in a written play to separate the name of the speaker from what he says.

Compare the punctuation after the greeting of a friendly letter with the punctuation after the greeting of a personal letter. Refer to the sample letters on page 290 and 291.

Call attention to the illustration of a scene from a school play. Mention that the children are acting out a folktale that is in their textbook. Encourage the children to identify the characters portrayed by the actors and the folktale. You may want to refer to the folktale on pages 56–61. Note that the setting is altered from the illustration in the text and that the folktale in the text is a narrative with dialogue, but not a play.

Colons

A **colon** (:) is used after the greeting in a business letter. Read these greetings.

Gentlemen: Dear Governor Roosevelt:
Dear Sir: My dear Mr. Glasgow:

Which greetings would you use when writing to the president of a company when you don't know his name? For help in writing business letters, turn to the section about Letters, page 290.

A colon is also used to help show what each person says in a play. In the picture, the children are putting on a play about the folktale on page 56 of this book. At the top of the next page is a part of the play they're acting out.

Demonstrate the use of colons:
a. after the greeting in a business letter.
b. to write dialogue for a play.

YAM: Well, at last you're here. You never weeded me, but now you're here with your weeding stick to dig me up for market. Go away and leave me alone!

FARMER (*turning to cow with surprised look*): Did you say something?

(*Cow keeps on chewing and says nothing.*)

DOG: It wasn't the cow who spoke to you. It was the yam. The yam says leave me alone.

Exercises

A. Show how you would write the greeting of a business letter to these people.

1. the governor of your state
2. the president of Standard Oil Company
3. the head of a reading department of a publishing house
4. the superintendent of schools in your school district
5. the principal of your school
6. a friendly letter to your Aunt Jane
7. a business letter to Mr. Day, president of Hi-Light Co.
8. a friendly letter to Mary Lou
9. a business letter to the Able Travel Agency
10. a friendly letter to your teacher

B. Now see if you can write the speaking parts of a play. Reread the myth Perseus and Atlas on page 97 of this book. Then find the exact words that Perseus and Atlas said to one another. (You'll find them on page 98.) Copy these words as you would write them for a play. Then make up something for Perseus to say as he opens the gate of the garden. Finally, write something for the people to say as they enter it.

Skillsbook: Colons and Commas, page 21

Call attention to the use of colons in the partial script for the scene of the play—page 308. You may want to note that the lines for the actors are quotations from the folktale.

Answers

EXERCISE A
1. Dear Governor: (names will vary)
2. Dear Sir:
3. Dear Sir:
4. Dear Mr./Dr./Miss/Mrs.: (names will vary)
5. Dear Mr./Miss/Mrs.: (names will vary)
6. Dear Aunt Jane,
7. Dear Mr. Day:
8. Dear Mary Lou,
9. Gentlemen:
10. Dear Mr./Miss/Mrs., (names will vary)

EXERCISE B
Accept any reasonable interpretation of the play. Be sure that quotations from page 98 are quoted exactly.

The comma is presented as a mark of punctuation that is used:

1. between the name of a city and the name of a state or a country.
2. between the numeral that stands for day of the month and the numeral for the year when writing a date.
3. after the greeting and after the closing of a friendly letter.
4. between words written in a series.

Call attention to each statement about the use of a comma and the examples of its use.

States and countries in the display:

Illinois and California are states.
France and Kenya are countries.

Today's date will vary with the day the lesson is used.

Greetings for letters to parents:

Dear Mother/Mom,
Dear Father/Dad,
Dear Mother/Mom and Father/Dad,

Closings for letters to parents:

Your son/daughter,
Love,

Accept any other reasonable closing.

Commas go after every word in a series, except for the conjunction (*and* and *or*) and the last word in the series.

Adding commas to the displayed words in a series:

Tom, John, Ray, Bob, and Ted will be at the party.

I like strawberry, chocolate, and vanilla ice cream.

Kathy eats ketchup with hot dogs, potatoes, and eggs.

Commas

A **comma** (,) is always used between the names of a city and the name of a state or a country.

Chicago, Illinois	Paris, France
Los Angeles, California	Nairobi, Kenya

Which names are those of states? Which ones are countries?

A comma is always used between the day of the month and the year when writing a date.

October 2, 1962	January 1, 1984
April 1, 1812	July 4, 1776

How would you write today's date?

A comma is always used after the greeting and after the closing of a friendly letter.

Dear Sam,	Sincerely yours,
Dear Anna,	Love,

How would you write the greeting and closing of a letter to your parents?

A comma is used between words when you have words in a series.

Susan, Lee, Kathy, and Joe
red, blue, yellow, gray, or brown

Do commas go after every word in this list? Which two words in each list don't have commas after them?

Now read these sentences. Which words in each one are part of a series? Where would you put commas?

Tom John Ray Bob and Ted will be at the party.
I like strawberry chocolate and vanilla ice cream.
Kathy eats ketchup with hot dogs potatoes and eggs.

Demonstrate the use of commas:
a. to separate words in series.
b. to separate the numeral that stands for the day from the numeral for the year in a date.
c. to separate the name of a city from the name of a state.
d. after the greeting of a friendly letter and after the closing of all letters.

Exercises

A. Which of these phrases need commas? Copy the ones that do, and put the commas where they belong.

1. July 22 2001
2. Lincoln Nebraska
3. Susie Johnson
4. Yours truly
5. Jim David Cindy and Kurt
6. Dear Pam
7. needles and pins
8. Atlanta Georgia
9. apples pears and plums
10. April 26 1904

B. Write the answers to each of these questions. Don't forget to put in commas if you need them.

1. What will be the date ten years from today?
2. When were you born? Give the month, day, and year.
3. What are the names of four musical instruments?
4. What are three different kinds of things you can read?
5. What are the names of three teachers in your school?

Exclamation Marks

An **exclamation mark** (!) is used by a writer to show surprise or great feeling. A period is usually used at the end of a statement. A question mark is usually used at the end of a question. But an exclamation mark may be used in place of a period or a question mark. Read these sentences.

My money is gone!
This is what you woke me up to see!
What was that!
Who hit me!

Tell what feelings each sentence shows. Which sentences are statements? Which ones are questions?

Demonstrate the use of exclamation marks to show great feeling.

Skillsbook: Commas and Exclamation Marks, page 22

Answers

EXERCISE A
1. July 22, 2001
2. Lincoln, Nebraska
4. Yours truly,
5. Jim, David, Cindy, and Kurt
6. Dear Pam,
8. Atlanta, Georgia
9. apples, pears, and plums
10. April 26, 1904

EXERCISE B
Answers will vary. Check answers for the correct use of commas.

The exclamation mark is presented as a mark of punctuation that is used to show surprise or great feeling.

The displayed sentences may show surprise or anger.

Displayed sentences that could be statements:

My money is gone.
This is what you woke me up to see.

Displayed sentences that could be questions:

What was that?
Who hit me?

Answers

EXERCISES A AND B

Accept any reasonable story content. Note the use of exclamation marks and accept any reasonable use of them.

Periods are presented as marks of punctuation that are used:

1. to end a sentence which is a statement or a command.
2. to end an abbreviation.
3. after each initial.

Note the statements about the use of a period and the examples that follow each rule.

Note the difference between a statement and a command. The subject of a command is *you*.

For more work with abbreviations, turn to pages 246–254.

For more work with initials, see pages 288–289.

Exercises

A. Write a short story in which you tell about something that made you angry. Tell what you said when you were angry. Use exclamation marks at the end of sentences that you want to show great feeling.

B. Write a short story in which you tell about a surprise you had. Tell what you said when you were surprised. Use marks of exclamation at the end of sentences to show that you were surprised.

Periods

A **period** (.) goes at the end of all sentences that are statements or commands.

Statements: Jody has some new goldfish.
I live in the house on the hill.

Commands: Bring me the newspaper.
Close the door on your way outside.

A period usually goes at the end of an abbreviation. (Turn to the section about Abbreviations, page 246.)

Mr.	oz.	Apr.	N.Y.
Rev.	lb.	Feb.	Ga.
Ave.	qt.	Dec.	Calif.

A period goes after initials that stand for names. (See the section about Initials, page 288.)

O. Henry	Samuel L. Clemens	T. C. Steele
A. Lincoln	Dwight D. Eisenhower	U. S. Grant

Demonstrate the use of periods:
a. to end sentences that are statements or commands.
b. to end abbreviations and initials.

Exercises

A. Copy these sentences and put periods where they're needed. Some sentences will need more than one period.

1. Take that ball outside if you're going to bounce it
2. My Uncle John wears suspenders to hold his pants up
3. Dr and Mrs Gordon are coming to tea this afternoon
4. Without periods, the abbreviations Sat, Sun, and Wed would spell other words
5. A A Milne and T S Eliot are both famous writers
6. My birthday and Sarah's birthday are both on Feb 12

B. Follow these directions.

1. Write three short sentences about water.
2. Write three short commands.
3. Write abbreviations for the first four months of the year.
4. Sign your paper with initials for all but your last name.

Question Marks

A **question mark** (?) is used to show a reader that a question is being asked. Read these questions.

Do you have a pet parrot?   Where is it kept?
When do you eat dinner?   What will you eat?

Now try to turn these statements into questions.

I saw a good TV show last night.
The people left the town before the volcano erupted.
When Ted fell out of the tree, he broke his arm.
Question marks are used at the end of questions.

Demonstrate the use of question marks to end sentences that ask questions.

Skillsbook: Periods and Question Marks, page 23

Answers

EXERCISE A

1. Take that ball outside if you're going to bounce it.
2. My Uncle John wears suspenders to hold his pants up.
3. Dr. and Mrs. Gordon are coming to tea this afternoon.
4. Without periods, the abbreviations Sat., Sun., and Wed. would spell other words.
5. A. A. Milne and T. S. Eliot are both famous writers.
6. My birthday and Sarah's birthday are both on Feb. 12.

EXERCISE B

Accept any responses that use periods correctly and follow the specific directions.

A question mark is presented as a mark of punctuation that is used to show that a question is being asked.

Making questions from statements in the display:

Did you see the good TV show that I saw last night?

Did the people leave town before the volcano erupted?

Did Ted break his arm when he fell from the tree?

Where are question marks used?

313

Answers

Quotation marks are presented as marks of punctuation that are used to enclose the exact words that someone says.

The words that aren't in quotation marks in the display tell who said something.

Inserting quotation marks in sentences in the display on page 315:

The guard said, "Thank you, and come again."

"Thank you, and come again," said the guard.

"Thank you," said the guard, "and come again."

Exercises

A. Here are the answers to some questions. Write a question to go with each answer. (The first one is done for you.)

1. I'm fine. *How are you?*
2. Sharon likes to eat Norwegian food.
3. Dad went downtown to see a silent movie.
4. I'm not going to answer that question.
5. It's on the floor where you threw it.

B. Here are some more answers. Think up matching questions. Remember they can be silly or sensible.

1. Go down two blocks and then turn right.
2. He's rather heavy and a little bald.
3. It starts about seven o'clock.
4. I'll ask my mother.
5. It's in the refrigerator.

Quotation Marks

Quotation marks (" ") are marks of punctuation that are used to show the exact words that people say. Quotation marks are placed before and after the words you are quoting. For example, Mark was writing a story about Sam. He wanted Sam to say it was time for him to go home. Here's how he could write it for Sam to say.

Sam said, "It is time for me to go home."
"It is time for me to go home," said Sam.
"It is time," said Sam, "for me to go home."

Which words in each of these sentences don't have quotation marks around them?

Demonstrate the use of quotation marks to enclose the exact words of a speaker.

Where should quotation marks go in these sentences?

The guard said, Thank you, and come again.
Thank you, and come again, said the guard.
Thank you, said the guard, and come again.

Exercises

A. Now copy these sentences and put quotation marks where they are needed.

1. Sally said, I am hungry.
2. My brother said, I want to go home.
3. I don't like to watch television, said Jerome.
4. Is this the right way to tie a tie? asked Tom.
5. Susan has her shoes on the wrong feet! exclaimed Alice.
6. Tina said, I go to school Monday through Friday.
7. So what? said Jimmy.
8. Who knows, Mrs. Livingstone asked, how to spell *phthisis*?
9. Mark exclaimed, I have a hole in my sleeve!
10. I know how to use quotation marks, said Melanie.

B. Here are some more sentences for you to copy and put the quotation marks where they are needed.

1. Is something wrong? asked John.
2. Miss Simpson said, It was nice of you to drop by.
3. Did I do something wrong? inquired Melissa.
4. Renie said, I want to be an artist when I grow up.
5. I need a new pair of socks, said David.
6. Yes, Amanda said, I understand that.
7. Sandy exclaimed, Look at that huge sandwich!
8. Where did Andy go? asked the teacher.
9. I don't like hospitals, said Julie.
10. Mother called, Are you ready to go yet?

Skillsbook: Quotation Marks, page 24

Answers

EXERCISE A
1. Sally said, "I am hungry."
2. My brother said, "I want to go home."
3. "I don't like to watch television," said Jerome.
4. "Is this the right way to tie a tie?" asked Tom.
5. "Susan has her shoes on the wrong feet!" exclaimed Alice.
6. Tina said, "I go to school Monday through Friday."
7. "So what?" said Jimmy.
8. "Who knows," Mrs. Livingston asked, "how to spell phthisis?"
9. Mark exclaimed, "I have a hole in my sleeve!"
10. "I know how to use quotation marks," said Melanie.

EXERCISE B
1. "Is something wrong?" asked John.
2. Miss Simpson said, "It was nice of you to drop by."
3. "Did I do something wrong?" inquired Melissa.
4. Renie said, "I want to be an artist when I grow up."
5. "I need a new pair of socks," said David.
6. "Yes," Amanda said, "I understand that."
7. Sandy exclaimed, "Look at that huge sandwich!"
8. "Where did Andy go?" asked the teacher.
9. "I don't like hospitals," said Julie.
10. Mother called, "Are you ready to go yet?"

315

Sounds and Letters (Pages 316–318)

Call attention to the illustration at the top of the page. Have the children identify the sounds made by a dog and a bird and the letters that stand for the sounds in the illustration.

These sound-letter relationships for consonant sounds are presented:

/b/ spelled *b* or *bb* (b̲ig, ru̲b̲ber, cab̲)
/f/ spelled *f*, *ff*, *ph*, or *gh* (f̲ish, muf̲f̲, p̲h̲one, laug̲h̲)
/j/ spelled *j*, *g*, *ge*, or *dge* (j̲eep, g̲entle, pag̲e, ed̲g̲e)
(When /j/ is the initial sound in a word and is followed by *e* or *i*, it may be spelled *j* or *g*. At the end of words, /j/ is usually spelled *ge* or *dge*. In *page*, the /j/ may be said to be spelled *g* and the *e* may be part of the vowel-consonant-*e* pattern for /ā/.)
/k/ spelled *c*, *k*, or *ck* (c̲all, pea̲k̲, pic̲nic, bric̲k̲)
/n/ spelled *n*, *kn*, or *gn* (n̲ame, seen̲, k̲n̲ee, g̲n̲ash)
/r/ spelled *r*, *wr*, or *rh* (r̲ead, star̲, w̲r̲eck, r̲h̲yme)
/s/ spelled *s*, *ss*, or *c* (s̲ay, gues̲s̲, c̲ent, nights̲, bus̲)
/z/ spelled *z*, *zz*, *s*, *ze*, (z̲oo, buz̲z̲, shoes̲, snee̲z̲e̲)
/ch/ spelled *ch* or *tch* (c̲h̲ick, reac̲h̲, wat̲c̲h̲)
/sh/ spelled *sh* (s̲h̲ow, rus̲h̲, s̲h̲arp, fis̲h̲)

The letter *c* stands for /k/ and /s/. (A *c* usually stands for /k/ when it is followed by *a*, *o*, or *u* as in *cat*, *cot*, *cut*. A *c* often stands for /s/ when it is followed by *i*, *e*, or *y* as in *city*, *cent*, or *cycle*.)

The letter *x* stands for /ks/ and /z/.
The letter *q* with *u* stands for /kw/.

Sounds and Letters

Most consonant sounds are spelled with one letter in our alphabet. But sometimes more than one letter stands for the same sound. The letters and symbols below show how sounds are written in dictionaries. Tell which letters in each word stand for the sound shown before the words.

/b/ big, rubber, cab
/f/ fish, muff, phone, laugh
/j/ jeep, gentle, page, edge
/k/ call, peak, picnic, brick
/n/ name, seen, knee, gnash
/r/ read, star, wreck, rhyme
/s/ say, guess, cent, nights, bus
/z/ zoo, buzz, shoes, sneeze
/ch/ chick, reach, watch
/sh/ show, rush, sharp, fish

The letters *c, x,* and *q* stand for the same sounds as some other letters. What sounds do *c, x,* and *q* stand for in these words?

caller	prefix	quart
center	xylophone	quick

What letters usually stand for each of these sounds?

Objectives: Sounds and Letters
Demonstrate the phoneme-grapheme correspondences that are listed on pages 316–318.

316

The letter *c* may stand for the sound /k/ as in *caller* or /s/ as in *center*. The letter *x* may stand for the /z/ in *xylophone* or the /ks/ in *prefix*. The letter *u* always follows *q* and *qu* stands for the sound /kw/ in *quick*.

There are five vowel letters in our alphabet—*a, e, i, o,* and *u*. But there are more than five vowel sounds. Often *y* stands for the sounds /ē/, /ī/, or /i/. Sometimes several letters are placed together to stand for the sound. Read these words and tell which letters stand for the sound shown before the words.

/a/ rap, laugh
/ā/ same, pain, say, break, vein, weigh, baby

/e/ when, bread
/ē/ see, cream, she, these, even

/i/ win
/ī/ kite, pie, try, sight, tiger

/o/ not
/ō/ pole, coat, woe, go, snow, open

/u/ cup, son
/ü/ Sue, root, chew, rule
/ū/ use, few, music, union

There is one special letter pattern that fits all the vowels. A vowel, a consonant, and an *e* at the end of a word usually means the vowel sound is the same as the vowel letter name in this letter pattern.

slāte   thēme   rīde   jōke   cūte

The schwa (ə) is a special symbol. Any vowel letter may stand for this sound. But it's usually used only in words of more than one syllable.

These sound-letter relationships for vowel sounds are presented:

/a/ spelled *a* and *au* (rap, laugh)
/ā/ spelled *a*-consonant-*e*, *ai*, *ay*, *ea*, *ei*, *eigh*, *a* (same, pain, say, break, vein, weigh, baby)
/e/ spelled *e* and *ea* (when, bread)
/ē/ spelled *ee*, *ea*, *e*, *e*-consonant-*e* (see, cream, she, these, even)
/i/ spelled *i* (win)
/ī/ spelled *i*-consonant-*e*, *ie*, *y*, *igh*, *i* (kite, pie, try, sight, tiger)
/o/ spelled *o* (not)
/ō/ spelled *o*-consonant-*e*, *oa*, *oe*, *o*, *ow* (pole, coat, woe, go, snow, open)
/u/ spelled *u* or *o* (cup, son)
/ü/ spelled *ue*, *oo*, *ew*, or *u*-consonant-*e* (Sue, root, chew, rule)
/ū/ spelled *u*-consonant-*e*, *ew*, or *u* (use, few, music, union)

Call attention to the vowel-conso-nant-*e* pattern in the display of words.

Note the symbol for the schwa sound. You may refer to the pronunciation key on page 280 to identify the sound represented by the symbol.

The displayed words at the top of the page each have two syllables. The unaccented syllable in each of the words has the schwa sound.

Letters that stand for the schwa sound in the displayed words:

children   disease   ribbon
alone   careful   confuse
caller   meaning   subtract
came   around   sailor

There are no schwa sounds in *came* or in *meaning*.

Answers

EXERCISE A

1. /s/—city, cats
2. /i/—dim
3. /ü/—grew
4. /k/—stickler
5. /ə/—ago
6. /ə/—golden
7. /e/—fed
8. /ā/—stay
9. /o/—rod
10. /ks/—fox

EXERCISE B

1. /ī/—dry, night
2. /ē/—greet, cream
3. /n/—sign, knot
4. /ō/—goat, slow
5. /ə/—written, above
6. /f/—phone, laugh
7. /ū/—mew, usage
8. /ā/—eight, break
9. /ə/—success, divide
10. /ə/—connect, probably

Read these words and notice the underlined letter and the sound that the schwa stands for in each word.

about (ə bout′)   taken (tāk′ ən)   April (ā′ prəl)
lemon (lem′ ən)   circus (ser′ kəs)

How many syllables are there in each word? Is it the accented syllable or the unaccented syllable that has the schwa sound?

The schwa sound stands for a vowel sound similar to the sound of *u* in *cup* in unaccented syllables. Which of these words has a schwa sound? What letter stands for this sound?

children	disease	ribbon
alone	careful	confuse
caller	meaning	subtract
came	around	sailor

Exercises

A. Copy each word that has the sound shown at the beginning of the line. Circle the letters that stand for this sound.

1. /s/: city, cats
2. /i/: dime, dim
3. /ü/: grew, use
4. /k/: stickler, center
5. /ə/: also, ago
6. /ə/: golden, goody
7. /e/: feed, fed
8. /ā/: stay, strand
9. /o/: rod, rode
10. /ks/: fox, sock

B. Write the letter and symbol for the sound that is the same in each pair of words.

1. dry   night
2. greet   cream
3. sign   knot
4. goat   slow
5. written   above
6. phone   laugh
7. mew   usage
8. eight   break
9. success   divide
10. connect   probably

Skillsbook: Sounds and Letters, page 25

Synonyms

Synonyms are words that have similar meanings. One word can be used in place of the other word without changing the meaning of the sentence.

Read these sentences and the underlined synonyms in each one.

The dog is lost, and we must <u>hunt</u> for it.
The dog is lost, and we must <u>search</u> for it.
The dog is lost, and we must <u>look</u> for it.

Now read these pairs of sentences. Then tell which word in the second sentence is a synonym for the underlined word in the first sentence.

I live in a <u>house</u> on Church Street.
My home is a cheerful place to live.

Don't eat too much chocolate, or you will be <u>sick</u>.
Dick is ill with a cold.

That was a <u>foolish</u> thing to do.
That silly parrot giggles all the time.

Synonyms (Pages 319–320)

Synonyms are presented as words that have similar meanings.

Call attention to the illustration at the top of the page. Have the children discuss the scene. Note the synonyms they use in describing the scene. Call attention to these synonyms after reading the first two paragraphs on the page.

These synonyms are presented:

hunt, search, look
house, home
sick, ill
foolish, silly

Synonyms in the displayed sentences:

house—home
sick—ill
foolish—silly

Objectives: Synonyms
1. Describe synonyms in operational terms.
2. Demonstrate the use of synonyms in context.

Answers

EXERCISE A

1. Outfits. Clothing comes in all colors and sizes.
2. Dawn. In the beginning of this book there is a myth.
3. Knock. Rap out the rhythm you hear in this song.
4. Sailor. Did you see the tattoo on the arm of that seaman?
5. Bleach. There isn't anything you can use to whiten it.
6. Outside. No, it is still light outdoors.
7. Close. Billy slams the door but it never shuts tightly.
8. Breeze. The wind rolled our garbage can down the street.

EXERCISE B

Accept any reasonable synonyms in reasonable sentences.
1. evening—dusk, night
2. talk—speak, converse, tell
3. huge—large, vast, enormous, big, gigantic
4. woods—forest, trees
5. fine—sheer, thin, nice
6. dine—eat, sup
7. start—begin, initiate, beginning
8. shop—purchase, buy, store
9. small—tiny, little
10. every—each, all

Exercises

A. Read each pair of sentences. Then copy the underlined word in the first sentence and all of the second sentence. In the sentence you copied, underline a word that is a synonym for the word you copied. (The first one is done for you.)

1. People wear different outfits to do different things.
   Clothing comes in all colors and sizes.
   Outfits. Clothing comes in all colors and sizes.

2. The sun announces the dawn of a new day.
   In the beginning of this book there is a myth.

3. Did you hear someone knock at the door?
   Rap out the rhythm you hear in this song.

4. A sailor spends most of his life on the sea.
   Did you see the tattoo on the arm of that seaman?

5. Mother says it's no use trying to bleach this shirt.
   There isn't anything you can use to whiten it.

6. Is it dark yet outside?
   No, it is still light outdoors.

7. I always close the screen door when I go outside.
   Billy slams the door but it never shuts tightly.

8. Pam's hair was flung about by a gentle breeze.
   The wind rolled our garbage can down the street.

B. Copy these words and write a synonym for each one. Then use each synonym in a sentence.

1. evening	6. dine
2. talk	7. start
3. huge	8. shop
4. woods	9. small
5. fine	10. every

Skillsbook: Synonyms, page 27

Usage: The Meaning

The scientists who study language know that people in different parts of the country talk in different ways. Even in the same city or town, people don't always talk the same way. Scientists use the word **usage** to mean "the way people use words when they speak and write."

Hundreds of years ago, people came from Europe to live in our country. They didn't all come from the same place. Many people came from England and Scotland. But even these people didn't speak English in exactly the same way. So people had different usage before they came to America.

These people went to different parts of our country. They didn't use words in the same way. After coming to America, people still had different usage.

Even though our country has been settled for more than two hundred years, we find that people still don't talk in exactly the same way. But in any one area, there are many people who do speak in much the same way. Scientists have divided the country into areas to show where people speak differently. This map shows some of these areas of the country. Find the area where you live.

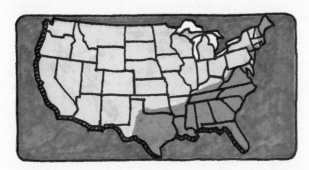

Objectives: Usage, The Meaning
1. Describe standard usage and non-standard usage in operational terms.
2. Distinguish between standard usage and non-standard usage in obvious situations.
3. Describe spoken usage and written usage in operational terms.

Usage: The Meaning (Pages 321–326)

Call attention to the meaning of *usage:* the way people use words when they speak and write.

Note that dialect areas on the map may differ from areas on other dialect maps.

Have the children identify the map as a map of the contiguous United States. Refer to the blue area on the map as the New England area (Northern on some dialect maps), to the red area as the Southern area, to the purple area as the New York City area, and to the yellow area as the western area (Midland on some dialect maps). Compare the settlers of these areas:

New England: religious refugees from England: Pilgrims at Plymouth, Massachusetts; Roger Williams in Rhode Island.

New York City: Swedish and Dutch traders; Swedes along Delaware River; Peter Minuit established Swedish colony of New Amsterdam; Henry Hudson's explorations; Peter Stuyvesant took over Swedish colony for the Dutch.

South: English nobleman and Spanish; Lord Baltimore in Maryland; James Oglethorpe in Georgia; Sir Walter Raleigh and John Smith in Virginia; Ponce de León in Florida; Cortez in Mexico; De Soto; Cabrillo in California.

West: a mixture of English, Welsh, Dutch, German, Scotch, Irish, French, and Swedish stocks; William Penn in Pennsylvania; French fur-trading posts along the Mississippi River; Cavelier, La Salle, and Joliet; settlers who moved west from the Atlantic seaboard and Gulf of Mexico; Daniel Boone in Ohio Valley; Lewis and Clark explorations along the Mississippi River; Joseph Smith and Brigham Young in Utah.

Note original stock of settlers and time of settlement of local areas.

Call attention to the variation in sounds of the words in the display. Note that in the examples only the vowel sound in each word varies from area to area, but consonant sounds may vary as well. Some people, in the New York City area, may substitute a *d* for a *th* (/dis/ for *this*); in parts of Ohio and Indiana, you may hear an *r* inserted in a word (/wərsh/ for *wash*); New Englanders sometimes say /kū′ bər/ for *Cuba* and /kä/ for *car*.

Besides differences in pronunciation, differences in usage may involve the use of different words to say the same thing:

cantaloupe, lope, melon, muskmelon
sick (to, in or on) his stomach
corn bread, johnny cake, corn pone

And the choice of words may indicate something about the sex, age, education, and occupation of the speaker, as well as his geographical or ethnic origin. For example, females are more likely to use such descriptive words as *lovely* or *darling* than males; elderly people may still refer to an *electric refrigerator* as an *icebox*; teenagers may refer to their *bedrooms* as *pads* or *gigs*; educated people may use words with more shades of meanings and literary references to make metaphors; the language of a particular occupation influences descriptive phrases, such as a sailor referring to *his wife* as *his first mate*.

Differences may also involve such things as past tense of verbs, plural nouns, and syntax:

I *et* lunch.
He *do* the job for you.
What do *youse* want?
Two *girl* came to see me.
This is a *more* prettier hat.
This *here* dog is a chow.
Tom won't go *without* I go.

Many people in your area will sound alike—or almost alike—when they talk. They'll use the same words to talk about the same things. They'll say these words in about the same way. But what about the people in another area? Would they sound the same as people in your area? Probably not. And if you listen closely as they talk, you might hear some of the differences in the way they say things.

Suppose two people are talking. One is from eastern New England, and the other is from the southern part of the United States. Here are some words you might hear them say in a different way:

Written Words	Spoken words in	
	New England	South
due	/dü/	/dū/
dog	/dôg/ or /däg/	/dô′ əg/
pin	/pin/	/pi′ ən/
pen	/pen/	/pin/
five	/fīv/	/fä′ əv/
bath	/bäth/	/ba′ ith/

(Try to describe how to say these words. Use the pronunciation key on page 280 if you need help.)

There are thousands of other differences, too. And the people in these areas also sound different from the people who live in other areas of the country.

Here are three questions to think about:

Is any way of speaking better than all the others?
Is any way "right" where other ways are "wrong"?
Is one usage <u>always</u> "better" than another?

The answer to all these questions is <u>No</u>.

In the United States, people have different usage. No way of speaking is always "right" or always "better" than another way.

Spoken Usage

Suppose you were watching a program on television. Suppose it was a program about cowboys and ranchers in Texas. Try to describe how the cowboys would sound. Do you think it would sound "funny" if one of the cowboys sounded like a person from New England or New York City? If you do, try to explain why.

If the actors were very good, then some of them might sound different from the others. And that's important. Even in the same city—or town—people don't sound alike. They have different usage.

Here's another important fact about the way people talk. In every part of the country, there's a **standard usage.** Usually, the standard in one part of the country is a little different from the standard in another part.

Now suppose you want to learn about standard spoken usage in some part of the country. Here's what you could do. First, you'd listen to different people talk. You should listen for words like these:

creek	news	which	hog
radish	bottle	coffee	car
water	weather	marry	pen
can't	catch	bird	barn

In different parts of the country, these words are pronounced in different ways. (Right now, scientists are writing books that show the different ways people say these words.)

You should also ask questions, like these, to find out what different words people use to say the same thing.

Suppose the time is 10:45. What word would you use if you said, "It's quarter _____ eleven"?

(Some people say, "till"; some say, "to"; and some say, "of.")

Note that all of these examples of usage are non-standard and are used to talk with people who have the same usage. However, some forms of non-standard usage may sound "funny" to those who have a different usage. A speaker or writer must take into consideration the usage of his audience. His usage "tunes in" or "tunes out" people.

Spoken Usage

Cowboys are not usually associated with New England or New York City. So a cowboy who spoke with a New England dialect or with a New York City dialect would sound "funny."

Variations of pronunciation of words in the display:

creek /krēk/, /krik/
radish /rad′ish/ /red′ish/
water /wôt′ər/, /wät′ər/, /wäd′er/
can't /känt/, /kant/
news /nüz/, /nūz/
bottle /bot′l/, /bod′l/
weather /weᴛн′ər/, /wed′ər/·
catch /kech/, /kach/
which /hwich/, /wich/
coffee /kô′fē/, /kä′fē/
marry /mar′ē/, /mer′ē/
bird /bėrd/, /bu′id/, /bud/
hog /hôg/, /hog/
car /kär/, /kä/
pen /pen/, /pin/
barn /bän/, /bärn/

Note that time *before* the hour may be indicated by *till*, *to*, or *of*.

Other words for *gutters, troughs,* or *eaves troughs,* may be *eaves spouts, spouts, spouting, water troughs, water gutters,* or *eaves.*

Another word for *faucet* may be *hydrant.*

Additional samples of different ways to say the same thing are:

fire hall, fire house, fire station

chipmunk, ground squirrel, grinnie

stone, seed, pit, kernel, heart

green beans, string beans, snap beans, snaps, beans

become ill, take sick, get sick, be taken sick or ill, come down

reckon, guess, figure, figger, imagine

Suppose you're building a house. What are the "metal things" you put at the edge of the roof?

(Some people say, "gutters"; some say, "troughs"; some say, "eaves troughs." And there are five or six other ways to say the same thing.)

Suppose you want to get a drink of water from the kitchen sink. What word would you use to tell what you turned on to get the water?

(Some people say, "faucet"; some say, "spigot" or "spicket"; some say, "tap.")

If you listened very carefully, you would soon learn that people don't talk the same way—even in the same city or town! So here's a problem. If people don't talk the same way—even in the same town, then which way is the <u>standard way</u> of talking?

Here's how the scientists solved the problem. They say that <u>some</u> people in a city speak in the standard way. They have <u>standard usage</u>. The other people in the city—the ones who speak in a different way—have **non-standard usage.** Usually, the scientists say that the mayor, the doctors and lawyers, and the teachers have standard usage. Anyone who speaks almost the same as they do also has standard usage.

If people don't speak the standard way for some city or town, then we say that they have <u>non-standard usage</u>. But here's an important fact. Anyone can learn to speak in more than one way! (Actors do it all the time.) If someone's usage is non-standard, he can learn to speak the standard way if he really wants to.

Most of the time, you don't need to think about standard spoken usage. You probably talk almost the same as your friends do. But suppose your usage is non-standard for the place where you live. With your friends, it won't be important. You may even use "slang." (If you're not sure what "slang" is, then look for its meaning in a dictionary.) But in school, it's probably a good idea to use the standard way of talking so that <u>anyone</u> can understand you.

Written Usage

People use language when they speak and when they write. We say that there are two kinds of standard usage:

standard spoken usage   standard written usage

You already know that there are different kinds of standard spoken usage in different parts of the country. But in <u>all</u> parts of the country, standard written usage is about the same.

The poems and stories in this book have been written by many different people. But when you read them, you

Note the distinction between *standard usage* and *non-standard usage* in a particular place: standard usage is the way most of the educated people in the community speak; non-standard usage is the way that the people who speak differently from most of the educated people speak.

Call attention to usage as immaterial when speaking with friends and relatives, but important when communicating with people that you don't know very well.

Written Usage

Note that standard written usage, unlike standard spoken usage, is just about the same all over the country. This is true because people have learned the conventions of writing. Schools have helped to standardize written usage.

Usage: Standard Written Forms
(Pages 326–336)

There are frequently variations in agreement of subject and verb between standard and non-standard written usage. The purpose of this section is to make the children aware of the standard written forms of verbs and pronouns and of the variations in these forms that they use in their own writing. This section is not intended to teach or drill standard written English or to label one form better than another. It is designed only to present the standard forms so that the children will have a knowledge of them. It is hoped that they will use this section as a reference for standard written usage.

probably can't tell where the writers are from. Almost all the writers used standard usage when they wrote the poems and stories.

People don't always talk and write in the same way. This means that standard <u>written</u> usage is sometimes a little different from standard <u>spoken</u> usage. Even when a person uses standard spoken usage (for his city), he may need to learn to write in standard written usage. That's one thing that people learn in school.

Here's something to think about. You learned to talk before you came to school. You already had one kind of usage —spoken usage—before you started school. But you probably learned to write after you came to school. This made it easier for you to learn the standard way of writing.

Suppose the way you talk is the same as the standard way for your city or town. Then it's easy for you to learn the standard way of writing.

Usage: Standard Written Forms

When scientists study usage, they sometimes use the word **forms.** There are many non-standard forms of English. And there are three kinds of words where the non-standard forms are sometimes very different from the standard ones: verb forms, "be" words, and pronoun forms.

Objectives: Usage, Standard Written Forms
Distinguish between standard and non-standard usage to show agreement of subject and verb, tenses, and sentence position of pronouns.

When people write books, newspapers, and compositions, they try to use the standard forms of these words. As you read, you can see if these are the forms you use when you write.

Verb Forms

In standard written usage, there's a special way that the subject and verb of a sentence go together. There's also a special word to use when you talk about subjects and verbs. The word is **agreement.** When people write in the standard way, they always make the verb agree with the subject.

Adding *s* to Verbs

Here are some sentences that use the verb *walk*.

I walk fast.	He walks slowly.
You walk quickly.	She walks to school.
We walk together.	The fish walks on its tail.
They walk every day.	It walks funny.
Dogs walk sideways sometimes.	

In the sentences in the first column, there's no *s* at the end of the verb *walk*. But in the second column, there is an *s* at the end of the verb.

In standard English, there are rules that say when to add *s* to a verb and when not to add *s*. We can show the rules this way:

1. With the pronouns *he, she,* and *it,* and with a noun that means "only one," we sometimes use *s* on the verb.
2. With the pronouns *I, you, we,* and *they* and also with a noun that means "more than one," we never use *s* at the end of a verb.

You may want to have the children complete each of the numbered exercises on the following pages before reading this part of the text. Have them file their responses to compare their instinctive responses with the responses they will make after studying the text.

Read and discuss each part of the standard written forms presented. Have the children complete each exercise and try to apply the rules or forms of agreement used in standard written usage. Help them see how to use the rules and examples to apply them to different but similar situations. Help them see that they can write in the standard way if they want to.

Answers

1. Bill *speaks* quickly. Ann <u>speaks</u> slowly.
2. My mother *works* hard. We <u>work</u> together sometimes.
3. John *eats* slowly. I <u>eat</u> slowly, too.
4. Goats *climb* hills. My cat <u>climbs</u> trees.
5. John *rides* the bus. We <u>ride</u> the subway.
6. They *sing* together. Sherman <u>sings</u> when he walks.
7. Birds *feast* on berries. They often <u>feast</u> on our berries.
8. Ted and Sue *like* hard candies. I <u>like</u> soft ones.
9. The dog *runs* after the boys. The boys <u>run</u> away.
10. Bob *studies* history. Kevin and Don <u>study</u> history, too.
11. Do you *keep* your room clean? Pam <u>keeps</u> her room clean.
12. I can't *draw* a tree. But Simon <u>draws</u> trees very well.
13. We *enjoy* eating pizza. Margaret <u>enjoys</u> eating pizza, too.
14. I don't *know* the answer. But Phillip <u>knows</u> it.
15. The king *wears* a crown. All kings <u>wear</u> crowns.
16. The king *lives* in a castle. The queen <u>lives</u> there, too.

(Actually, Rule 1 is only part of the rule that the scientists have studied. You don't use *s* with auxiliaries like *he can* or *she will*. And you don't use *s* when you're writing about some time "before right now." If this is a problem for you, then your teacher can help you.)

■ Here are some sentences that you can use to find out if you write verbs in the standard way. In the second sentence in each pair of sentences, the verb is missing. Use the underlined verb in the standard way to complete the second sentence.

1. Bill <u>speaks</u> quickly. Ann _____ slowly.
2. My mother <u>works</u> hard. We _____ together sometimes.
3. John <u>eats</u> slowly. I _____ slowly, too.
4. Goats <u>climb</u> hills. My cat _____ trees.
5. John <u>rides</u> the bus. We _____ the subway.
6. They <u>sing</u> together. Sherman _____ when he walks.
7. Birds <u>feast</u> on berries. They often _____ on our berries.
8. Ted and Sue <u>like</u> hard candies. I _____ soft ones.
9. The dog <u>runs</u> after the boys. The boys _____ away.
10. Bob <u>studies</u> history. Kevin and Don _____ history, too.
11. Do you <u>keep</u> your room clean? Pam _____ her room clean.
12. I can't <u>draw</u> a tree. But Simon _____ trees very well.
13. We <u>enjoy</u> eating pizza. Margaret _____ eating pizza, too.
14. I don't <u>know</u> the answer. But Phillip _____ it.
15. The king <u>wears</u> a crown. All kings _____ crowns.
16. The king <u>lives</u> in a castle. The queen _____ there, too.

Adding *ed* and *d* to Verbs

There are several different ways we can use verbs to show that something has already happened. With one kind of verb—called a regular verb—we usually follow the rules on the next page.

Skillsbook: Adding -s to Verbs, page 28

1. We add *ed* to show that something has happened. If there's already an *e* at the end of a regular verb, we only add *d*.

> We <u>play</u> in the yard. They <u>played</u> indoors.
> We <u>live</u> in Ohio now. We <u>lived</u> in Iowa last year.

2. Sometimes with a regular verb, we need to double the final letter before we add *ed*.

> They always <u>slam</u> the door. They <u>slammed</u> it again.

3. If we have a regular verb that ends in a consonant and then a *y*, we need to change the *y* to *i* before we add *ed*.

> I <u>worry</u> a lot. Today, I <u>worried</u> about school.

■ Here are some more pairs of sentences. In the second sentence in each pair, the verb is missing. Use the underlined verb in the first sentence in the standard way to complete the second sentence.

1. Jim and Bill <u>play</u> football. Last week, they _____ twice.
2. I <u>save</u> money every week. I _____ twenty dollars last year.
3. Mary and Ann <u>skip</u> rope. They _____ rope three times today.
4. Art and Sam <u>carry</u> wood for the fireplace. Yesterday, they _____ ten armloads.
5. Mr. Davis and Mr. Gray <u>drop</u> animal food from helicopters. Last winter, they _____ a thousand bales of hay for cattle.
6. The butchers <u>carve</u> meat for their customers. They _____ three turkeys for Mrs. Samuel's party.
7. The twins <u>cry</u> at night. Last night they _____ for an hour.
8. My mother said, "Now <u>listen</u> carefully to my directions." I _____ carefully.
9. The teacher said, "Lee, <u>try</u> to find the answer to this question." I _____ to find it in an encyclopedia.
10. I said, "Mike, <u>whisper</u> your secret in my ear." And Mike _____ his secret in my ear.

Answers

ADDING *ed* AND *d* TO VERBS

1. Jim and Bill *play* football. Last week, they <u>played</u> twice.
2. I *save* money every week. I <u>saved</u> twenty dollars last year.
3. Mary and Ann *skip* rope. They <u>skipped</u> rope three times today.
4. Art and Sam *carry* wood for the fireplace. Yesterday, they <u>carried</u> ten armloads.
5. Mr. Davis and Mr. Gray *drop* animal food from helicopters. Last winter, they <u>dropped</u> a thousand bales of hay for cattle.
6. The butchers *carve* meat for their customers. They <u>carved</u> three turkeys for Mrs. Samuel's party.
7. The twins *cry* at night. Last night they <u>cried</u> for an hour.
8. My mother said, "Now *listen* carefully to my directions. I <u>listened</u> carefully.
9. The teacher said, "Lee, *try* to find the answer to this question." I <u>tried</u> to find it in an encyclopedia.
10. I said, "Mike, *whisper* your secret in my ear." And Mike <u>whispered</u> his secret in my ear.

Skillsbook: Adding -*ed* and -*d*, page 29

"HAVE" WORDS AND REGULAR VERBS

1. Bob *has* asked for candy. He <u>has</u> asked for gum, too.
2. The boys <u>have/had</u> walked there. They <u>have/had</u> walked a mile and a half.
3. That star <u>has</u> shared my secret. It <u>has</u> winked at me.
4. We <u>have/had</u> talked for hours. I <u>have/had</u> learned a lot.
5. She <u>has/had</u> dropped the vase. Gail <u>has/had</u> picked it up.
6. Bill <u>has/had</u> laughed at you. You <u>have/had</u> laughed at him.

"Have" Words and Regular Verbs

Besides adding *ed* (the "past tense") to show that something has already happened, we can also use a "have" word as an auxiliary. (See page 144.)

> The girl <u>has walked</u> a mile.
> She <u>has walked</u> quickly.
> Two other girls <u>have walked</u> with her.
> They <u>have walked</u> a mile.

> The boy <u>had climbed</u> Black Mountain.
> He <u>had climbed</u> it last summer.
> We <u>had watched</u> him.
> You <u>had watched</u> him, too.

It's easy to use a "have" word with a regular verb. When you write the verb itself, you follow the regular rules for showing that something has already happened. For the "have" word that comes before the verb, you follow these rules.

1. With the pronouns *he, she,* and *it,* and with a noun that means "only one," use <u>has</u> or <u>had</u>.
2. With the pronouns *I, you, we,* and *they,* and also with a noun that means "more than one," use <u>have</u> or <u>had</u>.

■ Use these sentences to find out if you know the standard way of writing "have" words with regular verbs. Use a "have" word to complete each sentence.

1. Bob *has* asked for candy. He _____ asked for gum, too.
2. The boys _____ walked there. They _____ walked a mile and a half.
3. That star _____ shared my secret. It _____ winked at me.
4. We _____ talked for hours. I _____ learned a lot.
5. She _____ dropped the vase. Gail _____ picked it up.
6. Bill _____ laughed at you. You _____ laughed at him.

Irregular Verbs

Sometimes <u>irregular verbs</u> are difficult. Most of the time when you have an irregular verb, you need to remember two forms. The simple past tense form is spelled one way. And the form that goes with a "have" word is spelled another way. There aren't very many irregular verbs. But the ones we do use are important, and we use them over and over again. Here are some examples:

Verb	Past Tense	"Have" Word	Example
1. eat			We <u>eat</u> grits every day.
	ate		I <u>ate</u> the pickle.
		eaten	He <u>has eaten</u> lunch.
2. go			I <u>go</u> to school early.
	went		I <u>went</u> to the park.
		gone	I <u>have gone</u> there, too.
3. see			I <u>see</u> my dentist today.
	saw		We <u>saw</u> a play today.
		seen	John <u>has seen</u> the wind.
4. come			Please <u>come</u> to my party.
	came		I <u>came</u> to school early.
		come	I <u>have come</u> to see you.
5. run			We <u>run</u> races.
	ran		They once <u>ran</u> a mile.
		run	I <u>have run</u> a mile.

■ On the next two pages, there's a list of irregular verbs and some sentences. Use the sentences to find out if you know the standard way of writing irregular verbs. Use the underlined verb in the first sentence in the past tense form to complete the second and third sentences.

Answers

IRREGULAR VERBS

1. The wind *blows* the trees. It <u>blew</u> one tree down. The wind <u>has blown</u> for two days.

2. We *begin* a new lesson tomorrow. Juan <u>began</u> to sneeze. The rose <u>has begun</u> to bloom.

3. Anne *swims* very fast. I <u>swam</u> across the pool. We <u>have swum</u> here already.

4. Please *write* to me. I <u>wrote</u> to him last week. We <u>have written</u> five plays.

5. I *shake* all over when I sneeze. Yesterday we <u>shook</u> hands. I <u>have shaken</u> this rug already.

6. We *know* you are here. I <u>knew</u> the answer yesterday. I <u>have known</u> him for years.

7. Nathan *takes* piano lessons. Hannah <u>took</u> them last year. O.P. <u>has taken</u> lessons, too.

8. Some people *drive* too fast. We <u>drove</u> to Iowa last year. I <u>have driven</u> ten miles to see you.

9. Rocks *sink* in the water. Ed <u>sank</u> his new boat. He <u>has sunk</u> five boats now.

10. The tide *rises* slowly. The thermometer <u>rose</u> two degrees. It <u>has risen</u> quickly.

11. Please *ring* the bell. I <u>rang</u> it yesterday. I <u>have rung</u> it many times.

Verb	Past Tense	"Have" Word	Verb	Past Tense	"Have" Word
ring	rang	rung	sing	sang	sung
begin	began	begun	swim	swam	swum
sink	sank	sunk	drink	drank	drunk
take	took	taken	shake	shook	shaken
blow	blew	blown	know	knew	known
grow	grew	grown	drive	drove	driven
rise	rose	risen	write	wrote	written
ride	rode	ridden	fall	fell	fallen
give	gave	given	draw	drew	drawn

1. The wind <u>blows</u> the trees. It _____ one tree down. The wind _____ _____ for two days.

2. We <u>begin</u> a new lesson tomorrow. Juan _____ to sneeze. The rose _____ _____ to bloom.

3. Anne <u>swims</u> very fast. I _____ across the pool. We _____ _____ here already.

4. Please <u>write</u> to me. I _____ to him last week. We _____ _____ five plays.

5. I <u>shake</u> all over when I sneeze. Yesterday we _____ hands. I _____ _____ this rug already.

6. We <u>know</u> you are here. I _____ the answer yesterday. I _____ _____ him for years.

7. Nathan <u>takes</u> piano lessons. Hannah _____ them last year. O.P. _____ _____ lessons too.

8. Some people <u>drive</u> too fast. We _____ to Iowa last year. I _____ _____ ten miles to see you.

9. Rocks <u>sink</u> in the water. Ed _____ his new boat. He _____ _____ five boats now.

10. The tide <u>rises</u> slowly. The thermometer _____ two degrees. It _____ _____ quickly.

11. Please <u>ring</u> the bell. I _____ it yesterday. I _____ _____ it many times.

12. We <u>sing</u> every Thursday. John _____ very softly. We _____ _____ that song before.

13. Corn <u>grows</u> at night. Fred _____ two inches. I _____ _____ since last year.

14. Please <u>drink</u> your milk. Sue _____ her milk. She _____ _____ five glasses today.

15. Please <u>give</u> me some water. I already _____ you some. I _____ _____ you six glasses.

16. We <u>draw</u> pictures on Friday. I _____ a cat last week. I _____ _____ sixty cats.

17. Leaves <u>fall</u> slowly. Robin _____ off her seat. I _____ _____ out of bed twice.

18. Lester <u>rides</u> a bike to school. We _____ horses in Ohio. I _____ _____ on a yak in Florida.

More Irregular Verbs

Some people use forms of *do* that are different from the standard written forms. The forms are also different when they use both *do* and *n't.* Here are the rules for the standard forms:

1. With the pronouns *he, she,* and *it,* and also with a noun that means "only one," use *does* or *did* and also use *doesn't* and *didn't.*

> He <u>does</u> want to go.   She <u>doesn't</u> want to leave.
> He <u>did</u> his homework.   It <u>didn't</u> help very much.

2. With the pronouns *I, you, we,* and *they,* and also with a noun that means "more than one," use *do* or *did* and also use *don't* and *didn't.*

> I <u>do</u> the dishes every day.   I <u>don't</u> like soap.
> We <u>did</u> the best we could.   But <u>we didn't</u> win the game.

Skillsbook: Irregular Verbs, page 30

12. We *sing* every Thursday. John <u>sang</u> very softly. We <u>have sung</u> that song before.

13. Corn *grows* at night. Fred <u>grew</u> two inches. I <u>have grown</u> since last year.

14. Please *drink* your milk. Sue <u>drank</u> her milk. She <u>has drunk</u> five glasses today.

15. Please *give* me some water. I already <u>gave</u> you some. I <u>have given</u> you six glasses.

16. We *draw* pictures on Friday. I <u>drew</u> a cat last week. I <u>have drawn</u> sixty cats

17. Leaves *fall* slowly. Robin <u>fell</u> off her seat. I <u>have fallen</u> out of bed twice.

18. Lester *rides* a bike to school. We <u>rode</u> horses in Ohio. I <u>have ridden</u> on a yak in Florida.

Answers

1. I like pizza, and Phil <u>does</u>, too.
2. Mel wants a snake, but his mother <u>doesn't</u> like them.
3. I was late, and Becky <u>didn't</u> come at all.
4. I like ants more than my sister <u>does</u>.
5. Sue wants to sing, but the <u>girls</u> <u>don't</u> want to.
6. Don bought a balloon, and so <u>did</u> Mary Alice.
7. Mother likes the seashore, but I <u>don't</u> like it.
8. Charles insists that he <u>did</u> see you in town.
9. Martha said she wouldn't do it, and she <u>didn't</u>.
10. What <u>does</u> that funny word mean?
11. It may <u>sound</u> funny to you, but it <u>doesn't</u> to me.
12. If you <u>do</u> this work for me, then I'll help you.

■ Here are some sentences to help you find out if you know the standard forms of *do*. If there's an **N'T** before the sentence, use the *n't* form of *do* to complete the sentence.

1. I like pizza, and Phil _____, too.
2. N'T: Mel wants a snake, but his mother _____ like them.
3. N'T: I was late, and Becky _____ come at all.
4. I like ants more than my sister _____.
5. N'T: Sue wants to sing, but the girls _____ want to.
6. Don bought a balloon, and so _____ Mary Alice.
7. N'T: Mother likes the seashore, but I _____ like it.
8. Charles insists that he _____ see you in town.
9. N'T: Martha said she wouldn't do it, and she _____.
10. What _____ that funny word mean?
11. N'T: It may sound funny to you, but it _____ to me.
12. If you _____ this work for me, then I'll help you.

Forms of "Be" Words

Some people who speak a non-standard usage don't use "be" words in the way that other people do. For many people, "be" words are much more difficult than irregular verbs. Here are some of the most important standard forms of "be" words.

I <u>am</u> happy.
I <u>was</u> sad yesterday.

You <u>are</u> a hero.
You <u>were</u> late today.

We <u>were</u> early last week.
We <u>are</u> early again.

Sarah <u>is</u> a good reader.
She <u>was</u> first in the class.

Sam <u>is</u> always hungry.
He <u>was</u> born that way.

The room <u>is</u> clean now.
It <u>was</u> messy this morning.

The dogs <u>are</u> noisy.
They <u>were</u> in the bedroom.

■ Here are some pairs of sentences that will help you find out if you know the standard "be" words. In the first sentence, the "be" word is underlined. But the "be" word is missing in the second sentence. Try to add a standard "be" word to the second sentence to complete it.

1. I am hungry. My brother _____, too.
2. Paul was busy. Last week, he _____ busy, too.
3. The pies were good. The apple pie _____ the best.
4. Gus is awake. We thought he _____ asleep.
5. Those crackers are yours. This one _____ mine.
6. The bus is late. I _____ tired.
7. The red one is good. But the blue ones _____ better.
8. This box is square. Those coffee cans _____ round.
9. The men were busy. They _____ happy to be working.
10. Joy is a good bike rider. I _____ a good rider, too.
11. Kathy was in the kitchen. She _____ busy baking a cake.
12. My family and I were at the zoo. We _____ there today.
13. My father's surprise was a new car. It _____ a red one.
14. Jack, Pete, Sammy, and Mike were on the football field this afternoon. Tonight, they _____ too tired to watch TV.
15. Sandy, Carol, and Phyllis were at the game. They _____ happy to see Sammy make a touchdown.
16. The children were happy. Their mothers _____ happy, too.
17. John is a tall boy, but his brother _____ much taller.
18. Were you there yesterday? Paul and I _____ there, too.

Pronoun Forms

There aren't very many pronouns in English. But sometimes people have trouble using them. One easy way to think about pronouns is to use the position picture. There's one on page 113. You probably remember that a nominal in the first position is called the *subject of a sentence*.

Answers

FORMS OF "BE" WORDS

1. I *am* hungry. My brother is, too.
2. Paul *was* busy. Last week, he was busy, too.
3. The pies *were* good. The apple pie was the best.
4. Gus *is* awake. We thought he was asleep.
5. Those crackers *are* yours. This one is mine.
6. The bus *is* late. I am tired.
7. The red one *is* good. But the blue ones are better.
8. This box *is* square. Those coffee cans are round.
9. The men *were* busy. They were happy to be working.
10. Joy *is* a good bike rider. I am a good rider, too.
11. Kathy *was* in the kitchen. She was busy baking a cake.
12. My family and I *were* at the zoo. We were there today.
13. My father's surprise *was* a new car. It was a red one.
14. Jack, Pete, Sammy, and Mike *were* on the football field this afternoon. Tonight, they are/were too tired to watch TV.
15. Sandy, Carol, and Phyllis *were* at the game. They were happy to see Sammy make a touchdown.
16. The children *were* happy. Their mothers were happy, too.
17. John *is* a tall boy, but his brother is much taller.
18. *Were* you there yesterday? Paul and I were there, too.

Answers

1. Sam watched the movie. Then <u>he</u> went to bed.

2. Sue and I like games. <u>We</u> also like books.

3. I found Bill. I gave <u>him</u> your note.

4. Dave likes hats. <u>He</u> even wears one to bed.

5. Here are some mushrooms. I found <u>them</u> under a rock.

6. Ed dropped a book. Mary picked <u>it</u> up.

7. Ann got a bike. She let me ride <u>it</u> to the store.

8. Maria needed a pencil. I gave <u>her</u> mine.

9. Joe saw Fred and me. He told <u>us</u> about the ball game.

10. My father told me to study. So <u>I</u> did.

Here are the pronouns we use in the first position—the subject position—of a basic sentence.

<u>I</u> overslept.   <u>She</u> was sorry.
<u>He</u> sneezed.   <u>We</u> like pizza.
<u>You</u> are early.   <u>It</u> is raining.
<u>They</u> lost.

We can have pronouns in the first position of a sentence. And we can also have them in the third position. Most of the time, the pronouns that go in the third position are different from those that go in the first position. Here are the standard pronoun forms that people use in the third position of sentences.

Barbara found <u>me</u>.   Ruth met <u>her</u>.
Mary saw <u>him</u>.   Ginny visited <u>us</u>.
Janet called <u>you</u>.   Jean lost <u>it</u>.
            Vera saw <u>them</u>.

■ Here are some pairs of sentences that you can use to find out if you know standard pronoun forms. Read the first sentence. Then use a first-position pronoun or a third-position pronoun to complete the second sentence. (The first exercise is done for you.)

1. Sam watched the movie. Then *he* went to bed.
2. Sue and I like games. _____ also like books.
3. I found Bill. I gave _____ your note.
4. Dave likes hats. _____ even wears one to bed.
5. Here are some mushrooms. I found _____ under a rock.
6. Ed dropped a book. Mary picked _____ up.
7. Ann got a bike. She let me ride _____ to the store.
8. Maria needed a pencil. I gave _____ mine.
9. Joe saw Fred and me. He told _____ about the ball game.
10. My father told me to study. So _____ did.

Skillsbook: Pronouns, page 31

Index

Statement of Goals

(Continued from page x)

Language

Demonstrates an awareness of the nature and kinds of sentences through one or more of the following:

Chapters 1–5

1. Distinguishing between sentences and non-sentences.
2. Ordering given words to create sentences.
3. Describing a sentence as consisting of a nominal and a verb phrase.

Chapters 6–9

  Objectives 1–3 listed previously

4. Identifying the subjects and predicates of sentences.
5. Distinguishing between statements and questions.
6. Changing given basic sentences into yes-or-no questions.

Chapters 10–13

  Objectives 1–6 listed previously

7. Distinguishing between regular yes-or-no questions and tag questions.
8. Changing given sentences into tag questions.
9. Changing given sentences into negative statements.
10. Identifying questions and negative statements as derived sentences.
11. Recognizing that a derived sentence results when two basic sentences are combined.

Chapters 14–16

  Objectives 1–11 listed previously

12. Describing Q, Q_{tag}, and N'T as morphemes that we can add to sentences.

Demonstrates an understanding of some of the categories of the lexicon of the sentence model through one or more of the following:

Chapters 1–5

1. Defining a lexicon as consisting of a set of nominals and a set of verb phrases.
2. Distinguishing among regular nominals, pronouns, and names.
3. Recognizing that a regular nominal consists of a determiner and a noun.
4. Suggesting examples of regular nominals, pronouns, and names.
5. Identifying regular nominals, pronouns, and names in given sentences.

Chapters 6–9

Objectives 1–5 listed previously
6. Recognizing that some verb phrases consist of a verb followed by a nominal.
7. Identifying the verb in given basic sentences.
8. Identifying the nominal in the verb phrases of a given sentence.
9. Recognizing that the nominal in a verb phrase can be a regular nominal, a pronoun, or a name.
10. Distinguishing between subject pronouns and pronouns that are used after verbs.
11. Recognizing that some verb phrases consist of a "be" word followed by an adjective.

12. Suggesting adjectives to be used after "be" words in given sentences.
13. Recognizing that an adverbial can consist of a simple word or a group of words.
14. Distinguishing among adverbials that tell "when," "where," or "how."
15. Identifying adverbials in given basic sentences.
16. Adding adverbials to given sentences.

Chapters 10–13
Objectives 1–16 listed previously
17. Naming words which can function as auxiliaries in sentences.
18. Identifying auxiliaries in given sentences.
19. Adding auxiliaries to given basic sentences.
20. Including prefixes and suffixes among the types of morphemes.
21. Identifying the number of morphemes contained within a given word.
22. Combining two or more morphemes to produce words.

Chapters 14–16
Objectives 1–22 listed previously
23. Identifying the plural morpheme in nouns.
24. Identifying the past tense morpheme in verbs.
25. Adding the plural morpheme to given regular and irregular nouns.
26. Adding the past tense morpheme to given regular and irregular verbs.

Demonstrates an awareness that everyone has internalized rules for making and combining basic sentences through one or more of the following:

Chapters 1–5

1. Combining given nominals with given verb phrases to create basic sentences.
2. Recognizing that young children use *and* to combine sentences.
3. Using *wh-* words to combine sentences with identical first position nominals.
4. Describing the steps involved in combining sentences.

Chapters 6–9

Objectives 1–4 listed previously

5. Recognizing when the "special adjective way" can be used to combine sentences with identical first-position nominals.
6. Combining given sets of sentences with identical first-position nominals, using the regular way or the "special adjective way," whichever is appropriate.
7. Explaining how the "special adjective way" of combining sentences differs from the regular way.

Chapters 10–16

Objectives 1–7 listed previously

8. Using the regular way to insert a sentence after a third-position nominal.
9. Using the "special adjective way" to insert a sentence before a nominal in the third position of the matrix.
10. Recognizing that, wherever there's a nominal in a sentence, another sentence can be inserted.
11. Distinguishing between when to use *who* and when to use *which* (or *that*) in combining sentences.

Related Topics

Demonstrates an understanding of some of the uses of the dictionary through one or more of the following:

Chapters 1–5

1. Using a dictionary to determine the meanings of words.
2. Locating homographs in a dictionary.
3. Using a dictionary to find the meanings of given homographs.
4. Locating the two parts of the definitions of a noun.
5. Using a dictionary to determine the group that a particular thing belongs to.
6. Using a dictionary to determine the special features that distinguish a particular thing from other members of the same group.
7. Using pictures in a dictionary, as well as the picture captions, to clarify the meanings of words.

Chapters 6–9

Objectives 1–7 listed previously

8. Indicating that a dictionary can be used to determine the pronunciation and spelling of a word as well as the meaning.
9. Noting some of the symbols used in a dictionary to indicate pronunciation.
10. Using the short form of a pronunciation key to pronounce unfamiliar words.
11. Describing how dictionaries indicate the accented syllables in words.
12. Identifying the vowel letter (or letters) that the schwa stands for in the unaccented syllables of given words.
13. Describing how a dictionary can be used to determine the spellings of words.

Demonstrates an understanding of the arrangement of books in a library through one or more of the following:

Chapters 10–13

1. Describing the order applied to the arrangement of books in a library.
2. Locating needed titles in both fiction and nonfiction sections of the library.
3. Describing how fiction books are arranged.
4. Describing how nonfiction books are arranged.
5. Distinguishing among author cards, title cards, and subject cards in the card catalogue.
6. Using the card catalogue to locate nonfiction books.